THE ORIGINAL ANNUAL OF THE WORLD'S FINEST WRISTWATCHES

First published in the United States in 2017 by

TOURBILLON INTERNATIONAL
A MODERN LUXURY COMPANY

11 West 25th Street, 8th Floor
New York, NY 10010
Tel: +1 (212) 627-7732 Fax +1 (312) 274-8418
www.modernluxury.com/watches

In association with RIZZOLI INTERNATIONAL PUBLICATIONS, INC.

300 Park Avenue South, New York, NY 10010

ISBN: 978-0-8478-5966-5

PRINTED IN ITALY

COVER: ASTRONOMIA SKY (JACOB & CO.)

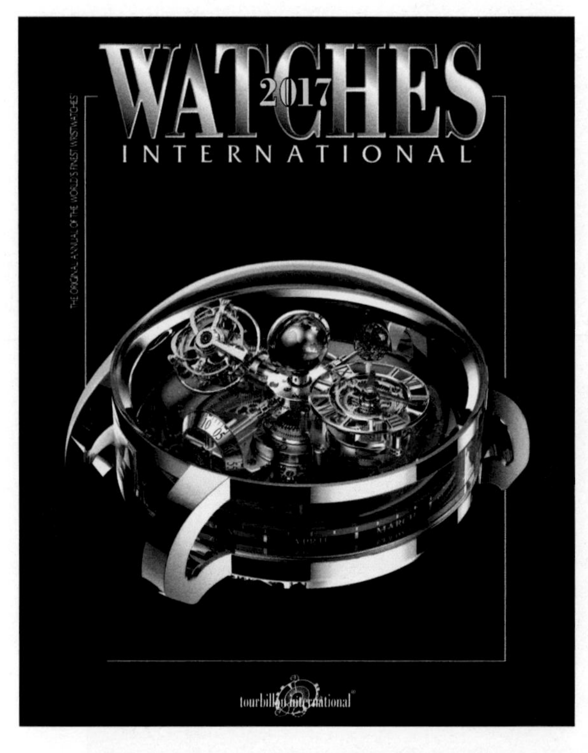

AUDEMARSPIGUET.COM

TO BREAK THE RULES, YOU MUST FIRST MASTER THEM.
THE VALLÉE DE JOUX. FOR MILLENNIA A HARSH, UNYIELDING ENVIRONMENT; AND SINCE 1875 THE HOME OF AUDEMARS PIGUET, IN THE VILLAGE OF LE BRASSUS. THE EARLY WATCHMAKERS WERE SHAPED HERE, IN AWE OF THE FORCE OF NATURE YET DRIVEN TO MASTER ITS MYSTERIES THROUGH THE COMPLEX MECHANICS OF THEIR CRAFT. STILL TODAY THIS PIONEERING SPIRIT INSPIRES US TO CONSTANTLY CHALLENGE THE CONVENTIONS OF FINE WATCHMAKING.
ROYAL OAK PERPETUAL CALENDAR
IN CERAMIC
AUDEMARS PIGUET
Le Brassus

An Ever-Evolving Fascination

It's truly stunning that watchmaking, a centuries-old art form so deeply founded on tradition, manages to fascinate its audience year after year. Stunning—but unsurprising, when one considers the spirit upon which it is founded. Innovation has a timeless quality to it. No matter the era, the ability to reinvent and reimagine captivates us to our core. In that way, haute horology is a profoundly timeless craft, as innovation is never antiquated. Every year, these visionaries, inventors and fearless designers build upon the past by refusing to accept that everything has been done. From groundbreaking materials and artistic techniques to unfathomable exploits in engineering and unprecedented display configurations, innovations continually ensure a rebirth of the industry.

Watches International takes great pride in sharing the perpetually growing story of watchmaking with our readers. Those who have never been introduced to this world get a riveting insight in the many facets that make haute horology the special universe that it is. They learn to develop an enthusiasm that will fascinate them for the rest of their lives. Seasoned aficionados learn of all the new frontiers that have been conquered by the virtuosos of time. Even watchmakers may draw inspiration from their peers' achievements and ingenuity, propelling them to new heights of imagination.

Passion is of paramount importance for *Watches International*. In many ways, teaching someone to develop a deep connection with such a sophisticated art form enriches their lives with new ways of experiencing the world. There's an undeniable beauty in that. So thank you for allowing us to share with you our undying passion.

Michael Dickey

Letter from the Publisher

I Can't Live without Men... and Men Can't Live without their Watches!

Just between you and me, I have a secret: I love men. I can't live without them! A firm handshake, the scent of eau de cologne and seasoned leather, and a kind smile make my heart go pitter-patter. I like to think the feeling is mutual, but what men really can't live without... is their watches. They have a special relationship: each complication offers a taste of a universe, an experience, a life well lived. Each watch tells a story, summoning up faces, people, histories and ideas.

If you ask a man about his love for watches, he will almost certainly begin by telling you about the pleasure of informing his eight-year-old classmates that "the little hand tells the hours and the big hand tells the minutes," or about the time his father brought him to a watch store for the first time, when he was a young man and the world seemed to stretch out at his feet and go on forever. He might tell you about his wife—a woman who understands the power of symbolism, and who, for their fortieth wedding anniversary, gave him a gift to transcend time: a wristwatch destined to be passed down to future generations.

Some people understand the masculine inclination for watches as the result of a cold calculation, detached from any emotional implications... some people think it's a kind of social golden ticket that also provides a boost to one's own self-regard. But if we take a closer look, those are never the only reasons. If we don't understand why men love their watches, maybe it's because men, and the forces that drive them, aren't so different from the timepieces they adore. For those of us (like me) who can't live without men but find ourselves wondering about their secret inner lives, men are an endlessly fascinating, elusive subject: virile, powerful, yet still faced with the passing of time, with no choice but to be as elegant as possible in the process.

I find myself asking men all the time why they chose the watch they wear. The last man I asked, a close friend just about to acquire a watch he'd dreamed of for ages, was a bit taken aback by my question. I had to use all my wiles, and a great deal of intuition, to get at the real reason he was so entranced by this watch—what lay behind the reliability and design qualities that he extolled to me. I'm still not sure I totally understand... nor even that he was telling me the truth. Clearly, a man and his watch are bound by invisible ties...

Caroline Childers

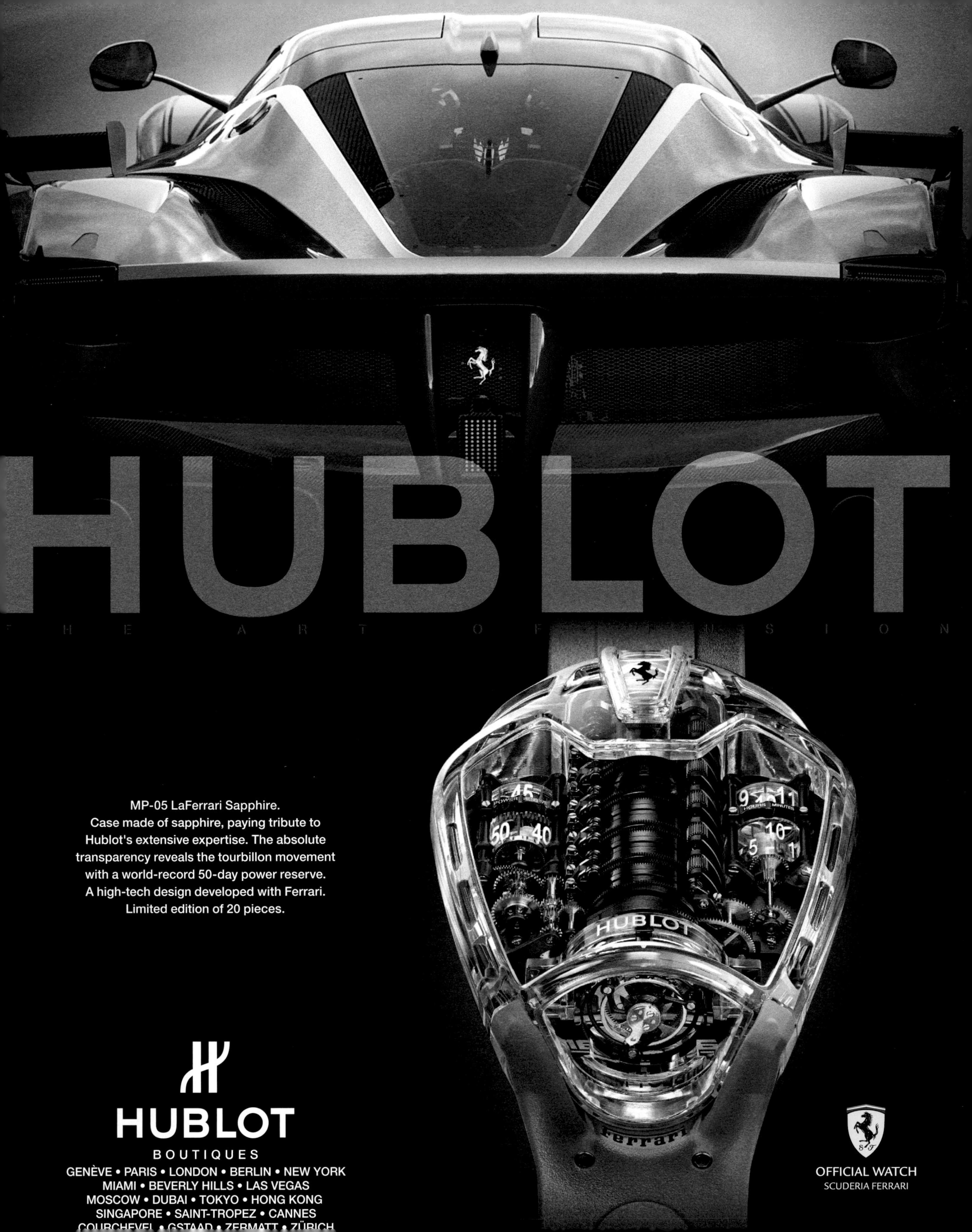

Tambour Automatic Chronograph

THE ORIGINAL ANNUAL OF THE WORLD'S FINEST WRISTWATCHES

TOURBILLON INTERNATIONAL
A MODERN LUXURY COMPANY
ADMINISTRATION, ADVERTISING SALES, EDITORIAL, BOOK SALES

11 West 25th Street, 8th Floor • New York, NY 10010
Tel: +1 (212) 627-7732 Fax: +1 (312) 274-8418

Caroline Childers
PUBLISHER

Michel Jeannot
EDITOR IN CHIEF

EDITORS	Merry Longthorne Elise Nussbaum Samson Crouhy
ART DIRECTOR	Mutsumi Hyuga
JUNIOR ASSISTANT EDITOR	Amber Ruiz
TRANSLATIONS	Caroline Elbaz Susan Jacquet
VICE PRESIDENT OF OPERATIONS	Sean Bertram
PRODUCTION DIRECTOR	Tim Maxwell
DIRECTOR OF INFORMATION TECHNOLOGY	Scott Brookman
NATIONAL CIRCULATION MANAGER	Amanda Higgins
NATIONAL DISTRIBUTION MANAGER	Hector Galvez
SALES ADMINISTRATOR	Ralph Gago

WEB DISTRIBUTION
www.modernluxury.com/watches

PHOTOGRAPHY
Photographic Archives
Property of Tourbillon International, a Modern Luxury Company

MODERN **LUXURY**

Lew Dickey
CHAIRMAN

Michael Dickey
CHIEF EXECUTIVE OFFICER

CHIEF OPERATING OFFICER	John Dickey
SENIOR COUNSEL	Ashley Herd

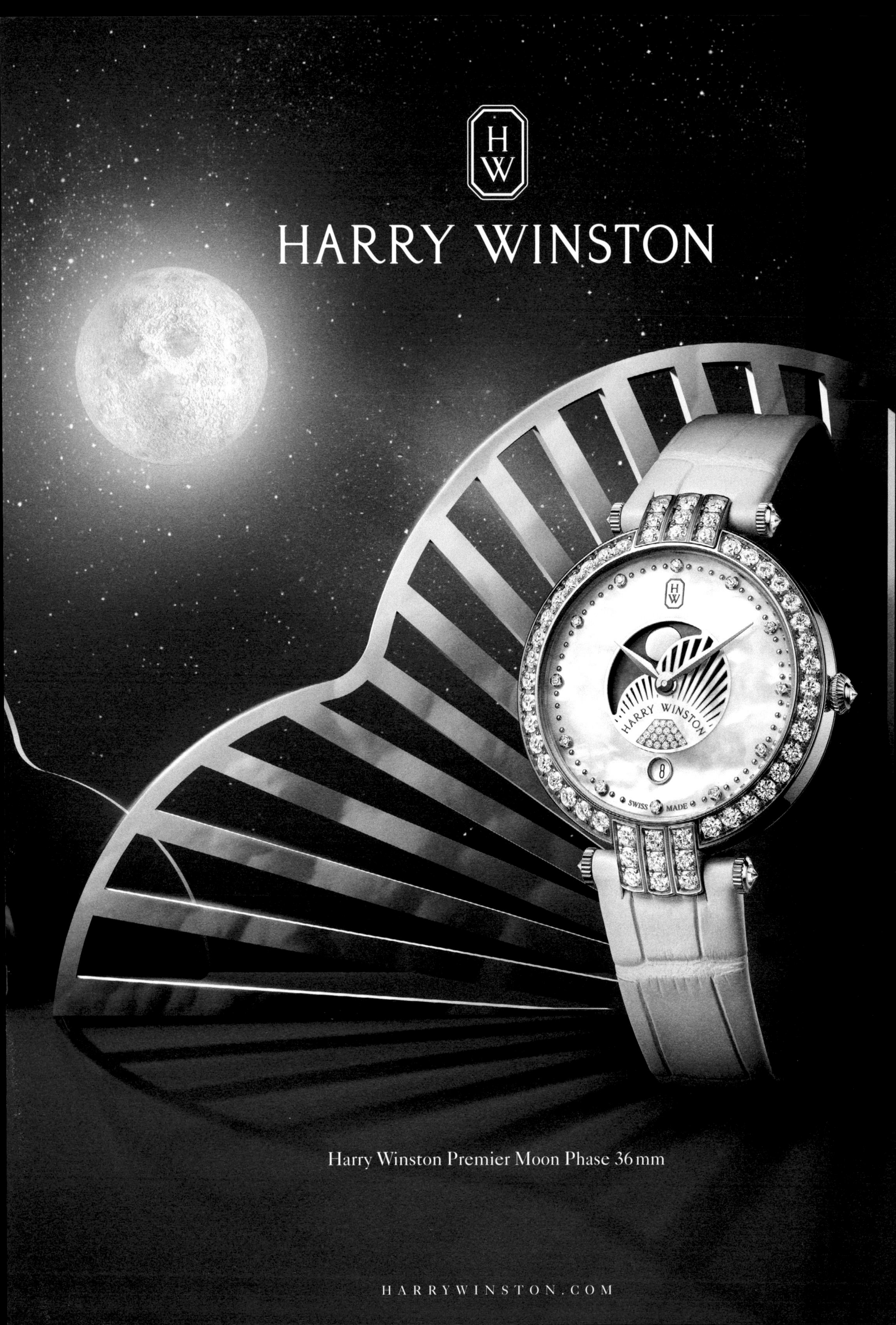

QUATRE
Grosgrain & Clou de Paris
Bracelets

[Letter from the Editor in Chief]

What engine is driving your car?

The world of horology is a profoundly masculine one, and a very odd industry. The watch itself is a peculiar object—if you don't believe me, try to imagine the imposing body of a Mercedes pushed forward by a Fiat 500 motor! It's impossible: the combination is ridiculous on its face. However, this kind of mismatch is common in watchmaking, and even worse—it is coming back in style as a business strategy.

Allow me to explain. In the 20th century, for many decades, the watchmaking industry was organized in the following way: manufactures produced movements that prestigious brands purchased to sell in watches under their own names. The quartz crisis then swept through the industry, taking with it most of the jobs and manufacturing capacities. Shortly afterwards, a certain Nicolas G. Hayek accepted the job (on very favorable terms, but candidates were not exactly clamoring for the position) of cleaning up the still-smoking ruins of the two most important groups in Swiss horology, ASUAG (comprising ETA and Longines) and SSIH (comprising Omega and Tissot). Their fusion led to the birth of SMH, later renamed the Swatch Group.

Mechanical horology started to get back on track, tripling its sales numbers over 20 years. Over these two profitable decades, Swatch Group (via ETA) was the reigning provider of movements, crowned as such by practically the entire Swiss watchmaking industry, with a few rare and notable exceptions, such as Rolex. Brands such as Vacheron Constantin, Audemars Piguet, Breguet, IWC, TAG Heuer and a multitude of others (the vast majority, in fact) did not make their own movements... and no one was complaining. In fact, the same mechanical movement (reliable, mass-produced and inexpensive at ETA) could just as well equip a $1,000 watch as a timepiece at $15,000 or even more!

Then, one day, Swatch Group decided that it no longer wanted to be horology's "supermarket," and cut its deliveries, causing a panic in this tightly knit world. The elite brands had no choice but to accelerate a process that some of them had already begun: building their own manufacturing facilities, getting R&D teams up and running, and producing their own movements (often ten times more expensive than those they had previously purchased). From now on, the "engine" driving an IWC would no longer resemble that of a Breitling, and each brand would have its own caliber, according to the image and resources of each company. In other words, the engine of a Citroën 2CV would no longer be pressed into service for a Mercedes. Nobody found cause to quarrel with this strategy.

Today, watchmaking is experiencing a brutal slowdown, and ETA is much more open to supplying its own competitors (once again). Some are saying (once again) that the body is more important than the motor that drives it. The manufactures are oversized, and those Fiat 500 engines are (once again) very fashionable with the financiers.

Michel Jeannot

LA ESMERALDA TOURBILLON, PINK GOLD CASE, 44 MM

Boutique Rolex Étoile A Star is Born

A boutique devoted entirely to Rolex has opened in the heart of Paris's Triangle d'Or, in the eighth arrondissement, just steps away from the Champs-Elysées. Since the beginning of 2017, it has offered a broad selection of watches from Rolex's Oyster and Cellini collections.

ROLEX
ROLEX
arije

ROLEX

The Rolex Experience

This superb $150m^2$ location incorporates the recent innovations of Rolex boutiques all over the world, while preserving the specific architectural legacy of the 19th century in a legendary neighborhood that has become the very symbol of Parisian elegance and luxury.

It is a space with a unique character, a subtle marriage of materials and lights, infused with both modernity and warmth. An architecture punctuated by bay windows, theatrical presentations, and clear views all harmonize with the use of elegant materials such as brushed, bronzed brass framing the built-in showcases, delicately grained walnut wood, the striated stone of the walls and the cream-colored leather that graces the furniture and inner partitions. The effect creates an atmosphere of restrained warmth, in which technology is incorporated discreetly in order to highlight elegance and a convivial ambience.

Whether it comes to welcoming customers, advising them, or seeing that their watches are in perfect working order, everything contributes to transforming each visit into an exceptional, Rolex-quality experience.

A Wide Selection of Watches

It is in this understated, refined atmosphere that the brand showcases a wide array of classic and professional Rolex models from the Oyster collection, as well as the Cellini collection, which was relaunched in 2014.

Among the major new models, visitors are able to admire the next generation of the archetypal classic watch, the Datejust 41, in a Rolesor version, as well as the latest version of the legendary chronograph, the Cosmograph Daytona, in 904L steel, equipped with a black ceramic monobloc Cerachrom bezel.

Besides these new additions to the Oyster line, the boutique also offers customers a chance to discover the latest iterations of the Oyster Perpetual Day-Date, "the Watch of Presidents," originally launched in 1956.

About Rolex

Leading brand of the Swiss watch industry, Rolex, headquartered in Geneva, enjoys an unrivaled reputation for quality and expertise the world over. Its Oyster and Cellini watches, all certified as Superlative Chronometers for their precision, performance and reliability, are symbols of excellence, elegance and prestige. Founded by Hans Wilsdorf in 1905, the brand pioneered the development of the wristwatch and is at the origin of numerous major watchmaking innovations, such as the Oyster, the first waterproof wristwatch, launched in 1926, and the Perpetual rotor self-winding mechanism invented in 1931. Rolex has registered over 400 patents in the course of its history. A truly integrated and independent manufacturing company, Rolex designs, develops and produces in-house all the essential components of its watches, from the casting of the gold alloys to the machining, crafting, assembly and finishing of the movement, case, dial and bracelet. Rolex is also actively involved in supporting the arts, sports, exploration, the spirit of enterprise, and the environment through a broad palette of sponsoring activities, as well as philanthropic programs.

Oyster Perpetual Day-Date 36 (Rolex)

Bulgari

Vacheron Constantin

IWC

Breguet

Harry Winston

CHANEL
CORUM
LA CHAUX-DE-FONDS · SUISSE
Chopard
BVLGARI
CHAUMET
PARIS
ROGER DUBUIS
HORLOGER GENEVOIS
Bell & Ross
TIME INSTRUMENTS
6 PLACE VENDÔME
REPOSSI
PARIS
BOUCHERON
PARIS
FREDERIQUE CONSTANT
GENEVE
FRANCK MULLER
GENEVE
Glashütte
ORIGINAL
BREGUET
BAUME & MERCIER
MAISON D'HORLOGERIE GENEVE 1830
MONT BLANC
Pomellato
JACOB & CO
GENÈVE
TAG Heuer
SWISS AVANT-GARDE SINCE 1860
de GRISOGONO
GENEVE
MESSIKA
PARIS
HERMÈS
PARIS
OMEGA
2
BLANCPAIN
MANUFACTURE DE HAUTE HORLOGERIE
GP
GIRARD-PERREGAUX
MECHANICS OF TIME SINCE 1791
VACHERON CONSTANTIN
Manufacture Horlogère. Genève, depuis 1755.
Cartier
Breguet
Depuis 1775
AUDEMARS PIGUET
Le Brassus
GUY ELLIA
PIAGET
IWC
SCHAFFHAUSEN
HUBLOT
HARRY WINSTON
PIAGET
Pomellato
PIAGET
JAQUET DROZ
SWISS WATCHMAKER SINCE 1738
Chopard
AUDEMARS PIGUET
Le Brassus
GUY ELLIA
Breguet
Depuis 1775
ARNOLD & SON
SINCE 1764
VACHERON CONSTANTIN
Manufacture Horlogère. Genève, depuis 1755.
CHANEL
GP
GIRARD-PERREGAUX
MECHANICS OF TIME SINCE 1791
Cartier
JACOB & CO
GENÈVE
Glashütte
ORIGINAL
1
FREDERIQUE CONSTANT
GENEVE
OMEGA
HERMÈS
PARIS
BOUCHERON
PARIS
TAG Heuer
SWISS AVANT-GARDE SINCE 1860
BVLGARI
BLANCPAIN
MANUFACTURE DE HAUTE HORLOGERIE
3
Bell & Ross
TIME INSTRUMENTS
ROGER DUBUIS
HORLOGER GENEVOIS
CHAUMET
PARIS
de GRISOGONO
GENEVE
FRANCK MULLER
GENEVE
JAQUET DROZ
SWISS WATCHMAKER SINCE 1738
IWC
SCHAFFHAUSEN
ARNOLD & SON
SINCE 1764
de GRISOGONO
GENEVE
HUBLOT
6 PLACE VENDÔME
REPOSSI
PARIS
MONT BLANC
HARRY WINSTON
BAUME & MERCIE
MAISON D'HORLOGERIE GENEVE 1

1. Piaget

2. Breguet

3. de GRISOGONO

4. Cartier

5. Bulgari

4

5

Audemars Piguet at Arije

The celebrated haute horology brand Audemars Piguet has also chosen Arije's plum location in the Triangle d'Or, at 46 rue Pierre Charron, to pursue its strategy of expansion. Upon entering this new boutique, visitors are ensconced in the brand's original, artistic universe, where they can find Audemars Piguet's entire collection, as well as models that are exclusive to the store.

Since its establishment in 1875, the Brassus company has made a priority of maintaining a close relationship with its international clientele. This elite group of people is passionate about the traditional horological expertise upon which Audemars Piguet has built its superb reputation. It is in this spirit of tradition that Audemars Piguet and Arije, partners for many years, will guide the direction of this new showcase.

Royal Oak Tourbillon Extra-Plat Edition Spéciale
(Audemars Piguet)

MAGIC
GOLD
HUBLOT
GENEVE

HUBLOT

Ricardo Guadalupe

CEO of Hublot

DIEGO MARADONA ▼

ACTIVE INNOVATION

In 2012, when Hublot signed a partnership with Ferrari, the new relationship was completely unmapped. This year, on the 70th anniversary of the Scuderia, a fourth Hublot Ferrari watch marks the occasion, the result of a true creative collaboration between the watchmaking and automobile design teams. **Basking in the success of the collaboration, Hublot CEO Ricardo Guadalupe details the brand's latest developments.** The in-house UNICO calibers currently account for almost half of the company's production, and since 2016, Hublot has been offering industrially produced sapphire watches for the first time in watchmaking history.

How has Hublot evolved in the last year?

Hublot has further progressed in 2016. Despite a gloomy year for the industry in general, we actually increased our sales by about 5%. Why? Probably because we are both creative and active! In addition, the fluctuations in the Chinese market—which represents only 8% of our sales—didn't really affect us. What was once a weakness has become an opportunity! However, we would like to increase this number to 20% of sales, and we're working hard on that.

If you had to choose just one, what would you say is the event that best represents 2016 for Hublot?

No contest: bringing Pelé and Maradona together for the first time! We managed to get these two soccer legends on the same pitch to play our "friendship match" at Paris's Palais Royal. Up until the last minute, I could hardly believe it was going to happen. What a memorable moment!

"Hublot's calling is innovation and creativity."

▲ BIG BANG UNICO SAPPHIRE ALL BLACK

And for your watches?

Our calling is innovation and creativity. We try to make products that our competitors are not offering. All Black just celebrated its sapphire-themed ten-year anniversary with the launch of a Hublot Big Bang Unico Sapphire in a white version and another in black sapphire (the All Black). This is an historic accomplishment, since we have succeeded in creating an industrial process for making a sapphire watch in relatively large quantities—500 pieces! In addition, until now, sapphire watches were only available at stratospheric prices. This one has a relatively "reasonable" price of 55,000 Swiss francs (CHF). It is an exceptional model, which is inspiring remarkable passion. I strongly believe in developing the use of sapphire in high-end horology over the course of the next five to ten years. This material opens up an immense array of possibilities, for example in terms of colored sapphire.

What will be Hublot's biggest moments in 2017?

In the field of sponsorship, our two pillars are soccer—which was front and center in 2016—and Ferrari, which celebrates its 70th anniversary this year! We will be associated with the worldwide coverage of this anniversary, which is also an important part of our Baselworld 2017 approach. A commemorative piece was specially designed by the automotive team, under the leadership of Flavio Manzoni, Design Director at Ferrari. Partnerships today require true collaboration at all levels; it's no longer enough to slap a logo on a dial! This very interesting watch has an aspect that is very "Ferrari," while still remaining "Hublot." It is not a Big Bang, nor a Classic Fusion, but instead a wholly new concept: a limited edition with a price point around 150,000 CHF.

▲ BIG BANG FERRARI TITANIUM LIMITED EDITION

Any other partnerships in the works?

Besides soccer and the Ferrari partnership, we are exploring numerous different arenas. For example, we collaborated with the tattoo studio Sang Bleu for a special Big Bang. We are also making forays into music and art, worlds that our clients also move in. Hublot aims to be as diverse as the lives of its clientele, and our communications approach must be interdisciplinary. We can't just stick to one or two fields.

What are the strongest points of Hublot's collections?

The Big Bang and the Classic Fusion account for 90% of our sales, with 60% for the former and 30% for the latter. The Classic Fusion, a discreet hours-minutes-seconds model, is our entry point for the collection. With prices between 6,000 and 15,000 CHF, it's very attractive from a commercial standpoint. Big Bang has a price point beginning at 10,000 CHF. The rest of our range comprises the Spirit of Big Bang, which features a tonneau shape and corresponds to 6% of sales, along with concept watches and complications, such as the Ferrari and tourbillons, representing a small percentage but with a relatively high value.

▲ BIG BANG SANG BLEU

▲ BIG BANG MECA-10

Is Hublot increasing its proportion of in-house movements?

We are mainly equipping our Big Bangs with our UNICO chronograph movement. We also have the MECA 10, which has 10 days of power reserve. We created 1,000 units in 2016, but expect to increase that. Forty percent of our production is currently equipped with in-house movements, and we started with zero! We plan to raise that figure to about 70% over the next five years.

What percentage of Hublot's production is women's watches?

Our watches are 72% men's models, 28% women's models. For a brand like Hublot, that is satisfactory. But we are aiming for 30% or even 40% in the feminine market. For us, women represent a new clientele to win over, and we are reaching out to them with innovations in terms of color or materials, such as embroidery, denim or the bright colors of Pop Art. The use of sapphire would also be particularly well suited to a women's watch.

Have the modes of communication changed?

Yes, all of our communication platforms are closely linked with digital, with images. Young people don't read much. We focus our efforts on beautiful visuals, so as to distinguish them from standard photos of a watch on the wrist, which anyone can easily post. These new, professional images are very expensive, but guarantee high-quality visuals and videos.

And what is on the horizon for your distribution network?

We have about 800 points of sale, including 78 boutiques. We are looking to reduce that number to 700, with about 100 boutiques.

▲ CLASSIC FUSION BERLUTI SCRITTO PLATINUM

▶ CLASSIC FUSION AEROFUSION CHRONOGRAPH CONCRETE JUNGLE

HUBLOT

Hublot expands its growing reach into the sporting world with a new and exciting partnership. The first brand to partner with both a European soccer club and an American football team, the Swiss watchmaker proudly joins forces with the four-time Super Bowl champion New York Giants. By becoming the team's Official Watch and Timekeeper, Hublot unites its historic pedigree and pioneering spirit with the team's rich winning tradition.

Underneath a stunning view of the unmistakable city skyline, Hublot and the New York Giants hosted Manhattan's first "luxury tailgate." An elevated take on one of football's most cherished pre-game customs, the event provided guests with a stunning catering menu by award-winning executive chef Jean-Paul Bourgeois while New York DJ Paul Sevigny honored his favorite team with a special set. The star-studded guest list, highlighted by New York Giants wide receiver Victor Cruz and Jean-François Sberro, Managing Director, Hublot of America, celebrated the event beneath an illuminated marquee of "Hublot Loves Football" that evoked a classic Times Square mood.

Grand, elegant and decisively "New York" in atmosphere, the event marked a rousing beginning to what is sure to be a captivating partnership between two leaders in their respective fields. The "luxury tailgate" also served as the perfect opportunity for Jean-François Sberro and Victor Cruz to introduce an exclusive new timepiece inspired by the New York Giants. An enlightening Q&A with Cruz followed, facilitated by former Giants star, TV personality, and Hublot Friend of the Brand Jesse Palmer.

◀ Jean-François Sberro, Ricardo Guadalupe and New York Giants owner Jonathan Tisch at a New York Giants game.

The Classic Fusion Aerofusion Limited New York Edition (in titanium or the brand's King Gold) is the watchmaker's first reference inspired by the New York Giants. The limited-edition self-winding timepiece, whose riveting skeletonized architecture is inspired by the New York City skyline, honors the high-achieving football team with numerous accents in the squad's iconic blue tones. Presented in a full-size authentic New York Giants helmet autographed by Victor Cruz, the 45mm wristwatch complements two centrally driven hour and minute hands with a red-tipped stem gliding across the openworked dial as it indicates the seconds of the HUB1155 caliber's chronograph. Two subdials, at 3 and 9 o'clock, display the small seconds and chronograph's 30-minute counter, respectively, while the date is easily identified via a skeletonized disc that orbits the dial to align itself appropriately with a highly legible white backdrop at 6 o'clock. The caseback, which features vintage imagery on its sapphire crystal, boasts an individual engraving with each timepiece's numbered limited edition. The Classic Fusion Aerofusion further proves its pedigree with a stunning blue football-inspired strap in calfskin leather stitched onto a blue version of the brand's signature rubber backing.

Alongside collaborative creations and a number of premium events, Hublot's partnership with the New York Giants includes a robust presence on game days. From a "Hublot Countdown to Kickoff" video as Giants players prepare to take the field at MetLife Stadium, to Hublot's sponsoring of Giants' coach's timeouts, to beautifully designed Hublot clocks indicating the time in club and suite areas at the stadium, the partnership truly integrates each party into the activities and very core of the other.

▲ Jean-François Sberro and Hublot Friends of the Brand Victor Cruz and Jesse Palmer at the Hublot Loves Football "luxury tailgate" event. *(top left)*

▲ Jean-François Sberro, Managing Director of Hublot of America and Mike Stevens, Senior Vice President and Chief Marketing Officer of the New York Giants. *(top right)*

At a London-themed gala in Hollywood's Sony Pictures Studios, Hublot and the legendary Chelsea FC united to present the manufacture's first watch created for the English soccer club. Celebrating the team's North American Tour, Hublot, the Official Watch of the recent UEFA EURO 2016™, bolstered its presence in and support of the global sport with the U.S. unveiling of the Classic Fusion Chronograph Chelsea FC, the Official Watch of Chelsea FC.

Housed in a 45mm titanium case, the self-winding timepiece imbues its rugged, masculine construction with regal elegance, thanks to its dial's eye-catching design. At 12 o'clock on the face, Chelsea FC's lion appliqué establishes its stately posture atop a sunray-finished backdrop in the blue synonymous with the iconic club. A pair of twin counters provides a vibrant contrast against the dial's main color while creating a harmony of tones with the watch's hands, hour markers and case. Driven by the HUB1143 caliber, the Classic Fusion Chronograph Chelsea FC indicates the hours, minutes and chronograph seconds via a central axis while the small seconds and 30-minute totalizers are displayed at 3 and 9 o'clock. The timepiece displays the date via an aperture at 6 o'clock and boasts a sapphire crystal caseback printed with Chelsea FC's logo.

▶ Entry of the Sony Pictures Studio. *(right)*

▶ Chelsea FC players in front of a British double decker "Hublot Loves Football" bus. *(far right)*

Hublot celebrates Usain Bolt's groundbreaking accomplishments

with a pair of timepieces that embody the power and colorful energy of the fastest man in the world.

World-record holder in the 100m, 200m and 4 x 100m sprints, Bolt built upon his already unprecedented career by punctuating Rio's 2016 Olympic Games with his third consecutive series of gold medals in the same sprinting events. The winner of nine Olympic gold medals, the Jamaican legend is honored with a timepiece of dazzling vivacity. The Big Bang Unico Usain Bolt Yellow Gold dresses itself in a fitting ensemble—an 18-karat gold case with shiny gold calfskin strap. On the openworked dial, the 45mm timepiece pays further homage to the sprinter with a palette in black, gold and green: the colors of his beloved Jamaica. Visible through the unobstructed dial-side construction, the HUB1242 UNICO Manufacture movement drives a display of the hours, minutes, small seconds, chronograph totalizer, date at 3 o'clock and chronograph seconds by way of a central hand shaped like a lightning bolt in honor of the champion's nickname. At 9 o'clock, the small seconds subdial is adorned with the silhouette of Usain Bolt striking his signature victory pose. The movement boasts a 72-hour power reserve and a flyback chronograph with column wheel. The timepiece's golden strap is embossed with a silhouette of the Jamaican flag.

The Big Bang Unico Usain Bolt Ceramic takes on the celebration with a more restrained color scheme, in black. Yet the material is anything but traditional, with the choice of high-tech ceramic for the case. Adorned with six H-shaped gold screws that celebrate Bolt's triumphant career, the watch's bezel finds an elegant harmony with the dial, which honors the colors of Jamaica. The Big Bang Unico Usain Bolt Ceramic is worn on a black rubber and Schedoni-leather strap embossed with the Jamaican flag.

▲ Big Bang Unico Usain Bolt. *(top left and center)*

▲ Ricardo Guadalupe, CEO, and Usain Bolt, fastest man in the world. *(top right)*

Collaborating with renowned tattoo artist Maxime Büchi,

founder of the multidisciplinary artistic platform Sang Bleu, Hublot combines the craft of haute horology with the equally expansive art form of tattooing.

The Big Bang Sang Bleu rejects traditional codes of design at every turn, establishing a sense of mystery and multi-dimensionality by eschewing hands entirely. Driven by the HUB1213 UNICO Manufacture movement, the self-winding timepiece decorates its dial with a combination of juxtaposed geometric shapes, comprised of a number of straight lines and reminiscent of Leonardo da Vinci's famed Vitruvian Man. However, the thoughtful composition is not merely a visual exhibition; the three superimposed octagonal discs that make up the geometric sculpture revolve around the central axis to indicate the time through a captivating choreography. As the largest disc indicates the hours, the smaller one above it displays the minutes. Both are enhanced with SuperLumiNova tips to ensure optimal legibility within the design's unusual architecture. The Hublot/Maxime Büchi creation completes its hands-free presentation with a display of the seconds via a third disc, the smallest of the trio, positioned in the center of the dial. The Big Bang Sang Bleu houses its hypnotic artwork within a 45mm titanium case engraved with a geometric Maxime Büchi design and honors the structural harmony of the dial by replacing the traditional circular Big Bang bezel with a perfect hexagon.

On May 6, 2016, in Chicago, Illinois, Hublot took its vision of "Art of Fusion" to a stunning level, blending Swiss haute horology, contemporary art and the motoring genius exemplified by Ferrari.

The event, hosted in partnership with Lake Forest Sportscars and watch retailer Geneva Seal, brought guests directly into the world of distinguished Chicago-based artist Hebru Brantley. Providing a rare look inside the artist's workspace, the celebration allowed attendees to explore his creative process, featuring finished works as well as unfinished paintings. Sharing the stage with Brantley's creations, Hublot's latest collections found a perfect home inside the artist's studio, admired for their exquisite craftsmanship by guests enjoying hors d'oeuvres and cocktails named after the watchmaker's iconic timepieces: Classic Fusion, Big Bang and All Black. The Official Watch and Official Timekeeper of Scuderia Ferrari, Hublot took the opportunity to treat its guests to a spellbinding showcase of the Italian motoring legend's California T in iconic red. The fascinating event marked a brilliant step on Hublot's journey through the "Art of Fusion," a journey that brings multi-dimensional worlds together through a unified language.

▲ Images from the Hublot Loves Art event with Hebru Brantley. *(top)*

#MP05LAFERRARI

The Swiss watchmaker takes its passion for Ferrari

sports cars and groundbreaking artistic endeavors to new heights with the release of the MP-05 LaFerrari movie.

Atop the roof of Los Angeles' Ace Museum, 50 guests, some even seated comfortably in Ferraris, enjoyed a drive-in-cinema experience of unique luxury and thrill. September 7, 2016, thus marked the world premiere of an animated movie with special effects and designs of the highest level. The film tells the riveting story of the MP-05 LaFerrari's HUB9005.H1.PN.1 caliber, a breathtaking 637-component mechanical movement whose 11 series-coupled barrels endow the timepiece with a record-breaking 50-day power reserve. In the movie, the FXX K supercar, the motoring triumph that inspired the MP-05 LaFerrari Sapphire's design, must complete a circuit in 50 seconds; as the vehicle passes checkpoints, the watch is simultaneously being constructed in a lab by a high-tech 3D scanner.

By collaborating with Digital Domain, a creator of innovative film visuals, Hublot immortalizes the MP-05 LaFerrari Sapphire through a medium that allows the watchmaker to capture the brilliance of its timepiece and give it a shining role alongside a mesmerizing co-star. As the FXX K completes its lap, the timepiece is finally completed, and upon the approach of a watchmaker, its tourbillon comes to life, encapsulating one of horology's most enthralling moments: the first tick of a mechanical masterpiece.

▲ The Ferrari 458 Italia.

▲ MP-05 La Ferrari movie screening event.

HUBLOT
POWER RESERVE
FIVE DAYS

"...and OMEGA is the watch
that went to the Moon."

Ω
OMEGA

Summary

Summary

PIAGET
AUTOMATIC

Westime

From international timepiece collectors, to customers who are considering their first purchase of a watch, Westime's four boutiques in Southern California and newest location in Miami cater to them all by offering a broad and deep selection of today's most desirable watches.

For three decades Westime has distinguished itself as the ultimate retail destination specializing in extraordinary watches. John Simonian, a third-generation watch expert with a passion for mechanical timepieces, founded Westime in 1987 when he opened the first boutique on Los Angeles's West Side. From its earliest days, Westime catered to a clientele that ranged from Hollywood celebrities and professional athletes, to the region's influential residents and international business travelers. Westime has since earned the return business of discriminating clients from around the globe.

Today, Westime's five locations reflect the iconic styles of their surrounding neighborhoods. The 2,000 ft^2 Beverly Hills boutique is part of the Two Rodeo shopping district on world famous Rodeo Drive. This location features a welcoming façade of red brick and floor-to-ceiling windows. Six showcase towers seem to stand at attention in the windows, until—like the hourly changing of the guard—they automatically rotate 180º to present a new selection of fine timepieces to browsers. Within the boutique, showcases of varying shapes, sizes and colors are arranged in a series of intimate "neighborhoods," allowing each of the 40 watch and jewelry brands on display to reside in a unique setting. Freestanding showcases, seating areas and an espresso bar create a relaxing environment that encourages customers to discover products at their leisure. Westime's signature capital W appears subtly throughout the interior design, while a deconstructed version of the company's watch gear logo inspires the blue and cream mosaic patterns seen in the boutique's custom terrazzo-tile floor.

SERPENTI (Bvlgari) ▸

▲ Westime Beverly HIlls

▲ Westime Sunset

▲ Westime Malibu

▲ Westime La Jolla

Westime Sunset is the largest boutique in the family. Its location on Sunset Boulevard in West Hollywood places it among the chic restaurants and boutiques of Sunset Plaza and the legendary nightclubs of the Sunset Strip. The 6,600 ft^2 Westime Sunset store reflects the bold buildings and signage of the neighborhood. Perforated and backlit metal panels wrap the asymmetrical façade, while a front wall of windows allows passersby to see the brightly lit scene inside. Asymmetrical angles and high-contrast materials including glass, Venetian plaster, steel, walnut and polished concrete create a gallery-like setting inside the two-story space. Custom corners for Audemars Piguet, Breitling, Omega, TAG Heuer, Zenith, Bulgari and Buben & Zörweg enhance the shopping experience for fans of those popular brands.

Westime La Jolla is located north of San Diego in one of the country's most beautiful seaside communities. The light-filled store resides among charming shops, galleries and cafes on elegant Prospect Street, just steps from the Pacific Ocean. The boutique's gray slate flooring, natural wood and glass watch showcases, and open floor plan invite customers to browse casually. The experienced Westime staff provides special services such as watch repairs and water resistance tests.

Westime's fourth boutique in Southern California resides along Malibu's sun-drenched shores. Located within the open-air Malibu Country Mart, Westime Malibu joins such luxury lifestyle neighbors as Ralph Lauren, Calypso St. Barth and Mr. Chow. The boutique's décor complements Malibu's famously laid-back style of luxury. Whitewashed panels and sea-blue awnings frame Westime's oversized front windows. A cluster of Adirondack chairs provides the perfect spot for shoppers to take in the view of Westime's window displays while enjoying a rest in the sunshine. Inside the boutique, a sand and cream design scheme creates a serene backdrop for backlit displays, as well as glass cases containing a tightly edited selection of watches and jewelry.

Westime looked east for its newest location, and opened Westime Miami early this year in the South Florida city's new downtown shopping mecca, Brickell City Centre.

Westime also operates Richard Mille, Audemars Piguet, and Hublot boutiques in select cities. The company is proud to support numerous charitable causes including After-School All-Stars, Scripps, and Special Olympics.

Westime is frequently noted as one of a dozen multi-brand retailers in the world that influences trends in the watchmaking industry. Led by John Simonian and his son Greg, the company is dedicated to offering the most important creations from traditional watch brands, while also promoting the new guard in haute horology. At Westime's boutiques, there is always something new to discover.

RM 11-02 JET BLACK
(Richard Mille)

ROYAL OAK TOURBILLON WESTIME LIMITED EDITION
(Audemars Piguet)

UR-210 CLOU DE PARIS
(Urwerk)

BRANDS CARRIED

AUDEMARS PIGUET	ERNST BENZ	MAÎTRES DU TEMPS
BELL & ROSS	FABERGÉ	MB&F
BLANCPAIN	FIONA KRUGER	MCT
BREGUET	FRANCK MULLER	MONTEGRAPPA
BREITLING	GIRARD-PERREGAUX	NIXON
BRM	GIULIANO MAZZUOLI	OMEGA
BUBEN & ZÖRWEG	GLASHÜTTE ORIGINAL	REUGE
BULGARI	GREUBEL FORSEY	RICHARD MILLE
CARL F. BUCHERER	HAMILTON	ROLAND ITEN
CHOPARD	HARRY WINSTON	RUDIS SYLVA
CHRISTOPHE CLARET	HAUTLENCE	SHAMBALLA JEWELS
DE BETHUNE	H. MOSER & CIE	TAG HEUER
DE GRISOGONO	HUBLOT	TISSOT
DEVON	HYT	TUDOR
DEWITT	JACOB & CO.	ULYSSE NARDIN
DIOR	LONGINES	URWERK
DÖTTLING	LOUIS MOINET	ZENITH

CLASSIC FUSION HERO VILLAIN
(Hublot)

HM8
(MB&F)

MIAMI
Brickell City Centre
701 South Miami Avenue, Suite 167C • Miami, FL 33131
T: 786-347-5353

BEVERLY HILLS
216 North Rodeo Drive • Beverly Hills, CA 90210
T: 310-888-8880

MALIBU
3832 Cross Creek Road • Malibu, CA 90265
T: 310-456-2555

LA JOLLA
1227 Prospect Street • La Jolla, CA 92037
T: 858-459-2222

SUNSET
8569 West Sunset Blvd. • West Hollywood
CA 90069
T: 310-289-0808

info@westime.com / www.westime.com

Greg Simonian

President of Westime

EASTERN EXPANSION

Even as it celebrates an expansion to the East Coast with its opening of a new boutique in Miami, Westime **PRESERVES THE SPECIAL TOUCH THAT SEPARATES IT FROM OTHER HIGH-END WATCH RETAILERS**. The family-run business demonstrates a profound understanding that behind the luxury lies an intense passion for horological art, exclusivity and exciting innovations. In that sense, Westime has firmly become a gallery-like institution connecting enthusiasts to the world of haute horology with a spectacular blend of variety, personalized service and unique creations.

What does it mean for Westime to have opened its first boutique outside of California with the launch of Westime Miami?

It definitely marks a new chapter for our family company, and means Westime is bi-coastal! While the opening of our downtown Miami boutique is entry into a new market, serving new customers, I am continually reminded of how many clients we already know in South Florida because they travel the world and have already shopped at Westime in California.

As Westime continues to grow, both in prestige and with new locations, how does the brand maintain the personal, family-owned touch that makes it such a unique retailer?

Growing without losing sight of what made a company great to begin with is a challenge that anyone on an upward trajectory faces, Westime included. My father, John Simonian, and I are very much involved in every aspect of the business and are committed to plenty of cross-country flights to keep our fingers on the pulse of all boutiques, and to spread the gospel.

◄ Zenith Pilot Type 20 Extra Special Limited Edition exclusively at Westime

"We strive to offer something to excite every watch enthusiast, as well as newcomers to the world of mechanical watches."

▸ **GREG SIMONIAN**

▲ Event at Westime Sunset.

▲ At the fourth annual Westime Charity Night at the home of Arnold Schwarzenegger, supporting After-School All-Stars, Westime president Greg Simonian presents a Richard Mille RM 030 limited edition to the grand prize winner, Chris Budack.

Do different Westime locations possess their own individual personalities? Which principles and qualities are universal throughout all the stores?

Most definitely. Our boutiques are designed to complement their specific communities and the preference of customers who shop there. Westime Malibu, for example, is small in terms of square footage but with its high open ceilings, sunshine-filled windows, and constant gentle ocean breezes it feels like a corner of a beach town, which it is. Westime Sunset, in West Hollywood, has a very modern, asymmetrical architecture that complements the iconic Mel's Diner next door as well as numerous luxury high-rises nearing completion in the trendy neighborhood. And Westime Miami represents a new design concept too. Enter Westime to discover expansive showcases for each of our watch brands, and linger in comfortable chairs in a rotunda in the center of the store. Then, branch off to explore two connecting mono-brand stores that are also owned and operated by Westime: Richard Mille Miami, and Audemars Piguet Miami. Across all locations, Westime presents a unique and surprising selection of watches, attentive service, a low-pressure shopping environment that leans toward a gallery experience, and expert skills of on-site watchmakers.

What part does philanthropy play in Westime's vision? How does the company leverage its numerous partnerships into a greater charitable impact?

Philanthropy is part of our DNA, and an important part of any business's relationship with the community it serves. We are eager to support local causes in our communities, from raffles, to gala fundraisers, to fun-runs and event sponsorships. And we are very proud to be entering our fifth year hosting a fundraising gala night at the home of Governor Arnold Schwarzenegger in support of the national children's charity he founded: After-School All-Stars.

What type of variety should customers expect when they enter a Westime boutique? How often does Westime add new brands to its locations?

We strive to offer something to excite every watch enthusiast, as well as newcomers to the world of mechanical watches. We love it when people allow themselves to explore and stumble upon a complication, or a brand, or a limited edition they never imagined seeing in person! And we also carry the most popular models. We don't add new watch collections casually. On the occasions that we do, you can rest assured that we have gotten to know the watch-

Why is it important for Westime to be such a leader when it comes to exclusive and limited edition timepieces?

Luxury products today are manufactured on a nearly mass level, and distributed in major cities around the world in the exact… same… way. The excitement of shopping while traveling really diminishes if the products available are identical to what you can find at home. We have to offer customers something special, something different, and of course a higher level of service than they find everywhere else.

What steps is Westime taking to match and complement its brick-and-mortar success within the digital/online world?

This year sees the relaunch of Westime.com, making it very easy to browse our inventory, contact a sales representative directly with any questions, and educate oneself about watches. It's also a fun place to follow Westime's event news, and browse our catalogs and newsletters. We are also committed to featuring our own original watch photography when it comes to social media sites.

Does Westime have anything special in the works as it prepares to celebrate its 30th anniversary?

To absorb our big growth spurt!

▲ Westime co-hosted an event in Beverly Hills with Los Angeles Confidential, honoring successful women and celebrating actress Kate Beckinsale.

LONGINES
La Grande Classique de Longines

LONGINES®

Web Site Directory

ALPINA	www.alpina-watches.com
ARNOLD & SON	www.arnoldandson.com
ATELIERS DEMONACO	www.ateliers-demonaco.com/
AUDEMARS PIGUET	www.audemarspiguet.com
BLANCPAIN	www.blancpain.com
BOUCHERON	www.boucheron.com
BREGUET	www.breguet.com
BVLGARI	www.bulgari.com
CARL F. BUCHERER	www.carl-f-bucherer.com
CARTIER	www.cartier.com
CHOPARD	www.chopard.com
CHRISTOPHE CLARET	www.christopheclaret.com
CORUM	www.corum.ch
DE GRISOGONO	www.degrisogono.com
FREDERIQUE CONSTANT	www.frederique-constant.com
GIRARD-PERREGAUX	www.girard-perregaux.com
GLASHÜTTE ORIGINAL	www.glashuette-original.com
GREUBEL FORSEY	www.greubelforsey.com
GUY ELLIA	www.guyellia.com
HARRY WINSTON	www.harrywinston.com
HUBLOT	www.hublot.com
JACOB & CO.	www.jacobandco.com
JAEGER-LECOULTRE	www.jaeger-lecoultre.com
JAQUET DROZ	www.jaquet-droz.com
LONGINES	www.longines.com
LOUIS VUITTON	www.louisvuitton.com
MANUFACTURE ROYALE	www.manufacture-royale.com
OMEGA	www.omegawatches.com
PATEK PHILIPPE	www.patek.com
PERRELET	www.perrelet.com
PIAGET	www.piaget.com
RICHARD MILLE	www.richardmille.com
ROGER DUBUIS	www.rogerdubuis.com
ROLEX	www.rolex.com
TAG HEUER	www.tagheuer.com
VACHERON CONSTANTIN	www.vacheron-constantin.com
ZENITH	www.zenith-watches.com

RELATED SITES

BASELWORLD	www.baselworld.com
SIHH	www.sihh.org

AUCTION HOUSES

CHRISTIE'S	www.christies.com
SOTHEBY'S	www.sothebys.com

Stephen Forsey

Co-Founder of Greubel Forsey

A STRIKING BREAKTHROUGH

This is the moment that aficionados and collectors of Greubel Forsey had been waiting for: **ROBERT GREUBEL'S AND STEPHEN FORSEY'S INTERPRETATION OF A COMPLICATION THAT RANKS AMONG THE MOST DIFFICULT TO CONSTRUCT—THE GRAND STRIKE**. This year, these two extraordinary watchmakers finally satisfied these hopes, presenting the brand's first grand strike model. Focused on perfection and determined to interpret this major complication in their own way, they are releasing it after a decade of research. The Greubel Forsey Grande Sonnerie thus possesses exceptional, even unprecedented, qualities for this type of complication: water resistance to 30m and 11 security functions. This standout model also boasts excellent acoustic properties, which remain the heart of the matter with this type of watch.

To begin with, how did Greubel Forsey fare in 2016, a year that saw decreased sales for the industry as a whole?

For us, 2016 was a year fairly similar to any other year. It is all relative, because our production remains stable, at about 100 units per year. That is why we are not really affected by economic fluctuations. If certain markets slow down, we focus on healthier ones. In any event, we cannot satisfy demand. This strategy requires a lot of work, but has the advantage of consistency and respect for our values, which really helped us weather the financial crisis in 2008. In 2016, South and North America represented our top market, with a nice showing in Southeast Asia as well. And we are making sure to concentrate on our strong points, such as creativity, while still communicating well.

◂ **GRANDE SONNERIE**

"We had kept our silence on striking watches… until this year!"

◂ STEPHEN FORSEY

How has your relationship with collectors evolved over the years?

We take great care to build a real relationship with them, rather than approach sales from a marketing point of view. This is why we are present in about 35 countries, where our clients are. That doesn't mean, however, that every Greubel Forsey piece is available in every point of sale. Retailers take on the role of our ambassadors, and we build real relationships with them that enable us to remain close to collectors. Our clients' interest has remained strong for more than a decade and they have long been clamoring for a striking watch.

A wish you've finally granted this year with the Grande Sonnerie!

Yes, this creation is the result of 11 years of research. We wanted to be completely confident about it. As with all our other complications, we began with examining the current state of the art, an approach that included taking an historic inventory of such models and considering all the classic technical specifications. If Greubel Forsey were to create such a complication, what would be its qualities? What would a collector want to see? Then, in the "final" phase of testing, Robert Greubel wore it for three years. Funnily enough, he actually had it on his wrist at a previous SIHH, naturally slightly concealed beneath his sleeve, and no one noticed!

That said, what are the essential qualities of the Grande Sonnerie as interpreted by Greubel Forsey?

Above all, exceptional acoustics. That is quite a feat for a timepiece that is water resistant to 30m. In fact, a watertight case muffles the sound... However, our grand strike is loud enough to be heard, even over competing sounds, such as in a car or an airplane. We also focused on additional security devices. There are 11 of them that protect the mechanism, for example in case someone tries to set the time while the striking is going on. Finally, comfort was essential. The entire caliber—which includes our 24-second tourbillon and comprises a grand total of 935 components—is housed within an asymmetrical Greubel Forsey case with the usual dimensions: 43.5mm in diameter and 16.13mm thick. It's a true grand strike wristwatch—a feat of miniaturization rarely seen in horology!

How did you approach the acoustic aspect?

We wanted a really rich, sustained sound. We were already experienced in the field, mostly through restoration work, and we knew the necessary specifications. A physicist and several engineers work in our extremely well-equipped laboratory. The resonance cage is in titanium, with two monobloc cathedral gongs on three levels. These "shaped" gongs also curve around the opening for the tourbillon, situated between 7 and 9 o'clock. We also maximized the striking strength of the hammers, as well as deliberating at length on the cadence of the strike. In fact, because the strike is automatic, it leaves time to count the chimes, without leaving too many pauses. Finally, we use a silent striking regulator to ensure an extremely pure sound that lasts throughout the entire chime.

Could you talk more about the striking mechanism, which is visible on the dial?

We didn't have any historical constraints, so we chose this location on the dial side. The openings on the hammers and chimes require very sophisticated finishing of these elements. The striking mechanism also possesses a separate winding and power reserve, independent from the rest of the mechanism! Our collectors actually prefer manual-winding pieces, which help them create a relationship with the watch. So we disassociated the two winding systems, a decision that also enabled us to assure sufficient power reserve for both. The watch itself is manually wound, while the striking mechanism is self-winding. While it is being worn, the strike is wound automatically by a platinum rotor, endowing it with a power reserve of 20 hours in grand strike mode. The mechanism has three modes in all: grand strike (sounds the hours and quarter hours), small strike (sounds the hours only) and silent. It is also possible to hear the time on demand, with the minute repeater activated by pressing on the crown.

How many of these watches will you produce?

We will create five to eight per year, with the first units delivered this year.

Before we go, how is the "Naissance d'une montre" (Birth of a watch) project developing?

The school-watch created by Michel Boulanger was sold at auction in 2016 for $1.4 million. Collectors saw it as a kind of sponsorship, and a chance to anticipate the future. In fact, 20 years from now, who will be able to service the watches in their collections? In Mexico, there are already no longer any watchmaking schools! At SIAR (Salón Internacional Alta Relojería) in Mexico, Boulanger instructed three Mexican watchmakers in traditional hand-decorating techniques. We now need to disseminate such watchmaking skills more widely...

◀ ▶ GRANDE SONNERIE

GENEVE

Ricardo Guadalupe

CEO of Hublot

ACTIVE INNOVATION

In 2012, when Hublot signed a partnership with Ferrari, the new relationship was completely unmapped. This year, on the 70th anniversary of the Scuderia, a fourth Hublot Ferrari watch marks the occasion, the result of a true creative collaboration between the watchmaking and automobile design teams. **Basking in the success of the collaboration, Hublot CEO Ricardo Guadalupe details the brand's latest developments.** The in-house UNICO calibers currently account for almost half of the company's production, and since 2016, Hublot has been offering industrially produced sapphire watches for the first time in watchmaking history.

DIEGO MARADONA ▸

How has Hublot evolved in the last year?

Hublot has further progressed in 2016. Despite a gloomy year for the industry in general, we actually increased our sales by about 5%. Why? Probably because we are both creative and active! In addition, the fluctuations in the Chinese market—which represents only 8% of our sales—didn't really affect us. What was once a weakness has become an opportunity! However, we would like to increase this number to 20% of sales, and we're working hard on that.

If you had to choose just one, what would you say is the event that best represents 2016 for Hublot?

No contest: bringing Pelé and Maradona together for the first time! We managed to get these two soccer legends on the same pitch to play our "friendship match" at Paris's Palais Royal. Up until the last minute, I could hardly believe it was going to happen. What a memorable moment!

"Hublot's calling is innovation and creativity."

◂ RICARDO GUADALUPE

▸ PELÉ

◄ BIG BANG FERRARI KING GOLD

▲ BIG BANG UNICO SAPPHIRE ALL BLACK

And for your watches?

Our calling is innovation and creativity. We try to make products that our competitors are not offering. All Black just celebrated its sapphire-themed ten-year anniversary with the launch of a Hublot Big Bang Unico Sapphire in a white version and another in black sapphire (the All Black). This is an historic accomplishment, since we have succeeded in creating an industrial process for making a sapphire watch in relatively large quantities—500 pieces! In addition, until now, sapphire watches were only available at stratospheric prices. This one has a relatively "reasonable" price of 55,000 Swiss francs (CHF). It is an exceptional model, which is inspiring remarkable passion. I strongly believe in developing the use of sapphire in high-end horology over the course of the next five to ten years. This material opens up an immense array of possibilities, for example in terms of colored sapphire.

What will be Hublot's biggest moments in 2017?

In the field of sponsorship, our two pillars are soccer—which was front and center in 2016—and Ferrari, which celebrates its 70th anniversary this year! We will be associated with the worldwide coverage of this anniversary, which is also an important part of our Baselworld 2017 approach. A commemorative piece was specially designed by the automotive team, under the leadership of Flavio Manzoni, Design Director at Ferrari. Partnerships today require true collaboration at all levels; it's no longer enough to slap a logo on a dial! This very interesting watch has an aspect that is very "Ferrari," while still remaining "Hublot." It is not a Big Bang, nor a Classic Fusion, but instead a wholly new concept: a limited edition with a price point around 150,000 CHF.

Any other partnerships in the works?

Besides soccer and the Ferrari partnership, we are exploring numerous different arenas. For example, we collaborated with the tattoo studio Sang Bleu for a special Big Bang. We are also making forays into music and art, worlds that our clients also move in. Hublot aims to be as diverse as the lives of its clientele, and our communications approach must be interdisciplinary. We can't just stick to one or two fields.

What are the strongest points of Hublot's collections?

The Big Bang and the Classic Fusion account for 90% of our sales, with 60% for the former and 30% for the latter. The Classic Fusion, a discreet hours-minutes-seconds model, is our entry point for the collection. With prices between 6,000 and 15,000 CHF, it's very attractive from a commercial standpoint. Big Bang has a price point beginning at 10,000 CHF. The rest of our range comprises the Spirit of Big Bang, which features a tonneau shape and corresponds to 6% of sales, along with concept watches and complications, such as the Ferrari and tourbillons, representing a small percentage but with a relatively high value.

Is Hublot increasing its proportion of in-house movements?

We are mainly equipping our Big Bangs with our UNICO chronograph movement. We also have the MECA 10, which has 10 days of power reserve. We created 1,000 units in 2016, but expect to increase that. Forty percent of our production is currently equipped with in-house movements, and we started with zero! We plan to raise that figure to about 70% over the next five years.

▼ BIG BANG MECA-10

▲ BIG BANG SANG BLEU

◂ CLASSIC FUSION AEROFUSION CHRONOGRAPH CONCRETE JUNGLE

What percentage of Hublot's production is women's watches?

Our watches are 72% men's models, 28% women's models. For a brand like Hublot, that is satisfactory. But we are aiming for 30% or even 40% in the feminine market. For us, women represent a new clientele to win over, and we are reaching out to them with innovations in terms of color or materials, such as embroidery, denim or the bright colors of Pop Art. The use of sapphire would also be particularly well suited to a women's watch.

Have the modes of communication changed?

Yes, all of our communication platforms are closely linked with digital, with images. Young people don't read much. We focus our efforts on beautiful visuals, so as to distinguish them from standard photos of a watch on the wrist, which anyone can easily post. These new, professional images are very expensive, but guarantee high-quality visuals and videos.

And what is on the horizon for your distribution network?

We have about 800 points of sale, including 78 boutiques. We are looking to reduce that number to 700, with about 100 boutiques.

▸ CLASSIC FUSION BERLUTI SCRITTO PLATINUM

#DontCrackUnderPressure

Jean-Claude Biver

President of LVMH Group's Watches Division and CEO of TAG Heuer

CONNECTION AND SYNERGY

In 2016, TAG Heuer posted double-digit growth—the best in its history!—despite the struggling sales of the watchmaking industry as a whole. The brand's CEO, Jean-Claude Biver, notably leads the company via clear positioning: **INNOVATION AND HIGH SUBJECTIVE VALUE, CONTRASTING WITH REASONABLE PRICES THAT PLACE ITS PRODUCTS FIRMLY IN THE AFFORDABLE LUXURY CATEGORY**. Since the beginning of 2017, Biver has also been applying his vision to guiding the destiny of Zenith, in addition to being President of Hublot and heading the entire watch division at French luxury group LVMH.

Are you planning on creating new synergies within the watch division at LVMH?

My new functions at the helm of Zenith will allow me to familiarize myself with its strategy and industrial capacities. Each of the brands in the group has mastered certain aspects, and of course it is more advantageous to be supplied internally than externally. Hublot produces 20,000 movements per year, manufactures its own cases and creates its own alloys, driven by a particularly dynamic R&D department. This year, TAG Heuer will roll out 120,000 mechanical movements, 300,000 cases and 500,000 dials. Clearly, such large-scale production facilities afford significant potential for mutual cooperation. In addition, TAG Heuer and Hublot are very well situated in terms of distribution, which will also support Zenith's development.

◄ TAG HEUER CONNECTED

▲ BERNARD ARNAULT CHAIRMAN AND CEO OF LVMH

"With the connected watch, TAG Heuer's image is suddenly 20 years younger!"

▼ JEAN-CLAUDE BIVER

◄ TAG HEUER MONZA CHRONOGRAPH CALIBRE 17

▲ CARRERA CHRONOGRAPH CALIBRE HEUER 01

◄ TAG HEUER CONNECTED

What positioning is TAG Heuer adopting?

Avant-garde and a leader in the market for accessible, luxury Swiss watches, TAG Heuer offers watches whose perceived value is twice their price! Our three main collections—Aquaracer, Carrera and Formula One—respond to these imperatives perfectly: their perceived value is two to three times their actual price.

What is the secret of TAG Heuer's growth, in an environment that is otherwise so gloomy?

We are investing more, even as our competitors are investing less. At the product strategy level, we are drawing a younger clientele with a strong entry-level range, priced between $1,000 and $3,000. The highest end of our product line (over $50,000) has been whittled down to a few conversation pieces. We have a muscular midrange offering ($3,000 to $6,000)—with a lot of in-house movements and innovations. Finally, you'll see a limited haute horology line, between $10,000 and $20,000.

How would you analyze the current public attitude towards luxury watches?

In the beginning, a watch was just a timekeeping instrument! Today, it represents status, style, design, even eternity. One of our major challenges continues to be the education of our clients. We want them to comprehend all these different dimensions. That's how we will continue to sell watches! The wearable technology trend is also opening up new perspectives for historic brands.

Why did you bet on the connected watch?

To build the future, we have to innovate! TAG stands for Technologie d'Avant-Garde—added to Heuer, a name that dates to 1860. We do better than simply replicate tradition. We continue the avant-garde legacy. By definition, youth is disruptive—and so are we in looking firmly towards the future! Thanks to the connected watch, our image has enjoyed an incredible rejuvenating effect.

◂ TAG HEUER FORMULA 1 200 M

How is the connected watch evolving this year?

From a single model at its launch, we now offer it as a complete collection, with different combinations of functions, colors, materials, finishes, sizes and prices.

What about production?

In 2016, we delivered 60,000 smart watches. We committed the error of underestimating the product's potential, which forced us to stagger the delivery process. This year, we won't make the same mistake. Deliveries will be made on a global scale, thanks to an available stock of 30,000 to 40,000 units. Over the year, we will produce about 100,000 units. What's more, starting this year, the assembly of the microprocessors will be done in-house—the first telecom assembly line in Switzerland!

How is 2017 shaping up for TAG Heuer in the mechanical watch market?

We are going to write a new chapter in horological history, thanks to a breakthrough in the field of metallurgy! This represents a very important new milestone for watchmaking.

How is TAG Heuer faring with collectors?

Vintage models benefit from our dynamism, such as the Autavia, which has been rereleased. Collectors also love the performance of the Mikrograph, powered by the first mechanical caliber with an integrated column wheel, which displays 1/100ths of a second using a central hand.

As far as sponsorship goes, Hublot and TAG Heuer seem to have the world of soccer all sewn up!

Yes, these two brands can rest assured of being the only ones in the sport. Hublot covers the more prestigious events, like the World Cup, the Euro and the Champions League. TAG Heuer partners with all the events, leagues and national teams, as well as the star players. This corresponds perfectly with the brand's image of accessible luxury. Soccer enables us to reach a wide audience: the clients of today and tomorrow! The sport is also gaining unprecedented popularity in China, since the government has encouraged top entrepreneurs to invest in the sport. Player transfers in China are now the most expensive in the world!

What are the other fields in which TAG Heuer has sponsorships?

We are partnering with the China Space Agency, notably for the exploration of Mars. We provide the clocks in the control rooms and ensure the countdowns. We will have access to the models of lunar and Martian vehicles, for example, for display in our boutiques. A dedicated TAG Heuer model will also be developed. Aside from that, TAG Heuer is visible wherever our clients are! In the great automobile races, but also in skiing, with the Patrouille des Glaciers, as well as in marathons, surfing, and even cycling, with the BMC Racing Team.

Which markets do you consider to be your top priorities?

The United States, China and Japan. In terms of distribution, the number of boutiques has remained stable over the last five years. In addition to the boutiques, TAG Heuer can be found at many retailers. A luxury brand must plan for the long term, according to the particularities of each market.

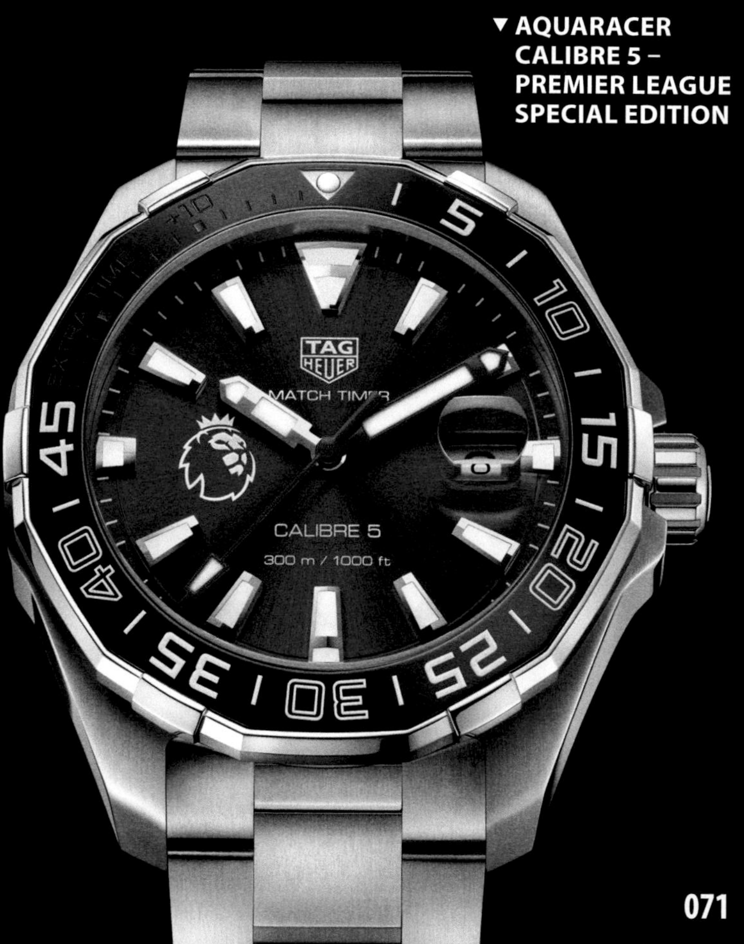

▾ AQUARACER CALIBRE 5 – PREMIER LEAGUE SPECIAL EDITION

#DontCrackUnderPressure
Red Bull
TOTAL
TAG Heuer
Pepe Jeans
Arai
RICCIARDO
VERSTAPPEN
WINGS
GIVES
RAUCH

TAG HEUER
TAGHeuer
SWISS AVANT-GARDE SINCE 1860

TACHYMETRE
400 300 240 200 170 150 135 120 110 100 90 85 80 75 70 65
TAG HEUER
CARRERA
HEUER 01

RANGE ROVER

Jean-Claude Biver

President of LVMH Group's Watches Division and interim CEO of Zenith

INTO THE SPOTLIGHT

Zenith is currently perhaps the least visible brand of LVMH Group's Watches Division. In taking the helm for the time being, Jean-Claude Biver plans to **REVITALIZE THE BRAND AND SET IT ON THE RIGHT COURSE**.

▲ JEAN-CLAUDE BIVER

"We are going to make a big push with the iconic El Primero movement."

You've just taken over at Zenith, in addition to your other responsibilities at TAG Heuer and Hublot. What is your plan for Zenith?

The plan for Zenith is to find a new CEO before the end of the year, ideally before the summer. As for TAG Heuer, I will stay on as CEO for a few more years. But make no mistake: I will still be very involved with Zenith after the brand has a new CEO.

The Zenith Manufacture possesses two in-house mechanical movements: the famous El Primero chronograph and the Elite movement. What will your strategy be for mechanical movements?

You're familiar with the quality of these two movements; we are naturally going to focus on the iconic and legendary El Primero caliber, as well as the Elite movement, which is less well known but extremely reliable. These are the two essential components of both Zenith and its collections, so these two movements will definitely remain the pillars of Zenith's collections in the future.

But it doesn't seem as though you're going to leave it at that...

That's true! I'm not at liberty to say more, because the big announcement is at Baselworld, but I can already tell you that we are presenting two exceptional new models. They will definitely be remembered as milestones in the history of the chronograph.

What do you mean by that?

At this point, all I can reveal is that we are presenting a novel, revolutionary chronograph movement, equipped with a new escapement. Zenith has often been a pioneer in chronograph movements, and will continue to be so in the future.

What are you doing for the collections?

We are clarifying, reducing and simplifying our range of products, giving Zenith's collections a unifying identity. Zenith's watches should be recognizable at a glance. This element will be fundamental for the brand's success.

▲ EL PRIMERO CHRONOMASTER 1969 COHIBA

In terms of marketing, what are your goals for Zenith?

First of all, we need to understand that Zenith has three exceptional assets: its history, its creations and its expertise. The brand does not in fact need to invent or search for external marketing elements, when it already has so much to say. This is wonderful, and clearly we are going to capitalize on that. Zenith is probably one of the rare brands that can base its marketing strategy solely on its own qualities, so that is the direction in which we will orient our marketing.

Which are Zenith's strongest markets at the moment?

Overall, we are strongest in America, Japan, China and England. But we are going to develop and support the brand all over the world.

President of LVMH Group's Watches Division, President of Hublot, CEO of TAG Heuer, and now interim CEO of Zenith. Doesn't it get to be a bit too much?

No, because I'm not alone, and I can count on extremely talented, motivated and innovative colleagues. My closest collaborators are a team, and this team is my strength. Without them, I wouldn't be able to lead a single brand. But with my passion and the support of my team, we are going to do the hard work necessary for Zenith to reclaim its rightful place in the watchmaking world.

▲ HERITAGE PILOT TON-UP

▲ EL PRIMERO ORIGINAL

▶ ELITE CHRONOGRAPH CLASSIC

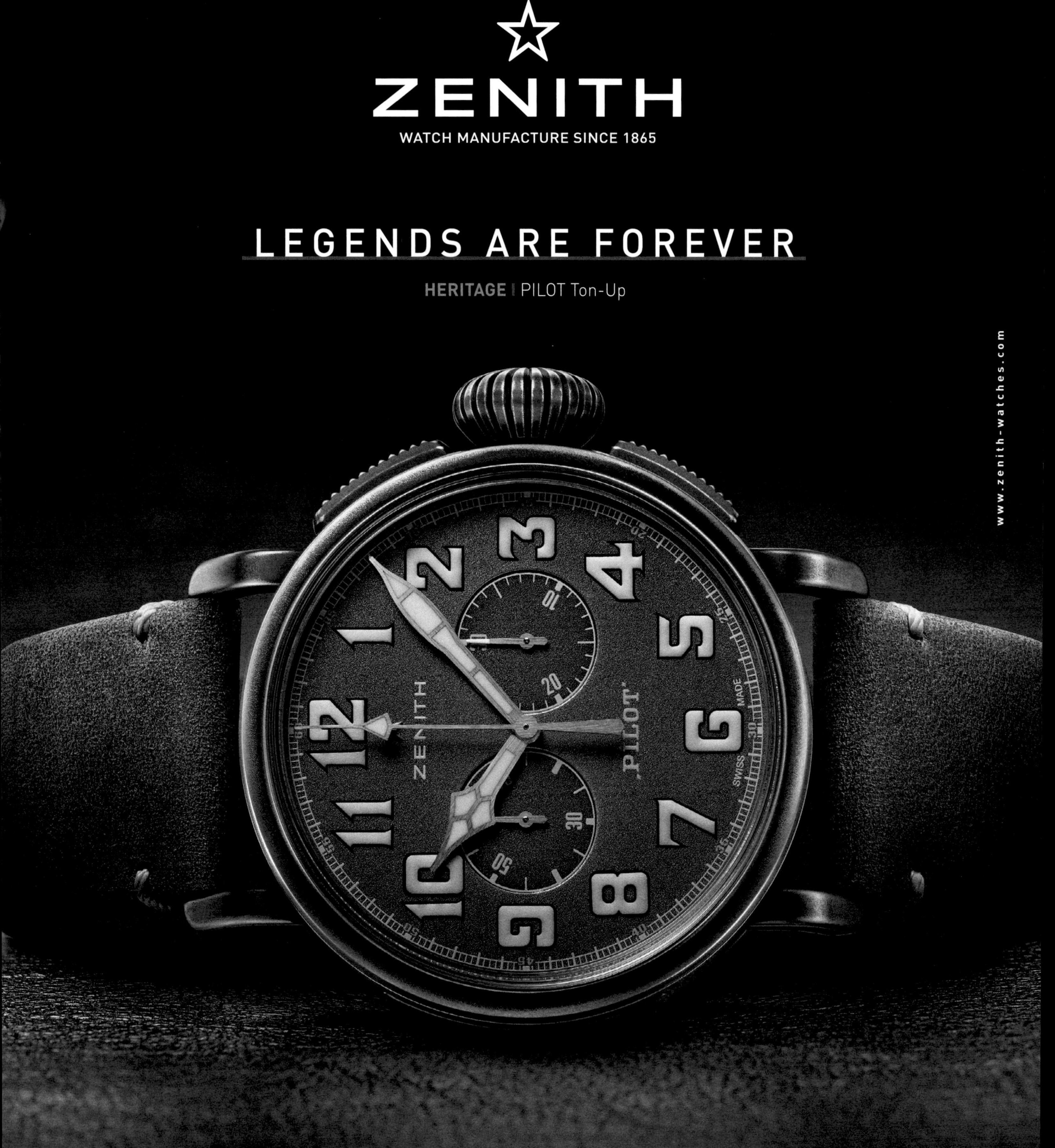

"Richard Mille is a brand that keeps its promises."

◂ RICHARD MILLE

Richard Mille

CEO of Richard Mille

PLAYFUL WATCHES, A SERIOUS BRAND

The fact that a given year is very much like the previous one can be a very positive thing when it comes to business. The strategic consistency of Richard Mille, founder and president of the brand bearing his name, has enabled the company to achieve controlled growth distinguished by its almost metronomic regularity. Largely thanks to his creativity, the brand has attracted an enviable new clientele over the last few years, among the younger generation as well as in the market for women's watches. However, **THE COMPANY STILL MAINTAINS A FIRM FOCUS ON THE UNCOMPROMISING QUALITY OF ITS WATCHES, AS WELL AS THEIR RARITY**—which Mille sees as the secret of true luxury.

Let's talk about your strategy, which has allowed you to make continued progress, despite the industry's current crisis...

My strategy has not changed one iota. I like creativity, but I also like constancy! The Richard Mille brand should always innovate and favor technology, with watches that are comfortable on the wrist. I insist on taking all aspects seriously: strategy, products, developments, quality, after-sales service. Richard Mille is a brand that keeps its promises, with a true consistency concerning its positioning, sales volume, creativity and quality.

As you like to express it, Richard Mille is a "serious" brand. Why is that?

We guarantee a phenomenal level of horological quality and strong resistance, even in highly technically demanding limited editions. Our quality procedures are like nothing else in watchmaking. Our watches undergo dynamic tests, with tests relating to impacts, aging... because Richard Mille watches are meant to be worn! It's not enough to say that (Romain) Grosjean races with his Richard Mille on, or that (Rafael) Nadal and (Bubba) Watson play wearing theirs. The watches have to actually stand up to these conditions! The branding has to match reality. We even receive congratulatory letters about our after-sales service. What's more, we are the only brand to guarantee our watches against minor shocks for five years!

◀ RM 38-01 BUBBA WATSON G-SENSOR TOURBILLON

RM 50-01 ▶ G-SENSOR LOTUS F1 ROMAIN GROSJEAN

▲ RM 037

Are you continuing to increase production?

Yes, our production volume and sales numbers are continuing to grow, but we still can't satisfy demand. In any case, Richard Mille doesn't enter into that logic (of rapid growth). You know, at my age, I've acquired a cautious attitude (laughs)! Especially since luxury should not become debased, but instead remain synonymous with consistency, as I said, as well as rarity. To talk numbers, in 2015 we produced about 3,200 units, then 3,500 in 2016—for a sales volume of 225,160,000 Swiss francs (CHF) and an average price of 180,000 CHF. This year, we will probably produce about 4,000 watches.

How has your distribution network evolved?

This year, we are opening new boutiques in Moscow, New York, Seoul, Taipei, Osaka, Kobe, Toronto and Saint Barth; we had delayed the openings in order to better control our growth. Richard Mille boutiques have very high sales, as do our multi-brand retailers. However, we have cut our number of points of sale in half, from 150 to 75. In fact, we couldn't deliver enough products, and we needed more space: 150 to $200m^2$. The collection has expanded, the whole range has evolved, because I have a strategy in mind for harmoniously dividing our sales numbers between the different lines. Currently, even though the RM 11 chronograph is our bestseller, our collection includes several other successful models: the RM 030, RM 35-01, RM 29, RM 050 and RM 055 for men, and the RM 07-01 and RM 037 for women.

How is the demand for women's watches?

In 2015, we produced a little under 500 women's watches. In 2016, that number grew to more than 800. But that wasn't enough—demand has exploded! We've been working on it for a long time, and put a lot of effort into marketing, but over the last three years, it's paid off.

How did Richard Mille evolve in 2016?

Over the last few years, our clientele has come to include more women, as well as larger numbers of young clients. These are the clients we always dreamed of having. Our existing clientele remains very faithful, and every day new clients come in, some of them between 18 and 20 years old! It's a sign of security for our future. While I'm very adventurous when it comes to creation, I remain extremely careful about our business model. Richard Mille has become one of horology's top brands, but remains revolutionary. That is very important to me.

◂ RM 07-01

What are some of the other avenues of progress for the company?

We have considerable potential for development in Russia, China, Japan, Eastern Europe and Northern Europe, where we don't have much of a presence, or sometimes any presence at all. In the countries where we have points of sale, we are making significant progress. When the rest of the world was investing in China in 2008, I chose to invest in the US. We worked hard to make inroads in this market, and today, Richard Mille is a well-known brand in the United States. We have just one boutique in China, in Shanghai, and it is doing extremely well, so our path is wide open there. Same thing in Russia, another place where we are taking our time.

What new models are you presenting in 2017?

In January, we launched our new McLaren watch, and we will release many new models around summertime. These days, I don't unveil all my latest pieces at the Salon International de la Haute Horlogerie in Geneva at the beginning of the year—I will launch marketing operations only after we have half the pieces in stock. Then, I deliver as many units as I can over the next six months. We have also rejuvenated our top seller, the RM 11-03. It's a strategy that I will be extending to our other models, such as the highly popular, ultra-thin RM 67. All of our women's watches, as well as the RM 67, are equipped with in-house movements. Of course, we continue to work with Renaud & Papi and Vaucher Manufacture, but we will be increasing the number of watches powered by our own calibers.

▲ RM 11-03

▼ RM 67-01

What partnerships do you have coming up?

John Malkovich, the brilliant actor of stage and screen, has signed on with us, as has Margot Robbie, who played a notable role in *The Wolf of Wall Street*. We are very open-minded, but we remain strongly involved in the world of automobiles, especially with McLaren, an excellent partnership.

◀ JOHN MALKOVICH

AUCKLAND
SAMOA
HONOLULU
MARQUESAS
L.ANGELES
NEW YORK
ST JOHN'S
CARACAS
RIO DE J.
LA PAZ
S.GEORGIA
AZORES
GMT
LONDON
GENEVA
ATHENS
MOSCOW
NEPAL
BANGKOK
DHAKA
KARACHI
KABUL
DELHI
11 12 13 14 15 16 17 18 19 20

WATCHES for Men

by Michel Jeannot

When we speak of timepieces, the first image that comes to mind is that of a men's watch. Without summarizing the entirety of horological history, suffice it to say that instruments designed to measure time or astronomical functions were for a very long time an exclusively masculine preserve. Women were not completely brushed aside, but their watches were first and foremost considered as jewelry that displayed the time almost as an afterthought. (This also explains why the first early 19th century wristwatches were created for feminine wrists only.) Even today, watches aimed at female watch lovers represent just one category among others in the vast universe of horological products, alongside classic or sports watches. From this we may deduce that, like it or not (and with all due respect to women), the conversation about watches is still largely led by and for men.

▸ **Overseas Chronograph**
(Vacheron Constantin)

▸ **Cosmograph Daytona**
(Rolex)

◂ **Aquaracer**
(TAG Heuer)

◂ **RM 056 Jean Todt 50th Anniversary**
(Richard Mille)

▸ **Pilot Type 20 Annual Calendar**
(Zenith)

I: Classic Watches: The Value of Precision

Let us enter this world together, a world where the back room is redolent of machine oil, where mechanical prowess stems as much from extreme industrialization as from watchmakers' dexterity, a world which still fascinates us with its ability to use technology as old as the invention of the spring. In a word, welcome to the sphere of mechanical horology, where parts are now machined to micron-level precision, and performance is measured in a handful of seconds by comparing with the highly accurate time kept by today's atomic clocks. Better still, performance is now controlled and certified according to ever stricter margins and criteria. This is probably the main issue facing "classic" watches, fitted with two or sometimes three hands and often eschewing a date display entirely. How can a watch with only the minimalist design of a round case stand out from the crowd, especially when its sole function is to tell the time?

This question becomes even more pertinent as classic watches retake cenclassicism is in vogue again, as a result of the effort to refocus on entry-level horology, which had been ignored and nearly forgotten. By "classic," we mean charming, elegant, simple and functional. Two variables have spurred watch brands to engage in fascinating rivalries. The first finds its main challenge in a slimming regime—a watch's thinness is synonymous with elegance and comfort. But these modelesque proportions are not accessible to just any watchmaker. To reduce the thickness of a caliber, one must rethink all of the components with one important constraint: the loss of bulk must not in any way be obtained at the detriment of the watch's robustness and reliability.

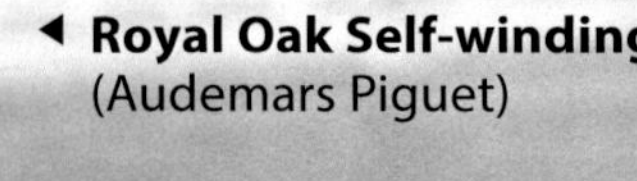

◀ **Royal Oak Self-winding**
(Audemars Piguet)

▼ **Classic Fusion Special Edition "The Watch Gallery"**
(Hublot)

◂ **Villeret Large Date**
(Blancpain)

▸ **Epure 42mm**
(Boucheron)

▾ **Palatial Classic Atomatic**
(Jacob & Co.)

▸ **Octo Ultranero**
(Bulgari)

▾ **Senator Excellence**
(Glashütte Original)

New Retro Ladies

Historically, certain houses have earned a significant reputation within this complex domain—for example, Piaget, which notably holds the record for the slimmest automatic movement in the world (the 1208P, 2.35mm thick) and the thinnest manual-winding watch ever created (Altiplano 900P, 3.65mm). And those are only two examples from the 25 or so ultra-thin models developed by the Manufacture, of which a dozen have achieved records for thinness over the last few years. But for some time now, other horologers have begun to explore this territory, as seen at the 2016 Baselworld Watch & Jewellery Show.

▸ **Altiplano**
(Piaget)

PIAGET
Mécanique
P00000
SWISS MADE
0003000
Au750
PIAGET
TWENTY (20) JEWELS
900P
SWISS MADE

Among this crowd, Bulgari stands out for its Octo Finissimo line, notably equipped with the Solotempo BVL 193 caliber (3.70mm). The L.U.C XPS 1860 from Chopard (caliber L.U.C 96.03-L, 3.30mm) and the Classique 7147 from Breguet (Caliber 502.3SD, 2.40mm) play in the same league. Not to mention the Elite 6150 from Zenith (Caliber Elite 6150, 6.92mm) or the Slim d'Hermès (Caliber H1950, 2.60mm), which also display amazing prowess.

▲ **Octo Finissimo**
(Bulgari)

▶ **BVL 193 caliber**
(Bulgari)

▼ **L.U.C XPS 1860**
(Chopard)

▶ **Classique 7147**
(Breguet)

▲ **Elite 6150**
(Zenith)

▶ **Slim d'Hermès and Caliber H1950**
(Hermès)

Aesthetics were never the be-all and end-all here. Models that would have simply been described as "minimalist" a few years ago are now held to higher standards, developing a second theme: precision and accuracy, as provided by mechanical movements. One might be tempted to say that there's nothing new about that: isn't that in fact what watches are for? But the industrial processes used in mass production complicate this question. Though a skilled adjuster can fine-tune watches in limited editions (given enough time), it is a completely different issue when brands produce hundreds of thousands of units. Since the rebirth of the mechanical watch in the 1990s, the use of new materials such as silicon has helped watchmakers largely overcome this pitfall of wide-scale production. Given this context, the criteria of the Swiss Official Chronometer Testing Institute (the famous COSC), may no longer be sufficient. A venerable, neutral, independent institution whose creation dates to 1876, the COSC delivers a certification of chronometric accuracy based on an international norm from the 1970s stipulating that at the end of a battery of tests performed on the watch, a mechanical model must not deviate from the correct time by more than -4 or +6 seconds per day.

▲ **Manero Peripheral**
(Carl F. Bucherer)

▶ **L.U.C Tourbillon QF Fairmined**
(Chopard)

▲ **Oyster Perpetual Yacht-Master 40**
(Rolex)

New Retro

Fondation Qualité Fleurier

La haute horlogerie certifiée

le 27 septembre 2004

Some believe that the industry should go a step further, by submitting finished watches to even more stringent testing. That is indeed why the Geneva Hallmark, enacted in cantonal law in 1886 —essentially as a weapon against counterfeiting — was completely reworked in 2011 to become one of the most demanding labels in the industry. The same philosophy of label in 2001. Individual brands have also been joining in the endeavor, as shown by the actions of Omega.

▲ **Excalibur 42**
(Roger Dubuis)

◀ **Patrimony Retrograde Day-Date**
(Vacheron Constantin)

▲ **Globemaster** (Omega)

▼ **Seamaster Planet Ocean** (Omega)

Three years ago, the brand presented a new certification, developed in collaboration with the Institut federal de métrologie (Swiss Federal Institute of Metrology) that notably included strict criteria for the areas of anti-magnetic protection and accuracy requirements of 0 to +5 seconds. After the first Globemaster in 2015, the first model to be certified Master Chronometer, or the "highest standard of excellence in the Swiss watchmaking industry" according to the brand, Omega arrived at Baselworld 2016 with no fewer than six Master Chronometer movements, including the entirety of the new Seamaster Planet Ocean line. Rolex responded in kind by announcing at the same event that it had extended its Superlative Chronometer certification to the entirety of its production, specifying that: "The certification applies to the fully assembled watch, after casing the movement, guaranteeing superlative performance on the wrist in terms of precision, power reserve, waterproofness and self-winding. The precision of a Rolex Superlative Chronometer after casing is of the order of −2/+2 seconds per day, or more than twice that required of an official chronometer."

◂ **Oyster Perpetual Day-Date 40**
(Rolex)

XII

II: Watches with Useful Functions: The Rise of the Calendar

This paean to classicism, which allows brands to market timepieces that are simpler and therefore accessible to a wider audience, accompanies the use of more "functional" materials, such as steel. No shame there. Since Audemars Piguet's 1972 launch of the Royal Oak, steel has earned its bona fides as a noble metal, perfectly adapted to the standards demanded by haute horology maisons. At Geneva's 2016 Salon International de la Haute Horlogerie (SIHH), steel was a powerful presence, even among brands that usually present their newest collections exclusively in gold. The new Drive de Cartier appeared in a steel version, with hours, minutes, small seconds and date driven by the 1904-PS MC caliber, and the Clé de Cartier came out in steel for the first time.

▲ **Royal Oak** (Audemars Piguet)

▶ **Palatial Classic Manual Big Date Colored Dial** (Jacob & Co.)

◂ **Drive de Cartier**
(Cartier)

▾ **Clé de Cartier**
(Cartier)

◂ **1904-PS MC Caliber**
(Cartier)

JACOB & Co

▸ **Bubble Collection**
(Corum)

▾ **Signature 1**
(Greubel Forsey)

The material seems poised to conquer new territories. Greubel Forsey, for example, released its first steel watch in 2016: the Signature 1, the first step in the company's strategy of showcasing one of its talented watchmakers and proposing more "accessible" pieces. In a completely different sector of the market, Corum is following a parallel path with the Bubble collection, which is now making a comeback, mainly in steel versions, after having faded from the scene.

CORUM
CORUM

Needless to say, brands that have long recognized the wonders of steel have wryly noted the sudden passion for this material among brands that had long considered it “trivial.” Longines is one of these early adopters. This watch brand, which is among the very few horologers to see sales of over a billion Swiss francs, confirms its positioning with, among others, an automatic-winding RailRoad, inspired by a 1960 model with a 40mm steel case and an engraved caseback. Similar game is afoot at TAG Heuer, whose Carrera Heuer-01, the house’s signature chronograph, is equipped with a new in-house movement, housed in a modular case with 12 steel-based components that allow for multiple combinations of colors and materials.

▶ **Carrera Heuer-01**
(TAG Heuer)

▼ **RailRoad**
(Longines)

TACHYMETRE
CHRONOGRAPH
TAG HEUER
CARRERA
HEUER 01
SWISS

PARIS

CIRCLE « LA PETITE »

Dotée d'un boîtier ultra-plat de 45 ou 52 millimètres de diamètre pour 6 millimètres d'épaisseur pour la première et 7 millimètres pour l'autre, cette montre d'une extrême convexité épouse parfaitement le poignet de toutes les dames. Son boîtier se décline en or blanc, rose ou jaune avec lunette sertie ou entièrement serti. Son cadran au galbe parfait et à la finition poli-miroir ou satinée se définit au choix avec index en appliques, index sertis ou encore entièrement serti neige.

With an ultra-flat case of 45 or 52 millimetres in diameter and 6 millimetres thickness for the first and 7 millimeters for the other, this watch literally envelops women's wrist thanks to its impressive convexity. This case is available in white gold, rose gold and yellow gold, with a bezel set or full set. Its dial with a perfect curve and with a gold mirror or a gold matte aspect is available with simple markers, jewel-set markers or completely set.

Useful complications are a good match for this utilitarian-seeming material. Once a watch ventures beyond time and date read-off, a world of functions opens up, among them those whose immediate practicality wins over a wide audience, such as extra time zones or annual calendars (which require just one correction per year). In 2015, the annual calendar had already celebrated its grand comeback to mechanical horology, notably at Jaeger-LeCoultre (Master Calendar) and IWC (Portuguese Annual Calendar). Simpler and thus less fragile than a perpetual calendar, it still allows for highly original dial choreography, particularly since it is often paired with a chronograph, as with Ulysse Nardin in 2016 (Marine Chronograph Annual Calendar), or with a second time zone, for instance the Blancpain Villeret Annual Calendar GMT, whose steel version made its debut at Baselworld.

◂ **Master Calendar**
(Jaeger-LeCoultre)

▾ **Portuguese Annual Calendar**
(IWC)

▲ **Marine Chronograph Annual Calendar**
(Ulysse Nardin)

▶ **Villeret Annual Calendar GMT**
(Blancpain)

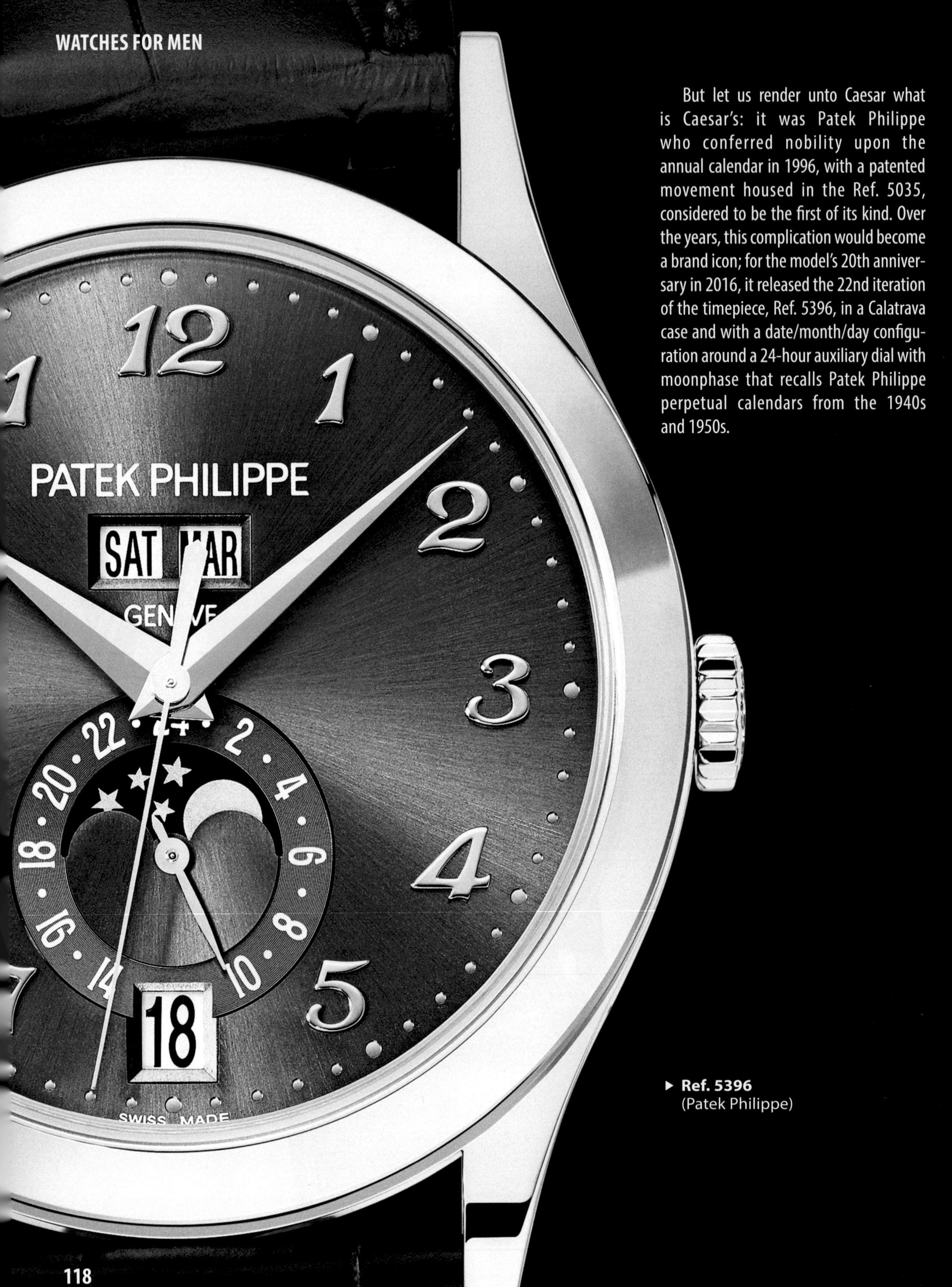

But let us render unto Caesar what is Caesar's: it was Patek Philippe who conferred nobility upon the annual calendar in 1996, with a patented movement housed in the Ref. 5035, considered to be the first of its kind. Over the years, this complication would become a brand icon; for the model's 20th anniversary in 2016, it released the 22nd iteration of the timepiece, Ref. 5396, in a Calatrava case and with a date/month/day configuration around a 24-hour auxiliary dial with moonphase that recalls Patek Philippe perpetual calendars from the 1940s and 1950s.

▸ **Ref. 5396**
(Patek Philippe)

PATEK PHILIPPE
GENEVE
SAT
MAR
18
SWISS MADE

PARIS

« JUMBO CHRONO»

Mises en valeur par un imposant boîtier de 50 x 11,5 mm , les finitions et les caractéristiques de la Jumbo Chrono font de cette pièce unique un modèle d'élégance et de subtilité. Agrémentés d'un fond glace Saphir, les quatre cadrans indicateurs sont animés par un mouvement automatique chronographe avec roue à colonne, conçu par "Manufacture Blancpain", et offrant une réserve de marche de 45 heures. Ses ponts, son cadran et sa lunette en or gris pvd noir microbillé sertie de 323 brillants pour 7.93 carats et sa boucle déployante sont assortis d'un bracelet Alligator.

Highlighted by an impressive case 50 x 11.5 mm, the finishes and the features of the Jumbo Chrono make of this unique piece a model of elegance and subtlety. Orned with a sapphire crystal back case, the four dials are driven by an automatic movement, chronograph with column wheel, designed by "Manufacture Blancpain", and offering a power reserve of 45 hours. Its bridges, its dial and its bezel in black matte pvd treatment set with 323 brilliants for 7.93 carats and its deployant clasp embellished by an alligator strap

When Patek Philippe's patent on the annual calendar expired in 2006, more and more watch brands began to release their own versions of the complication, and a decade later, it has become a touchstone. SIHH 2016 offered ample evidence of the phenomenon, with pieces such as the Montblanc Heritage Chronométrie Annual Calendar Chronograph, the IWC Big Pilot's Watch Annual Calendar Edition "Le Petit Prince," and the Baume & Mercier Clifton Chronograph Complete Calendar. Omega went in a different aesthetic direction with its Globemaster, adding an annual calendar to the watch's first iteration. The resulting piece boasts an enlarged 41mm case and the same "pie pan" dial form, whose 12 facets bear the names of the months, indicated by a blued hand.

▼ **Globemaster**
(Omega)

▶ **Heritage Chronométrie Annual Calendar Chronograph**
(Montblanc)

▶ **Nº Uno Annual Calendar**
(de GRISOGONO)

▶ **Clifton Chronograph**
(Baume & Mercier)

◂ **Big Pilot's Watch Annual Calendar Edition "Le Petit Prince"**
(IWC)

▲ **Grande Seconde Dual Time**
(Jaquet Droz)

▶ **Ref. 5930G**
(Patek Philippe)

▲ **Pilot's Watch Timezoner Chronograph**
(IWC)

Another popular additional function, this one for travelers: the time zone display, such as the Grande Seconde Dual Time from Jaquet Droz, or the even more cosmopolitan Ref. 5930G from Patek Philippe (the brand's major new 2016 release), which accompanies the world-time function with a chronograph. For usefulness and practicality, IWC comes out on top for its Pilot's Watch Timezoner Chronograph, which combines a ring of city names (as a world-time watch does) with a rotating bezel that transmits the rotational movement to the inside of the watch. The result, in the brand's own words, is "a world time watch that shows its owner a new time zone and the time of day together with the 24-hour display and the new date, all with a simple twist of the wrist." If needed, the chronograph is on hand to measure the system's efficacy…

▲ **Escale Worldtime**
(Louis Vuitton)

◂ **1966 ww.tc**
(Girard-Perregaux)

1888

MADE OF LUCERNE

CARL F. BUCHERER
Travel Tec
GMT

III: Grand Complications: A New Record

This focus on simplicity and functionality should not, however, obscure the efforts of watchmakers to make history with the ultimate collection of complications. We are referring here to perpetual calendars with astronomical indications, as well as the category of striking watches and minute repeaters: two mechanical achievements that, when combined with a chronograph, transform a timepiece into the classic example of what watchmaking tradition refers to as a "grand complication." And that's not even counting tourbillons and karussels, devices linked to the regulating organ that counteract the effects of gravity on the movement's function. They have enjoyed an overwhelming surge of popularity in recent years and are now mastered by almost every watchmaking Manufacture. To stand out in this domain, horologers must now display extraordinary creativity, such as that shown by Arnold & Son, which recently added the UTTE Skeleton to its Instrument collection: it is the thinnest skeletonized tourbillon watch on the market, with a 3.30mm-thin movement housed in an 8.34mm case. For its part, Audemars Piguet has decided to honor this complication via an unusual collection of eight original pieces in the Royal Oak and Jules Audemars lines that represent innovative interpretations in the world of ultra-thin models, skeletonization and the combination of functions. The crowning glory of this collection, the Jules Audemars Tourbillon Openworked in platinum, is particularly outstanding.

◀ **UTTE Skeleton**
(Arnold & Son)

▲ **Jules Audemars Tourbillon Openworked**
(Audemars Piguet)

◀ **Classique Tourbillon Quantième Perpétuel**
(Breguet)

◀ **Tourbillon Magistere II**
(Guy Ellia)

▶ **Androgyne**
(Manufacture Royale)

Great design also demands originality, as seen in Guy Ellia's Tourbillon Magistère II, Manufacture Royale's Androgyne and Louis Vuitton's Flying Tourbillon Watch, the airiest in its category. Originality and high technology working together is the hallmark of Harry Winston's Histoire de Tourbillon saga. Chapter 7, unveiled at the beginning of 2016, showcases the ballet of two bi-axial tourbillons that evolve in space through different positions. To reconcile the functioning of these two rotating regulating organs, the caliber integrates a spherical differential in order to optimize the machine's efficiency.

◀ **Chapter 7**
(Harry Winston)

◀ **Flying Tourbillon**
(Louis Vuitton)

▶ **Epic SF-24 Tourbillon**
(Jacob & Co.)

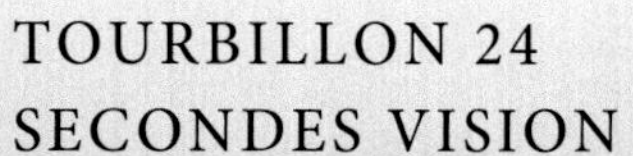

Cartier, which has achieved a remarkable technical breakthrough in mechanical haute horology over the last ten years by putting its own stamp on traditional complications, was drawn to another form of rotation that inspired the keystone of the brand's 2016 collections, the true horological masterpiece named Rotonde de Cartier Astromystérieux Calibre 9462 MC. In Cartier's mystery clocks, a specialty of the house at the beginning of the 20th century, the hands appeared between two sapphire crystals, as if suspended in midair, with no apparent connection to the mechanical ensemble that powered them. The Rotonde Astromystérieux pushes the prowess of this horological architecture one step further, with supplementary rotating discs serving to make the entire movement rotate around the dial center, as if weightless.

▲ **Rotonde de Cartier Astromystérieux Calibre 9462**
(Cartier)

When it comes to grand complications, even though 2016 was not as fertile a year as the ones before (due to the global economic situation), it nonetheless brought its share of surprises. Among them was Patek Philippe's Grandmaster Chime Ref. 6300, which joins the Genevan Manufacture's current collections. This timepiece, equipped with 20 complications (including five audible ones) housed inside a patented, double-faced case, dethroned the Sky Moon Tourbillon Ref. 6200 as Patek Philippe's most complicated wristwatch and one of the most complicated in the world. For its 175th anniversary in 2014, the brand unveiled a collection of limited-edition commemorative watches. Among them was the Grandmaster Chime, the Manufacture's first wristwatch with large and small strike, with just seven examples produced at this time, in entirely hand-engraved gold cases. It was exactly this model that made its appearance in 2016, equipped with a redesigned case, which was conceived for everyday use. The brand noted, "given its extreme complexity, which only allows for a very limited annual production, Ref. 6300 will remain a very rare watch."

▲ **Grandmaster Chime Ref. 6300** (Patek Philippe)

▶ **Sky Moon Tourbillon Ref. 5002** (Patek Philippe)

◂ **Sky Moon Tourbillon Ref. 6200**
(Patek Philippe)

▼ ▶ **Reference 57260**
(Vacheron Constantin)

The Grandmaster Chime Ref. 6300 is nonetheless not as rare as the Reference 57260, a unique piece unveiled by Vacheron Constantin in honor of its 260th anniversary, which is, as of this writing, the most complicated watch ever made. At the end of 2015, the Genevan Manufacture introduced it to the world: "Reference 57260, bearing the Hallmark of Geneva, is a double-dial horological masterwork of hitherto unimaginable complication and technical innovation." We couldn't say it better ourselves. Some convincing numbers make the case: protected by 10 patents, this timepiece comprises 57 complications, which are powered by 2,826 components for a total weight of nearly a kilogram. It took eight years of development and three watchmakers to complete this exceptional piece in the Cabinet des Cabinotiers, Vacheron Constantin's workshop, which creates bespoke watches for the brand's clients and collectors.

VACHERON CONSTANTIN
5775
MAR
APR
MAY
JUN
JUL
AUG
SEP
OCT
NOV
DEC
JAN
FEB
PISCES
ARIES
TAURUS
GEMINI
CANCER
LEO
VIRGO
LIBRA
SCORPIO
SAGITTARIUS
CAPRICORN
AQUARIUS
WINTER
SPRING
SUMMER
AUTUMN
SAT SUN MON TUE WED THU FRI
DAY LENGTH
NIGHT LENGTH
SUNRISE
SUNSET
N
E
W

Clearly, the complication competition has just reached a new level. After Breguet's 1827 Marie-Antoinette, a piece that included all the complications known at the time, it was the Leroy 01, completed in 1904, that long held the title of the most complicated watch in the world. That is, until the Patek Philippe Calibre 89, designed for the 150th anniversary of the company (in 1989), came along to set a new record for pocket-watches, with 33 complications and 1,728 components. The wristwatch world picked up the baton again rather quickly in 2006, when Vacheron Constantin revealed its Tour de l'Ile and the model's 16 complications. Three years later, Franck Muller's Eternitas Mega 4 became the most complex, with 36 "functions." Breguet's Grande Complication Hommage à Nicolas Hayek couldn't quite snatch the crown in 2013, possessing only 35 complications, and neither could Patek Philippe Grandmaster Chime. How long will Reference 57260 hold this much-coveted title?

▲ **1827 Marie-Antoinette** (Breguet)

▲ **Calibre 89**
(Patek Philippe)

▲ **Leroy 01** (Breguet)

▼ **Tour de l'Ile** (Vacheron Constantin)

▼ **Aeternitas Mega 4**
(Franck Muller)

IV: Sporting Watches: Essential Chronographs

Since the chronograph has been recognized as a complication in its own right and indeed every bit as difficult to execute as a tourbillon, according to Michel Parmigiani, this function is no longer considered a simple enhancement for dials lacking animation. Recently it has even become the objective of research conducted with the goal of obtaining a precision unmatched in the world of mechanical movements. We are reminded of TAG Heuer's breakthroughs in this field with the Mikro line and its dual chain, which brought 5/10,000th of a second precision within the reach of a wrist-worn chronograph. Still counted among TAG Heuer's collections, the Carrera Mikrograph associates two escapements oscillating at 28,800 and 360,000 vph respectively, which allows 1/100th of a second measurements without interfering with the functioning of the movement base.

▸ **Carrera Mikrograph** (TAG Heuer)

▲ **Speedmaster Mark II Rio**
(Omega)

◀ **Speedmaster Bullhead Rio**
(Omega)

Watch brands still occupy a niche that continues to impress watch lovers attuned to the chronograph's ticking seconds hand. Rare indeed is the house that does not have a chronograph on the roster, especially since the complications can be interpreted in any register: from models imbued with stately classicism, such as the Admiral Chronograph Flyback from Ateliers deMonaco, to ultra-technical ones, such as the Carl F. Bucherer Patravi Traveltec Black, whose profoundly black color highlights a short countdown timer and three time zone displays powered by proprietary COSC-certified caliber CFB 1901.1. Not to mention the "tribute" watches, for example the Super KonTiki from Eterna, equipped with the house's first flyback chronograph caliber, which revisits the origins of the watch dating back to the 1940s, when six Eterna watches served as navigation instruments to the Norwegian ethnologist Thor Heyerdahl during his expedition across the Pacific in a wooden raft. Perrelet has also chosen the homage route, with its recent Turbine Chrono, which offers an original chronograph display with sapphire crystal disks, in order to avoid visually distorting its dial-side double-rotor mechanism (a signature of the brand since its launch in 1995).

▶ **Admiral Chronograph Flyback**
(Ateliers deMonaco)

▶ **Patravi Traveltec Black**
(Carl F. Bucherer)

▶ **Turbine Chrono**
(Perrelet)

▼ **Super KonTiki**
(Eterna)

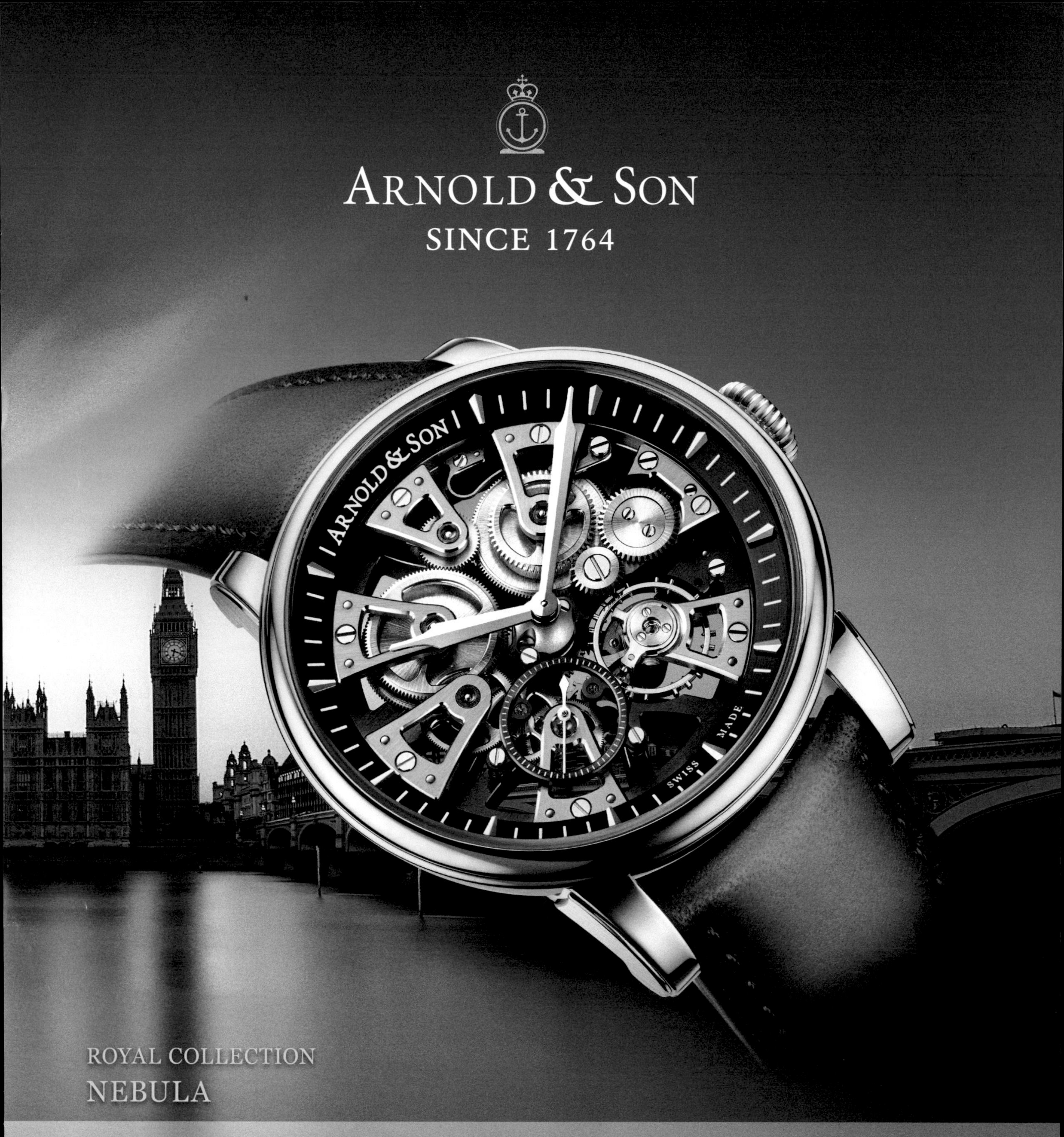

Even those companies whose fame is intimately linked with haute couture or jewelry are open to adding chronographs to their masculine models. Aesthetics are timeless, as proven by de GRISOGONO and its Grande Chrono N° 1, Harry Winston and its Ocean Chronograph Automatic 44mm, Boucheron and its Epure Chronograph in steel, as well as Dior and its Chiffre Rouge A02 and A05. At the other end of the spectrum from this approach, some houses have done their utmost to join the sports world, backed by chronographs, to the point where the quest for performance has become part of the DNA of these brands, whose names have become synonymous with one sport or another. This is exactly what Hublot did with soccer, forging a relationship so intimate it could be considered a textbook case for future brands. When Hublot first set its cap for soccer, no watchmakers were interested in the sport's stars, and even less in soccer itself, deemed too mass market. So Hublot began in 2006 by designing a watch for the Swiss national team. This first step opened up an entire field to Hublot, territory that it rapidly conquered by becoming, in 2008, the partner of the UEFA European Football Championship, then the FIFA World Cup. It was a brilliant play: at the world's biggest international competitions, the Hublot name is displayed on the referee boards, which signal substitutions and additional time periods. Given that the audience for these meets numbers in the billions for televised games, the Hublot name has traveled the entire planet, bringing with it products such as the famous Soccer Bang, a Big Bang Bi-Retrograde Chrono designed specifically for the soccer world.

▲ **Grande Chrono N° 1**
(de GRISOGONO)

▲ **Ocean Chronograph Automatic 44mm**
(Harry Winston)

▶ **Epure Chronograph**
(Boucheron)

▸ **Big Bang Unico Bi-Retrograde Chronograph UEFA EURO 201**
(Hublot)

▸ **Big Bang Bi-Retrograde Chrono**
(Hublot)

◂ **Big Bang Ferrari Limited Edition** (Hublot)

▸ **La Ferrari** (Hublot)

▾ **Rover** (Zenith)

Hublot has indeed not confined itself to soccer, also striking up a partnership with Ferrari. As the world of watchmaking and that of automobiles share a focus on performance, there have been a number of relationships between horologers and car companies: Breitling and Bentley, Zenith and Rover, Chopard and Porsche, as well as Bovet 1822's collaboration with Pininfarina, the renowned automobile designer. These are just a few examples among many, and allusions abound to classic racetracks such as Le Mans, Daytona and Panamerica, as well as legendary drivers: Michael Schumacher, Lewis Hamilton, Felipe Massa... The latter name has gained a special place at Richard Mille, which has developed a line of products for Massa, including the remarkable RM 056 Tourbillon Sapphire and the RM 050 Tourbillon Competition Chronograph, highly complex timepieces developed to resist the conditions in which this "friend of the brand" races.

▸ **Superfast Chrono Porsche 919 Jacky Ickx Edition** (Chopard)

▸ **RM 050 Felipe Massa** (Richard Mille)

V: Vintage Watches: An Outstanding Trend

Over the last few years, it has been impossible to ignore the proliferation of vintage-styled watches with clear references to timepieces past. For those nostalgic for the good old days, when all watches were mechanical, this is a wonderful development. Watch companies are quite skilled at keeping the flame alive, returning to the archives to create new models that seem to have traversed the years without a single sign of age. Jaeger-LeCoultre offers a magnificent example of this passion. The Manufacture's current success is largely due to its 1980s strategy of mining the potential of the Reverso, a watch developed in the 1930s for polo players. Ever since, the brand has continually produced Reverso watches in all different varieties of forms and models.

▲ **1931 Reverso**
(Jaeger-LeCoultre)

◄ **Reverso Tribute Gyrotourbillon**
(Jaeger-LeCoultre)

For the line's 85th anniversary, celebrated in 2016, the brand presented a completely reimagined collection, featuring all the year's new models. Considered in this way, anniversaries are good for shining the spotlight on these icons, inherited from the great watchmaking tradition, which will be "readied" for future generations. In 2016, two emblematic models celebrated their fortieth anniversaries: Chopard's Happy Diamonds (fundamentally, let us remember, a men's watch) and Patek Philippe's signature Nautilus model.

▲ **1980s Happy Diamonds**
(Chopard)

▲ **Happy Diamonds Duo**
(Chopard)

▶ **Nautilus Ref. 5976**
(Patek Philippe)

▶ **Nautilus Ref. 5711**
(Patek Philippe)

Manufactures have become adept in the art of dusting off older models, rejuvenating them while maintaining their core personality traits, an exercise mastered perfectly by Girard-Perregaux, which presented in 2016 two limited editions of its famous 1975 model Laureato to celebrate the company's 225th anniversary, as well as Rolex, which breathed new life into its Air-King, a piece that "epitomizes Rolex's privileged ties with the world of aviation during its golden age in the 1930s." The same analysis took place at Omega with its Speedmaster CK2998, of which the original, prized by collectors for its Alpha-style hands, dates back to 1959, or TAG Heuer, which presented a Heuer Monza in black PVD-treated steel in honor of its 40 years of existence. TAG Heuer also launched a veritable high-wire exercise in 2016 with the objective of reviving the Autavia, one of the brand's three great chronographs (along with the Carrera and the Monaco), which experienced its finest moments on the Formula 1 racetrack in the 1960s and 1970s. For the occasion, the brand launched an online competition, which allowed users to vote their choice from among 16 pre-selected Autavia models (of which 12 were historic models and 4 designed for the occasion). The competition began on March 17, the first day of Baselworld 2016, and ended with the crowning of the "Rindt" Autavia from 1966, named for the F1 Austrian champion Jochen Rindt, TAG Heuer's brand ambassador before the concept of that role was widespread. As a consequence of the vote, this model has been rereleased and presented at Baselworld 2017.

▲ **Laureato** (Girard-Perregaux)

▲ **Air-King** (Rolex)

▲ **Monza** (TAG Heuer)

▲ **Autavia** (TAG Heuer)

◂ **Speedmaster CK2998** (Omega)

If individual reference watches are lacking, retro inspiration guides the creation of new pieces and even new collections. At Zenith, the patina of time is an element in its Heritage Pilot Ton-up in the spirit of Café Racer, a chronograph that alludes to 1950s England, when young men would careen from café to café on stripped-down motorcycles. For Alpina, the touchstones are the watches created by the brand in the 1930s for the German Kriegsmarine. These models, boasting precision and shock-resistance, were used by the military to coordinate sea operations. Today they have been revived under the name KM-710. The design of legendary British sportscars Austin-Healey, produced between 1952 and 1972, served as inspiration for Vintage Rally from Frederique Constant (a brand recently acquired by Citizen along with Alpina and Ateliers deMonaco). Glashütte Original launched its own 20th Century Vintage line, which includes two collections dedicated, respectively, to the 1960s and 1970s, two "decades that changed the world through their ideals, their music, their architecture and design."

▼ **Heritage Pilot Café Racer**
(Zenith)

▲ **KM-710** (Alpina)

▶ **Retro Nº3** (de GRISOGONO)

▼ **20th Century Vintage** (Glashütte Original)

▶ **Vintage Rally** (Frederique Constant)

During the current rage for high-tech components, certain materials precisely convey a retro image. Bronze, for example, associated with techniques from the past, has recently gained great popularity in horology, not without practical reasons. An amagnetic metal, it offers a high resistance to corrosion, while taking on a natural patina with age, which makes each bronze watch a unique piece. Adopted very early on for naval construction, this material, once forged into propellers or diving helmets, found its natural extension in the world of diving watches. Panerai was a pioneer here, thrilling the hearts of its fans with an imposing Luminor Submersible 1950 3 Days Bronzo in 2011, then with a new automatic-winding version with power reserve two years later. Zenith joined in, releasing its Pilot Montre d'Aéronef Type 20 Extra Special Bronze in 2015, followed one year later by Oris (Carl Brashear Limited Edition), Tudor (Heritage Black Bay Bronze) and Hautlence (Vortex Bronze). In the universe of vintage watches, everything is up for grabs to lend an authentic allure to watches that might have come straight from our grandfathers' drawers.

▲ **Carl Brashear Limited Edition** (Oris)

◄ **Heritage Black Bay Bronze** (Tudor)

▼ **Luminor Submersible 1950 – 3 Days Bronzo** (Panerai)

▲ **Vortex Bronze** (Hautlence)

◄ **Pilot Montre d'Aéronef Type 20 Extra Special Bronze** (Zenith)

FREDERIQUE CONSTANT
GENEVE
horological smartwatch
delight
Gwyneth Paltrow
supports DonorsChoose
live your passion
foundation.frederiqueconstant.com

VI: Jewelry Watches: Precious Mechanics

We often hear that the watch is the only jewelry made for men, and this assertion, whatever truth it holds, is nonetheless taken literally by many of those who are passionate about horology. In certain markets, there is a distinct preference among men for timepieces that are both technical and bejeweled, as well as those dedicated to métiers d'art. Watchmakers might not (yet) take it upon themselves to develop gem-set men's watches for Spain or the United States (although such models are increasingly well received), but it is a different story in the Middle East, India or Mexico. This very particular offering is thus found only on the outer confines of haute horology, in territory where high fashion and even high jewelry do not venture, too busy earning their watchmaking stripes in a more classic masculine register. In these conditions, there is no question of reversing the pathway generally taken by watchmakers who shrink men's watches and set them with diamonds to make women's versions. It would be impossible to start with a woman's watch and make a version for men. For watch brands, this means that precious horology provides a creative territory—featuring its own codes and above all rare techniques—that is also intended for an audience of aficionados.

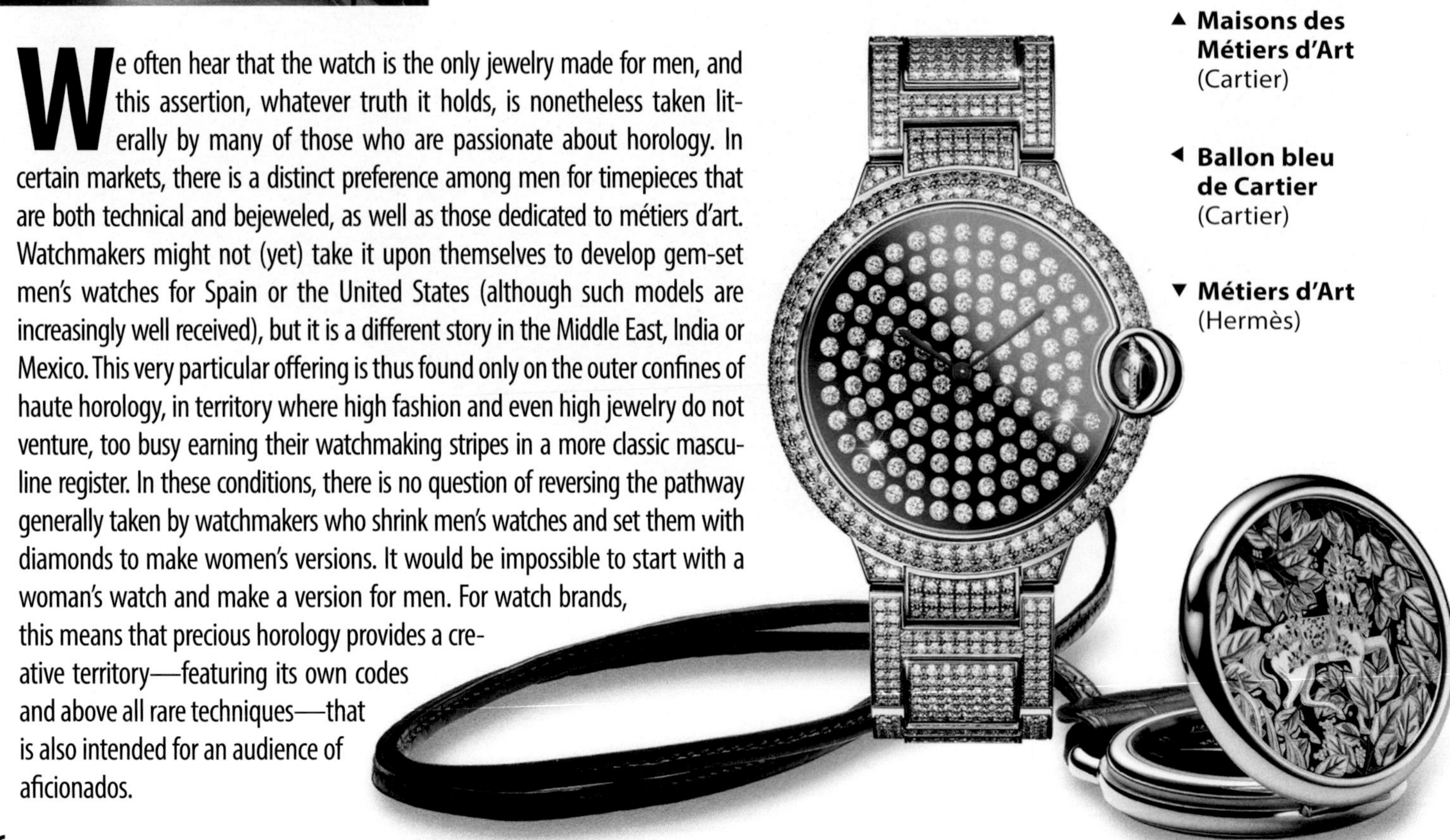

▲ **Maisons des Métiers d'Art** (Cartier)

◄ **Ballon bleu de Cartier** (Cartier)

▼ **Métiers d'Art** (Hermès)

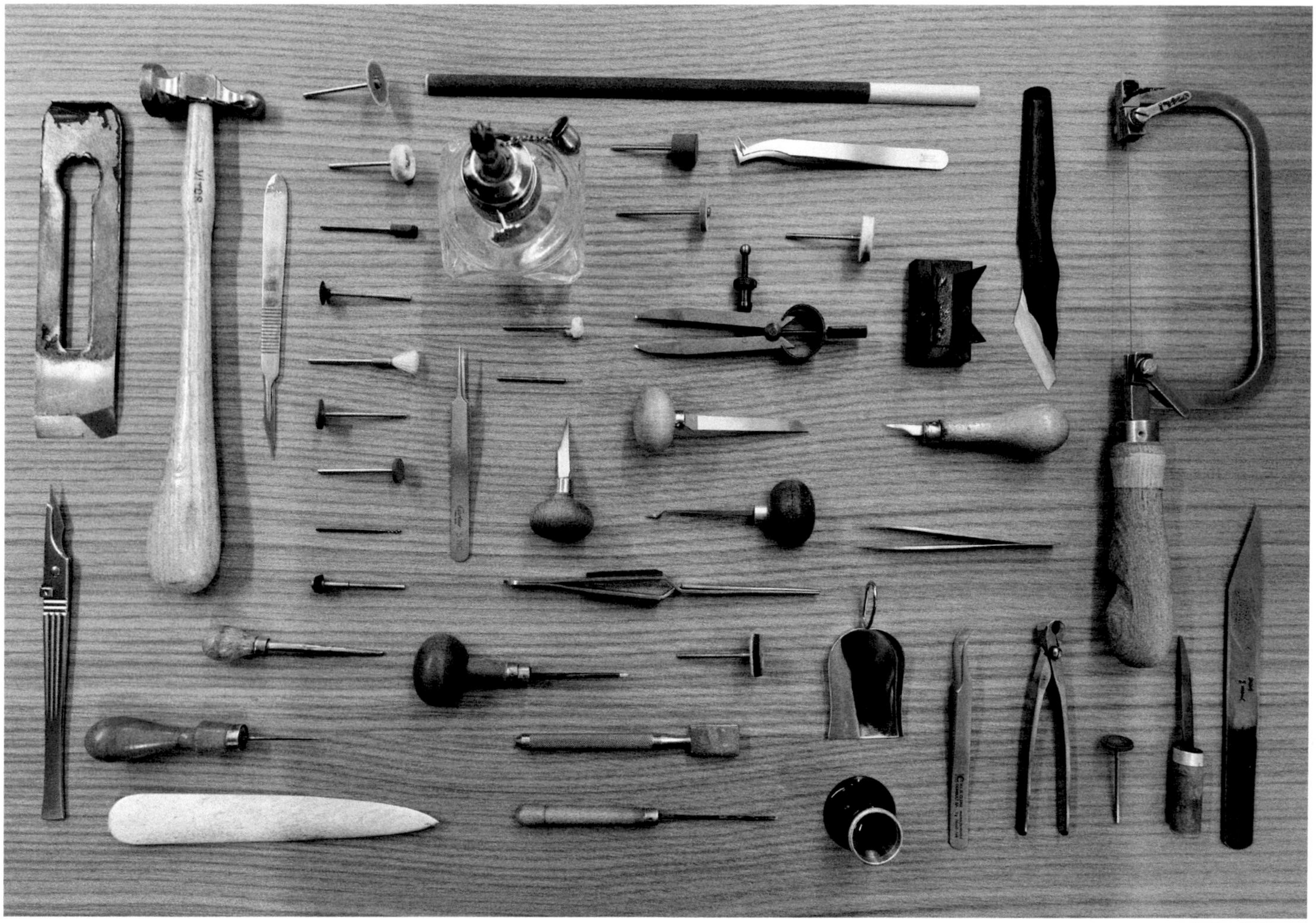

One need only look at the exceptional collections presented by Piaget under the title Mythical Journey to realize that the creation of watches such as these arises from its own distinct philosophy, in which the measurement of time is subordinate to métiers d'art that in fact have very little to do with the fairer sex. The Genevan Manufacture began this watchmaking odyssey in 2013 with "Silk Road," extending it in late 2015 with the presentation of "Secrets & Lights," a collection inspired by the symbolism of Venice and Samarkand. This collection featured 15 models interpreted in 93 jewelry creations and 38 watch models, which draw on techniques such as sculpture, gold engraving, micromosaic, gem-setting, Bulino engraving, enameling and even lacquer encrusted with eggshells and bits of feathers. Just one example in this dazzling series of masterpieces: the Piaget Protocol XXL, for which the Italian artisan Cesare Bella meticulously placed nearly 5,000 minuscule glass tesserae to create a breathtaking view of Santa Maria Della Salute overlooking the mouth of Venice's Grand Canal.

▲ **Maisons des Métiers d'Art** (Cartier)

▶ **Protocol XXL** (Piaget)

The mastery of métiers d'art is in this sense an incomparable opening for new modes of expression in horology. We speak here of techniques that go above and beyond gem-setting, and which very few houses count among their skills. This is why the same few names come up in any discussion of the topic: Blancpain's Métiers d'art collections, Jaquet Droz's Ateliers d'art lines, Van Cleef & Arpels's Complications Poétiques.

▲ **Ateliers d'Art** (Jaquet Droz)

▶ **Complications Poétiques** (Van Cleef & Arpels)

▶ **Métiers d'Art** (Blancpain)

▲ **Elégance Sartoriale** (Vacheron Constantin)

▲ **Métiers d'Art Villes Lumiéres** (Vacheron Constantin)

And Vacheron Constantin, an incomparable brand with its Métiers d'art lines, whose Mécaniques Ajourées and Elégance Sartoriale are intimately tied to the masculine universe. Hermès is another force in this world, as is Cartier, which two years ago inaugurated its Maison des Métiers d'art, a place where lost and even forgotten arts gain new life, with artisans working to sustain these extraordinary disciplines. In addition, at every SIHH, the company presents dazzling pieces that revisit techniques such as filigree or Etruscan granulation.

Highly "mechanical" brands clearly have a card to play in this game by setting their pieces with gems. The three-dimensional configuration of gear trains against a diamond backdrop makes for a transfixing visual effect. Between the gemstone and the mechanism, it is impossible to say which one is better placed to lay claim to this famous piece of eternity. Jacob & Co. demonstrated its mastery of this explosive art with pieces such as the Astronomia Tourbillon Baguette, "a poetic vision of the celestial world," and with its Quenttin Tourbillon Baguette, which offers 31 days of power reserve regulated by a vertical tourbillon. These are just two models among several that combine rare technical sophistication with a subversive aesthetic.

▲ **Astronomia Tourbillon Baguette**
(Jacob & Co.)

▶ **Quenttin Tourbillon Baguette**
(Jacob & Co.)

This explosive cocktail is also served up at Roger Dubuis, a brand that has made a specialty of "contemporary" skeletonization in its movements and its tourbillon, two particularities that marry beautifully in the Excalibur collection, an expression of the brand's powerful—even outrageous—style. At Roger Dubuis, the art of gem-setting is always in the mix, especially as the house was the first to incorporate unusual techniques: setting gems into rubber and carbon. This nonconformist approach is consistent with the image of the brand, for which a timepiece is much more than an instrument for displaying the hours and minutes. That is also the philosophy that inspires all the watches in these pages: they reflect everything that we are!

▶ **Excalibur Spider** (Roger Dubuis)

▼ **Excalibur** (Roger Dubuis)

As the arbiter of "jewelry for men," watches fulfill a particular, multifaceted function. Whether their focus is on simplicity or sophistication, elegance or rugged sportsmanship, high-tech breakthroughs or time-honored tradition, these high-end timepieces convey a complex vision of masculinity. Whatever a man values, however he sees himself, he is sure to find a timepiece that helps him express his unique personality.

▼ **Classic Fusion Berluti Scritto** (Hublot)

"MAN IS FREE AT THE INSTANT HE WANTS TO BE."

VOLTAIRE

COUNTING DOWN

Alpina presents two timepieces that **AFFIRM THE SWISS WATCHMAKER'S PLACE AS A LEADER IN SPORTING HAUTE HOROLOGY**.

Developed primarily as an authentic diving instrument, the self-winding Seastrong Diver Heritage is housed in a robust 42mm stainless steel case boasting water resistance to depths of 300m. Furthermore, the integration of scratch-resistant sapphire crystal endows the watch with the ability to face the toughest of environmental conditions. Positioned at 2 o'clock and designed for ease of use, a secondary crown allows the wearer to rotate the timepiece's internal 60-minute ring, ensuring accurate tracking of time spent under water and of the diver's remaining air supply. On the dial, a wealth of luminous elements grants the owner optimal legibility in the ocean's darker depths or in murky waters. Naturally, these crucial design features would be superfluous without a caliber of excellent precision. The Seastrong Diver Heritage is driven by the AL-525 caliber, a 26-jewel mechanical movement oscillating at a rate of 28,800 vph and safeguarded from shocks thanks to an Incabloc impact-protection device. Hours, minutes and seconds are told from the central axis with striking clarity while a tasteful date window, at 4 o'clock, gives the timepiece a touch of classical elegance.

The Seastrong Diver Heritage is presented in two variations, each with a unique personality. The first, with its silver-colored dial and black internal ring, plays off the sobriety of its tones to establish an understated, high-contrast personality. A second model, adorned with a dark gray dial and navy-colored internal ring, evokes the fascinating shades of the ocean's depths. Both models are worn on a water resistant black leather strap.

▲ ▶ **SEASTRONG DIVER HERITAGE**

This duo of authentic diver's timepieces boasts a rugged external construction that allows for optimal performance to depths of up to 300m beneath the surface.

The visual design of the Alpiner 4 Manufacture Flyback Chronograph echoes the sophistication of its engine with a bold full-black aesthetic.

Guided by the sage words of the adventurous pilot and poet Antoine de Saint-Exupéry, who stated that "perfection is attained, not when there is no longer anything to add, but when there is no longer anything to take away," Alpina presents a sophisticated timepiece whose caliber achieves its functional excellence thanks to the innovative paring down of its construction. The Alpiner 4 Manufacture Flyback Chronograph's AL-760 movement boasts a high-performance flyback chronograph composed of only 95 parts. The entire caliber, comprised of 233 components, boasts excellent magnetic and shock resistance. Rejecting convention, the self-winding timepiece replaces the traditional multiple-column-wheel design of the chronograph with a star-shaped alternative that, in combination with the operating lever, gives the timepiece its remarkable smoothness of operation. The visual design of the wristwatch echoes the high-tech sophistication of its internal engine with a full-black aesthetic as bold as it is contemporary. Beige luminous components stand out against the dark, masculine face, achieving ideal levels of contrast. The AL-760 caliber complements the hour-and-minute function with a hand-driven date subdial at 6 o'clock, small seconds at 9 o'clock and 30-minute-counter chronograph with central sweeping seconds. Thanks to its flyback construction, the chronograph may be stopped, reset and restarted with a single push of a button. The 44mm black-PVD-coated stainless steel timepiece is fitted with a peripheral telemeter scale and is worn on a black leather strap with beige stitching.

▲ **ALPINER 4 MANUFACTURE FLYBACK CHRONOGRAPH**

Less is more with this bold sporting wristwatch that boasts a complex flyback-chronograph module composed of a mere 96 of the 28,800 vph caliber's 233 components.

ALPINER MANUFACTURE 4 FLYBACK CHRONOGRAPH REF. AL-760BN5FBAQ6

Movement: automatic-winding AL-760 caliber; 38-hour power reserve; 32 jewels.
Functions: hours, minutes, seconds; date at 6; chronograph: 30-minute counter at 3, 60-second counter at 9.
Case: stainless steel with black PVD coating; Ø 44mm; scratch-resistant sapphire crystal; water resistant to 10atm
Dial: black; applied blue indexes; blue luminous coating; blue luminous-coated hour and minute hands.
Strap: black genuine leather with blue stitching.

Suggested price: $4,750
Also available: stainless steel case, silver sunray dial (ref. AL-760SB5AQ6).

STARTIMER PILOT AUTOMATIC CHRONOGRAPH REF. AL-725GR4S6

Movement: automatic-winding AL-725 caliber; 46-hour power reserve; 25 jewels.
Functions: hours, minutes, seconds; date at 3; chronograph: 30-minute counter at 12, 12-hour counter at 6.
Case: stainless steel; Ø 44mm; scratch-resistant antireflective sapphire crystal; water resistant to 10atm.
Dial: military matte green; white SuperLumiNova-coated hour and minute hands; Alpina red triangle signature on seconds hand.
Strap: brown genuine leather.

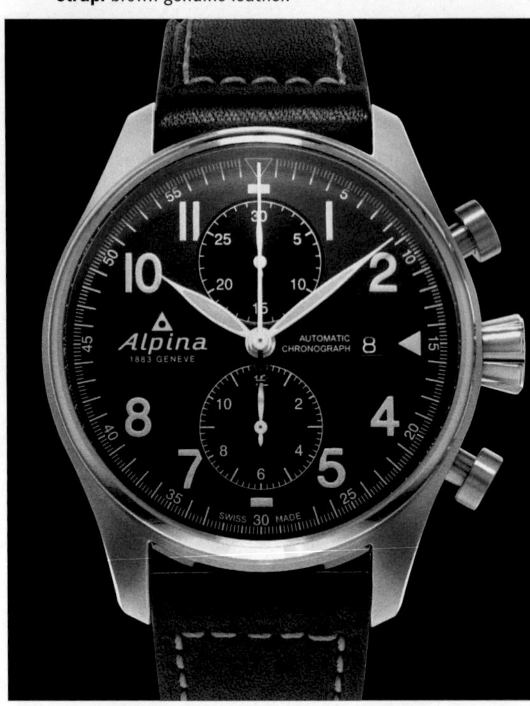

Suggested price: $1,995
Also available: stainless steel case, matte black dial, black genuine leather strap (ref. AL-725B4S6).

ALPINER AUTOMATIC 4 REF. AL-525NS5AQ6

Movement: automatic-winding AL-525 caliber; 36-hour power reserve; 26 jewels.
Functions: hours, minutes, seconds; date at 3.
Case: stainless steel; Ø 44mm; scratch-resistant sapphire crystal; water resistant to 10atm.
Dial: glacier blue sunray; applied luminous indexes; Alpina red triangle signature on seconds hand.
Strap: brown genuine leather.
Suggested price: $1,395

Also available: stainless steel case, black sunray dial, black leather strap (ref. AL-525BS5AQ6).

SEASTRONG DIVER HERITAGE REF. AL-525S4H6

Movement: automatic-winding AL-525 caliber; 38-hour power reserve; 26 jewels.
Functions: hours, minutes, seconds; date at 4.
Case: stainless steel; Ø 42mm; scratch-resistant "glass box" sapphire crystal; water resistant to 30atm.
Dial: silver; applied silvered indexes.
Strap: black water resistant leather.
Suggested price: $1,695

Also available: stainless steel case, dark blue dial, black leather strap (ref. AL-525G4H6).

SEASTRONG DIVER 300 AUTOMATIC — REF. AL-525LBBRG4V6

Movement: automatic-winding AL-525 caliber; 38-hour power reserve; 26 jewels.
Functions: hours, minutes, seconds; date at 3.
Case: stainless steel; Ø 44mm; red diving bezel; scratch-resistant sapphire crystal; engraved case back; water resistant to 30atm.
Dial: black; applied luminous indexes; white luminous hour and minute hands; Alpina red triangle signature on seconds hand.
Strap: rubberized nubuck leather.
Suggested price: $1,295
Also available: stainless steel case, blue diving bezel (ref. AL-525LBN4V6).

STARTIMER PILOT CHRONOGRAPH BIG DATE DESERT CAMOUFLAGE — REF. AL-372MLY4FBS6

Movement: quartz AL-372; 48-month battery life; 13 jewels.
Functions: hours, minutes, seconds; date at 6; chronograph: 10-hour counter at 2, 60-second counter at 6, 30-minute counter at 10.
Case: stainless steel with black PVD coating; Ø 44mm; scratch-resistant antireflective sapphire crystal; water resistant to 10atm.
Dial: matte desert camouflage; SuperLumiNova-coated hour and minute hands; Alpina red triangle signature on seconds hand.
Strap: technical fabric.
Suggested price: $1,150
Also available: stainless steel case with black PVD coating, black dial, black cordura strap (ref. AL-372B4FBS6).

HOROLOGICAL SMARTWATCH — REF. AL-285STD3C6

Movement: quartz AL-285 MMT caliber; 2+ years battery life.
Functions: hours, minutes; date at 6; activity tracking; sleep monitoring; sleep cycle alarms; get-active alerts; smart coaching; world time; cloud backup and restore.
Case: stainless steel; Ø 39mm; domed scratch-resistant sapphire crystal; water resistant to 10atm.
Dial: white guilloché set with 9 diamonds; white SuperLumiNova-coated hour and minute hands.
Strap: white genuine leather.
Suggested price: $1,050
Also available: stainless steel case, stainless steel bracelet (ref. AL-285STD3C6B).

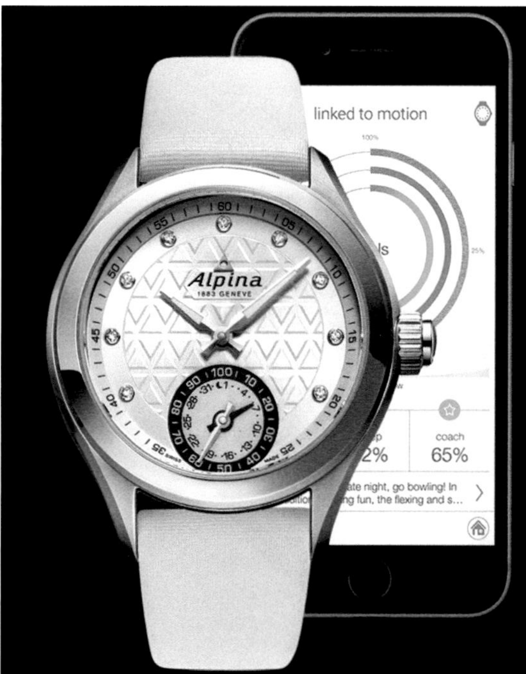

HOROLOGICAL SMARTWATCH — REF. AL-285NS5AQ6

Movement: quartz AL-285 MMT caliber; 2+ years battery life.
Functions: hours, minutes; date at 6; activity tracking; sleep monitoring; sleep cycle alarms; get-active alerts; smart coaching; world time; cloud backup and restore.
Case: stainless steel; Ø 44mm; domed scratch-resistant sapphire crystal; water resistant to 10atm.
Dial: blue sunray; SuperLumiNova-coated hour and minute hands.
Strap: brown genuine leather.
Suggested price: $1,050
Also available: stainless steel case, silvered dial, black leather strap (ref. AL-285S5AQ6).

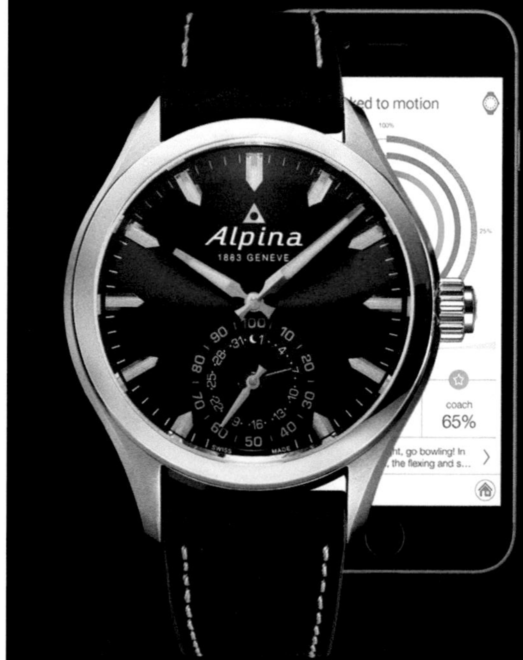

ARNOLD & SON
SINCE 1764

A VISIBLE HEART BEAT

Arnold & Son takes on the art form of openworked timepieces with **STUNNING DEXTERITY, AGILE IMAGINATION AND METICULOUS PRECISION**, carrying on a centuries-old legacy.

The Swiss horologer pairs triumphs of micro-mechanical engineering with a refusal to compromise. The UTTE Skeleton boasts record-breaking slenderness, a multi-dimensional design and an oversized centerpiece. Measuring a mere 8.34mm in thickness, the timepiece achieves this extraordinary dimension while prominently featuring a curved three-dimensional flying tourbillon on the lower half of the dial. The 14mm tourbillon cage thus bestows upon the wearer a vivid demonstration of horological dynamism, presenting the fascinating choreography within the clarity of an openworked design. Arnold & Son also refuses to sacrifice performance for the sake of the timepiece's standing as the thinnest skeleton tourbillon on the market. The UTTE Skeleton's hand-wound A&S8220 caliber achieves a massive 90-hour power reserve by integrating two skeleton barrels within the exquisitely finished architecture. The UTTE Skeleton is housed in a 42mm red-gold case that perfectly contrasts the cool tones and sharp lines of the watch's face, which is not only skeletonized but also decorated with guilloché Côtes de Genève.

◂ **UTTE SKELETON**
This masterpiece of skeletonization presents a 14mm tourbillon cage within a design of record-breaking slenderness.

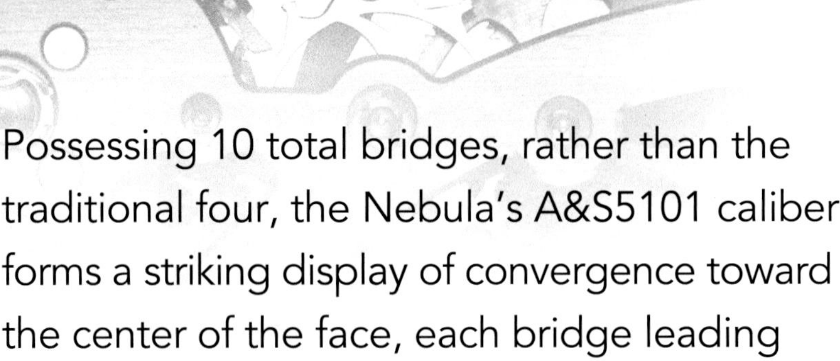

Possessing 10 total bridges, rather than the traditional four, the Nebula's A&S5101 caliber forms a striking display of convergence toward the center of the face, each bridge leading the eye toward a unified focal point.

Arnold & Son plays with multi-axial symmetry and meticulous ratios, presenting a sculptural timepiece inspired by the universe's astounding expansion. The 41.5mm 18-karat red-gold Nebula reveals seven bridges on the periphery of the openworked dial. Possessing 10 total bridges, rather than the four traditionally found in a mechanical timepiece, the A&S5101 caliber forms a striking display of convergence toward the center of the face, each bridge leading the eye toward a unified focal point. The hand-wound Nebula then takes symmetry to a fascinating level. Two mainspring barrels, at 10 and 2 o'clock, combine with the small seconds subdial and openworked oscillating balance wheel, near 7 and 5 o'clock, to compose a harmonious geometric tableau. Symmetry also guides the display visible through the watch's transparent caseback, where the caliber's skeletonized mainplate makes a vibrant appearance along with the movement's polished gears and solid-18-karat-gold chatons. The Nebula is worn on a brown or black hand-stitched alligator leather strap and boasts a generous 90-hour power reserve.

With the Eight-Day Royal Navy, Arnold & Son pays a visually and mechanically contemporary tribute to the manufacture's intimate ties to 18th-century marine chronometry. A master watchmaker and ceaseless innovator, John Arnold devoted himself to the pursuit of precise timekeeping at sea—a crucial challenge of the era, as mariners sought methods of determining longitude with necessary accuracy. Arnold and his son soon became decisive players in the success of the Royal British Navy as well as that of some of the world's most distinguished marine explorers. Equipped with a highly efficient twin-barrel construction, the 43mm Eight-Day Royal Navy honors John Arnold's historic achievements with a combination of classical arrangements and modern aesthetic codes. Two subdials, positioned at 12 and 6 o'clock, subtly echo the design of Arnold & Son's celebrated 18th-century chronometers. Indicating the small seconds and revealing the date through a discreet aperture, the 6 o'clock counter offers a perfect complement to the display, at 12 o'clock, of the A&S1016 caliber's colossal 192-hour power reserve. A radiant blue guilloché decoration on the dial adorns the stainless steel timepiece with a colorful nod to the manufacture's rich heritage, while providing a stunning backdrop for a central display of the hours and minutes.

▲ **NEBULA** *(top)*

Symmetry is at the forefront of this astronomy-inspired timepiece that uniquely incorporates seven of its bridges into a stunning and distinctive dial-side design.

▲ **EIGHT-DAY ROYAL NAVY** *(bottom)*

This homage to John Arnold's 18th-century marine-chronometry achievements indicates its impressive eight-day power reserve atop a guilloché royal blue dial.

NEBULA — REF. 1NEAS.B01A.D134A

Movement: manual-winding A&S5101 caliber; Ø 31.5mm, thickness: 4.04mm; 90-hour power reserve; 24 jewels; 21,600 vph; two mainspring barrels; screwed balance wheel; decoration: NAC-treated bridges and black ADLC-treated mainplate with haute horology finishing, chamfered bridges with polished edges and brushed surfaces, chamfered wheels with A&S three-spoke design and polished edges, gold chatons, screws with beveled and mirror-polished heads.
Functions: hours, minutes; small seconds at 7.
Case: stainless steel; Ø 41.5mm, thickness: 8.73mm; antireflective sapphire crystal; sapphire crystal caseback; water resistant to 3atm.
Dial: skeletonized; anthracite-colored chapter ring.
Strap: hand-aged anthracite calf leather.
Suggested price: $14,500
Also available: 18K red-gold case, light gray chapter ring, brown alligator leather strap (ref. 1NEAR.S01A.D135A).

8-DAY ROYAL NAVY — REF. 1EDAS.S01A.D135A

Movement: manual-winding A&S1016 caliber; Ø 33mm, thickness: 4.7mm; 192-hour power reserve; 33 jewels; 21,600 vph; double barrel; decoration: palladium-treated nickel-silver movement, mainplate featuring haute horology finishing: skeletonized hand-chamfered bridges with polished edges, Côtes de Genève rayonnantes, fine circular graining, circular-grained wheels, blued screws, screwed gold chatons, screws with beveled and mirror-polished heads.
Functions: hours, minutes; small seconds and date at 6; power reserve indicator at 12.

Case: stainless steel; Ø 43mm; antireflective sapphire crystal; sapphire crystal caseback; water resistant to 3atm.
Dial: silver guilloché polished lacquer.
Strap: brown hand-aged calf leather.
Suggested price: $12,950
Also available: blue dial, blue calf leather strap (ref. 1EDAS.U01A.D136A).

8-DAY ROYAL NAVY — REF. 1EDAS.B01A.D134A

Movement: manual-winding A&S1016 caliber; Ø 33mm, thickness: 4.7mm; 192-hour power reserve; 33 jewels; 21,600 vph; double barrel; decoration: palladium-treated nickel-silver movement, mainplate featuring haute horology finishing: skeletonized hand-chamfered bridges with polished edges, Côtes de Genève rayonnantes, fine circular graining, circular-grained wheels, blued screws, screwed gold chatons, screws with beveled and mirror-polished heads.
Functions: hours, minutes; small seconds and date at 6; power reserve indicator at 12.

Case: stainless steel; Ø 43mm; antireflective sapphire crystal; sapphire crystal caseback; water resistant to 3atm.
Dial: black guilloché polished lacquer.
Strap: black hand-aged calf leather.
Suggested price: $12,950

HM DRAGON & FENGHUANG — REF. 1LCAP.M08A.C110A/C111A

Movement: manual-winding A&S1001 caliber; Ø 30mm, thickness: 2.7mm; 90-hour power reserve; 21 jewels; 21,600 vph; double barrel; decoration: rhodium-treated nickel-silver movement with haute horology finishing: hand-chamfered bridges with polished edges, fine circular graining and Côtes de Genève rayonnantes, blued screws with beveled and mirror-polished heads.
Functions: hours, minutes.
Case: 18K rose gold; Ø 40mm; antireflective sapphire crystal; sapphire crystal caseback; water resistant to 3atm.

Dial: red dragon and fenghuang on white mother-of-pearl.
Strap: hand-stitched brown alligator leather.
Note: limited edition of 5 pieces.
Suggested price: $25,950
Also available: diamond-set bezel; black alligator leather strap.

HMS1 — REF. 1LCAW.S09A.C111W

Movement: manual-winding A&S1001 caliber; Ø 30mm, thickness: 2.7mm; 90-hour power reserve; 21 jewels; 21,600 vph; double barrel; decoration: rhodium-treated nickel-silver movement with haute horology finishing: hand-chamfered bridges with polished edges, fine circular graining and Côtes de Genève rayonnantes, blued screws with beveled and mirror-polished heads.
Functions: hours, minutes; small seconds at 6.
Case: 18K white gold; Ø 40mm; antireflective sapphire crystal; sapphire crystal caseback; water resistant to 3atm.
Dial: silvery white guilloché.
Strap: hand-stitched black alligator leather.
Suggested price: $18,950
Also available: 18K rose-gold case, brown alligator leather strap (ref. 1LCAP.S10A.C110A).

TES BLUE — REF. 1SJAR.V01A.C112A

Movement: manual-winding A&S8100 caliber; Ø 32.6mm, thickness: 6.3mm; 80-hour power reserve; 19 jewels; 21,600 vph; decoration: nickel-silver and sapphire movement, palladium-treated bridges and blue CVD-treated mainplate with haute horology finishing: hand-chamfered bridges with polished edges, A&S specific pattern engraved on the mainplate, circular satin-finished wheels with hand-chamfered and polished edges, screwed gold chatons, mirror-polished tourbillon cage and bridge, screws with beveled and mirror-polished heads.
Functions: hours, minutes; tourbillon at 6.
Case: 18K white gold; Ø 44mm; antireflective sapphire crystal; sapphire crystal caseback; water resistant to 3atm.
Dial: blue; open.
Strap: hand-stitched blue alligator leather.
Note: limited edition of 25 pieces.
Suggested price: $162,200
Also available: black alligator leather strap.

TB88 GUNMETAL — REF. 1TBAS.B98A.T113A

Movement: manual-winding A&S5003 caliber; Ø 37.8mm, thickness: 5.9mm; 100-hour power reserve; 32 jewels; 18,000 vph; double barrel; Breguet spring; decoration: nickel-silver movement, NAC gray-treated bridges and mainplate with haute horology finishing: manually-chamfered bridges and steel parts with polished edges and brushed surfaces, chamfered and circular satin-finished wheels, screws with beveled and mirror-polished heads.
Functions: hours, minutes; true beat seconds at 8.
Case: sandblasted stainless steel with dark gray DLC coating; Ø 46mm; antireflective sapphire crystal; sapphire crystal caseback; water resistant to 3atm.
Dial: skeletonized.
Strap: cordura 1100 with calf leather lining.
Note: limited edition of 5 pieces.
Suggested price: $41,500

TEC1 — REF. 1CTAR.G01A.C112R

Movement: automatic-winding A&S8305 caliber; Ø 35mm, thickness: 8.83mm; 55-hour power reserve; ceramic ball bearing; 28,800 vph; decoration: palladium-treated with haute horology finishing: hand-chamfered bridges with polished edges, fine circular graining and Côtes de Genève rayonnantes, all chronograph levers are satin-finished with hand-chamfered and polished edges, circular satin-finished wheels, blued screws with beveled and mirror-polished heads; hand-engraved 22K red-gold skeletonized rotor with brushed surfaces and chamfered polished edges.
Functions: hours, minutes; tourbillon at 12; chronograph: central seconds hand, 60-minute counter at 6.
Case: 18K red gold; Ø 45mm; antireflective sapphire crystal; sapphire crystal caseback; water resistant to 3atm.
Dial: anthracite.
Strap: hand-stitched brown alligator leather.
Suggested price: $99,900
Also available: black alligator leather strap.

CONSTANT FORCE TOURBILLON — REF. 1FCAR.B01A.C112C

Movement: manual-winding A&S5119 caliber; Ø 36.8mm, thickness: 6mm; 90-hour power reserve; 39 jewels; 21,600 vph; double barrel; decoration: nickel-silver and steel movement, palladium-treated bridges and NAC gray-treated mainplate with haute horology finishing: hand-chamfered bridges with polished edges and brushed surfaces, screwed gold chatons, screws with beveled and mirror-polished heads.
Functions: hours, minutes; true beat seconds and constant force between 7 and 8; tourbillon between 4 and 5.
Case: 18K red gold; Ø 46mm; antireflective sapphire crystal; sapphire crystal caseback; water resistant to 3atm.
Dial: anthracite open.
Strap: hand-stitched brown bottier alligator leather with patina.
Note: limited edition of 28 pieces.
Suggested price: $197,500

HM PERPETUAL MOON — REF. 1GLAS.U02A.C122S

Movement: manual-winding A&S1512 caliber; Ø 34mm, thickness: 5.35mm; 90-hour power reserve; 27 jewels; 21,600 vph; double barrel; decoration: nickel-silver movement, rhodium-treated with haute horology finishing: manually-chamfered bridges with polished edges, fine circular graining and Côtes de Genève rayonnantes, blued screws with polished and chamfered edges.
Functions: hours, minutes; perpetual moonphase at 12; second moonphase indicator on the caseback.
Case: stainless steel; Ø 42mm; antireflective sapphire crystal; sapphire crystal caseback; water resistant to 3atm.

Dial: translucent blue lacquered guilloché; back dial: fine circular graining, rhodium-treated, rendition of the 8 phases of the moon.
Strap: hand-stitched black alligator leather.
Suggested price: $16,950
Also available: brown alligator leather strap.

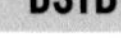

HM DOUBLE HEMISPHERE PERPETUAL MOON — REF. 1GLAR.U03A.C122A

Movement: manual-winding A&S1512 caliber; Ø 34mm, thickness: 5.35mm; 90-hour power reserve; 27 jewels; 21,600 vph; double barrel; decoration: nickel-silver movement, rhodium-treated with haute horology finishing: manually-chamfered bridges with polished edges, fine circular graining and Côtes de Genève rayonnantes, blued screws.
Functions: hours, minutes; two perpetual moonphase indicators; third moonphase indicator on the caseback.
Case: 18K red gold; Ø 42mm; antireflective sapphire crystal; sapphire crystal caseback; water resistant to 3atm.

Dial: translucent blue lacquered guilloché; back dial: fine circular graining, rhodium-treated, rendition of the 8 phases of the moon.
Strap: hand-stitched brown alligator leather.
Suggested price: $31,000
Also available: black alligator leather strap.

DSTB — REF. 1ATAR.S01A.C120A

Movement: automatic-winding A&S6003 caliber; Ø 38mm, thickness: 7.39mm; 45-hour power reserve; 32 jewels; 28,800 vph; decoration: palladium-treated with haute horology finishing: hand-chamfered bridges and polished edges, fine circular graining and Côtes de Genève rayonnantes, NAC gray-treated dial plate with traditional English frosted finish, circular satin-finished wheels, blued screws with beveled and mirror-polished heads, red-gold-treated satin-finished true beat seconds bridges with hand-chamfered and polished edges, solid 22K red-gold guilloché oscillating weight.
Functions: off-centered hours, minutes; true beat seconds.

Case: 18K red gold; Ø 43.5mm; antireflective sapphire crystal; sapphire crystal caseback; water resistant to 3atm.
Dial: silvery opaline.
Strap: hand-stitched brown alligator leather.
Note: limited edition of 125 pieces.
Suggested price: $48,550
Also available: black alligator leather strap.

TB DRAGON — REF. 1ARAP.B04A.C120P/121P

Movement: automatic-winding A&S6103 caliber; Ø 30.4mm, thickness: 7.79mm; 45-hour power reserve; 30 jewels; 28,800 vph; ceramic ball bearing; decoration: rhodium-treated with haute horology finishing: hand-chamfered bridges with polished edges, fine circular graining and Côtes de Genève rayonnantes, brushed and skeletonized oscillating weight, blued screws with beveled and mirror-polished heads.
Functions: hours, minutes at 9; true beat seconds.
Case: 18K rose gold; Ø 44mm; antireflective sapphire crystal; sapphire crystal caseback; water resistant to 3atm.
Dial: black; engraved 22K solid rose-gold appliqué with hand-painted textures and shades.
Strap: hand-stitched black alligator leather.
Note: limited edition of 28 pieces.
Suggested price: $36,750
Also available: brown alligator leather strap.

GOLDEN WHEEL — REF. 1HVAR.M01A.C120A

Movement: automatic-winding A&S6018 caliber; Ø 37.2mm, thickness: 8mm; 45-hour power reserve; 29 jewels; 28,800 vph; decoration: palladium-treated with haute horology finishing: hand-chamfered bridges with polished edges, fine circular graining and Côtes de Genève rayonnantes, dial plate black ADLC-treated with Côtes de Genève, circular satin-finished wheels, blued screws with beveled and mirror-polished heads, solid 22K red-gold guilloché oscillating weight.
Functions: jumping digital hours; minutes at 12; true beat seconds.
Case: 18K red gold; Ø 44mm; antireflective sapphire crystal; sapphire crystal caseback; water resistant to 3atm.
Dial: silvery and white mother-of-pearl.
Strap: hand-stitched brown alligator leather.
Note: limited edition of 125 pieces.
Suggested price: $47,500
Also available: black alligator leather strap.

TIME PYRAMID — REF. 1TPAS.S01A.C124S

Movement: manual-winding A&S1615 caliber; Ø 37mm, thickness: 4.4mm; 90-hour power reserve; 27 jewels; 21,600 vph; double barrel; decoration: skeletonized nickel-silver movement, NAC gray-treated with haute horology finishing: hand-chamfered bridges with polished edges, Côtes de Genève, circular satin-finished wheels, blued screws.
Functions: hours, minutes, seconds; double power reserve indicators at 3 and 9.
Case: stainless steel; Ø 44.6mm; antireflective sapphire crystal; translucent-gray-coated sapphire caseback; water resistant to 3atm.
Dial: sapphire; circular satin-finished dial frame with chamfered and polished edges; blued hands; hour and minute hands with white SuperLumiNova.
Strap: hand-stitched black alligator leather.
Suggested price: $31,900

UTTE DRAGON — REF. 1UTAR.M01P.C320A

Movement: manual-winding A&S8200 caliber; Ø 32mm, thickness: 2.97mm; 90-hour power reserve; 29 jewels; 21,600 vph; decoration: nickel-silver movement, rhodium-treated with haute horology finishing: unique hand-engraved tourbillon bridge, hand-chamfered bridges with polished edges, fine circular graining and Côtes de Genève rayonnantes, circular satin-finished wheels with hand-chamfered and polished edges, blued screws with beveled and mirror-polished heads.
Functions: hours, minutes at 12; tourbillon at 6.
Case: 18K red gold; Ø 42mm; antireflective sapphire crystal; sapphire crystal caseback; water resistant to 3atm.
Dial: hand-painted miniature on white mother-of-pearl.
Strap: hand-stitched brown alligator leather.
Note: one-of-a-kind piece.
Suggested price: $85,900
Also available: black alligator leather strap.

ATELIERS

DEMONACO

A REFINED LOOK INSIDE

Ateliers deMonaco strikes **A RIVETING BALANCE OF CLASSICAL ACCENTS, UNIQUE MODERN INTERPRETATIONS AND CALIBERS OF THE HIGHEST MECHANICAL STANDARDS**. With its three newest presentations, the manufacture delights horology enthusiasts with brilliant takes on transparency, multi-dimensionality and luxurious play of light.

With the Admiral Chronographe Flyback, the Swiss watchmaker delights wearers with a sumptuous view of the sophisticated, hand-decorated dMc-760 caliber.

Housed in a three-piece, 18-karat rose-gold case, the self-winding movement allows its owner to stop, reset and restart the chronograph with a single press of a button. The 42mm timepiece complements its flyback chronograph's central seconds and 30-minute counter (at 3 o'clock) with a small seconds subdial (at 9 o'clock) that asserts the watch's elegant sense of balance and symmetry. This visual sobriety bears a vibrant result, as the dial, entirely composed of sapphire crystal, reveals the exquisite composition of the movement without distraction. Ten Roman numerals complete the frontal display. Through the caseback, the wearer is treated to another stunning view of the 28,800 vph movement, as well as its luxurious hand-engraved 22-karat-gold rotor. The Admiral Chronographe Flyback is worn on a hand-stitched alligator strap and is limited to 88 pieces.

◂ **ADMIRAL CHRONOGRAPHE FLYBACK**

This timepiece's sapphire dial allows for a fascinating view of the patented dMc-760 caliber with flyback chronograph.

▸ **RONDE DE MONTE-CARLO** *(top)*

The Ronde de Monte-Carlo plays off the shimmering beauty of its diamond-set case with a dial in radiant mother-of-pearl.

▸ **TOURBILLON OCULUS 1297** *(bottom)*

Driven by one of the most accurate tourbillon calibers in the world, this titanium wristwatch adorns its dial with a captivating motif in relief achieved using a sophisticated laser technique.

The Ronde de Monte-Carlo's dial responds to the shimmer of its surrounding frame with a design that irresistibly reflects each incoming ray of light.

The Ronde de Monte-Carlo plays with a magnificent combination of radiant materials to adorn the feminine wrist with a breathtaking display of elegance.

Composed of 31 parts, including a titanium core, the 18-karat white- or rose-gold case sets a scintillating tone thanks to its magnificent setting of 300 diamonds on the bezel. The self-winding timepiece's dial responds to the shimmer of its surrounding frame with a blue or mother-of-pearl design (in blue or white) that irresistibly reflects each incoming ray of light. At the heart of the watch, the dMc-700 caliber animates a three-hand display of the hours, minutes and seconds with excellent precision, boasting a silicon escape wheel and oscillation frequency of 28,800 vph. Turning over the 39mm timepiece reveals the meticulous construction of the movement, including its hand-decorated bridges, perlage adornment and 22-karat rose-gold, hand-engraved rotor. A fifth available model enrobes its case completely with a breathtaking setting of 617 diamonds.

Notes of elegant classicism combine with avant-garde technical expertise to give the Tourbillon Oculus 1297 its stunning personality. Housed in a 44mm titanium case, the self-winding timepiece presents a brilliantly precise tourbillon without obstruction at 6 o'clock thanks to the integration of a transparent sapphire bridge and off-centered positioning of the hours and minutes on the upper half of the face. The wearer is thereby treated to a magnificent exhibition of the exquisite construction of the Tourbillon XP 1 caliber, which boasts a silicon escape wheel and lever. This multi-layered dial-side architecture, highlighted by the enlightening view of the movement's high-precision heartbeat, is further accentuated by Ateliers deMonaco's use of a five-axis laser machine to adorn the royal blue dial with a vibrant motif of lozenges in relief. Through the 88-piece limited edition timepiece's sapphire crystal caseback, the owner may admire the movement's numerous hand finishes and hand-engraved 22-karat-gold oscillating weight. The Tourbillon Oculus 1297 is finished with a discreet small seconds hand atop the tourbillon's aperture and is worn on a hand-stitched alligator strap that echoes the rich, colorful personality of the dial.

ADMIRAL CHRONOGRAPHE FLYBACK – SAPHIR REF. DMC-CHR-SPH-RG

Movement: automatic-winding dMc-760 caliber; 38-hour power reserve; 32 jewels; 28,800 vph; hand-perlage decoration on bridges; 22K gold hand-engraved rotor.
Functions: hours, minutes; small seconds at 9; chronograph: central seconds hand, 30-minute counter at 3.
Case: 18 rose gold; Ø 42mm, thickness: 13.3mm; antireflective sapphire crystal; sapphire crystal caseback; water resistant to 3atm.
Dial: sapphire; PVD-plated diamond-cut applied Roman numeral indexes; dauphine-shaped hands.

Strap: hand-stitched alligator leather; 18K gold ardillon buckle.
Note: limited edition of 88 pieces.
Suggested price: $27,100

ADMIRAL CHRONOGRAPH FLYBACK – SAPHIR REF. DMC-CHR-SPH-WG

Movement: automatic-winding dMc-760 caliber; 38-hour power reserve; 32 jewels; 28,800 vph; hand-perlage decoration on bridges; 22K rose-gold hand-engraved rotor.
Functions: hours, minutes; small seconds at 9; chronograph: central seconds hand, 30-minute counter at 3.
Case: 18K white gold; Ø 42mm, thickness: 13.3mm; antireflective sapphire crystal; sapphire crystal caseback; water resistant to 3atm.
Dial: sapphire; PVD-plated diamond-cut applied Roman numeral indexes; dauphine-shaped hands.

Strap: hand-stitched alligator leather; 18K gold ardillon buckle.
Note: limited edition of 88 pieces.
Suggested price: $28,200

TOURBILLON OCULUS 1297 REF. DMC-TB-OCBL-RL-TI

Movement: automatic-winding Tourbillon XP 1 caliber; 28,800 vph; curved chamfered and hand-perlage decoration on bridges; 22K gold hand-engraved rotor.
Functions: off-centered hours and minutes; small seconds on tourbillon at 6.
Case: titanium; Ø 44mm, thickness: 13.1mm; sapphire crystal; sapphire crystal caseback; water resistant to 3atm.
Dial: blue lozenge pattern; dauphine-shaped hands.
Strap: hand-stitched alligator leather; titanium folding buckle.
Note: limited edition of 88 pieces.
Suggested price: $56,700

TOURBILLON RONDE D'OR – GRAND PRIX DE MONACO MAI 1966 REF. DMC-TB-GP2-WG

Movement: automatic-winding Tourbillon XP 1 caliber; 28,800 vph; curved chamfered and hand-perlage decoration on bridges; 22K gold hand-engraved rotor.
Functions: hours, minutes; small seconds on tourbillon at 6.
Case: 18K white gold; Ø 44mm, thickness: 13.1mm; sapphire crystal; sapphire crystal caseback; water resistant to 3atm.
Dial: solid gold; hand-engraved showing Grand Prix de Monaco Mai 1966; dauphine-shaped hands.
Strap: hand-stitched alligator leather; 18K gold folding buckle.

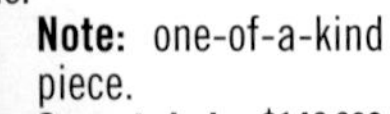

Note: one-of-a-kind piece.
Suggested price: $146,600

POINCON DE GENEVE – SAPHIR REF. DMC-PDG-SPH-WG

Movement: manual-winding dMc-708 caliber; 38-hour power reserve; 18 jewels; 28,800 vph; hand-perlage decoration on bridges.
Functions: hours, minutes, seconds.
Case: 18K white gold; Ø 40mm, thickness: 9.2mm; antireflective sapphire crystal; sapphire crystal caseback; water resistant to 3atm.
Dial: sapphire; PVD-plated diamond-cut applied Roman numeral indexes; dauphine-shaped hands.
Strap: hand-stitched alligator leather; 18K gold ardillon buckle.
Note: limited edition of 18 pieces.
Suggested price: $24,100

RONDE DE MONTE-CARLO REF. DMC-MC-DMPW-RGP

Movement: automatic-winding dMc-700 caliber; 42-hour power reserve; 26 jewels; 28,800 vph; hand-perlage decoration on bridges; 22K rose-gold hand-engraved rotor.
Functions: hours, minutes, seconds.
Case: 18K rose gold; Ø 39mm, thickness: 11mm; set with 617 diamonds (2.93 carats); antireflective sapphire crystal; sapphire crystal caseback; water resistant to 3atm.
Dial: white mother-of-pearl; applied Roman numeral indexes and 8 diamonds (0.03 carat); dauphine-shaped hands.
Strap: hand-stitched alligator leather; 18K gold and titanium folding buckle.
Note: limited edition of 88 pieces.
Suggested price: $64,600

RONDE DE MONTE-CARLO REF. DMC-MC-LMPW-WGD

Movement: automatic-winding dMc-700 caliber; 42-hour power reserve; 26 jewels; 28,800 vph; hand-perlage decoration on bridges; 22K rose-gold hand-engraved rotor.
Functions: hours, minutes, seconds.
Case: 18K white gold; Ø 39mm, thickness: 11mm; set with 300 diamonds (1.33 carats); antireflective sapphire crystal; sapphire crystal caseback; water resistant to 3atm.
Dial: white mother-of-pearl; applied Roman numeral indexes; dauphine-shaped hands.
Strap: hand-stitched alligator leather; 18K gold and titanium folding buckle.
Note: limited edition of 88 pieces.
Suggested price: $25,400

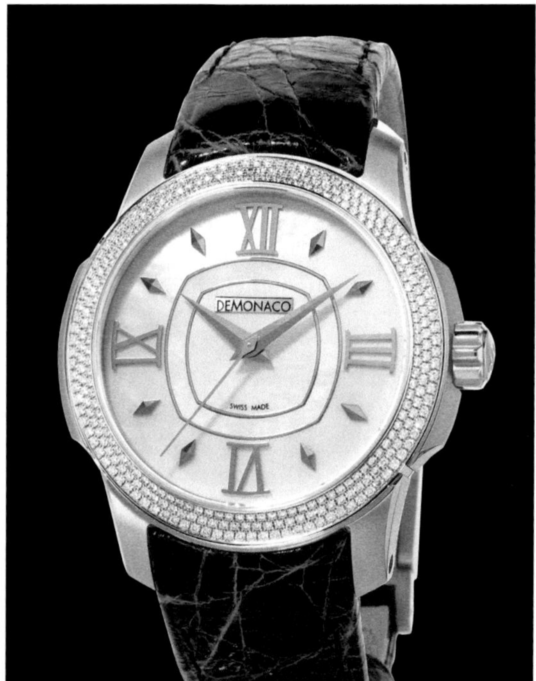

RONDE DE MONTE-CARLO REF. DMC-MC-LMPBL-RGD

Movement: automatic-winding dMc-700 caliber; 42-hour power reserve; 26 jewels; 28,800 vph; hand-perlage decoration on bridges; 22K rose-gold hand-engraved rotor.
Functions: hours, minutes, seconds.
Case: 18K rose gold; Ø 39mm, thickness: 11mm; set with 300 diamonds (1.33 carats); antireflective sapphire crystal; sapphire crystal caseback; water resistant to 3atm.
Dial: blue mother-of-pearl; applied Roman numeral indexes; dauphine-shaped hands.
Strap: hand-stitched alligator leather; 18K gold and titanium folding buckle.
Note: limited edition of 88 pieces.
Suggested price: $23,700

AUDEMARS PIGUET

Le Brassus

NEW LEAVES ON A STORIED TREE

Audemars Piguet boasts one of the richest histories in all of haute horology, but **IT IS A CONSTANT APPETITE TO REINVENT AND MODERNIZE ITS CELEBRATED TRADITIONS THAT HAS CONTINUALLY AFFIRMED ITS POSITION AT THE APEX OF THE ART FORM**. By dressing two iconic collections in unique materials and finishes, the manufacture further energizes its already fascinating legacy.

The new Royal Oak Frosted Gold is more than an homage to the manufacture's 1976 creation of the first Royal Oak for women: it is the celebration of an undying spirit of horological elegance that refuses to be restrained. When Jacqueline Dimier transposed the collection to the feminine wrist in the 1970s, she did so without compromising the timepiece's decisive character. Instead of following the conventions of ladies' horology, she embraced the Royal Oak's distinctive personality and adorned the wearer with a powerful creation that imbued the watch's strength of character with graceful femininity.

◂ ▸ **ROYAL OAK FROSTED GOLD**

This ladies' timepiece's enthralling texture is achieved by way of a gold-hammering process known as the Florentine technique.

The Royal Oak Frosted Gold proudly furthers Jacqueline Dimier's vision of ladies' haute horology and adorns its owner with a statement of strength and feminine sensibility.

By collaborating with Florentine designer Carolina Bucci, Audemars Piguet breathes a new energy into the timekeeping icon while preserving its cherished design codes. The manufacture enriches the spirit of the Royal Oak with a fascinating new texture, achieved through an ancient gold hammering method known as the Florentine technique. Consisting of beating the gold with a diamond-tipped tool, the Florentine technique forms minuscule indentations on the surface that result in a sparkling effect reminiscent of diamond dust. Carolina Bucci's expertise in the craft allows for a final product that glitters with every ray of light without affecting the flexibility and softness of the structure.

Housed in a 37 or 33mm case in hammered pink or white gold, the Royal Oak Frosted Gold brings to the warm or cool tones of its precious metal an irresistible charisma. The dial joins the festival of texture, yet with a geometric perfection that completely—yet harmoniously—opposes the unpredictable pattern of the case's finish. A "Grande Tapisserie" pattern, composed of countless perfect squares, acts as the backdrop for the timepiece's timekeeping indications. Two Royal Oak hands, coated with a luminescent material for optimal visibility, indicate the hours and minutes while a slender hand displays the running seconds of the 280-component 3120 caliber. Endowed with a 60-hour power reserve and an oscillation frequency of 21,600 vph, the self-winding movement completes its demonstration with an aperture, at 3 o'clock, that briefly interrupts the eye-catching motif with a revelation of the date. The resplendent product of a brilliant meeting of minds by Audemars Piguet and Carolina Bucci, the Royal Oak Frosted Gold proudly furthers the legacy of Jacqueline Dimier's vision of haute horology for women and adorns its owner with a statement of feminine strength and sensibility.

The leap-year display is deeply rooted in the legacy of the manufacture, a tradition that finds new expression on the Royal Oak Perpetual Calendar. The first watchmaker to create a perpetual calendar wristwatch with leap-year indication, in 1955, Audemars Piguet extends this rich heritage with a timepiece as fascinating in its mechanical sophistication as in its outer architecture. The self-winding timepiece dresses its comprehensive display in a chic 41mm hand-finished black ceramic case and bracelet that boast exceptional levels of resistance to temperature variations, scratches and general aging. The dial completes the riveting, dark allure of the watch with a combination of black elements and a slate-gray "Grande Tapisserie" motif. At 12 o'clock, joining a display of the month in a multi-purpose subdial, a prominent, hand-guided leap-year indication pays subtle tribute to the manufacture's rich legacy. Two counters, at 3 and 9 o'clock, complement the design with displays of the date and day respectively. A fourth subdial, positioned at 6 o'clock, breaks through the elegant darkness to showcase the phases of the moon amidst a stunning, starry night sky. Audemars Piguet also turns the flange of the dial into a numbered scale used to indicate the current week of the year by way of a centrally driven arrow-tipped hand—a rare and exciting twist on the perpetual calendar concept.

The black ceramic Royal Oak Perpetual Calendar, which automatically compensates for the range of varying lengths of the months, is powered by the extraordinary 5134 caliber. Composed of 374 parts, the self-winding movement is visible through the timepiece's glare-proof sapphire crystal caseback.

▶ **ROYAL OAK PERPETUAL CALENDAR**

Housed in a contemporary black ceramic case, this self-winding timepiece boasts a perpetual calendar complete with prominent leap-year indication and week-of-the-year indication.

AUDEMARS PIGUET
SAT SUN MON TUE WED THU FRI
NOV JAN MAR MAY JUL SEP
SWISS MADE

ROYAL OAK PERPETUAL CALENDAR — REF. 26574ST.OO.1220ST.02

Movement: self-winding Manufacture 5134 caliber.
Functions: hours, minutes; perpetual calendar: day at 9, date at 3, month and leap year at 12; astronomical moon at 6.
Case: stainless steel; Ø 41mm; screw-locked crown; glareproofed sapphire crystal and caseback.
Dial: blue with "Grande Tapisserie" pattern; blue inner bezel; white-gold applied hour markers; Royal Oak hands with luminescent coating.
Bracelet: stainless steel; AP folding clasp.

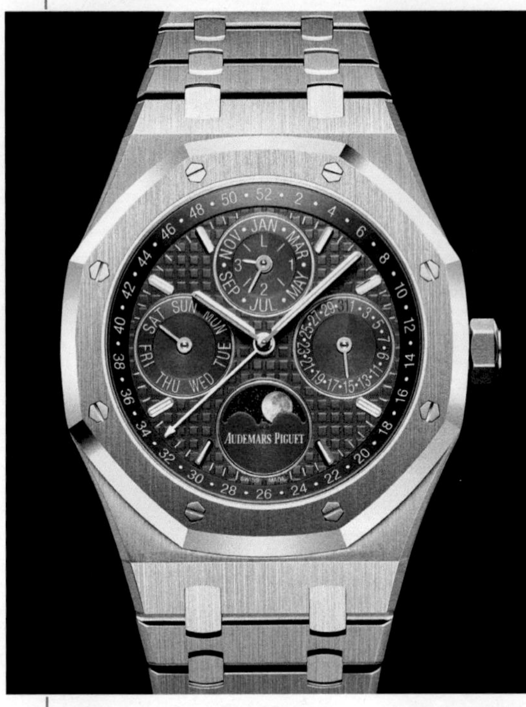

ROYAL OAK DOUBLE BALANCE WHEEL OPENWORKED — REF. 15407ST.OO.1220ST.01

Movement: self-winding 3132 caliber.
Functions: hours, minutes, seconds.
Case: stainless steel; Ø 41mm; screw-locked crown; glareproofed sapphire crystal and caseback.
Dial: openworked slate gray; pink-gold applied hour markers; Royal Oak hands with luminescent coating.
Bracelet: stainless steel; AP folding clasp.

ROYAL OAK CHRONOGRAPH — REF. 26331IP.OO.1220IP.01

Movement: self-winding 2385 caliber.
Functions: hours, minutes; small seconds at 6; date between 4 and 5; chronograph: central seconds hand, 30-minute counter at 3, 12-hour counter at 9.
Case: titanium; polished 950 platinum bezel and links; screw-locked crown; glareproofed sapphire crystal.
Dial: slate gray with "Grande Tapisserie" pattern; blue counters; white-gold applied hour markers; Royal Oak hands with luminescent coating.
Bracelet: titanium; polished 950 platinum links; titanium AP folding clasp.

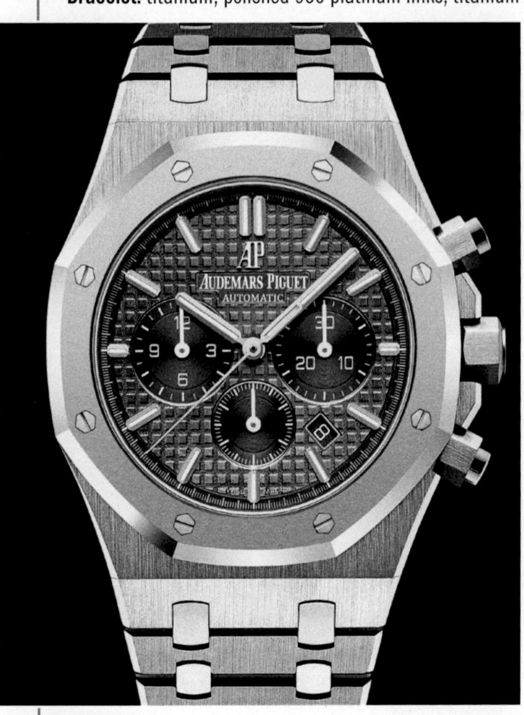

ROYAL OAK OFFSHORE CHRONOGRAPH — REF. 26470OR.OO.A002CR.01

Movement: self-winding 3126/3840 Manufacture caliber.
Functions: hours, minutes; small seconds at 12; date at 3; chronograph: central seconds hand, 30-minute counter at 9, 12-hour counter at 6.
Case: 18K pink gold; Ø 42mm; black ceramic screw-locked crown and pushpieces; glareproofed sapphire crystal and caseback.
Dial: pink-gold-toned with "Méga Tapisserie" pattern; black inner bezel; black counters; black Arabic numerals with luminescent coating; pink-gold Royal Oak hands with luminescent coating.

Strap: hand-stitched large square scale black alligator leather; 18K pink-gold pin buckle.

ROYAL OAK CHRONOGRAPH REF. 26331OR.OO.D315CR.01

Movement: self-winding 2385 caliber.
Functions: hours, minutes; small seconds at 6; date between 4 and 5; chronograph: central seconds hand, 30-minute counter at 3, 12-hour counter at 9.
Case: 18K pink gold; screw-locked crown; glareproofed sapphire crystal.
Dial: blue with "Grande Tapisserie" pattern; pink-gold-toned counters; pink-gold applied hour markers; Royal Oak hands with luminescent coating.
Strap: hand-stitched large square scale blue alligator leather; 18K pink-gold AP folding clasp.

ROYAL OAK OFFSHORE CHRONOGRAPH REF. 26405CE.OO.A002CA.02

Movement: self-winding 3126/3840 Manufacture caliber.
Functions: hours, minutes; small seconds at 12; date at 3; chronograph: central seconds hand, 30-minute counter at 9, 12-hour counter at 6.
Case: black ceramic; black ceramic bezel; black ceramic screw-locked crown; glareproofed sapphire crystal; glareproofed titanium sapphire crystal caseback.
Dial: black with "Méga Tapisserie" pattern; black inner bezel; black counters; pink-gold applied hour markers; Royal Oak hands with luminescent coating.
Strap: black rubber; titanium pin buckle.

ROYAL OAK OFFSHORE CHRONOGRAPH REF. 26470ST.OO.A820CR.01

Movement: self-winding 3126/3840 Manufacture caliber.
Functions: hours, minutes; small seconds at 12; date at 3; chronograph: central seconds hand, 30-minute counter at 9, 12-hour counter at 6.
Case: stainless steel; black ceramic screw-locked crown and pushpieces; glareproofed sapphire crystal and caseback.
Dial: brown with "Méga Tapisserie" pattern; brown inner bezel; brown counters; Arabic numerals with beige luminescent coating; pink-gold Royal Oak hands with beige luminescent coating.
Strap: hand-stitched large square scale brown alligator leather; stainless steel pin buckle.

ROYAL OAK CHRONOGRAPH REF. 26331ST.OO.1220ST.03

Movement: self-winding 2385 caliber.
Functions: hours, minutes; small seconds at 6; date between 4 and 5; chronograph: central seconds hand, 30-minute counter at 3, 12-hour counter at 9.
Case: stainless steel; screw-locked crown; glareproofed sapphire crystal.
Dial: silver-toned with "Grande Tapisserie" pattern; black counters; white-gold applied hour markers and Royal Oak hands with luminescent coating.
Bracelet: stainless steel; AP folding clasp.

ROYAL OAK EXTRA-THIN — REF. 15202ST.OO.1240ST.01

Movement: self-winding 2121 Manufacture caliber.
Functions: hours, minutes; date at 3.
Case: stainless steel; Ø 39mm; glareproofed sapphire crystal and caseback.
Dial: blue with "Petite Tapisserie" pattern; white-gold applied hour markers; Royal Oak hands with luminescent coating.
Bracelet: stainless steel; AP folding clasp.

ROYAL OAK SELFWINDING — REF. 15400ST.OO.1220ST.01

Movement: self-winding 3120 Manufacture caliber.
Functions: hours, minutes, seconds; date at 3.
Case: stainless steel; Ø 41mm; screw-locked crown; glareproofed sapphire crystal and caseback.
Dial: black with "Grande Tapisserie" pattern; white-gold applied hour markers; Royal Oak hands with luminescent coating.
Bracelet: stainless steel; AP folding clasp.

MILLENARY HAND-WOUND — REF. 77248BC.ZZ.A111CR.01

Movement: hand-wound 5201 Manufacture caliber.
Functions: hours, minutes; small seconds at 6.
Case: 18K white gold; Ø 39.5mm; entirely set with diamonds; crown set with a blue cabochon sapphire; glareproofed sapphire crystal and caseback.
Dial: diamond-paved white-gold off-centered disc; anthracite printed Roman numerals; white mother-of-pearl small seconds counter with diamond-set ring; blued gold hands; set with 136 brilliant-cut diamonds (approx. 0.26 carat).
Strap: large square scale pearly dark gray alligator leather; 18K white-gold pin buckle set with diamonds.
Note: case and buckle set with 438 brilliant-cut diamonds (approx. 1.93 carats).

ROYAL OAK FROSTED GOLD — REF. 15454OR.GG.1259OR.01

Movement: self-winding 3120 Manufacture caliber.
Functions: hours, minutes, seconds; date at 3.
Case: hammered 18K pink gold; Ø 37mm; glareproofed sapphire crystal and caseback.
Dial: silver-toned with "Grande Tapisserie" pattern; pink-gold applied hour markers; Royal Oak hands with luminescent coating.
Bracelet: hammered 18K pink gold; AP folding clasp.

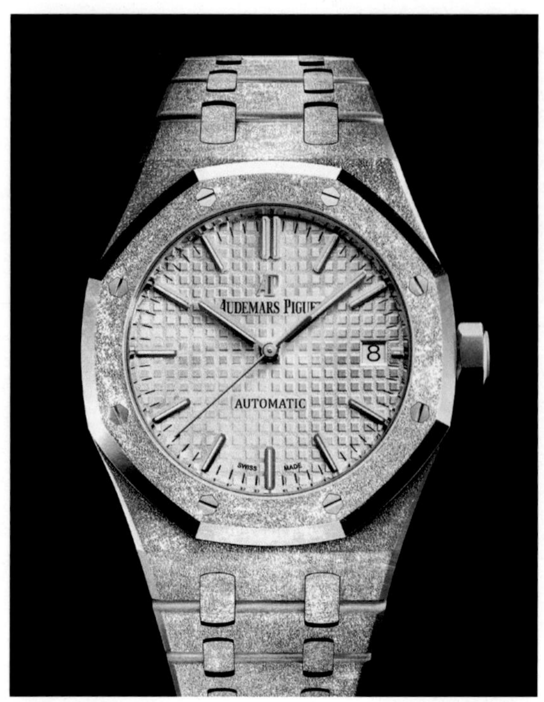

ROYAL OAK SELFWINDING REF. 15451OR.ZZ.1256OR.01

Movement: self-winding 3120 Manufacture caliber.
Functions: hours, minutes, seconds; date at 3.
Case: 18K pink gold; bezel set with 40 brilliant-cut diamonds (approx. 0.88 carat); screw-locked crown; glareproofed sapphire crystal and caseback.
Dial: silver-toned with "Grande Tapisserie" pattern; pink-gold applied hour markers; Royal Oak hands with luminescent coating.
Bracelet: 18K pink gold; AP folding clasp.

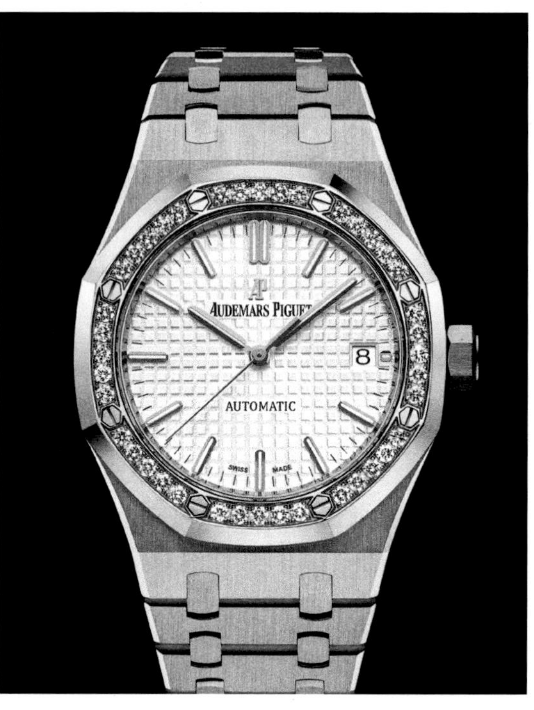

ROYAL OAK QUARTZ REF. 67651IP.ZZ.1261IP.01

Movement: 2713 caliber.
Functions: hours, minutes; date at 3.
Case: titanium; polished 950 platinum bezel set with diamonds; glareproofed sapphire crystal.
Dial: smoked blue with "Grande Tapisserie" pattern; white-gold applied hour markers; Royal Oak hands with luminescent coating.
Bracelet: titanium; polished 950 platinum links; titanium AP folding clasp.

ROYAL OAK OFFSHORE CHRONOGRAPH REF. 26231ST.ZZ.D002CA.01

Movement: self-winding 2385 caliber.
Functions: hours, minutes; small seconds at 6; date between 4 and 5; chronograph: central seconds hand, 30-minute counter at 3, 12-hour counter at 9.
Case: stainless steel; bezel set with diamonds; screw-locked crown; glareproofed sapphire crystal.
Dial: black with new "Lady Tapisserie" pattern; white-gold applied hour markers; Royal Oak hands with luminescent coating.
Strap: black rubber; stainless steel AP folding clasp.

ROYAL OAK QUARTZ REF. 67650ST.OO.1261ST.01

Movement: 2713 caliber.
Functions: hours, minutes; date at 3.
Case: stainless steel; Ø 33mm; glareproofed sapphire crystal.
Dial: black with "Grande Tapisserie" pattern; white-gold applied hour markers; Royal Oak hands with luminescent coating.
Bracelet: stainless steel; AP folding clasp.

BLANCPAIN

ELEGANCE & EXCELLENCE

With the Fifty Fathoms Bathyscaphe and the Villeret Quantième Annuel GMT, Blancpain **ENERGIZES AN ICONIC COLLECTION WITH INNOVATIVE MATERIALS AND STRIKES JUST THE RIGHT BALANCE OF CLASSICISM AND MODERNITY**.

By dressing the Fifty Fathoms Bathyscaphe in rich oceanic tones and high-tech materials, the renowned watchmaker brings a jolt of symbolic aesthetic energy to a timepiece with a decisive raison d'être: diving to the depths of the sea. Blancpain demonstrates impressive technical dexterity with its incorporation of a case in plasma-gray ceramic. Rugged, scratch resistant and lightweight, the state-of-the-art material endows the timepiece with a subtle metallic tone thanks to the manufacture's innovative production method. On the deep-blue dial, three hands and 12 hour markers, each luminously enhanced, provide exceptional legibility in the darkness and murky conditions of the water's depths—a requirement for an authentic diving instrument such as the Fifty Fathoms Bathyscaphe. The bezel follows suit, combining a striking design with crucial functionality. Unidirectional in rotation as to protect divers from dangerous timing changes, the plasma-gray ceramic bezel boasts a blue ceramic insert enhanced with Liquidmetal® hour markers for an unparalleled degree of clarity and reduced distortion. At the heart of the watch, the 1315 caliber provides a constant supply of energy over a five-day power reserve thanks to its remarkable integration of three series-coupled barrels. Fitted with a lightweight silicon balance spring impervious to magnetic interference, the self-winding movement also indicates the date through an aperture between 4 and 5 o'clock. Back on solid land from a journey of up to 300m below the surface, the owner may admire the 1315 caliber through the timepiece's sapphire crystal caseback.

The Villeret Quantième Annuel GMT makes brilliant use of the dial's open space, providing its wearer with a second time zone whose 24-hour layout leaves no doubt as to the day or night status of the chosen location.

The Villeret Quantième Annuel GMT uses the ingenious layout of its dial to imbue its classical design with visual intuitiveness and contemporary sophistication. Aligned at 2, 3 and 4 o'clock for a smooth, orderly read, the 6054F caliber's day, date and month apertures automatically account for months with 30 or 31 days. The self-winding timepiece thus backs up its seamless legibility with a delightful ease of use. At 8 o'clock on the elegant white dial, the Villeret Quantième Annuel GMT makes brilliant use of the face's open space, providing its wearer with a second time zone whose 24-hour layout leaves no doubt as to the day or night status of the chosen location. Turning the watch over reveals Blancpain's devotion to detail and craftsmanship at every level of the timepiece, as a sapphire crystal caseback allows an unobstructed view of the movement's construction, as well as its stunning yellow-gold oscillating weight. The Villeret Quantième Annuel GMT is housed in a classically elegant stainless steel case and worn on an alligator leather strap lined with Alzavel calfskin.

▸ **VILLERET QUANTIÈME ANNUEL GMT**

Automatically adjusting for months of 30 or 31 days, this stainless steel annual calendar enhances its elegant design with a 24-hour display of a secondary time zone.

◂ **FIFTY FATHOMS BATHYSCAPHE**

This genuine diver's timepiece houses its inspired oceanic design in a high-tech case composed of plasma-gray ceramic.

VILLERET 8-DAY COMPLETE CALENDAR — REF. 6639A-3631-55B

Movement: automatic-winding 6639 caliber; Ø 32mm, thickness: 7.6mm; 192-hour power reserve; 303 components; 35 jewels.
Functions: hours, minutes; small seconds on moonphase at 6; calendar: date via central hand, day and month at 12.
Case: 18K red gold; Ø 42mm, thickness: 13.03mm; sapphire crystal caseback; water resistant to 3atm.
Dial: cambered Grand Feu white enamel.
Strap: brown alligator leather.
Suggested price: $41,900
Also available: 18K red-gold bracelet (ref. 6639A-3631-MMB).

VILLERET ULTRA-SLIM — REF. 6651-1504-55

Movement: automatic-winding 1151 caliber; Ø 27.40mm, thickness: 3.37mm; 100-hour power reserve; 210 components; 28 jewels.
Functions: hours, minutes, seconds; date at 3.
Case: 18K white gold; Ø 40mm, thickness: 8.74mm; sapphire crystal caseback; water resistant to 3atm.
Dial: sunburst gray.
Strap: dark brown alligator leather.
Suggested price: $19,400

VILLERET ULTRA-SLIM — REF. 6653Q-1504-55

Movement: automatic-winding 7663Q caliber; Ø 27mm, thickness: 4.57mm; 65-hour power reserve; 244 components; 34 jewels.
Functions: hours, minutes; retrograde small seconds at 6; date via central hand.
Case: 18K white gold; Ø 40mm, thickness: 10.88mm; sapphire crystal caseback; water resistant to 3atm.
Dial: sunburst gray.
Strap: dark brown alligator leather.
Suggested price: $22,500

VILLERET ULTRA-SLIM — REF. 6670-1127-55B

Movement: automatic-winding 6054F caliber; Ø 32mm, thickness: 5.57mm; 72-hour power reserve; 367 components; 34 jewels.
Functions: hours, minutes, seconds; annual calendar: date at 3, day at 2, month at 4; second time zone at 8.
Case: stainless steel; Ø 40mm, thickness: 11.04mm; sapphire crystal caseback; water resistant to 3atm.
Dial: white.
Strap: black alligator leather.
Suggested price: $27,300
Also available: stainless steel bracelet (ref. 6670-1127-MMB).

VILLERET COMPLETE CALENDAR — REF. 6654A-1127-MMB

Movement: automatic-winding 6654 caliber; Ø 32mm, thickness: 5.5mm; 72-hour power reserve; 321 components; 28 jewels.
Functions: hours, minutes, seconds; moonphase at 6; calendar: date via central hand, day and month at 12.
Case: stainless steel; Ø 40mm, thickness: 10.94mm; sapphire crystal caseback; water resistant to 3atm.
Dial: white; silver-toned date ring.
Bracelet: stainless steel.
Suggested Price: $17,300
Also available: black alligator leather strap (ref. 6654A-1127-55B).

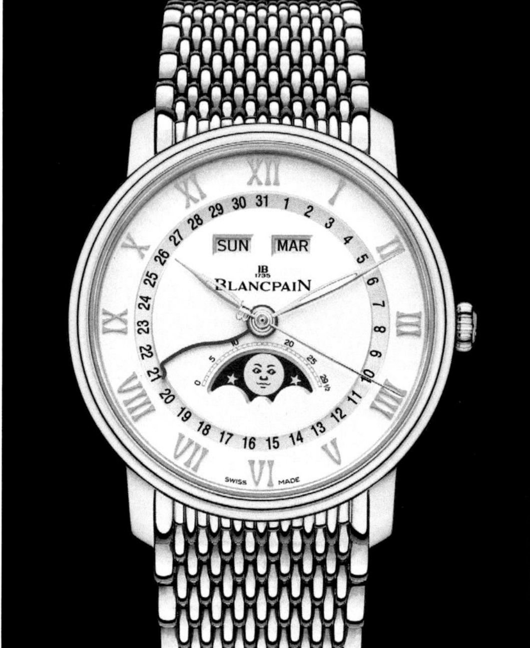

VILLERET LARGE DATE — REF. 6669-3642-55B

Movement: automatic-winding 6950 caliber; Ø 32mm, thickness: 4.75mm; 72-hour power reserve; 285 components; 35 jewels.
Functions: hours, minutes, seconds; large date at 6.
Case: 18K red gold; Ø 40mm, thickness: 10.88mm; sapphire crystal caseback; water resistant to 3atm.
Dial: opaline.
Strap: brown alligator leather.
Suggested price: $21,300
Also available: 18K red-gold bracelet (ref. 6669-3642-MMB).

VILLERET LARGE DATE — REF. 6669-1127-MMB

Movement: automatic-winding 6950 caliber; Ø 32mm, thickness: 4.75mm; 72-hour power reserve; 285 components; 35 jewels.
Functions: hours, minutes, seconds; large date at 6.
Case: stainless steel; Ø 40mm, thickness: 10.88mm; sapphire crystal caseback; water resistant to 3atm.
Dial: white.
Bracelet: stainless steel.
Suggested price: $14,050
Also available: black alligator leather strap (ref. 6669-1127-55B).

VILLERET 8-DAY PERPETUAL CALENDAR — REF. 6659-3631-55B

Movement: automatic-winding 5939A caliber; Ø 32mm, thickness: 7.25mm; 192-hour power reserve; 379 components; 42 jewels.
Functions: hours, minutes; small seconds on moonphase at 6; perpetual calendar: date at 3, day at 9, month and leap year at 12.
Case: 18K red gold; Ø 42mm, thickness: 13.50mm; sapphire crystal caseback; water resistant to 3atm.
Dial: cambered Grand Feu white enamel.
Strap: brown alligator leather.
Suggested price: $58,900
Also available: 18K red-gold bracelet (ref. 6659-3631-MMB); platinum case, black alligator leather strap (ref. 6659-3431-55B).

LE BRASSUS TOURBILLON CARROUSEL — REF. 2322-3631-55B

Movement: manual-winding 2322 caliber; Ø 35.30mm; thickness: 5.85mm; 168-hour power reserve; 379 components; 70 jewels.
Functions: hours, minutes; date at 3; tourbillon at 12; carrousel at 6; power reserve indicator on the bridge side.
Case: 18K red gold; Ø 44.60mm, thickness: 11.94mm; sapphire crystal caseback; water resistant to 3atm.
Dial: Grand Feu white enamel.
Strap: brown alligator leather.
Suggested price: $319,000

FIFTY FATHOMS AUTOMATIC — REF. 5015-1130-52

Movement: automatic-winding 1315 caliber; Ø 30.6mm, thickness: 5.65mm; 120-hour power reserve; 222 components; 35 jewels.
Functions: hours, minutes, seconds; date between 4 and 5.
Case: stainless steel; Ø 45mm, thickness: 15.50mm; sapphire crystal caseback; water resistant to 30atm.
Dial: black.
Strap: black sail-canvas.
Suggested price: $14,500

Also available: stainless steel bracelet (ref. 5015-1130-71); 18K red-gold case (ref. 5015-3630-52).

FIFTY FATHOMS BATHYSCAPHE CHRONOGRAPHE FLYBACK — REF. 5200-0130-NABA

Movement: automatic-winding F385 caliber; Ø 31.80mm, thickness: 6.65mm; 50-hour power reserve; 322 components; 37 jewels.
Functions: hours, minutes; small seconds at 6; date between 4 and 5; chronograph: central seconds hand, 30-minute counter at 3, 12-hour counter at 9.
Case: satin-brushed black ceramic; Ø 43.60mm, thickness: 15.25mm; sapphire crystal caseback; water resistant to 30atm.
Dial: black.
Strap: black NATO.
Suggested price: $17,200
Also available: black sail-canvas strap (ref. 5200-0130-B52A); satin-brushed stainless steel case (ref. 5200-1110-NABA); satin-brushed stainless steel case, black sail-canvas strap (ref. 5200-1110-B52A); satin-brushed stainless steel case, stainless steel bracelet (ref. 5200-1110-70B).

FIFTY FATHOMS BATHYSCAPHE — REF. 5000-0240-052A

Movement: automatic-winding 1315 caliber; Ø 30.6mm, thickness: 5.65mm; 120-hour power reserve; 227 components; 35 jewels.
Functions: hours, minutes, seconds; date between 4 and 5.
Case: satin-brushed gray ceramic; Ø 43.60mm, thickness: 13.83mm; sapphire crystal caseback; water resistant to 30atm.
Dial: blue.
Strap: blue sail-canvas.
Suggested price: $12,800

Also available: satin-brushed blue ceramic case, blue NATO strap (ref. 5000-0240-NAOA).

WOMEN ULTRA-SLIM LADYBIRD — REF. 0063E-1954-55A

Movement: automatic-winding 6150 caliber; Ø 15.70mm, thickness: 3.90mm; 40-hour power reserve; 180 components; 29 jewels; platinum oscillating weight set with 1 diamond (approx. 0.006 carat).
Functions: hours, minutes.
Case: 18K white gold; Ø 21.50mm, thickness: 8.23mm; set with diamonds (approx. 0.534 carat); sapphire crystal caseback; water resistant to 3atm.
Dial: mother-of-pearl; set with diamonds (approx. 0.011 carat).
Strap: purple alligator leather.
Note: 60th Anniversary piece; limited edition of 60 pieces.
Suggested price: $19,300

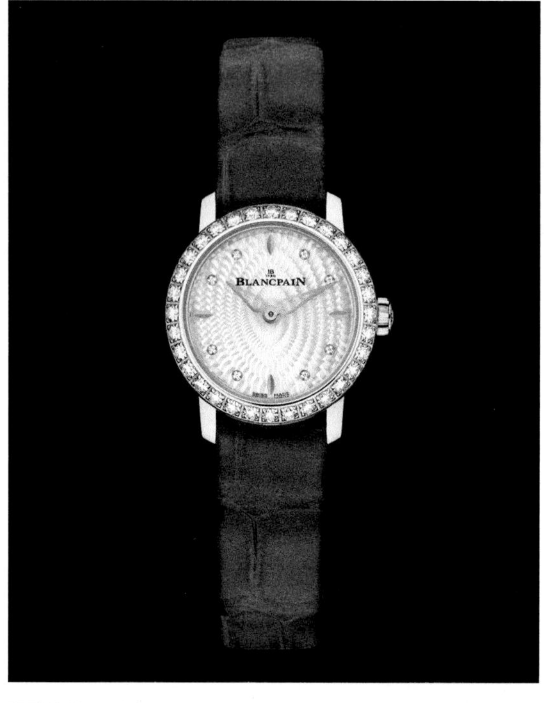

WOMEN ULTRA-SLIM LADYBIRD — REF. 0063C-2987-63A

Movement: automatic-winding 6150 caliber; Ø 15.70mm, thickness: 3.90mm; 40-hour power reserve; 180 components; 29 jewels.
Functions: hours, minutes.
Case: 18K red gold; Ø 21.50mm, thickness: 8.23mm; set with diamonds (approx. 0.534 carat); water resistant to 3atm.
Dial: sunburst opaline; set with diamonds (approx. 0.040 carat).
Strap: white ostrich leather.
Note: charms are removable.
Suggested price: $19,800

WOMEN COMPLETE CALENDAR — REF. 3663A-4654-55B

Movement: automatic-winding 6763 caliber; Ø 27mm, thickness: 4.9mm; 100-hour power reserve; 261 components; 30 jewels.
Functions: hours, minutes; small seconds on moonphase at 6; calendar: date via central hand, day and month at 12.
Case: stainless steel; Ø 35mm, thickness: 10.57mm; set with diamonds (approx. 1.74 carats); water resistant to 3atm.
Dial: mother-of-pearl; set with diamonds (approx. 0.019 carat).
Strap: white alligator leather.
Suggested price: $18,700
Also available: 18K red-gold case, white alligator leather strap (ref. 3663-2954-55B); blue mother-of-pearl dial (ref. 3663-4654L-52B).

WOMEN RETROGRADE CALENDAR — REF. 3653-2954-58B

Movement: automatic-winding 2650RL caliber; Ø 26.20mm, thickness: 5.37mm; 65-hour power reserve; 302 components; 32 jewels.
Functions: off-centered hours and minutes; retrograde date and moonphase at 12.
Case: 18K red gold; Ø 36mm, thickness: 10.75mm; set with diamonds (approx. 1.831 carats); sapphire crystal caseback; water resistant to 3atm.
Dial: mother-of-pearl; set with diamonds (approx. 0.010 carat).
Strap: white ostrich leather.
Suggested price: $41,300
Also available: 18K white-gold case (ref. 3653-1954L-58B).

BOUCHERON
PARIS

LIGHTHEARTED LUXURY

Boucheron **PLAYS WITH LIGHT, TEXTURES AND PRECIOUS MATERIALS TO ACHIEVE ITS OWN STYLE OF DISTINCTIVE ELEGANCE**. Playful, imaginative and luxurious, six new timepieces adorn the wrist with the undeniable DNA of the Parisian horologer, which opened its doors in 1858.

As its name implies, the Joy de Lumière adorns the wrist with scintillating light and jubilant luxury. Its dial, in radiant white mother-of-pearl, plays off a 17.6mm white-gold case set with 48 round diamonds as it hosts an understated display of hours and minutes via two silvered stems. The timepiece's refined personality extends to its bracelet, where 71 diamonds combine to form a slender thread of sparkling light. Preserving the watch's graceful geometry, the Joy de Lumière does not possess a crown for the setting of time, instead boasting a key activated by the push of a discreet button on the side of the case. An inscription on the caseback, stating "Je ne Sonne que les Heures Heureuses," confirms the effervescent spirit of the watch.

The Joy de Lumière Ricochet enlivens the regal, graduated design of its bracelet with riveting patterns composed of rock crystal and a total of 290 shimmering round diamonds. The imaginative composition creates a floating effect, showcasing each precious central stone to perfection. The dial complements the rock crystal design with a decadent full-pavé snow setting boasting an additional 114 round diamonds for a textured, vibrant appearance. The watch's 18-karat white-gold case follows the theme of the bracelet's rings with a diamond-set bezel and three jewels arranged in a pattern on either side of the structure. Foregoing the traditional crown system, the Joy de Lumière Ricochet is set using a waveform key crafted in white gold and adorned with 19 round diamonds.

▸ **JOY DE LUMIÈRE** *(left)*

This slender feminine wristwatch combines mother-of-pearl, white gold and diamonds for an elegant and luxurious design.

▸ **JOY DE LUMIÈRE RICOCHET** *(right)*

The bracelet of this diamond-paved watch reveals precious stones seemingly floating on a rock crystal bed for a dazzling effect.

BOUCHERON
BOUCHERON

Boucheron breathes life into the Ajourée Hopi's two floating hummingbirds with a breathtaking display of transparency and creative jewelry craftsmanship. Paved on both sides with a colorful combination of diamonds, sapphires and blackened gold, the two sculpted birds float above an off-centered dial. The latter, framed by a sparkling row of diamonds, echoes the vivid pink tone of the watch's satin strap with a mother-of-pearl face that plays off the exuberant shimmer of the design's precious stones. Along with creating a superb flow of light and transparency, the watch's skeletonized construction highlights the three-dimensional nature of the two protagonists in flight, further realized by their wings' positioning on either sides of the gem-set outer ring. The 38mm 18-karat pink-gold timepiece indicates the hours and minutes, boasts a total of 532 stones and is set with a key instead of a crown, maintaining the design's cohesive visual brilliance.

◂ **AJOURÉE HOPI**

Boucheron's imagination rises to new heights with this skeleton timepiece that features two floating three-dimensional hummingbirds composed of numerous colorful precious stones.

The skeletonized construction of the Ajourée creates a superb flow of light and transparency, as well as highlighting the three-dimensional nature of the two protagonists in flight.

Inspired by the iconic blue tones of India's famed city of Jodhpur, Boucheron presents a wristwatch that fuses aesthetic modernity with a color of unforgettable intensity. The Epure "Bleu de Jodhpur" is housed in a 42mm steel case enhanced with double gadroons on the side and beveled horns at 6 and 12 o'clock. Clean and contemporary in its geometry, the self-winding timepiece complements the deep hue of its dial with a blue sapphire cabochon at 12 o'clock, giving the face a welcome sense of three-dimensionality. At 6 o'clock, the SW300 caliber's date function is read through a subtle white aperture, while the hours, minutes and seconds are indicated from the central axis. A double gadroon on the watch face cleverly separates the sleek exterior aesthetic of a satin finish from an elegant Clous de Paris motif in the interior portion. Through the open caseback, the owner may view the inner workings of the timepiece's 28,800 vph caliber as well as its oscillating weight engraved with "1858 – Paris." The Epure "Bleu de Jodhpur" is worn on a blue alligator strap with large scales and stitches.

▸ EPURE "BLEU DE JODHPUR"

This elegant and contemporary self-winding timepiece pays tribute to India's Jodhpur with a blue tone of powerful depth and intensity.

The vibrant tribute to the Indian city and the famous blue that adorns many of its buildings' façades continues with a timepiece of elegant minimalism and contemporary design. The Reflet Small "Bleu de Jodhpur," limited to 88 pieces in honor of the night sky's ever-shifting 88 constellations, houses its six-jewel quartz movement in a steel case with vertical gadroons that provide a multi-dimensional luster and sense of modernity. A blue model presents its hours and minutes on a blue aventurine-glass dial that evokes the fascinating infinity of space. At 12 o'clock on the face, a single, sparkling diamond illuminates the scene like a full moon gracefully guarding its endless sky. At 3 o'clock, a blue sapphire cabochon echoes the spirit of the dial and leads the eye seamlessly into the hue of a blue alligator strap, whose white inner lining plays off the counter tones of the face.

A white version pays its respects to India's Taj Mahal with a dial composed of a fine layer of marble. Extremely unconventional in haute horology, the luxurious mineral gives the face an inimitable depth and organic texture. Two rows of diamonds, set onto the left and right sides of the case, frame the exhibition and accentuate the timepiece's lean aesthetic. This model is worn on a white alligator strap with blue inner lining and finished with a blue sapphire cabochon at 3 o'clock.

◂ REFLET SMALL "BLEU DE JODHPUR"

Blue aventurine glass, or a fine layer of marble, adorns the dynamic design of these wristwatches and gives them a fascinating sense of textural depth.

AJOUREE HIRUNDA JEWELRY WATCH — REF. WA017312

Movement: quartz ETA 01 caliber.
Functions: hours, minutes.
Case: white gold; Ø 38m; set with diamonds.
Dial: gray mother-of-pearl.
Strap: gray brushed satin.

AJOUREE HOPI JEWELRY WATCH — REF. WA017314

Movement: quartz ETA 01 caliber.
Functions: hours, minutes.
Case: pink and white gold; Ø 38mm; set with multicolored sapphires.
Dial: pink mother-of-pearl.
Strap: brushed pink satin.

EPURE LIERRE DE PARIS — REF. WA021402

Movement: automatic-winding GP 4000 caliber.
Functions: hours, minutes.
Case: white gold; Ø 41mm; set with diamonds.
Dial: gray; métier d'art.
Strap: gray alligator leather.

EPURE OLEA — REF. WA021430

Movement: automatic-winding GP 4000 caliber.
Functions: hours, minutes.
Case: white gold; Ø 41mm; set with diamonds.
Dial: white mother-of-pearl; métier d'art.
Strap: white alligator leather.

EPURE BLEU DE JODHPUR — REF. WA021209

Movement: automatic-winding SW300 caliber.
Functions: hours, minutes, seconds; date at 6.
Case: steel; Ø 42mm; blue sapphire cabochon crown; double gadroons on the side case.
Dial: blue; polished and silvered double gadroons.
Strap: blue alligator leather.

EPURE 42MM — REF. WA021106

Movement: automatic-winding GP4000 caliber.
Functions: hours, minutes, seconds; date at 6.
Case: pink gold; Ø 42mm; cabochon signature; double gadroons.
Dial: white.
Strap: brown alligator leather.

EPURE 38MM — REF. WA021202

Movement: automatic-winding GP4000 caliber.
Functions: hours, minutes, seconds; date at 6.
Case: steel; Ø 38mm; cabochon signature; double gadroons on the side case.
Dial: black.
Strap: black alligator leather.

EPURE CHRONOGRAPH 43MM — REF. WA021301

Movement: automatic-winding SW500 caliber.
Functions: hours, minutes, seconds; chronograph: 30-minute counter at 12, 12-hour counter at 6.
Case: steel; Ø 43mm; cabochon signature; double gadroons.
Dial: semi-matte silver.
Strap: black alligator leather.

REFLET SMALL — REF. WA030501

Movement: quartz.
Functions: hours, minutes.
Case: steel; cabochon signature; vertical gadroons.
Dial: white; Roman numerals.
Strap: black patent calf leather; interchangeable strap system.

REFLET LARGE — REF. WA030302

Movement: quartz.
Functions: hours, minutes.
Case: steel; one hematite cabochon; vertical gadroons.
Dial: anthracite.
Strap: gray alligator leather; interchangeable strap system.

REFLET MEDIUM — REF. WA030407

Movement: quartz.
Functions: hours, minutes.
Case: polished yellow gold; set with diamonds; vertical gadroons.
Dial: white lacquered.
Strap: black patent calf leather; interchangeable strap system.

REFLET SMALL — REF. WA030508 + WDA31027

Movement: quartz.
Functions: hours, minutes.
Case: polished yellow gold; set with diamonds; vertical gadroons.
Dial: yellow gold.
Bracelet: yellow gold; composed of 5 ranks of links with gadroon pattern; interchangeable strap system.

SERPENT BOHEME JEWELRY WATCH — REF. WA015504

Movement: quartz.
Functions: hours, minutes.
Case: white gold; Ø 18mm; set with diamonds.
Dial: white mother-of-pearl.
Strap: black brushed satin.

SERPENT BOHEME JEWELRY WATCH — REF. WA015501

Movement: quartz.
Functions: hours, minutes.
Case: yellow gold; Ø 18mm; set with diamonds.
Dial: white mother-of-pearl.
Bracelet: yellow gold.

JOY DE LUMIERE JEWELRY WATCH — REF. WA027203

Movement: quartz ETA E01.701/h3 caliber.
Functions: hours, minutes.
Case: white gold; Ø 17.6mm; set with diamonds.
Dial: white mother-of-pearl.
Bracelet: white gold; one row of bezel-set diamonds.

REFLET POMPON — REF. WA026010

Movement: quartz ETA 280.002 caliber; 5 jewels.
Functions: hours, minutes.
Case: white gold; 15x25mm, thickness: 6mm; set with 30 baguette-cut diamonds (approx. 1.1 carats) and 34 round diamonds (approx. 1.38 carats); domed sapphire crystal and caseback with Boucheron engraving.
Dial: fully paved with 180 snow-set diamonds (0.62 carat); white-gold hour and minute hands set with 1 diamond (approx. 0.15 carat).
Bracelet: white gold; paved with 3 rows of diamonds; white-gold full-paved jewelry clasp; white-gold pompon paved with diamonds and a row of 32 baguette diamonds (approx. 0.97 carat); set with 264 diamonds on bracelet, jewelry clasp and pompon (approx. 18.5 carats).

REVERENCE AND REVELATIONS

Celebrated for horological excellence since its founding in 1775, Breguet proves that **INNOVATION IS THE TRUEST OF ALL TRADITIONS, WITH THREE SOPHISTICATED AND INVENTIVE TIMEPIECES**.

Perfected after years of dedicated research in acoustics, the Tradition Répétition Minutes Tourbillon complements the remarkable sophistication of its caliber and design with an unprecedented purity of sound. To enhance sound transmission, Breguet completely reimagines its own 1783 invention, attaching the gong springs to the bezel and having them struck vertically from the movement toward the exterior. An acoustic chamber, built directly into the 44mm 18-karat rose-gold case, allows for impressive volume at no cost to sound quality. Yet Breguet wisely understands sound's fundamental companion: silence. The watch's integration of a magnetic strike governor ensures constancy of rotation speed while preventing any unwanted noises, as its construction ensures that none of the mechanical elements are in direct contact. An openworked dial-side design permits the owner to admire everything from the minute repeater's numerous innovations to the 565DR caliber's 60-second tourbillon and titanium baseplates and bridges. The visual exhibition extends to the back of the timepiece, where the platinum winding rotor's peripheral construction allows for a view of the movement's masterful finishes.

◂ **TRADITION RÉPÉTITION MINUTES TOURBILLON**

Six patents attest to the innovative nature of this exquisitely reinvented minute repeater.

The Classique Hora Mundi boasts an ingenious mechanical-memory module that allows the timepiece to adjust all indicators simultaneously.

The self-winding Classique Hora Mundi uses Breguet's ingenuity to take on the GMT concept from a dynamic, intuitive perspective. A first glance at the dial reveals only a single set of hands, in apparent opposition to the multiple-time-zone premise. However, Breguet perfectly captures, and even advances, the notion of the traveler's wristwatch. Just as the owner may only be in one location at once, so is his timepiece. Instead of using a subdial to indicate the second time zone, the Classique Hora Mundi boasts an ingenious mechanical-memory module that allows the timepiece to adjust all indicators simultaneously, upon a single switch from one time zone to another. The mechanism instantly transports hours, minutes, date and day/night display to their desired destination. The date, read through an aperture at 12 o'clock, features an added touch of imagination. A dragging disc sees the appropriate date framed by the circular tip of a hidden hand. As the disc glides across the aperture, so does the legible indicator. At midnight, however, the 77F0 caliber performs a spectacular trick, as the retrograde circular tip jumps instantaneously back to the left of the opening to accompany the next date on its 24-hour journey. On its silvered gold dial, the 18-karat white-gold timepiece melds modern design with three unique tributes to traditional craftsmanship: a principal "clou de Paris" motif and the 24-hour indicator's two guilloché patterns, flames for the upper half and a cross-weave décor on the lower section.

Sixty-eight brilliant-cut diamonds and an elegantly exposed movement provide an enticing appeal for Breguet's female followers. Housed in a diamond-set, 18-karat white-gold case, the Tradition Dame dazzles the keen horological eye with a fascinating multi-dimensional openworked architecture. The caliber's barrel, seen in the center of the dial, joins a stunning, layered display of the balance wheel and intermediate wheels, forming an arc from 4 to 8 o'clock. At 12 o'clock, the timepiece indicates the hours and minutes upon a breathtaking, meticulously engine-turned Tahitian-mother-of-pearl subdial. At 10 o'clock on the movement, the Tradition Dame indicates the seconds with a dynamic retrograde display that completes its passage across an arc from 11 to 9 o'clock before instantly reinitiating the journey from its original position. The 37mm wristwatch is driven by the 505SR caliber with inverted in-line lever escapement and is cleverly finished with the unusual placement of a movement jewel on the tip of the crown at 3 o'clock.

▲ **CLASSIQUE HORA MUNDI** *(top)*

A sophisticated mechanical-memory system allows every one of this dual-time wristwatch's indicators to travel instantly to a chosen location at the press of a button.

▲ **TRADITION DAME** *(bottom)*

This feminine timepiece reveals the full breadth of its mechanical sophistication within a multi-layered, openworked design.

TRADITION REPETITION MINUTES TOURBILLON — REF. 7087BR/G1/9XV

Movement: automatic-winding 565DR caliber; 16 lines; 80-hour power reserve; 58 jewels; Breguet balance wheel on Breguet silicon balance spring.
Functions: hours, minutes; minute repeater; tourbillon at 6.
Case: 18K rose gold; Ø 44mm; sapphire crystal caseback.
Dial: silvered 18K gold offset at 1:30; hours chapter with Roman numerals; blued steel Breguet open-tipped hands; individually numbered and signed Breguet.
Strap: brown leather.
Also available: 18K white-gold case, black leather strap (ref. 7087BB/G1/9XV).

TRADITION GMT — REF. 7067BB/G1/9W6

Movement: manual-winding 507 DRF caliber; 14 ½ lines; 50-hour power reserve; 215 components; 40 jewels; Breguet balance wheel on Breguet silicon balance spring.
Functions: hours, minutes; second time zone between 7 and 8; day/night indicator at 10.
Case: 18K white gold; Ø 40mm, thickness: 12.65mm; sapphire crystal caseback; water resistant to 3atm.
Dial: silvered 18K gold off-set at 12; hours chapter with Roman numerals; blued steel Breguet open-tipped hands.
Strap: black leather.

TRADITION DAME — REF. 7038BB/1T/9V6 DOOD

Movement: automatic-winding 505SR caliber; 14 ½ lines; 50-hour power reserve; 38 jewels; Breguet silicon balance spring; numbered and signed Breguet.
Functions: hours, minutes; retrograde seconds on movement face at 10.
Case: 18K white gold; Ø 37mm; bezel set with 68 brilliant-cut diamonds (approx. 0.895 carat); crown set with a watch movement jewel; water resistant to 3atm.
Dial: Tahitian mother-of-pearl offset at 12; hours chapter with Roman numerals; blued steel Breguet open-tipped hands.
Strap: red leather.

CLASSIQUE TOURBILLON QUANTIEME PERPETUEL — REF. 3795BR/1E/9WU

Movement: manual-winding 558QP3 caliber; 14 ½ lines; 50-hour power reserve; 21 jewels.
Functions: hours, minutes; small seconds on tourbillon at 6; day at 9; retrograde date at 12; month and leap year at 3.
Case: 18K rose gold; Ø 41mm; delicately fluted caseband; sapphire crystal caseback; water resistant to 3atm.
Dial: skeletonized in silvered 18K gold; individually numbered and signed Breguet; Roman numeral hour markers on a sapphire disc; open-tipped blued steel hands; welded lugs with screw bars.
Strap: brown leather; triple-blade folding clasp.
Also available: 950 platinum case (ref. 3795PT/1E/9WU).

CLASSIQUE TOURBILLON EXTRA-PLAT AUTOMATIQUE REF. 5377PT/12/9WU

Movement: automatic-winding 581DR caliber; 16 lines; 80-hour power reserve; 42 jewels.
Functions: hours, minutes; small seconds on tourbillon at 5; power reserve indicator at 9.
Case: platinum; Ø 42mm; delicately fluted caseband; sapphire crystal caseback; water resistant to 3atm.
Dial: silvered 18K gold; individually numbered and signed Breguet; Roman numeral hour markers; open-tipped blued steel hands; welded lugs with screw bars.
Strap: black leather; triple-blade folding clasp.
Also available: 18K rose-gold case (ref. 5377BR/12/9WU).

CLASSIQUE HORA MUNDI REF. 5727BB/12/9ZU

Movement: automatic-winding 77F0 caliber; 12 lines; 55-hour power reserve; 39 jewels; silicon balance spring.
Functions: hours, minutes, seconds; date at 12; 24-hour indicator between 3 and 4; city indicator at 6.
Case: 18K white gold; Ø 43mm; sapphire crystal caseback; water resistant to 3atm.
Dial: silvered 18K gold; hours chapter with Roman numerals; blued steel Breguet open-tipped hands; individually numbered and signed Breguet.
Strap: black leather.
Also available: 18K rose-gold case (ref. 5727BR/12/9ZU).

CLASSIQUE REF. 7147BR/12/9WU

Movement: automatic-winding 502.3SD caliber; 12 lines, thickness: 2.4mm; 45-hour power reserve; 35 jewels; Breguet silicon balance spring.
Functions: hours, minutes; small seconds between 5 and 6.
Case: 18K rose gold; Ø 40mm; sapphire crystal caseback; water resistant to 3atm.
Dial: silvered 18K gold; hours chapter with Roman numerals; blued steel Breguet open-tipped hands; individually numbered and signed Breguet.
Strap: brown leather.
Also available: 18K white-gold case (ref. 7147BB/12/9WU).

CLASSIQUE PHASE DE LUNE REF. 9088BB/29/964 DD0D

Movement: automatic-winding 537L caliber; 8 ¾ lines; 45-hour power reserve; 26 jewels; silicon balance spring.
Functions: hours, minutes; small seconds on moonphase at 6.
Case: 18K white gold; Ø 30mm; bezel and lugs set with 66 brilliant-cut diamonds (approx. 1.04 carats); sapphire crystal caseback; water resistant to 3atm.
Dial: Grand Feu enamel; hours chapter with Arabic numerals; blued steel Breguet open-tipped hands; individually numbered and signed Breguet.
Strap: blue leather.
Also available: 18K rose-gold case, guilloché dial, white leather strap; guilloché dial; mother-of-pearl dial (ref. 9088BB/52/964 DD0D); 18K rose-gold case, white leather strap (ref. 9088BR/29/964 DD0D).

HERITAGE GRANDE DATE — REF. 5410BR/12/9V6

Movement: automatic-winding 516GG caliber; 11 ½ lines; 65-hour power reserve; 30 jewels; silicon balance spring.
Functions: hours, minutes; small seconds at 6; date at 12.
Case: 18K rose gold; 45x32mm; water resistant to 3atm.
Dial: curved silvered 18K gold; hours chapter with luminescent Roman numerals; blued steel luminescent Breguet open-tipped hands; individually numbered and signed Breguet.
Strap: brown leather.

Also available: 18K white-gold case (ref. 5410BB/12/9V6).

HERITAGE PHASE DE LUNE RETROGRADE — REF. 8861BB/15/986 D000

Movement: automatic-winding 586L caliber; 13 ¾ lines; 36-hour power reserve; 38 jewels; Breguet balance wheel on silicon balance spring.
Functions: hours, minutes; moonphase between 12 and 1.
Case: 18K white gold; 35x25mm, thickness: 9.75mm; bezel set with 140 diamonds (approx. 1.14 carats); water resistant to 3atm.
Dial: cambered frosted silvered and natural mother-of-pearl; blued steel Breguet open-tipped hands.
Strap: red leather.

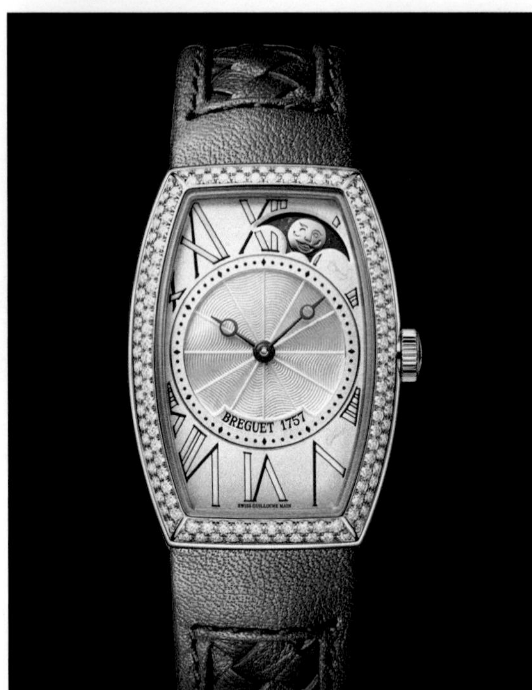

Also available: black leather strap (ref. 8861BB/11/386/D000); 18K rose-gold case, brown leather strap (ref. 8861BR/11/386/D000); 18K white-gold bracelet (ref. 8861BB/11/BB0/D000); 18K rose-gold case, 18K rose-gold bracelet (ref. 8861BR/11/RB0/D000).

MARINE GMT — REF. 5857BR/Z2/5ZU

Movement: automatic-winding 517F caliber; 13 ¾ lines; 72-hour power reserve; 28 jewels; Breguet balance wheel on silicon balance spring.
Functions: hours, minutes, seconds; date at 6; second time zone at 6; 24-hour indicator at 2.
Case: 18K rose gold; Ø 42mm, thickness: 12.25mm; sapphire crystal caseback; water resistant to 10atm.
Dial: silvered gold and black rhodium; gold Breguet open-tipped hands.
Strap: rubber.

TYPE XXI — REF. 3817ST/X2/3ZU

Movement: automatic-winding 584Q/2 caliber; 13 ½ lines; 48-hour power reserve; 26 jewels; silicon balance spring.
Functions: hours, minutes; small seconds at 9; date at 6; day/night indicator at 3; chronograph: central split seconds hands, 12-hour counter at 6.
Case: stainless steel; Ø 42mm; bidirectional rotating bezel; screw-down crown; sapphire crystal caseback; water resistant to 10atm.
Dial: slate gray; hours chapter with luminescent Arabic numerals; luminescent hands and dots; signed Breguet.
Strap: brown calfskin leather.

REINE DE NAPLES JOUR/NUIT REF. 8998BB/11/874/D00D

Movement: automatic-winding 78CS caliber; 9 ¾ x 13 ¼ lines; 57-hour power reserve; 45 jewels; Breguet balance wheel on silicon balance spring.
Functions: hours, minutes; day/night indicator.
Case: 18K white gold; 40.05x32mm, thickness: 10.6mm; bezel and flange set with 143 diamonds (approx. 1.45 carats); sapphire crystal caseback; water resistant to 3atm.
Dial: silvered gold.
Strap: black satin.
Also available: 18K rose-gold case (ref. 8998BR/11/874/D00D).

REINE DE NAPLES REF. 8918BB/58/864 D00D

Movement: automatic-winding 537/1 caliber; 8 ¾ lines; 184 components; 44-hour power reserve; 20 jewels; silicon balance spring.
Functions: hours, minutes.
Case: 18K white gold; 36.5x28.45mm, thickness: 10.05mm; bezel and flange set with 117 diamonds (approx. 0.99 carat); sapphire crystal caseback; water resistant to 3atm.
Dial: silvered gold; white natural mother-of-pearl; Breguet Arabic numerals; 1 pear-cut diamond (approx. 0.09 carat); blued steel Breguet open-tipped hands.
Strap: black satin.
Also available: 18K yellow-gold case; 18K rose-gold case; 18K rose-gold bracelet; 18K yellow-gold bracelet; 18K white-gold bracelet.

PERLES IMPERIALES REF. GJ29BB8924 5D58

Movement: automatic-winding 586/1 caliber; 6 ¾ lines; 38-hour power reserve; 29 jewels; Breguet balance on a silicon balance spring.
Functions: hours, minutes.
Case: 18K white gold ovoid; 34.4x28.7mm; crown set with a briolette diamond (approx. 0.28 carat); caseband set with 24 brilliant-cut diamonds (approx. 0.24 carat); surround set with 23 brilliant-cut diamonds (approx. 4.12 carats) and an Akoya pearl; flange set with 66 brilliant-cut diamonds (approx. 0.13 carat); chaton settings incorporating 15 brilliant-cut diamonds beneath the prongs (approx. 0.28 carat); sapphire crystal caseback.
Dial: mother-of-pearl; offset hours chapter with diamond markers at 3, 6, 9 and 12; blued steel Breguet open-tipped hands; Breguet medallion at 12.
Strap: satin; folding clasp set with 26 brilliant-cut diamonds (approx. 0.14 carat).
Also available: 18K rose-gold case (ref. GJ29BR8924TDT8).

BE CRAZY REF. GJ25BB8989DDDD

Movement: automatic-winding 586/1 caliber; 6 ¾ lines; 40-hour power reserve; 29 jewels; Breguet balance on a silicon spring.
Functions: hours, minutes.
Case: 18K white gold ovoid; 33x24.95mm; caseband set with more than 1,000 baguette-cut mobile diamonds; flange set in staggered rows with 56 baguette diamonds; sapphire crystal caseback.
Dial: 18K white gold; radial paving of 133 baguette-cut diamonds; blued steel Breguet open-tipped hands.
Bracelet: 18K white gold; paved with more than 200 baguette-cut diamonds.
Note: more than 80 carats of diamonds.

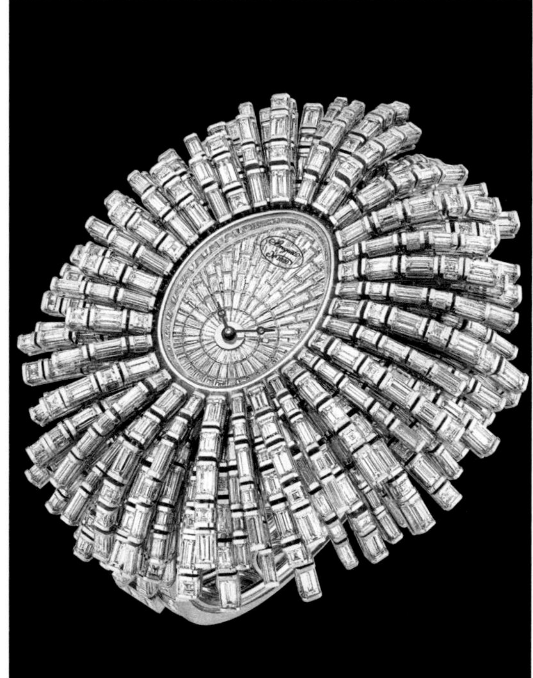

BVLGARI

LIFE WITHOUT LIMITS

Bulgari **DISPLAYS ITS INNOVATIVE SPIRIT WITH FOUR TIMEPIECES THAT PUSH THE BOUNDARIES OF THE HOROLOGICAL ART**. Whether drenched in diamonds, shaped to mimic the sinuous grace of a serpent or showcasing exceptional sophistication within ultra-thin dimensions, Bulgari's newest timepieces adorn the wrist with the apex of watchmaking possibility.

The Octo Finissimo Minute Repeater pushes the limits of slenderness and grand-complication watchmaking, placing the manufacture's expertise and pioneering ingenuity squarely in the spotlight. The slimmest minute repeater on the market, the 6.85mm-thick timepiece required an audacious approach to the revered complication; Bulgari reimagined the concept from the ground up to achieve optimal sound quality within record-breaking dimensions. While minute repeaters traditionally take advantage of a generous internal chamber to enhance acoustic diffusion, the 40mm timepiece required an innovative construction to offset its exceptionally diminutive size. By housing the timepiece in a titanium case, Bulgari capitalizes on the low-density metal's unique properties to ensure maximal quality of sound diffusion without the benefit of a large internal chamber. The watchmaker then put even the dial at the service of the watch's sonorous raison d'être. By replacing the hour markers and border of the off-centered small seconds with cut-out sections, the timepiece dramatically amplifies its resonant quality while treating the wearer to a glimpse into the movement's sophisticated architecture. The Octo Finissimo Minute Repeater also boasts circular-section gongs directly affixed to the case and a centrifugal strike governor fitted with two inertia blocks. Each of the BVL 362 caliber's 362 meticulously crafted components thus plays its part to perfection. The hand-wound wristwatch is limited to 50 pieces and features a transparent sapphire crystal caseback.

The record-breaking Finissimo Tourbillon brings tantalizing micro-mechanical complexity to the intense all-black personality of the manufacture's Octo Ultranero concept. Housed within a titanium case with black DLC treatment, the 40mm timepiece boasts the world's thinnest bridge-free flying-tourbillon caliber. Thanks to Bulgari's exceptional command of ultra-thin haute horology, the Finissimo Tourbillon brilliantly combines its intense black design with refined dimensions and one of watchmaking's most captivating complications. Piercing the black lacquered dial at 6 o'clock, the BVL 268 caliber's flying tourbillon takes the stage with its riveting dynamism and exquisite mechanical craftsmanship. The owner may admire the 1.95mm-thick movement's entirely hand-finished construction through a transparent sapphire crystal caseback—the case itself measures a mere 5mm in thickness. Two hands, skeletonized to complement the tourbillon's transparency, indicate the hours and minutes while echoing the golden tone of the hour markers and crown against the blackness of the dial, case and alligator-leather strap. The Finissimo Tourbillon boasts a 52-hour power reserve.

Thanks to Bulgari's exceptional command of ultra-thin haute horology, the Finissimo Tourbillon brilliantly combines its intense black design with refined dimensions and one of watchmaking's most captivating complications.

▲ OCTO FINISSIMO MINUTE REPEATER

Thanks to numerous innovative and imaginative architectural solutions, this timepiece achieves exceptional acoustic resonance and quality despite setting a new standard in slenderness for a minute repeater.

▶ FINISSIMO TOURBILLON

This black titanium timepiece is driven by the world's thinnest bridge-free flying-tourbillon caliber, measuring only 1.95mm in thickness and housed in a 5mm-thick case.

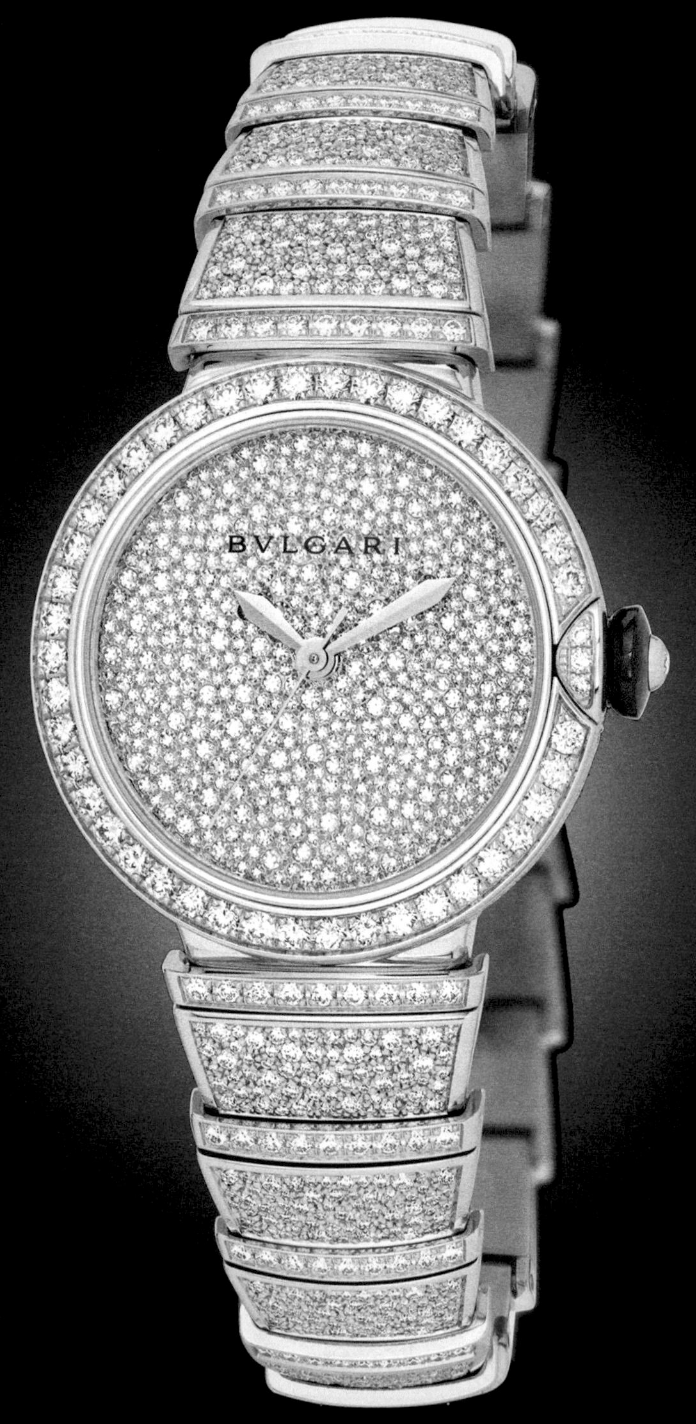

The watchmaker's fully snow-set LVCEA illuminates the feminine wrist with a statement of intense luxury and vivacity. Driven by the self-winding B77 caliber, the 33mm timepiece enlivens its 18-karat pink-gold case with a full snow-pavé setting of diamonds, on the band, complementing the bezel's shimmering arrangement of brilliant-cut stones. The scintillation spreads to the dial, where 487 additional diamonds create a breathtaking wintry backdrop for the timepiece's three-hand display of the hours, minutes and seconds. The LVCEA performs perhaps its greatest feat of luxury with its demonstration of opulent comfort—its stunning bracelet perfectly frames the body thanks to its harmonious row of articulated links, themselves snow-pavé set with 1,155 brilliant-cut diamonds for a play of light at every turn. Breaking from the dazzling dual-tone exhibition, the LVCEA's precious pink cabochon adds a flash of brilliant color that accentuates the watch's 10.9 carats of gems.

◂ **LVCEA**

The LVCEA brings light and life to its pink-gold case and articulated-links bracelet with a glorious setting of 1,859 scintillating gems.

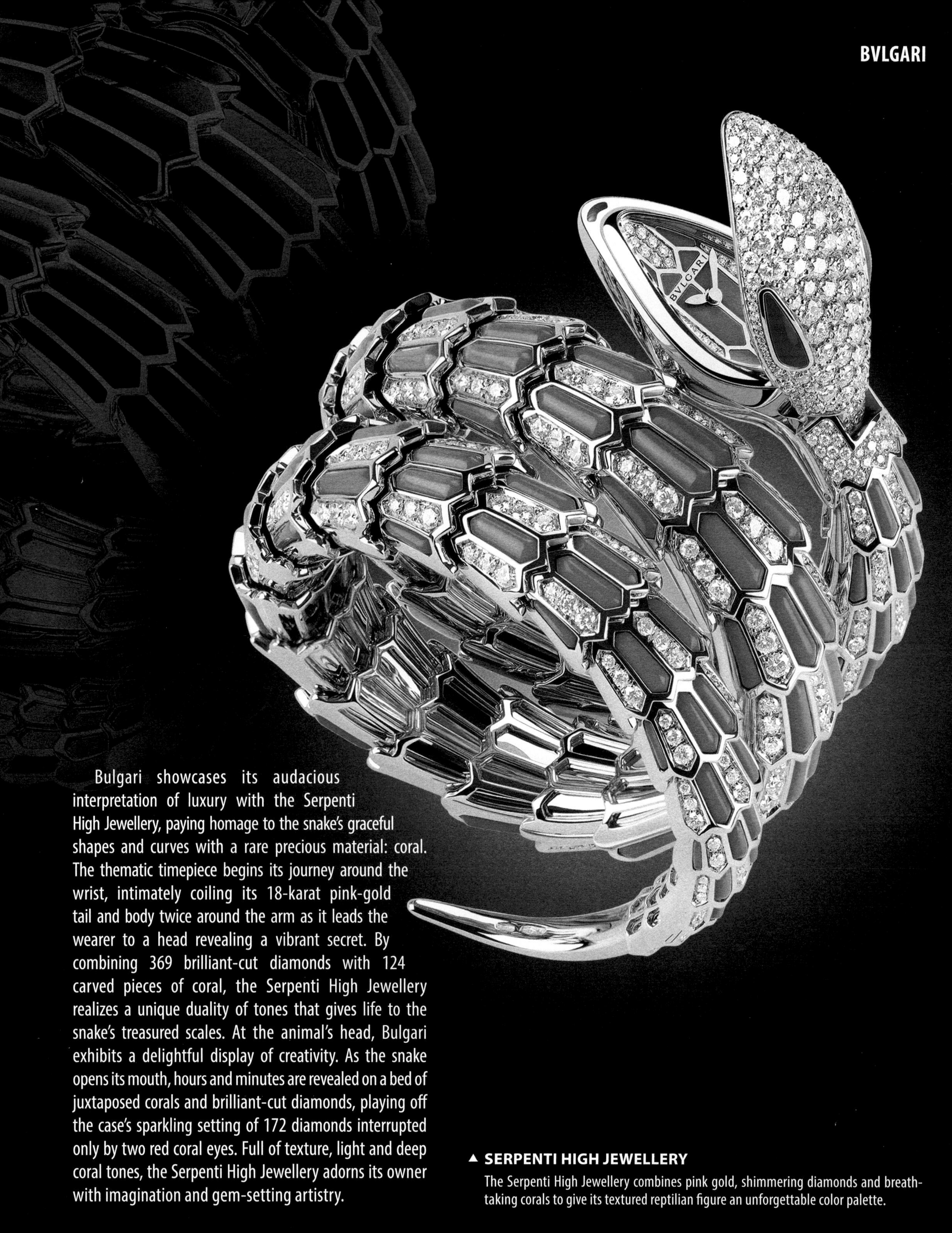

Bulgari showcases its audacious interpretation of luxury with the Serpenti High Jewellery, paying homage to the snake's graceful shapes and curves with a rare precious material: coral. The thematic timepiece begins its journey around the wrist, intimately coiling its 18-karat pink-gold tail and body twice around the arm as it leads the wearer to a head revealing a vibrant secret. By combining 369 brilliant-cut diamonds with 124 carved pieces of coral, the Serpenti High Jewellery realizes a unique duality of tones that gives life to the snake's treasured scales. At the animal's head, Bulgari exhibits a delightful display of creativity. As the snake opens its mouth, hours and minutes are revealed on a bed of juxtaposed corals and brilliant-cut diamonds, playing off the case's sparkling setting of 172 diamonds interrupted only by two red coral eyes. Full of texture, light and deep coral tones, the Serpenti High Jewellery adorns its owner with imagination and gem-setting artistry.

▲ **SERPENTI HIGH JEWELLERY**

The Serpenti High Jewellery combines pink gold, shimmering diamonds and breathtaking corals to give its textured reptilian figure an unforgettable color palette.

SERPENTI INCANTATI REF. 102538

Movement: quartz.
Functions: hours, minutes.
Case: 18K white gold; Ø 30mm; set with 112 brilliant-cut diamonds (approx. 2.36 carats); antireflective sapphire crystal.
Dial: 18K white gold; snow-set with 116 brilliant-cut diamonds (approx. 0.26 carat); blue-coated brass hands.
Strap: blue satin; 18K white-gold ardillon buckle set with 20 brilliant-cut diamonds (approx. 0.33 carat).
Also available: 18K pink-gold case set with 79 brilliant-cut diamonds (approx. 1.38 carats), 30 baguette-cut rubellites (approx. 1.06 carats) and 1 rubellite (approx. 1.02 carats), 18K pink-gold dial, brown satin strap (ref. 102537).

SERPENTI INCANTATI REF. 102541

Movement: manual-winding BVL 208 caliber; Ø 28.5mm, thickness: 5.08mm; 64-hour power reserve; 22 jewels; 21,000 vph.
Functions: hours, minutes; tourbillon at 6; power reserve indicator.
Case: 18K white gold; Ø 41mm; set with 227 brilliant-cut diamonds (approx. 2.15 carats) and 1 sapphire (approx. 0.15 carat); scratch-resistant antireflective sapphire crystal.
Dial: 18K white gold; 18K white-gold arch with graduated dots and blue PVD treatment; blue-coated brass hands.
Strap: blue alligator leather; 18K white-gold deployant buckle set with diamonds (approx. 0.28 carat).
Note: limited edition of 30 pieces.

SERPENTI INCANTATI REF. 102536

Movement: quartz.
Functions: hours, minutes.
Case: 18K pink gold; Ø 30mm; antireflective sapphire crystal.
Dial: 18K pink gold; snow-set with 116 brilliant-cut diamonds (approx. 0.26 carat); gold-plated brass hands.
Bracelet: 18K pink gold.
Note: case and bracelet set with 219 brilliant-cut diamonds (approx. 7.68 carats), 30 baguette-cut rubellites (approx. 1.2 carats) and 1 rubellite (approx. 1.2 carats).
Also available: 18K white-gold case, 18K white-gold dial, 18K white-gold bracelet, case and bracelet set with 251 brilliant-cut diamonds (approx. 8.67 carats) (ref. 102535).

SERPENTI REF. 102528

Movement: quartz.
Functions: hours, minutes.
Case: 18K pink gold; Ø 40mm; coated with green lacquer and set with 8 marquise-cut diamonds (approx. 3.4 carats) and 2 pear-shaped rubies (approx. 0.5 carat); scratch-resistant antireflective sapphire crystal.
Dial: 18K pink gold set with 82 brilliant-cut diamonds (approx. 0.43 carat); green-coated brass hands.
Bracelet: double-spiral 18K pink gold; set with 13 marquise-cut diamonds (approx. 3.44 carats) and coated with green lacquer.

SERPENTI — REF. 102526

Movement: quartz.
Functions: hours, minutes.
Case: 18K pink gold coated with black lacquer; Ø 40mm; set with 8 marquise-cut diamonds (approx. 3.4 carats) and 2 pear-shaped emeralds (approx. 0.45 carat); antireflective sapphire crystal.
Dial: 18K pink gold; set with 82 brilliant-cut diamonds (approx. 0.43 carat).
Bracelet: double-spiral 18K pink gold; set with 13 marquise-cut diamonds (approx. 3.44 carats) and coated with black lacquer.

SERPENTI TUBOGAS — REF. 102621

Movement: quartz.
Functions: hours, minutes.
Case: curved steel; Ø 35mm, thickness: 9mm; 18K pink-gold bezel set with brilliant-cut diamonds (approx. 0.29 carat); 18K pink-gold crown set with a cabochon-cut pink rubellite; antireflective sapphire crystal.
Dial: black opaline; guilloché soleil treatment; pink-gold-plated hands.
Bracelet: 5-twirl 18K pink gold and steel.

SERPENTI — REF. 102532

Movement: quartz.
Functions: hours, minutes.
Case: black ceramic; Ø 35mm, thickness: 9mm; 18K pink-gold bezel set with brilliant-cut diamonds (approx. 0.29 carat); 18K pink-gold crown set with a cabochon-cut ceramic element.
Dial: black lacquered; pink-gold-plated hands.
Bracelet: single-spiral 18K black ceramic; 18K pink-gold elements.
Also available: white ceramic case, white lacquered dial, 18K white ceramic bracelet (ref. 102613).

DIVAS' DREAM — REF. 102546

Movement: quartz.
Functions: hours, minutes.
Case: 18K pink gold; Ø 39mm; set with 209 brilliant-cut diamonds (approx. 5.04 carats); antireflective sapphire crystal.
Dial: white mother-of-pearl; gold-plated hands.
Strap: brown satin; 18K pink-gold 3-blade deployant buckle and round clasp set with 28 brilliant-cut diamonds (approx. 0.28 carat).
Also available: case set with 68 brilliant-cut diamonds (approx. 0.75 carat), mandarin garnets, tourmalines and pink opal elements, taupe satin strap (ref. 102420).

DIVAS' DREAM — REF. 102561

Movement: quartz.
Functions: hours, minutes.
Case: 18K white gold; Ø 30mm; set with 78 brilliant-cut diamonds (approx. 0.94 carat); 18K white-gold crown set with a tourmaline (approx. 0.108 carat); antireflective sapphire crystal.
Dial: diamond-pavé; set with 233 brilliant-cut diamonds (approx. 0.95 carat); rhodium-plated hands.
Strap: black satin; 18K white-gold ardillon buckle.

Also available: acetate brown anthracite dial made from natural cotton and wood fibers, taupe satin strap (ref. 102434).

PICCOLA LVCEA — REF. 102466

Movement: quartz.
Functions: hours, minutes.
Case: 18K white gold; Ø 23mm; set with 26 buff-cut emeralds (approx. 0.76 carat); 18K white-gold crown set with baguette and brilliant-cut diamonds; scratch-resistant antireflective sapphire crystal.
Dial: set with 84 baguette-cut diamonds (approx. 1.64 carats); blue hands.
Bracelet: 18K white gold; set with 210 baguette-cut diamonds (approx. 13.08 carats and 100 buff-cut emeralds (approx. 1.99 carats); 3-blade deployant buckle.

Also available: case set with 26 baguette-cut diamonds (approx. 1.03 carats), 18K white-gold crown set with a blue sapphire (approx. 0.54 carat) and diamond (approx. 0.02 carat), 18K white-gold bracelet set with 310 baguette-cut diamonds (approx. 14.01 carats) (ref. 102465); case set with 26 buff-cut rubies (approx. 1.11 carats), 18K white-gold bracelet set with 210 baguette-cut diamonds (approx. 13.08 carats) and 100 buff-cut rubies (approx. 2.82 carats) (ref. 102464).

LVCEA — REF. 102191

Movement: automatic-winding.
Functions: hours, minutes, seconds; date at 3.
Case: 18K pink gold; Ø 33mm; set with 43 brilliant-cut diamonds (approx. 1.2 carats); 18K pink-gold crown with a pink synthetic corundum and diamond (approx. 0.025 carat); antireflective sapphire crystal.
Dial: black opaline; guilloché soleil treatment; set with 11 diamond indexes (approx. 0.19 carat); pink-gold-plated hands.
Bracelet: 18K pink gold; set with 117 diamonds (approx. 2 carats); 3-blade deployant buckle and Bulgari logo.

Also available: gold-plated indexes with Roman numerals at 12 and 6, 18K pink-gold bracelet without diamonds (ref. 102260).

LVCEA — REF. 102476

Movement: automatic-winding.
Functions: hours, minutes, seconds; date at 3.
Case: steel; Ø 33mm, thickness: 9.87mm; 18K pink-gold bezel set with 43 brilliant-cut diamonds (approx. 1.2 carats); antireflective sapphire crystal.
Dial: white mother-of-pearl; set with 11 diamond indexes (approx. 0.2 carat).
Bracelet: steel and 18K pink gold; 3-blade deployant buckle with Bulgari logo.

OCTO FINISSIMO — REF. 102469

Movement: manual-winding BVL 128SK caliber; Ø 36mm, thickness: 2.35mm; 65-hour power reserve; 28 jewels; 28,800 vph.
Functions: hours, minutes; small seconds between 7 and 8; power reserve indicator between 9 and 10.
Case: steel treated with black DLC; Ø 40mm, thickness: 5.37mm; 18K pink-gold bezel; 18K pink-gold screw-down crown with ceramic insert; scratch-resistant antireflective sapphire crystal; sapphire crystal caseback; water resistant to 3atm.
Dial: skeletonized; faceted and skeletonized pink-gold-plated hands.
Strap: black alligator leather; titanium ardillon buckle treated with black DLC.

OCTO FINISSIMO TOURBILLON — REF. 102138

Movement: manual-winding BVL 268 caliber; Ø 32.6mm, thickness: 1.95mm; 52-hour power reserve; 13 jewels; 21,600 vph.
Functions: hours, minutes; tourbillon at 6.
Case: platinum; Ø 40mm, thickness: 5mm; crown with black ceramic insert; scratch-resistant antireflective sapphire crystal; sapphire crystal caseback.
Dial: black lacquer; skeletonized and faceted hands.
Strap: black alligator leather; platinum ardillon buckle.

OCTO ULTRANERO — REF. 102581

Movement: automatic-winding BVL 193 caliber; Ø 25.6mm, thickness: 3.7mm; 50-hour power reserve; 28 jewels; 28,800 vph; decoration: perlage, Côtes de Genève, chamfered finishing; double barrel.
Functions: hours, minutes, seconds; date at 3.
Case: steel treated with black DLC; Ø 41mm, thickness: 10.6mm; screw-down 18K pink-gold crown with ceramic insert; scratch-resistant antireflective sapphire crystal; sapphire crystal caseback; water resistant to 10atm.
Dial: black lacquered and polished; hand-applied pink-gold-plated indexes; faceted and skeletonized pink-gold-plated hands.
Strap: integrated rubber; steel ardillon buckle treated with black DLC.

OCTO ULTRANERO — REF.102630

Movement: automatic-winding BVL 328 caliber; Ø 30mm, thickness: 6.62mm; 50-hour power reserve; 31 jewels; 36,000 vph; decoration: perlage, Côtes de Genève, chamfered finishing.
Functions: hours, minutes; small seconds at 9; date between 4 and 5; chronograph: central seconds hand, 30-minute counter at 3, 12-hour counter at 6.
Case: steel treated with black DLC; Ø 41mm, thickness: 13.07mm; screw-down 18K pink-gold crown with ceramic insert; scratch-resistant antireflective sapphire crystal; sapphire crystal caseback; water resistant to 10atm.
Dial: black lacquered and polished with champlevé technique; hand-applied pink-gold-plated indexes; faceted and skeletonized pink-gold-plated hands.
Strap: integrated rubber; steel ardillon buckle treated with black DLC.

CARL F. BUCHERER

FINE SWISS WATCHMAKING

COMMITTED TO PRECISION

Carl F. Bucherer proves once again that **INNOVATION IS THE ESSENCE OF ITS DNA**. The Swiss watchmaker pushes the envelope with every facet of its mechanical movements, never compromising, always leading the way to the future of the art form.

Its newest movement, the CFB A2000, is the epitome of the brand's drive for perfection in the field of precision engineering and micro-mechanical aesthetics. Entirely manufactured in the brand's development workshops, the double-sided self-winding caliber builds on the groundbreaking advances of Carl F. Bucherer's celebrated CFB A1000, utilizing a peripherally arranged rotor. In the quest for optimal and consistent rates of accuracy, the CFB A2000 is fitted with an entirely free-breathing balance spiral that experiences no change in its effective length. Small weights, known as pivotable masselottes, sit on the four balance arms, calibrating the motion of the watch and controlling the inertia of the balance.

The caliber's delicate finishes additionally speak to Carl F. Bucherer's commitment to perfectionism throughout each creation. Adorned with Côtes de Genève on the bridges and balance cocks, the CFB A2000 pays tribute to the fine craftsmanship tradition of Swiss haute horology. The linearly designed movement oscillates at a frequency of 28,800 vph.

▸ **CFB A2000**

This new, sophisticated caliber boasts a peripherally arranged rotor and free-breathing balance spiral.

Adorned with Côtes de Genève on the bridges and balance cocks, the CFB A2000 pays tribute to the fine craftsmanship tradition of Swiss haute horology.

The Manero Peripheral marks the debut of the CFB A2000 caliber series with consummate elegance. Driven by the specially designed CFB A2050 iteration, the self-winding timepiece beats tastefully in a softly curved, multi-faceted 40.6mm case composed of luxurious 18-karat rose gold. On a matte black dial that plays off the rich warmth of the outer design, the Manero Peripheral achieves a graceful sense of texture using 13 raised wedge hour markers. Emanating from its center, two faceted lance hands indicate the hours and minutes, echoing the color notes of the case and indexes. A subdial at 6 o'clock, whose white indicators ensure flawless legibility against the dark background, displays the precise running seconds of the innovative 33-jewel caliber. At 3 o'clock, the CFB A2050 exhibits the date through a large highly readable white aperture. The timepiece's uncluttered dial-side aesthetic sets a fitting tone that extends to the domed sapphire crystal caseback, where the Manero Peripheral showcases the exquisite construction of its caliber without obstruction by incorporating a peripheral rotor. This rose-gold model is also available with a white dial that contrasts the precious metal with its noble tone and classical appeal.

Also presented is a version of the self-winding timepiece in a stainless steel case with matching raised wedge hour markers. This iteration, furnished with a white or matte-black dial, is worn on a Louisiana alligator leather strap or stainless steel bracelet. The Manero Peripheral thus rounds out the timeless luxury of rose gold with the contemporary feel of sleek steel. The timepiece boasts a power reserve of 55 hours.

▼ MANERO PERIPHERAL

This self-winding timepiece owes its extraordinary precision and consistency to the manufacture's new CFB A2050 caliber.

A ceaseless innovator since its founding in 1888, Carl F. Bucherer has always put the excellence of mechanical movements at the forefront of its efforts. With the opening of a new competence center in Lengnau, Switzerland, in the canton of Aargau, the heralded manufacture establishes the perfect infrastructural environment for enhanced verticalization. As the watchmaker continues to push advances in the field of haute horology, the new development strengthens its position of leadership, allowing for a meeting of the substantial growth in demand while fulfilling the brand's strict standards of excellence. This substantial step is hereby a testament to Carl F. Bucherer's vision of sustainable growth, committed to quality and innovative spirit as production increases.

▼ CARL F. BUCHERER NEW COMPETENCE CENTER

The opening of Carl F. Bucherer's new competence center marks an exciting development as the brand continues to innovate in the field of high-precision mechanical calibers.

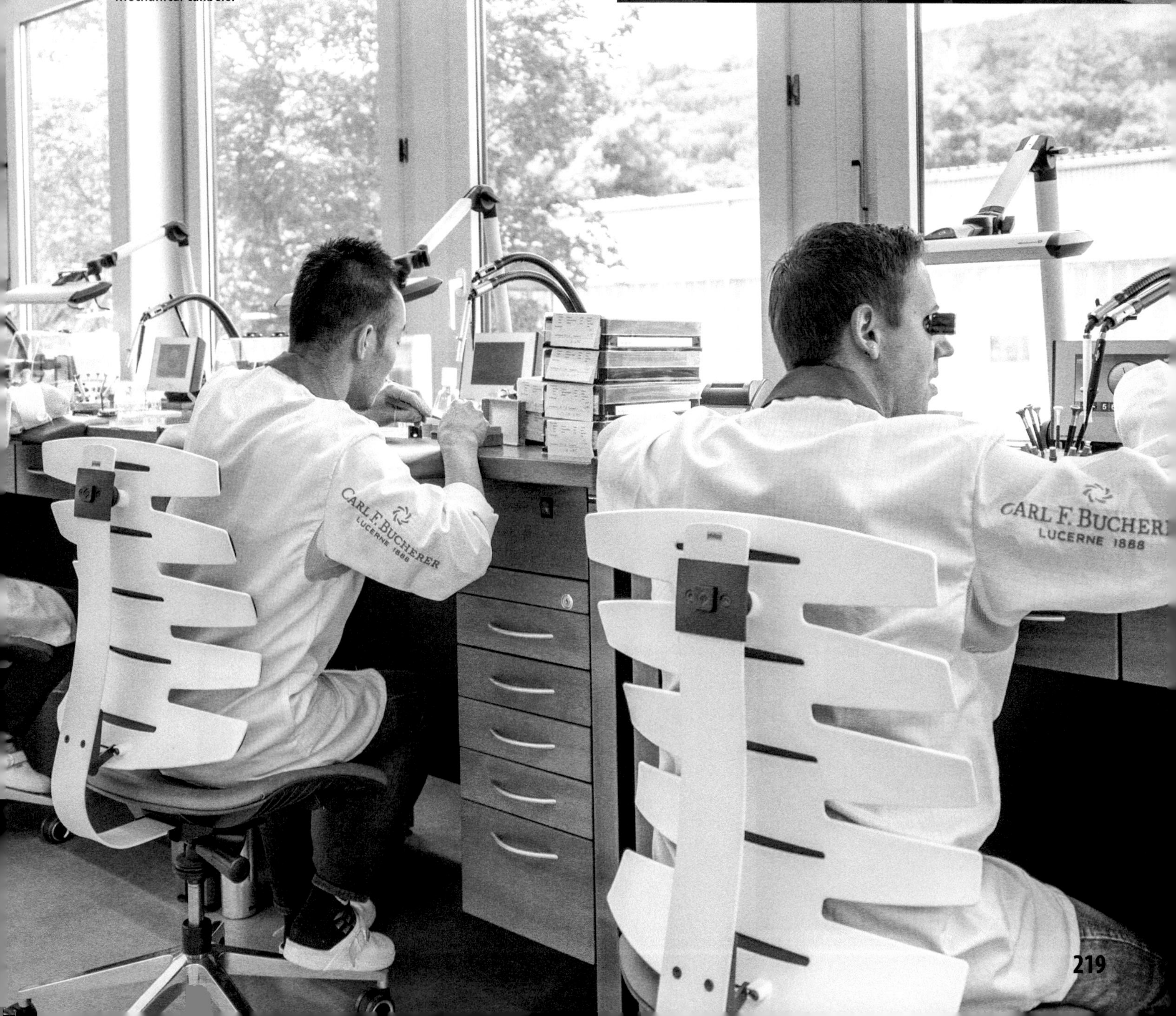

PATRAVI TRAVELTEC BLACK — REF. 00.10620.12.33.21

Movement: automatic-winding CFB 1901.1 caliber; Ø 28.6mm, thickness: 7.3mm; 42-hour power reserve; 39 jewels; COSC certified.
Functions: hours, minutes; small seconds at 3; date between 4 and 5; three time zones; chronograph: central seconds hand, 12-hour counter at 6, 30-minute counter at 9.
Case: stainless steel with black DLC coating; Ø 46.6mm, thickness: 15.5mm; screw-down crown; antireflective sapphire crystal; water resistant to 5atm.
Dial: black; nine applied hour indexes; stainless steel hands; red third time zone hand.
Bracelet: stainless steel with DLC coating; folding clasp in stainless steel with DLC coating.
Suggested price: $15,400

PATRAVI TRAVELTEC II — REF. 00.10633.08.33.01

Movement: automatic-winding CFB 1901.1 caliber; Ø 28.6mm, thickness: 7.3mm; 42-hour power reserve; 39 jewels; COSC certified.
Functions: hours, minutes; small seconds at 3; date between 4 and 5; three time zones; chronograph: central seconds hand, 12-hour counter at 6, 30-minute counter at 9.
Case: stainless steel; Ø 47.4mm, thickness: 15.9mm; screw-down crown; antireflective sapphire crystal; water resistant to 10atm.
Dial: black; nine applied hour indexes; stainless steel hands; red third time zone hand.

Strap: rubber; folding clasp with stainless steel comfort extension.
Suggested price: $12,900
Also available: stainless steel bracelet (ref. 00.10633.08.33.21).

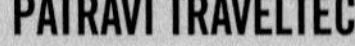

PATRAVI TRAVELTEC FOURX — REF. 00.10620.22.93.01

Movement: automatic-winding CFB 1901.1 caliber; Ø 28.6mm, thickness: 7.3mm; 42-hour power reserve; 39 jewels; COSC certified.
Functions: hours, minutes; small seconds at 3; date between 4 and 5; three time zones; chronograph: central seconds hand, 12-hour counter at 6, 30-minute counter at 9.
Case: 18K rose gold; Ø 46.6mm, thickness: 15.5mm; ceramic bezel; 18K rose-gold and rubber screw-down crown; antireflective sapphire crystal; water resistant to 5atm.
Dial: skeletonized; nine applied hour indexes; 18K rose-gold hands; red third time zone hand.

Strap: rubber; 18K rose-gold pin buckle.
Note: limited edition of 125 pieces.
Suggested price: $52,900
Also available: palladium case (ref. 00.10620.21.93.01).

PATRAVI TRAVELTEC — REF. 00.10620.08.53.21

Movement: automatic-winding CFB 1901.1 caliber; Ø 28.6mm, thickness: 7.3mm; 42-hour power reserve; 39 jewels; COSC certified.
Functions: hours, minutes; small seconds at 3; date between 4 and 5; three time zones; chronograph: central seconds hand, 12-hour counter at 6, 30-minute counter at 9.
Case: stainless steel; Ø 46.6mm, thickness: 15.5mm; screw-down crown; antireflective sapphire crystal; water resistant to 5atm.
Dial: blue; nine applied hour indexes; stainless steel hands; red third time zone hand.
Bracelet: stainless steel; stainless steel folding clasp.

Suggested price: $11,400
Also available: black dial, black calfskin leather strap (ref. 00.10620.08.33.01); black dial, 18K rose-gold bracelet (ref. 00.10620.03.33.21); silver dial, brown calfskin leather strap (ref. 00.10620.08.63.01); silver dial, stainless steel bracelet (ref. 00.10620.08.63.21); blue calfskin leather strap (ref. 00.10620.08.53.01); brown dial, 18K rose-gold bracelet (ref. 00.10620.03.93.21); brown dial, brown calfskin leather strap (ref. 00.10620.03.93.01).

PATRAVI SCUBATEC WHITE — REF. 00.10634.23.23.01

Movement: automatic-winding CFB 1950 caliber; Ø 26.2mm, thickness: 4.6 or 4.8mm; 38-hour power reserve; 25 or 26 jewels.
Functions: hours, minutes, seconds; date at 3.
Case: stainless steel; Ø 36.5mm, thickness: 11.37mm; stainless steel/ceramic bezel; screw-down crown; antireflective sapphire crystal; water resistant to 20atm.
Dial: white; stainless steel hands; eleven applied hour indexes.
Strap: rubber; stainless steel adjustable folding clasp.
Suggested price: $5,100
Also available: stainless steel bracelet (ref. 00.10634.23.23.21).

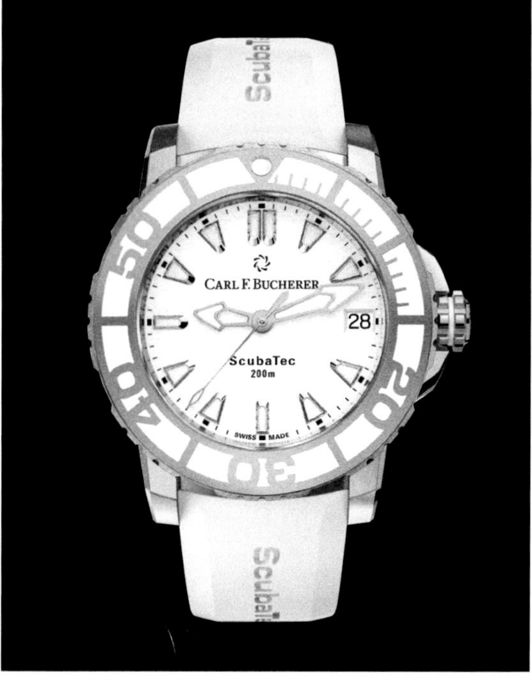

PATRAVI SCUBATEC ROSE GOLD — REF. 00.10632.22.33.01

Movement: automatic-winding CFB 1950.1 caliber; Ø 26.2mm, thickness: 4.6 or 4.8mm; 38-hour power reserve; 25 or 26 jewels; COSC certified.
Functions: hours, minutes, seconds; date at 3.
Case: 18K rose gold; Ø 44.6mm, thickness: 13.45mm; 18K rose-gold/ceramic bezel; screw-down crown; antireflective sapphire crystal; blackened titanium caseback; water resistant to 50atm.
Dial: black; 18K rose-gold hands; eleven applied hour indexes.
Strap: rubber; 18K rose-gold and blackened titanium adjustable diving clasp.
Suggested price: $24,800

PATRAVI SCUBATEC TWOTONE — REF. 00.10632.24.53.01

Movement: automatic-winding CFB 1950.1 caliber; Ø 26.2mm, thickness: 4.6 or 4.8mm; 38-hour power reserve; 25 or 26 jewels; COSC certified.
Functions: hours, minutes, seconds; date at 3.
Case: stainless steel; Ø 44.6mm, thickness: 13.45mm; 18K rose-gold/ceramic bezel; screw-down crown; antireflective sapphire crystal; water resistant to 50atm.
Dial: blue; 18K rose-gold hands; eleven applied hour indexes.
Strap: rubber; stainless steel adjustable diving clasp.
Suggested price: $9,800
Also available: white dial (ref. 00.10632.24.23.01); white dial, stainless steel/18K rose-gold bracelet (ref. 00.10632.24.23.21); stainless steel/18K-rose gold bracelet (ref. 00.10632.24.53.21); black dial (ref. 00.10632.24.33.01); black dial, stainless steel and 18K rose-gold bracelet (ref. 00.10632.24.33.21).

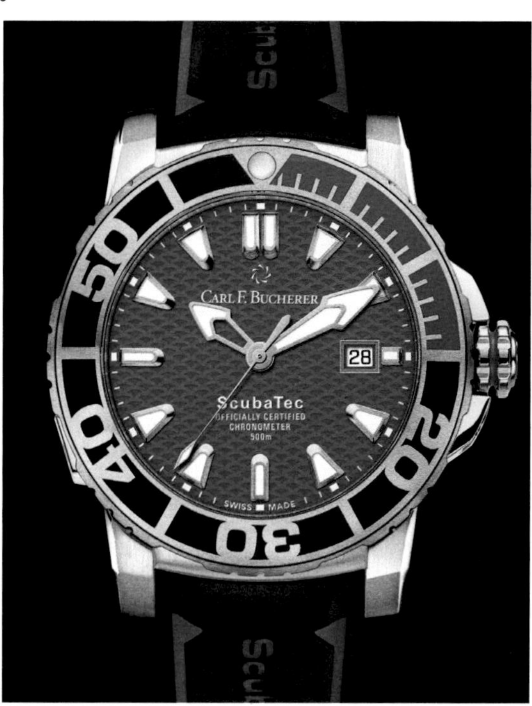

PATRAVI SCUBATEC — REF. 00.10632.23.33.01

Movement: automatic-winding CFB 1950.1 caliber; Ø 26.2mm, thickness: 4.6 or 4.8mm; 38-hour power reserve; 25 or 26 jewels; COSC certified .
Functions: hours, minutes, seconds; date at 3.
Case: stainless steel; Ø 44.6mm, thickness: 13.45mm; stainless steel/ceramic bezel; screw-down crown; antireflective sapphire crystal; water resistant to 50atm.
Dial: black; stainless steel hands; eleven applied hour indexes.
Strap: rubber; stainless steel adjustable diving clasp.
Suggested price: $6,400
Also available: stainless steel/ceramic bezel, black dial, stainless steel bracelet (ref. 00.10632.23.33.21); stainless steel/ceramic bezel, white dial, stainless steel bracelet (ref. 00.10632.23.23.21); blue dial (ref. 00.10632.23.53.01); blue dial, stainless steel bracelet (ref. 00.10632.23.53.21); red and black ceramic bezel (ref. 00.10632.23.33.02); red and black ceramic bezel, stainless steel bracelet (ref. 00.10632.23.33.22).

MANERO PERIPHERAL ROSE GOLD — REF. 00.10917.03.33.01

Movement: automatic-winding CFB A2050 caliber; Ø 30.6mm, thickness: 5.28mm; 55-hour power reserve; 33 jewels.
Functions: hours, minutes; small seconds at 6; date at 3.
Case: 18K rose gold; Ø 40.6mm, thickness: 11.2mm; domed antireflective sapphire crystal; sapphire crystal caseback; water resistant to 3atm.
Dial: black; 18K rose-gold hands; twelve applied hour indexes.
Strap: black Louisiana alligator leather; 18K rose-gold pin buckle.
Suggested price: $17,800

Also available: white dial (ref. 00.10917.03.23.01).

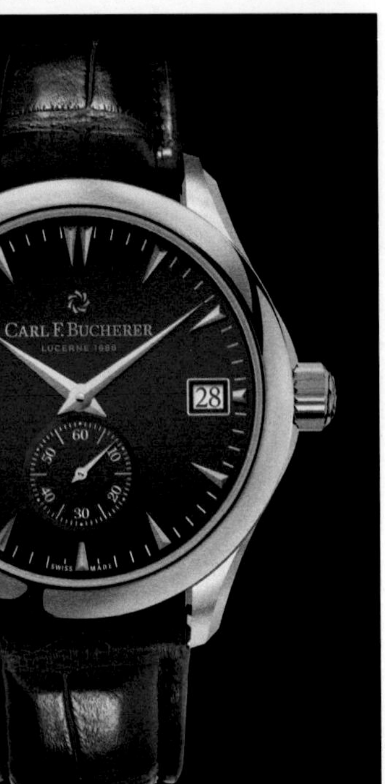

MANERO PERIPHERAL — REF. 00.10917.08.23.01

Movement: automatic-winding CFB A2050 caliber; Ø 30.6mm, thickness: 5.28mm; 55-hour power reserve; 33 jewels.
Functions: hours, minutes; small seconds at 6; date at 3.
Case: stainless steel; Ø 40.6mm, thickness: 11.2mm; domed antireflective sapphire crystal; sapphire crystal caseback; water resistant to 3atm.
Dial: white; stainless steel hands; twelve applied hour indexes.
Strap: brown Louisiana alligator leather; stainless steel pin lock folding clasp.
Suggested price: $7,200

Also available: stainless steel bracelet (ref. 00.10917.08.23.21); black dial, black alligator leather strap (ref. 00.10917.08.33.01); black dial, stainless steel bracelet (ref. 00.10917.08.33.21).

MANERO FLYBACK — REF. 00.10919.03.13.01

Movement: automatic-winding CFB 1970 caliber; Ø 30.4mm, thickness: 7.9mm; 42-hour power reserve; 25 jewels.
Functions: hours, minutes; small seconds at 9; date at 6; flyback chronograph: 30-minute counter at 3.
Case: 18K rose gold; Ø 43mm, thickness: 14.45mm; antireflective sapphire crystal; sapphire crystal caseback; water resistant to 3atm.
Dial: silver; 18K rose-gold hands; ten applied hour indexes.
Strap: brown Louisiana alligator leather; 18K rose-gold pin buckle.
Suggested price: $21,000

MANERO FLYBACK — REF. 00.10919.08.13.01

Movement: automatic-winding CFB 1970 caliber; Ø 30.4mm, thickness: 7.9mm; 42-hour power reserve; 25 jewels.
Functions: hours, minutes; small seconds at 9; date at 6; flyback chronograph: 30-minute counter at 3.
Case: stainless steel; Ø 43mm, thickness: 14.45mm; antireflective sapphire crystal; sapphire crystal caseback; water resistant to 3atm.
Dial: silver; stainless steel hands; ten applied hour indexes.
Strap: black Louisiana alligator leather; stainless steel pin lock folding clasp.
Suggested price: $8,700

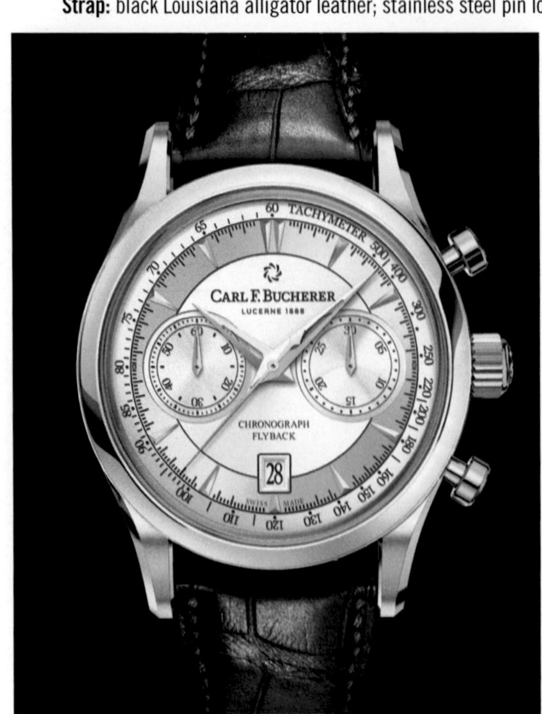

PATHOS SWAN LIMITED EDITION REF. 00.10590.03.90.31

Movement: quartz CFB 1851 caliber.
Functions: hours, minutes.
Case: 18K rose gold; Ø 34mm, thickness: 9.45mm; set with 254 FC TW VVS diamonds and 116 sapphires (4.15 carats); domed antireflective sapphire crystal; water resistant to 3atm.
Dial: 18K rose gold and mother-of-pearl; set with 31 FC TW VVS diamonds and 117 sapphires (0.6 carat); 18K rose-gold hands.
Bracelet: 18K rose gold; set with 240 FC TW VVS diamonds and 164 sapphires (7.75 carats); 18K rose-gold folding clasp.
Note: limited edition of 88 pieces.
Suggested price: $171,600

PATHOS DIVA ROSE GOLD REF. 00.10580.03.73.31.02

Movement: automatic-winding CFB 1963 caliber; Ø 20mm, thickness: 4.8mm; 38-hour power reserve; 25 jewels.
Functions: hours, minutes, seconds; date at 3.
Case: 18K rose gold; Ø 34mm, thickness: 9.65mm; set with 54 FC TW VVS diamonds (0.7 carat); domed antireflective sapphire crystal; water resistant to 3atm.
Dial: mother-of-pearl; 18K rose-gold hands; eleven 18K rose-gold applied hour indexes.
Bracelet: 18K rose gold; 18K rose-gold folding clasp.
Suggested price: $29,300
Also available: without diamonds (ref. 00.10580.03.73.21.02); decorative grid (ref. 00.10580.03.75.31.01); decorative grid without diamonds (ref. 00.10580.03.75.21.01).

PATHOS DESIRE LIMITED EDITION REF. 00.10590.02.99.31

Movement: quartz CFB 1851 caliber.
Functions: hours, minutes.
Case: 18K white gold; Ø 34mm, thickness: 9.45mm; set with 370 FC TW VVS diamonds (4.15 carats); domed antireflective sapphire crystal; water resistant to 3atm.
Dial: 18K white gold and mother-of-pearl; set with 96 FC TW VVS diamonds (0.5 carat); 18K white-gold hands; two 18K white-gold Roman numerals.
Bracelet: 18K white gold; set with 404 FC TW VVS diamonds (7.85 carats); 18K white-gold folding clasp.
Note: limited edition of 88 pieces.
Suggested price: $182,000

PATHOS DIVA REF. 00.10580.08.25.31.01

Movement: automatic-winding CFB 1963 caliber; Ø 20mm, thickness: 4.8mm; 38-hour power reserve; 25 jewels.
Functions: hours, minutes, seconds; date at 3.
Case: stainless steel; Ø 34mm, thickness: 9.65mm; set with 54 FC TW VVS brilliant-cut diamonds (0.7 carat); domed antireflective sapphire crystal; sapphire crystal caseback; water resistant to 3atm.
Dial: white; stainless steel hands; nine stainless steel applied indexes; three stainless steel Roman numerals.
Bracelet: stainless steel; stainless steel foldover clasp.
Suggested price: $10,000
Also available: stainless steel and 18K rose-gold case, without diamonds, stainless steel and 18K rose-gold bracelet (ref. 00.10580.07.25.21.01); stainless steel and 18K rose-gold case, stainless steel and 18K rose-gold bracelet (ref. 00.10580.07.25.31.01); without diamonds (ref. 00.10580.08.25.21.01).

Cartier

ANIMAL ATTRACTION

CARTIER SHOWCASES THE FULL BREADTH OF ITS ARTISTIC VIRTUOSITY with five distinctive timepieces. Whether capturing the vintage elegance of femininity, bringing a panther to life with a variety of artistic and horogical techniques, or leaving its audience in awe of a fascinating illusion, the Parisian watchmaker imbues each creation with the brand's unmistakable personality.

PANTHÈRE DE CARTIER WATCH

Jewelry first, timepiece second, the imposing 1980s icon that is the Panthère de Cartier watch is looking edgier than ever in this re-issue by Cartier.

An unabashed head-turner, the Panthère de Cartier watch slinks about the wrist in a rippling celebration of triumphant and carefree femininity.

Gleaming sun-kissed and golden on the wrist, it wears yellow gold with aplomb and features a flexible, chain-link bracelet. Instantly recognizable as Cartier, this jewelry watch is a child of the 1980s, but returns with a fresh sense of chic.

The Panthère de Cartier watch wows again, reviving all the exuberant decadence of the 1980s. Emblem of an era, this is a watch that belongs firmly in the spotlight. In any decade and whether day or night, its sensual bracelet and intuitive design glint with class and distinction that refuse to fade.

Nearly thirty years on, the Maison is reissuing the original Panthère de Cartier and this cult timepiece continues to capture the zeitgeist. The watch epitomizes the woman of today, who impresses with her sophisticated attitude and instinctive sense of style. She has impeccable taste and knows exactly what she wants. She curates her own cocktail of influences from every era, defining her own style with a distinctive spin on the classics.

Authentic and imposing, the Panthère de Cartier watch is a foregone conclusion. Worn as a bracelet, chain and good luck charm, this is a bejeweled accessory to mix and match; a watch designed to be worn in creative new ways and tailored to the personality of the wearer.

It goes with the flow and curls around the wrist in an unfettered movement. Gleaming. Winding its way...

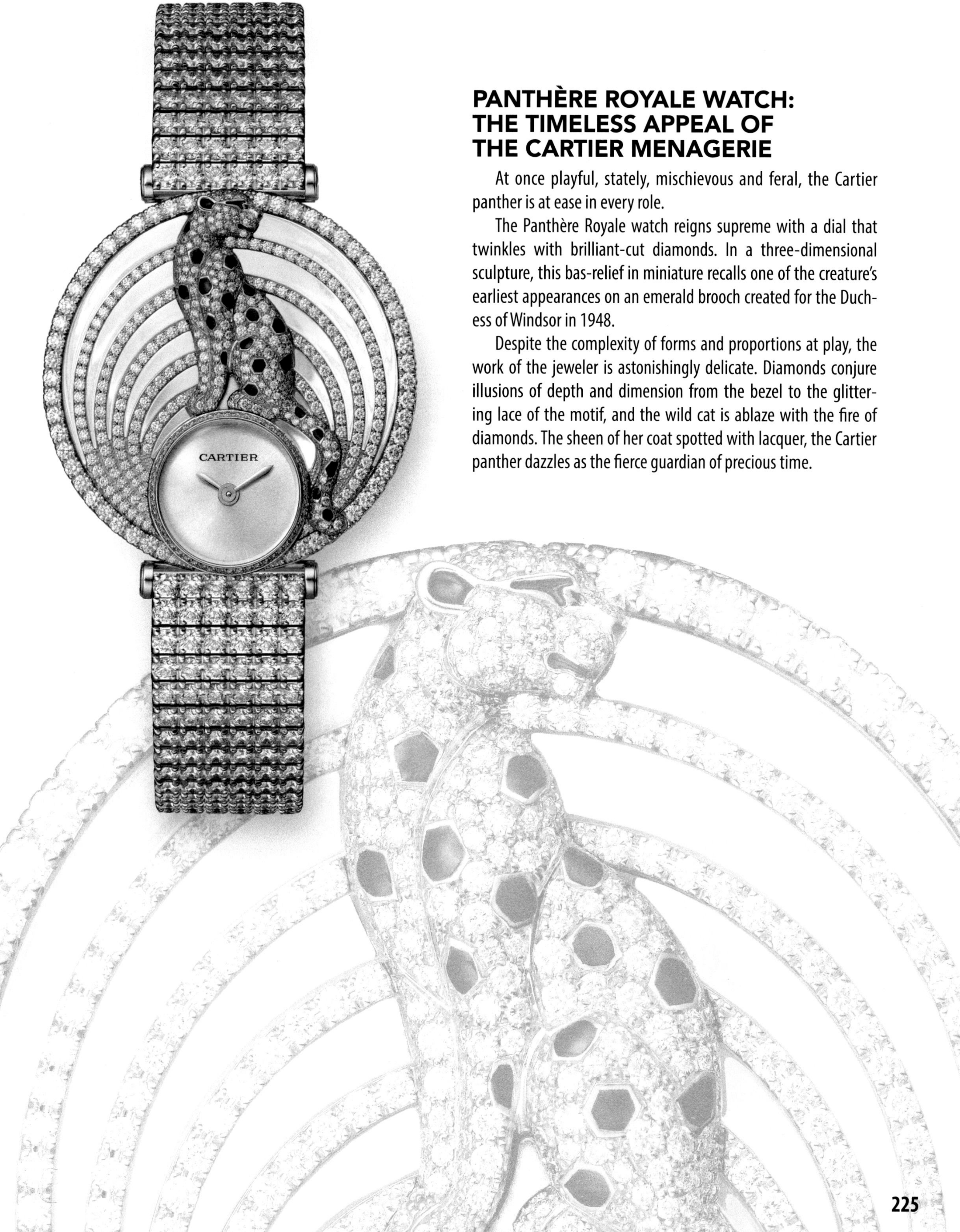

PANTHÈRE ROYALE WATCH: THE TIMELESS APPEAL OF THE CARTIER MENAGERIE

At once playful, stately, mischievous and feral, the Cartier panther is at ease in every role.

The Panthère Royale watch reigns supreme with a dial that twinkles with brilliant-cut diamonds. In a three-dimensional sculpture, this bas-relief in miniature recalls one of the creature's earliest appearances on an emerald brooch created for the Duchess of Windsor in 1948.

Despite the complexity of forms and proportions at play, the work of the jeweler is astonishingly delicate. Diamonds conjure illusions of depth and dimension from the bezel to the glittering lace of the motif, and the wild cat is ablaze with the fire of diamonds. The sheen of her coat spotted with lacquer, the Cartier panther dazzles as the fierce guardian of precious time.

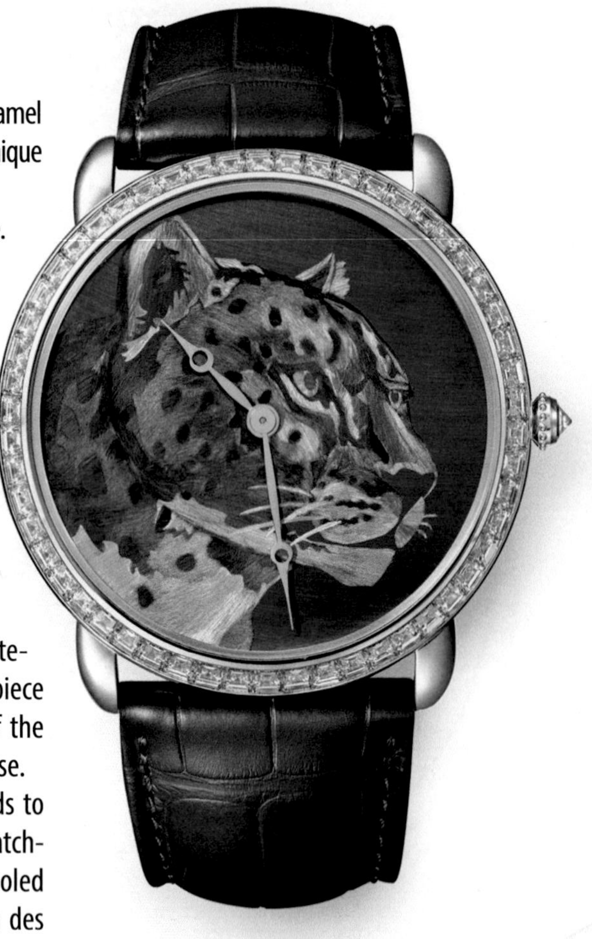

INNOVATIVE USE OF ARTISTIC CRAFTS: WATCHES ABLAZE WITH ANIMAL COLORS

Which artistic craft has Cartier mastered to create a dial with the luminosity of enamel and the precision of a miniature painting? This Ronde Louis Cartier watch pioneers a new technique in watchmaking: flamed gold, the latest addition to the repertoire of Cartier craftsmanship.

The flamed gold technique is inspired by the method of bluing watch hands in a flame. It requires a perfect mastery of intense heat since the most precise temperatures are needed to elicit the colors: the hottest flame produces blue; the coolest, beige. The pattern of the panther's coat is engraved—or "brushed"—onto the 18-karat-gold dial. The gold plate is heated in a flame to produce an initial color, and returned to the flame as many times as necessary until the full palette of colors has been produced.

This sensitive and exacting technique calls for tremendous foresight: since each return to the flame alters all of the colors, long hours of work can be undone in an instant.

The outcome of such minute, delicate handiwork—commanding staggering levels of concentration on the part of Cartier craftsmen—is suitably impressive. The depth of a rich animal palette ranging from beige to brown is contrasted with white-gold, apple-shaped hands. Cartier has chosen to pave the bezel of this exquisite timepiece in baguette-cut diamonds, a flash of fire that brilliantly illuminates the genius of the artwork. The creature is strikingly lifelike from the tops of the ears to the tip of the nose.

Flamed gold is the latest technique in a repertoire of Cartier crafts that extends to Etruscan granulation, enamel granulation and filigree work. Enriching the art of watch-making with techniques borrowed from other fields, artisan craftsmen have pooled their skills to create this innovative new display of talent by Cartier and its Maison des Métiers d'Art.

PANTHÈRE JOUEUSE PAVES THE WAY FOR COLLABORATION BETWEEN WATCHMAKING AND JEWELRY WORKSHOPS

The panther, the iconic animal of the Cartier menagerie, is in a playful mood in this new complication watch by the Maison.

In a dramatic scene powered by a brand-new complication, the mischievous creature appears to pounce from the dial in pursuit of a ball. The caliber moves as one with the body of the panther to bring this miniature theater to life. The minutes are indicated by the head and paw of the figure, while the hours are marked by the ball.

Exhibiting exquisite craftsmanship in a display of diamonds, black lacquer and emeralds, Cartier brings the panther to life with a new movement. The workshops have joined forces to channel the jewelry expertise of the Maison and its flair for rendering these strikingly lifelike three-dimensional creatures. The watch is transfigured by the presence of the panther and the hidden mechanism that marks the passage of time in a never-ending game.

ROTONDE DE CARTIER WATCH SKELETON MYSTERIOUS HOUR

For the first time by Cartier, skeleton work and a mysterious movement—two of the Maison's iconic Fine Watchmaking signatures—come together in the same watch. Cartier is launching this exceptional union of aesthetics and technical prowess with the Rotonde de Cartier watch and its calibre 9983 MC.

Asymmetrical and structured, this two-sided movement exploits the visible and invisible with the stylistic audacity that is an essential component of Cartier's design tradition.

THE INVISIBLE

The watch incorporates a mysterious movement, an in-house complication that was introduced more than a century ago with the first mystery clocks in 1912. Their mechanisms rely on an ingenious concept that Cartier has successfully transposed to the wrist. The hands are not directly linked to the movement, but are joined to two sapphire discs fitted with teeth around their circumference. These discs, activated by the movement, turn the hands: one disc for the minute hand and the other for the hour hand.

THE VISIBLE

Then there is the skeleton work, the product of a long Cartier tradition that began in the 1930s. It achieved signature status in 2009 with the creation of the skeleton watch with sculpted mechanism in the shape of Roman numerals. Unmistakable and instantly recognizable, it is protected by a patent, enabling Cartier to create a skeleton movement with an architecture that helps to tell the time. With the calibre 9983 MC, Cartier decided to reveal the gear train of the mysterious movement, which is usually hidden beneath the dial. This transparency exposes even the smallest details of the movement's architecture, but reveals nothing of the mysterious mechanism's magic.

THE PURITY OF THE ROTONDE DE CARTIER WATCH

Chosen for its balanced proportions and pure dimensions, the round shape of the Rotonde de Cartier watch provides the ideal setting for the original combination of these two signatures.

PANTHERE DE CARTIER SMALL MODEL REF. HPI01129

Movement: quartz.
Functions: hours, minutes.
Case: 18K white gold; 22x30mm, thickness: 6mm; set with brilliant-cut diamonds; 18K white-gold octagonal crown set with a diamond; water resistant to 3atm.
Dial: silver-finished; blued steel sword-shaped hands.
Bracelet: 18K white gold; set with brilliant-cut diamonds.
Price: available upon request.

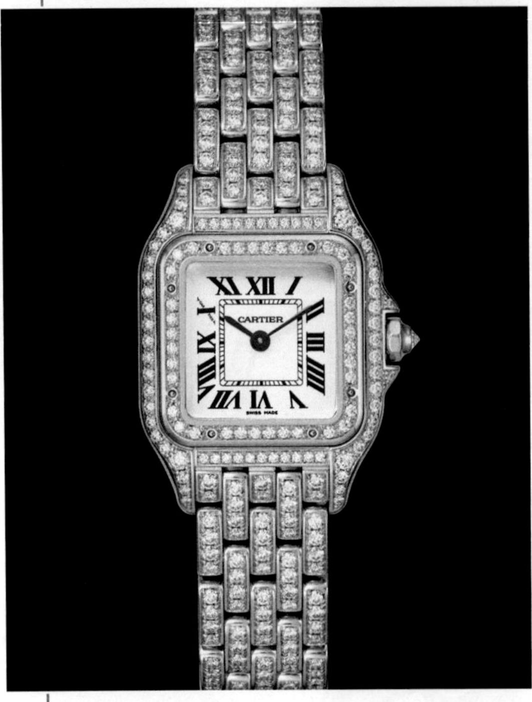

PANTHERE DE CARTIER MEDIUM MODEL REF. WJPN0009

Movement: quartz.
Functions: hours, minutes.
Case: 18K pink gold; 27x37mm, thickness: 6mm; bezel set with brilliant-cut diamonds; 18K pink-gold octagonal crown set with a diamond; water resistant to 3atm.
Dial: silver-finished; blued steel sword-shaped hands.
Bracelet: 18K pink gold.
Price: available upon request.

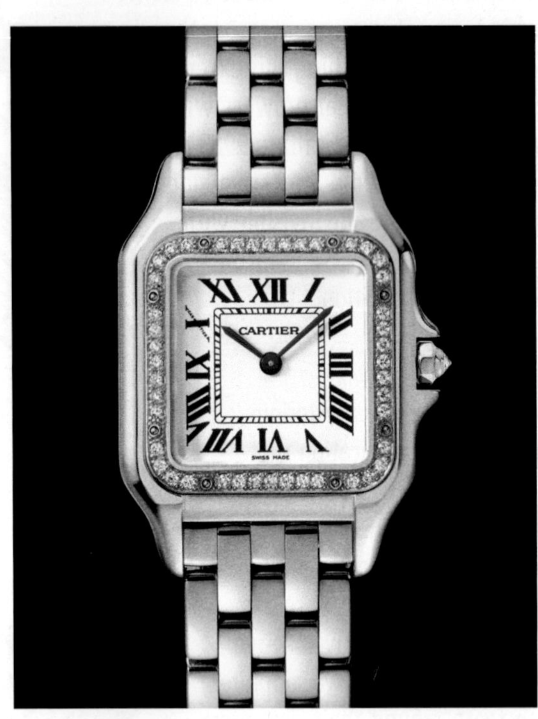

PANTHERE DE CARTIER SMALL MODEL REF. WJPN0006

Movement: quartz.
Functions: hours, minutes.
Case: 18K white gold; 22x30mm, thickness: 6mm; bezel set with brilliant-cut diamonds; 18K white-gold octagonal crown set with a diamond; water resistant to 3atm.
Dial: silver-finished; blued steel sword-shaped hands.
Bracelet: 18K white gold.
Price: available upon request.

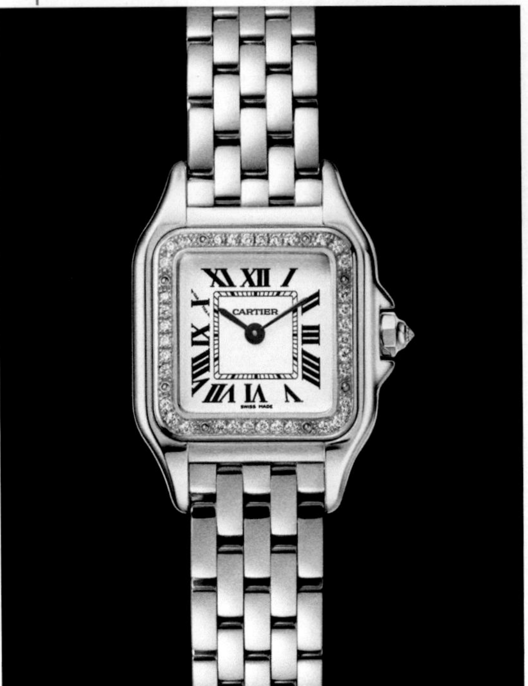

PANTHERE DE CARTIER MEDIUM MODEL REF. WGPN0009

Movement: quartz.
Functions: hours, minutes.
Case: 18K yellow gold; 27x37mm, thickness: 6mm; 18K yellow-gold octagonal crown set with a sapphire; water resistant to 3atm.
Dial: silver-finished; blued steel sword-shaped hands.
Bracelet: 18K yellow gold.
Price: available upon request.

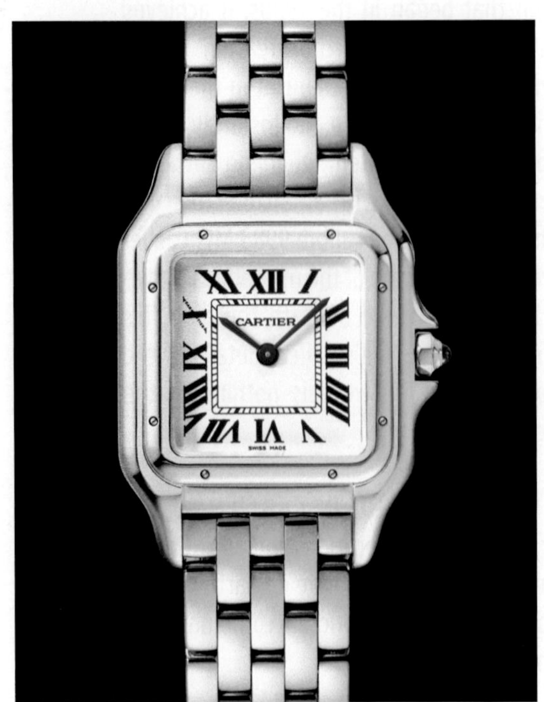

PANTHERE DE CARTIER SMALL MODEL — REF. WGPN0006

Movement: quartz.
Functions: hours, minutes.
Case: 18K pink gold; 22x30mm, thickness: 6mm; 18K pink-gold octagonal crown set with a sapphire; water resistant to 3atm.
Dial: silver-finished; blued steel sword-shaped hands.
Bracelet: 18K pink gold.
Price: available upon request.

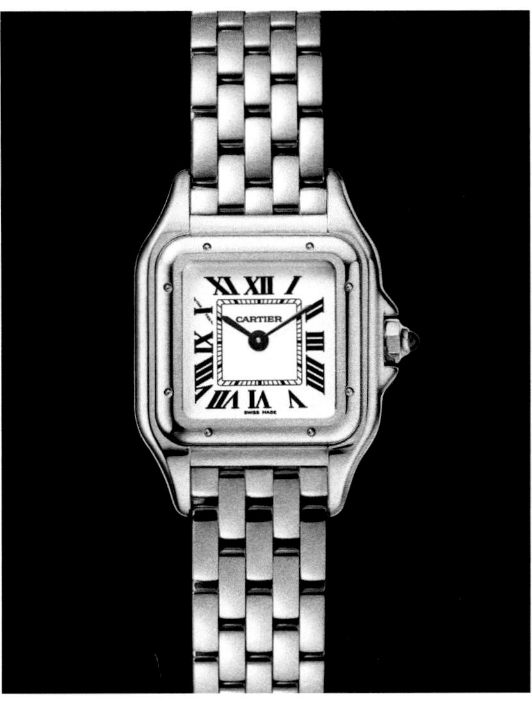

PANTHERE DE CARTIER MEDIUM MODEL — REF. WSPN0007

Movement: quartz.
Functions: hours, minutes.
Case: steel; 27x37mm, thickness: 6mm; steel octagonal crown set with a blue synthetic spinel; water resistant to 3atm.
Dial: silver-finished; blued steel sword-shaped hands.
Bracelet: steel.
Price: available upon request.

PANTHERE DE CARTIER SMALL MODEL — REF. W2PN0006

Movement: quartz.
Functions: hours, minutes.
Case: 18K yellow gold and steel; 22x30mm, thickness: 6mm; 18K yellow-gold octagonal crown set with a blue synthetic spinel; water resistant to 3atm.
Dial: silver-finished; blued steel sword-shaped hands.
Bracelet: 18K yellow gold and steel.
Price: available upon request.

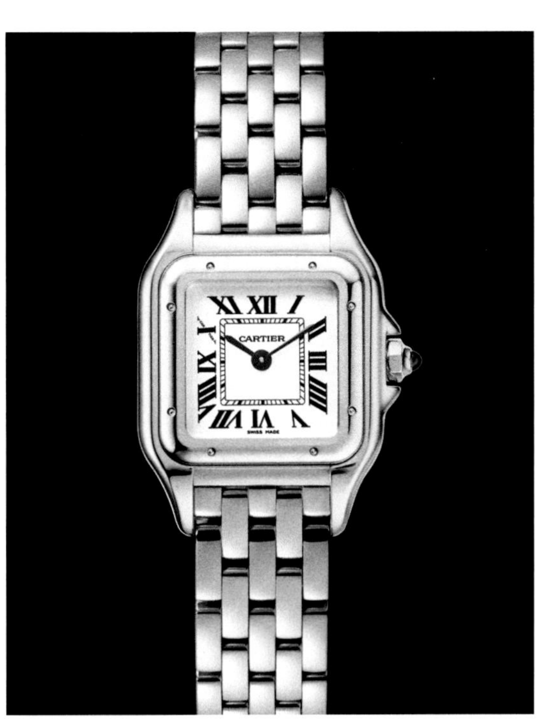

PANTHERE DE CARTIER MEDIUM MODEL — REF. W2PN0007

Movement: quartz.
Functions: hours, minutes.
Case: 18K yellow gold and steel; 27x37mm, thickness: 6mm; 18K yellow-gold octagonal crown set with a blue synthetic spinel; water resistant to 3atm.
Dial: silver-finished; blued steel sword-shaped hands.
Bracelet: 18K yellow gold and steel.
Price: available upon request.

ROTONDE DE CARTIER NIGHT & DAY — REF. HPI01010

Movement: manufacture automatic-winding 9912 MC caliber; 48-hour power reserve.
Functions: hours, minutes; day/night indicator; retrograde moonphase.
Case: 18K pink gold; Ø 40mm, thickness: 11.3mm; bezel set with brilliant-cut diamonds; 18K pink-gold beaded crown set with a diamond; sapphire crystal; sapphire crystal caseback; water resistant to 3atm.
Dial: 18K pink gold and mother-of-pearl; set with brilliant-cut diamonds and orange sapphires; steel hands with pink-gold finish.
Strap: brown alligator leather; 18K pink-gold folding clasp set with brilliant-cut diamonds.
Note: limited edition of 50 individually numbered pieces.
Price: available upon request.

CLE DE CARTIER CREATIVE SERTI VIBRANT — REF. HPI01101

Movement: manufacture automatic-winding 530 MC caliber.
Functions: hours, minutes.
Case: 18K white gold; Ø 40mm, thickness: 12.2mm; set with 447 brilliant-cut diamonds; 18K white-gold crown set with a sapphire and 28 brilliant-cut diamonds; sapphire crystal; sapphire crystal caseback; water resistant to 3atm.
Dial: 18K white gold with NAC treatment; set with 105 vibrating brilliant-cut diamonds and 105 rubies; blued steel sword-shaped hands.
Strap: wine-colored alligator leather; 18K white-gold double adjustable deployant buckle set with 43 brilliant-cut diamonds.
Note: limited edition of 30 individually numbered pieces.
Price: available upon request.

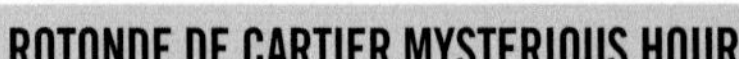

ROTONDE DE CARTIER MYSTERIOUS HOUR — REF. HPI01100

Movement: manufacture manual-winding 9984 MC caliber; 48-hour power reserve.
Functions: mysterious hours and minutes.
Case: 18K white gold; Ø 35mm, thickness: 11.1mm; bezel set with brilliant-cut diamonds; 18K white-gold beaded crown set with a diamond; sapphire crystal; sapphire crystal caseback; water resistant to 3atm.
Dial: stone marquetry; rhodiumized steel sword-shaped hands.
Strap: blue alligator leather; 18K white-gold folding clasp with brilliant-cut diamonds.
Note: limited edition of 50 individually numbered pieces.
Price: available upon request.

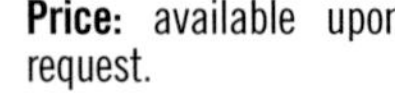

DRIVE DE CARTIER PANTHER DECOR — REF. HPI01099

Movement: manufacture automatic-winding 1904 MC caliber; 48-hour power reserve.
Functions: hours, minutes.
Case: 18K yellow gold; 40x41mm, thickness: 11.25mm; black enamel spots; 18K yellow-gold octagonal crown set with a faceted sapphire; sapphire crystal; sapphire crystal caseback; water resistant to 3atm.
Dial: 18K yellow gold; black enamel spots; steel sword-shaped hands with yellow-gold finish.
Strap: black alligator leather; 18K yellow-gold folding clasp.
Note: limited edition of 100 individually numbered pieces.
Price: available upon request.

DRIVE DE CARTIER MOONPHASE — REF. WGNM0008

Movement: manufacture automatic-winding 1904-LU MC caliber; 48-hour power reserve.
Functions: hours, minutes; moonphase at 6.
Case: 18K pink gold; 40x41mm, thickness: 12.15mm; 18K pink-gold octagonal crown set with a faceted sapphire; sapphire crystal; sapphire crystal caseback; water resistant to 3atm.
Dial: satin-finished guilloché; blued steel sword-shaped hands.
Strap: brown alligator; 18K pink-gold folding clasp.
Price: available upon request.

DRIVE DE CARTIER MOONPHASE — REF. WSNM0008

Movement: manufacture automatic-winding 1904-LU MC caliber; 48-hour power reserve.
Functions: hours, minutes; moonphase at 6.
Case: steel; 40x41mm, thickness: 12.15mm; steel octagonal crown set with a faceted synthetic spinel; sapphire crystal; sapphire crystal caseback; water resistant to 3atm.
Dial: satin-finished guilloché; blued steel sword-shaped hands.
Strap: black alligator leather; steel folding clasp.
Price: available upon request.

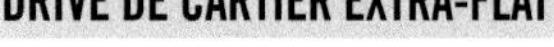

DRIVE DE CARTIER EXTRA-FLAT — REF. WGNM0007

Movement: manufacture manual-winding 430 MC caliber; 40-hour power reserve.
Functions: hours, minutes.
Case: 18K white gold; 38x39mm, thickness: 6.6mm; 18K white-gold octagonal crown set with a faceted sapphire; water resistant to 3atm.
Dial: satin-finished; blued steel sword-shaped hands.
Strap: gray alligator leather; 18K white-gold ardillon buckle.
Note: limited edition of 200 individually numbered pieces.
Price: available upon request.

DRIVE DE CARTIER EXTRA-FLAT — REF. WGNM0006

Movement: manufacture manual-winding 430 MC caliber; 40-hour power reserve.
Functions: hours, minutes.
Case: 18K pink gold; 38x39mm, thickness: 6.6mm; 18K pink-gold octagonal crown set with a faceted sapphire; water resistant to 3atm.
Dial: satin-finished; blued steel sword-shaped hands.
Strap: brown alligator leather; 18K pink-gold ardillon buckle.
Price: available upon request.

Chopard

FREEDOM OF MOVEMENT

Whether allowing precious stones to roam about the dial, capturing the measure of time in its smallest and largest increments, or reviving the irresistible aesthetics of vintage automobiles, Chopard demonstrates **A SUPERB BALANCE OF FINESSE, TECHNICAL SKILL AND VERSATILITY**.

▲ **HAPPY DIAMONDS**

Bound only by the desires of their wearer, 15 diamonds move freely around the mother-of-pearl dial of this sparkling ladies' timepiece.

With the Happy Diamonds, the Swiss horologer adorns the lady's wrist with shimmering luxury, freely roving around the dial to follow her every movement. The 18-karat white-gold timepiece begins its sparkling tale with a bezel embellished by a row of prong-set diamonds. Within the enclosure, 15 mobile stones of varying sizes are free to pirouette about a dial whose mother-of-pearl backdrop provides a radiant stage. Invented in 1976, the concept of moving diamonds brings scintillating vivacity to a timepiece as contemporary as it is timeless. In the center of the watch, a two-tier diamond-set bezel plays off the cushion shape of the case with its circular nature, subtly commanding attention without interrupting the visual exhibition. Indicating the hours and minutes on a mother-of-pearl inner dial, two hands conduct their own choreography, bound by the precise rules of time, unlike the irresistible gems that dance without inhibition just millimeters away.

The partner and official timekeeper of the unparalleled Mille Miglia rally, Chopard expresses its love of racing and vintage aesthetics with a timepiece evocative of the dashboard of a finely tuned classic car.

As devoted to time's largest increments as to its smallest intervals, the L.U.C Perpetual Chrono combines the vital precision of its column-wheel chronograph with the extraordinary sophistication of a perpetual calendar. Driven by the L.U.C Calibre 03.10-L, certified by both the COSC and Poinçon de Genève for its mechanical excellence, the 45mm timepiece achieves remarkable clarity thanks to a clever use of space and symmetry. At 9 o'clock, mirroring the geometry of the month, leap-year and 30-minute-counter subdial found at 3 o'clock, the timepiece unites the day/night indicator, day of the week and 12-hour counter in a single legible subsection. At 12 o'clock, a large twin-aperture display indicates the date, while a colorful opening on the lower half of the hand-guilloché dial reveals the running seconds atop a vibrant moon-phase display (which needs only one adjustment every 122 years). A central sweeping hand, red-tipped for optimal readability, indicates the column-wheel chronograph's seconds and may be stopped, reset and restarted with a single press of a button thanks to the movement's flyback functionality. The L.U.C Perpetual Chrono is housed in a case entirely composed of "Fairmined" 18-karat white gold, reflecting Chopard's devotion to responsible mining and to the support of mining communities throughout the world.

The Mille Miglia 2016 XL Race Edition pays unmistakable homage to the timeless design codes of vintage racing automobiles. The partner and official timekeeper of the Mille Miglia rally, in which the racecars all date between 1927 to 1957, Chopard expresses its love of racing and vintage aesthetics with a timepiece evocative of the dashboard of a finely tuned classic car. The generously sized 46mm wristwatch, housed in a stainless steel case, sets off its black dial with a number of luminous elements and clear contrasts. Driven by COSC-certified self-winding 03.05-C caliber, the watch's 28,800 vph chronograph indicates its sweeping seconds using a bright red stem that stands out perfectly from the entire design. Three subdials, representing the 12-hour and 30-minute counters of the chronograph, at 9 and 3 o'clock, as well as small seconds, at 6 o'clock, join a discreet date aperture in the lower-right quadrant to complete the animations on the dial. Surrounding them, a tachymeter scale, used in conjunction with the chronograph's sweeping hand, allows the wearer to measure velocities against set distances. The Mille Miglia 2016 XL Race Edition is limited to 1,000 pieces and worn on a finely weathered "Suportlo ™" calfskin strap.

▲ **L.U.C PERPETUAL CHRONO** *(top)*

Chopard's artistic ingenuity allows the dial of this hyper-sophisticated hand-wound timepiece to display a full perpetual calendar and flyback chronograph with remarkable clarity.

▲ **MILLE MIGLIA 2016 XL RACE EDITION** *(bottom)*

This tribute to the "world's most beautiful race," complete with chronograph and tachymeter scale, evokes the timeless elegance of vintage automobiles.

L.U.C PERPETUAL CHRONO — REF. 161973-1001

Movement: manual-winding L.U.C 03.10-L caliber; Ø 33mm, thickness: 8.32mm; 60-hour power reserve; 42 jewels; 28,800 vph; certified chronometer; Hallmark of Geneva; Côtes de Genève-adorned bridges.
Functions: hours, minutes; small seconds on moonphase at 6; perpetual calendar: date at 12, day at 9, month at 3, leap year at 2; day/night indicator at 10; chronograph: central seconds hand, 30-minute counter at 3, 12-hour counter at 9.
Case: 18K "fairmined" white gold; Ø 45mm, thickness: 15.06mm; 18K white-gold crown with L.U.C logo; antireflective sapphire crystal; water resistant to 3atm.
Dial: ruthenium-toned sunburst satin-brushed and hand-guilloché gold; rhodiumed Roman numerals and hour markers; rhodiumed dauphine-type hands; baton-type rhodiumed red-tipped sweep seconds hand.
Strap: hand-sewn black alligator leather; 18K white-gold "fairmined" pin buckle.
Note: limited edition of 20 pieces.
Suggested price: $85,000
Also available: 18K rose-gold "fairmined" pin buckle (ref. 161973-5001).

L.U.C PERPETUAL TWIN — REF. 168561-3001

Movement: automatic-winding L.U.C 96.51-L caliber; Ø 33mm, thickness: 6mm; 58-hour power reserve; 27 jewels; 28,800 vph; certified chronometer; Côtes de Genève-adorned bridges.
Functions: hours, minutes; small seconds at 6; perpetual calendar: date at 12, day at 9, month at 3, leap year between 2 and 3.
Case: stainless steel; Ø 43mm, thickness: 11.47mm; polished bezel and caseback; stainless steel crown with L.U.C logo; antireflective sapphire crystal; water resistant to 3atm.

Dial: silver-toned; rhodiumed dauphine-type hands; rhodiumed red-tipped triangular leap-year hands; rhodiumed Roman numerals.
Strap: hand-sewn black alligator leather; steel pin buckle.
Suggested price: $22,890

L.U.C XPS 1860 — REF. 161946-5001

Movement: automatic-winding L.U.C 96.01-L caliber; Ø 27.4mm, thickness: 3.3mm; 65-hour power reserve; 29 jewels; 28,800 vph; certified chronometer; Hallmark of Geneva; Côtes de Genève-adorned bridges.
Functions: hours, minutes; small seconds and date at 6.
Case: 18K rose gold; Ø 40mm, thickness: 7.2mm; polished bezel and caseback; 18K rose-gold crown with L.U.C logo; antireflective sapphire crystal; water resistant to 3atm.
Dial: silver-toned gold; hand-guilloché center with sunburst satin-brushed surround; gilt dauphine-type hands.
Strap: hand-sewn matte brown alligator leather; 18K rose-gold pin buckle.
Note: limited edition of 250 pieces.
Suggested price: $20,250
Also available: stainless steel case, $8,410 (ref. 168583-3001).

L.U.C XPS FAIRMINED — REF. 161920-5006

Movement: automatic-winding L.U.C 96.12-L caliber; Ø 27.4mm, thickness: 3.3mm; 65-hour power reserve; 29 jewels; 28,800 vph; certified chronometer; Côtes de Genève-adorned bridges.
Functions: hours, minutes; small seconds at 6.
Case: 18K "fairmined" rose gold; Ø 39.5mm, thickness: 7.13mm; polished case middle, bezel and caseback; 18K rose-gold crown with L.U.C logo; antireflective sapphire crystal; water resistant to 3atm.
Dial: slate-gray galvanic; gilt dauphine-type hour and minute hands; gilt small seconds hand.

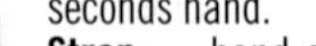

Strap: hand-sewn matte black alligator leather; 18K rose-gold pin buckle.
Note: limited edition of 250 pieces; Chopard boutique exclusive.
Suggested price: $18,900

L.U.C REGULATOR REF. 161971-5001

Movement: manual-winding L.U.C 98.02-L caliber; Ø 30.4mm, thickness: 4.9mm; 216-hour power reserve; 39 jewels; 28,800 vph; certified chronometer; Hallmark of Geneva; Côtes de Genève-adorned bridges.
Functions: minutes; hours at 3; small seconds at 6; date between 4 and 5; GMT at 9; power reserve indicator at 12.
Case: 18K rose gold; Ø 43mm, thickness: 9.78mm; polished bezel; 18K rose-gold crown with L.U.C logo; antireflective sapphire crystal; water resistant to 5atm.
Dial: sunburst satin-brushed silver-toned; gilt dauphine-type hour and minute hands; black triangular small seconds, GMT and power reserve hands.
Strap: hand-sewn brown alligator leather; 18K rose-gold pin buckle.
Suggested price: $33,530

L.U.C 1963 TOURBILLON REF. 161970-5001

Movement: manual-winding L.U.C 02.19-L1 caliber; Ø 29.7mm, thickness: 5.5mm; 216-hour power reserve; 33 jewels; 28,800 vph; certified chronometer; Hallmark of Geneva; Côtes de Genève-adorned bridges.
Functions: hours, minutes; small seconds on tourbillon at 6; power reserve indicator at 12.
Case: 18K rose gold; Ø 40mm, thickness: 10.6mm; polished bezel and caseback; 18K rose-gold crown with L.U.C logo; antireflective sapphire crystal; water resistant to 5atm.
Dial: white Grand Feu enamel; gilt dauphine-type hour and minute hands; gilt small seconds hand and power reserve indicator.
Strap: hand-sewn brown alligator leather; 18K rose-gold pin buckle.
Note: limited edition of 100 pieces.
Suggested price: available upon request.

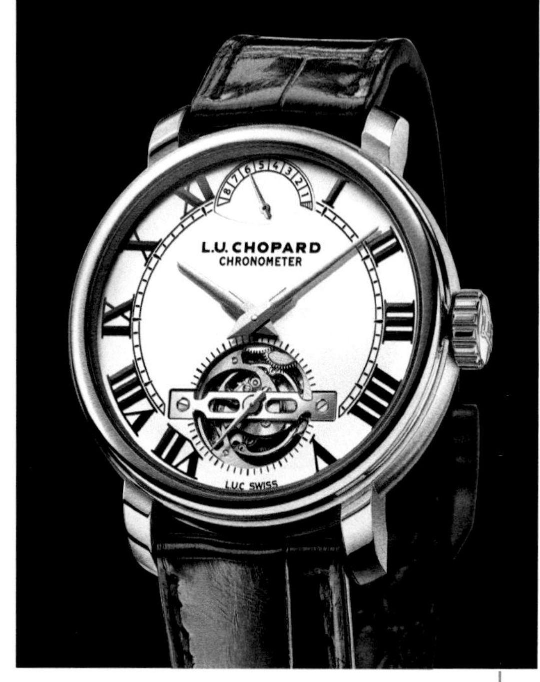

L.U.C QUATTRO REF. 161926-9001

Movement: manual-winding L.U.C 98.01-L caliber; Ø 28.6mm, thickness: 3.7mm; 216-hour power reserve; 39 jewels; 28,800 vph; certified chronometer; Hallmark of Geneva; Côtes de Genève-adorned bridges.
Functions: hours, minutes; small seconds and date at 6; power reserve indicator at 12.
Case: platinum; Ø 43mm, thickness: 8.87mm; 18K white-gold crown with L.U.C logo; antireflective sapphire crystal; water resistant to 5atm.
Dial: blue-gray sunburst satin-brushed; rhodiumed hour markers; rhodiumed hands.
Strap: hand-sewn navy blue alligator leather; 18K white-gold pin buckle.
Suggested price: $32,630
Also available: 18K rose-gold case, brown dial, brown alligator leather strap, $26,510 (ref. 161926-5003).

L.U.C XP 35MM ESPRIT DE FLEURIER PEONY REF. 131944-5001

Movement: automatic-winding L.U.C 96.23-L caliber; Ø 27.4mm, thickness: 3.3mm; 65-hour power reserve; 29 jewels; 28,800 vph.
Functions: hours, minutes.
Case: 18K rose gold; Ø 35mm, thickness: 7.5mm; 18K rose-gold crown with L.U.C logo; diamond-set flanks, lugs and case middle; antireflective sapphire crystal; water resistant to 3atm.
Dial: gold; coated with Tahitian mother-of-pearl; diamond-set peony motif; gilt dauphine-type hour and minute hands.
Strap: brushed pink canvas; diamond-set 18K rose-gold pin buckle.
Note: limited edition of 8 pieces; Chopard boutique exclusive.
Suggested price: $98,000

MILLE MIGLIA 2016 XL RACE EDITION — REF. 168580-3001

Movement: automatic-winding 03.05-C caliber; Ø 28.8mm; approx. 60-hour power reserve; 45 jewels; 28,800 vph; certified chronometer.
Functions: hours, minutes, seconds; date between 4 and 5; chronograph: 60-second counter at 6, 30-minute counter at 3, 12-hour counter at 9.
Case: stainless steel; Ø 46mm, thickness: 14.17mm; stainless steel crown; antireflective sapphire crystal; water resistant to 5atm.
Dial: circular satin-brushed black; SuperLumiNova-painted hour numerals; rhodiumed hour and minute hands; red sweep seconds hand.
Strap: brown "Suportlo®" calfskin leather; stainless steel folding clasp.
Note: limited edition of 1,000 pieces.
Suggested price: $9,800

MILLE MIGLIA GTS AUTOMATIC SPEED BLACK — REF. 168565-3002

Movement: automatic-winding Chopard 01.01-M caliber; Ø 28.8mm, thickness: 4.95mm; approx. 60-hour power reserve; 31 jewels; 28,800 vph; certified chronometer.
Functions: hours, minutes, seconds; date at 3.
Case: DLC-coated blackened steel; Ø 43mm, thickness: 11.43mm; bezel with aluminum insert with shiny black numerals; DLC-coated blackened steel crown; antireflective sapphire crystal; water resistant to 10atm.
Dial: velvet-finish matte black; faceted hands with SuperLumiNova; black metalized numerals and appliqués with SuperLumiNova; red sweep seconds hand.
Strap: rubber; inspired by 1960s Dunlop racing tires; beadblasted DLC-coated blackened stainless steel folding clasp.
Note: limited edition of 1,000 pieces.
Suggested price: $6,900

GRAND PRIX DE MONACO HISTORIQUE 2016 RACE EDITION — REF. 168570-3002

Movement: automatic-winding; Ø 37.2mm; approx. 46-hour power reserve; 25 jewels; 28,800 vph; certified chronometer.
Functions: hours, minutes, seconds; date at 3; chronograph: 60-second counter at 9, 30-minute counter at 12, 12-hour counter at 6.
Case: shotblasted titanium and stainless steel; Ø 44.5mm, thickness: 14.1mm; stainless steel bezel with gray inlay; titanium crown; antireflective sapphire crystal; caseback stamped with the Automobile Club de Monaco logo; water resistant to 10atm.
Dial: silver-toned snailed; painted metallic black hour and minute hands with SuperLumiNova; orange central sweep seconds hand; metallic black counter pointers.
Strap: gray Barenia calfskin with orange stitching.
Note: limited edition of 500 pieces.
Suggested price: $6,890
Also available: rose-gold case, limited edition of 100 pieces (ref. 161294-5001).

SUPERFAST CHRONO PORSCHE 919 BLACK EDITION — REF. 168535-3005

Movement: automatic-winding Chopard 03.05-M caliber; Ø 28.8mm; 60-hour power reserve; 45 jewels; 28,800 vph; certified chronometer.
Functions: hours, minutes, seconds; date between 4 and 5; chronograph: 60-second counter at 6, 30-minute counter at 3, 12-hour counter at 9; tachymeter scale.
Case: DLC-blackened titanium; Ø 45mm, thickness: 15.18mm; engraved and black-lacquered titanium bezel; matte black rubber-coated screw-down crown; antireflective sapphire crystal; water resistant to 10atm.
Dial: matte black; SuperLumiNova metallic black hour and minute hands; metallic hour markers; arrow-tipped central sweep seconds hand; red minute and hour counter hands; metallic black seconds counter hand.
Strap: black rubber; beadblasted DLC-blackened titanium folding clasp.
Note: limited edition of 100 pieces; Chopard boutique exclusive.
Suggested price: $14,370

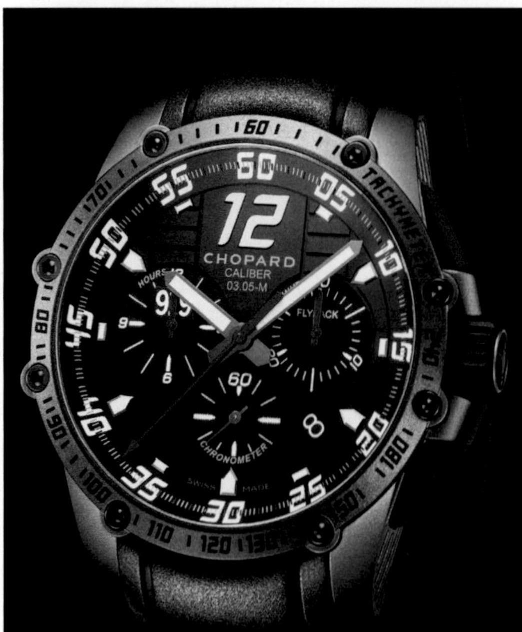

SUPERFAST PORSCHE MOTORSPORT 919 LIMITED VICTORY EDITION REF. 168535-6001

Movement: automatic-winding Chopard 03.05-M caliber; Ø 28.8mm; 60-hour power reserve; 45 jewels; 28,800 vph; certified chronometer.
Functions: hours, minutes, seconds; date between 4 and 5; chronograph: 60-second counter at 6, 30-minute counter at 3, 12-hour counter at 9; tachymeter scale.
Case: stainless steel; Ø 45mm, thickness: 15.18mm; 18K rose-gold bezel; screw-down crown with steering wheel in black rubber-molded stainless steel; antireflective sapphire crystal; water resistant to 10atm.
Dial: opaline silver-toned; metallic black hours, minutes and hour markers with SuperLumiNova; arrow-tipped central red sweep seconds hand; red chronograph hour and minute counter hands; metallic black chronograph seconds hand.
Strap: black rubber; polished stainless steel folding clasp.
Note: limited edition of 17 pieces; Chopard boutique exclusive.
Suggested price: $15,870

MILLE MIGLIA GTS POWER CONTROL REF. 168566-3001

Movement: automatic-winding Chopard 01.08-C caliber; Ø 28.6mm, thickness: 4.95mm; approx. 60-hour power reserve; 40 jewels; 28,800 vph; certified chronometer.
Functions: hours, minutes, seconds; date at 3; power reserve indicator at 9.
Case: stainless steel; Ø 43mm, thickness: 11.43mm; steel bezel with black aluminum insert; steel crown; antireflective sapphire crystal; water resistant to 10atm.
Dial: matte velvet-finish black; SuperLumiNova rhodiumed numerals and appliqués; rhodiumed hour and minute hands; red seconds hand.
Strap: rubber; inspired by 1960s Dunlop racing tires; steel folding clasp.
Suggested price: $6,640
Also available: 18K rose-gold case, rubber strap, $22,390 (ref. 161296-5001); steel bracelet, $8,250 (ref. 158566-3001).

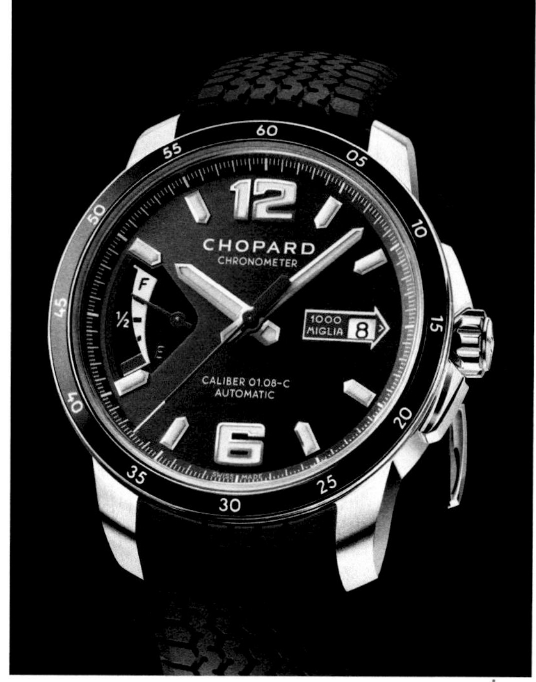

HAPPY DIAMONDS REF. 204368-1001

Movement: quartz.
Functions: hours, minutes.
Case: 18K white gold; Ø 37.85mm; bezel set with diamonds; crown set with diamonds; antireflective sapphire crystal; water resistant to 3atm.
Dial: mother-of-pearl; central ring set with diamonds; 15 moving diamonds.
Strap: black brushed canvas.
Note: limited edition of 150 pieces; Chopard boutique exclusive.
Suggested price: $48,500

HAPPY SPORT 36MM REF. 278582-3003

Movement: quartz.
Functions: hours, minutes, seconds; date between 4 and 5.
Case: stainless steel; Ø 36mm; bezel set with diamonds (1.96 carats); sapphire crown; antireflective sapphire crystal; water resistant to 3atm.
Dial: white; 4 Roman numerals; 5 moving diamonds.
Strap: interchangeable rubber.
Suggested price: $13,840
Also available: without diamonds on bezel, $4,940 (ref. 278582-3001).

NEVER CONFORM

No matter the theme, no matter the concept, Christophe Claret boldly **DEMONSTRATES TRANSFORMATIVE AUDACITY AND ANTI-CONFORMIST CREATIVITY** with every twist and turn of his inimitable path.

▲ **MAESTRO**

This multi-dimensional timepiece turns mechanical components into visual works of art thanks to an imaginative take on horological architecture.

Dynamic, multi-dimensional and vibrantly imaginative, the Maestro turns mechanical functionality into an irresistible visual work of art. The 42mm timepiece, endowed with a glass dome that doubles as a bezel, treats its owner to a breathtaking view of the watchmaker's mechanical creativity. Along with its multi-layered revelation of a number of the hand-wound DMC16 caliber's 342 components, including the balance wheel, cylindrical balance spring and Swiss lever escapement, the Maestro presents a captivating exhibition of Christophe Claret's unique vision of timekeeping. A patented dual-cone architecture, at 5 o'clock, indicates the date as the upper and lower portions rotate to display the tens and ones, respectively, within a sharp, colorful frame extending from a bridge at 6 o'clock. Endowed with semi-instantaneous jump functionality, the complication is topped with a ruby or sapphire for a luxurious final touch. The Maestro also serves as a clever companion for those seeking a daily reminder to perform a task they simply cannot afford to forget. The device, positioned between 3 and 4 o'clock, indicates the word MEMO until the simple press of a pusher pivots the module, only to be reset automatically each night via a semi-instantaneous jump system. Housed in a case in grade-5 titanium or 5N red gold, both versions of the timepiece are available in a limited edition of 88 pieces. Boasting a large seven-day power reserve, the Maestro blends creative complications, mechanical components and exquisitely designed bridges, completing its three-dimensional spectacle with a splendid view of one of the movement's two series-coupled barrels at 12 o'clock.

As hundreds of sparkling stones light with the fluttering butterflies, the Marguerite Sertie's mother-of-pearl dial transports its romance straight into the realm of daydreams.

Even in the most romantic of contexts, Christophe Claret adorns the wrist with his incomparable balance of watchmaking creativity and mechanical virtuosity.

The Marguerite Sertie enlivens its wearer's most enchanting adventures with a luxurious floral exhibition and a secret visual display meant just for her at the press of a button. Shimmering with more than 600 diamonds between the bezel, lugs and central flower, the 42.5mm timepiece transports its owner to a majestic meadow, indicating the hours and minutes by way of two floating butterflies around a scintillating daisy finished with a vibrant pistil ruby. As the hundreds of sparkling stones share each ray of incoming light with the fluttering butterflies, a mother-of-pearl dial lends depth and irresistible gleam to the entire design, transporting its romance straight into the realm of daydreams. While the white- or 5N red-gold timepiece displays Arabic numerals at 3, 6 and 9 o'clock in its passive state, a press of the pusher at 2 o'clock reveals a personalized message meant just for its wearer. Once the button is released, the secret is veiled once more thanks to Christophe Claret's ingenious incorporation of superimposed discs. Driven by the self-winding MT115 caliber, the Marguerite Sertie extends its romantic DNA to the caseback, where a spin of the oscillating weight brings the wearer back to a simpler time with a fitting game of "he loves me, he loves me not." The Marguerite comes in a total of 6 different versions, each one limited to 30 pieces.

▲ **MARGUERITE SERTIE**

More than 600 diamonds shed luxurious light onto this romantic timepiece that tugs on its wearer's heartstrings with a secret customizable message meant for her eyes only.

The Soprano epitomizes Christophe Claret's mastery of haute horology's most sophisticated pursuits, combining two revered complications within a design that leaves its wearer in awe of its skeletonized architecture and sonorous showcase. Poised with regal grace beneath an openworked Charles X-style bridge at 6 o'clock, the Soprano's finely sculpted tourbillon performs itcomplete rotation every 60 seconds thanks to the precise heartbeat of the 450-component TRD98 caliber. In typical Christophe Claret fashion, the timepiece goes one step further, boasting a Westminster-chime minute repeater enhanced for heightened complexity. Fitted with four cathedral gongs and four hammers, all visible through the dial-side exhibition, the audible complication produces a supreme quality of sound thanks to the manufacture's meticulous care for detail and inclusion of a patented invention that protects the minute repeater from excessive vibrations, consequently eliminating any unwanted buzzing. Optimal resonance is also achieved through the manufacture's choice of materials for the 45mm case. Available in 5N red gold and chocolate-brown PVD-treated titanium, white gold and black PVD-treated titanium or white gold and slate-blue PVD-treated titanium, and each version limited to 8 timepieces, the Soprano achieves its powerful low-pitch sound while endowing the visual design with an exterior perfectly in line with the daring dial-side revelation of the movement's sophisticated construction.

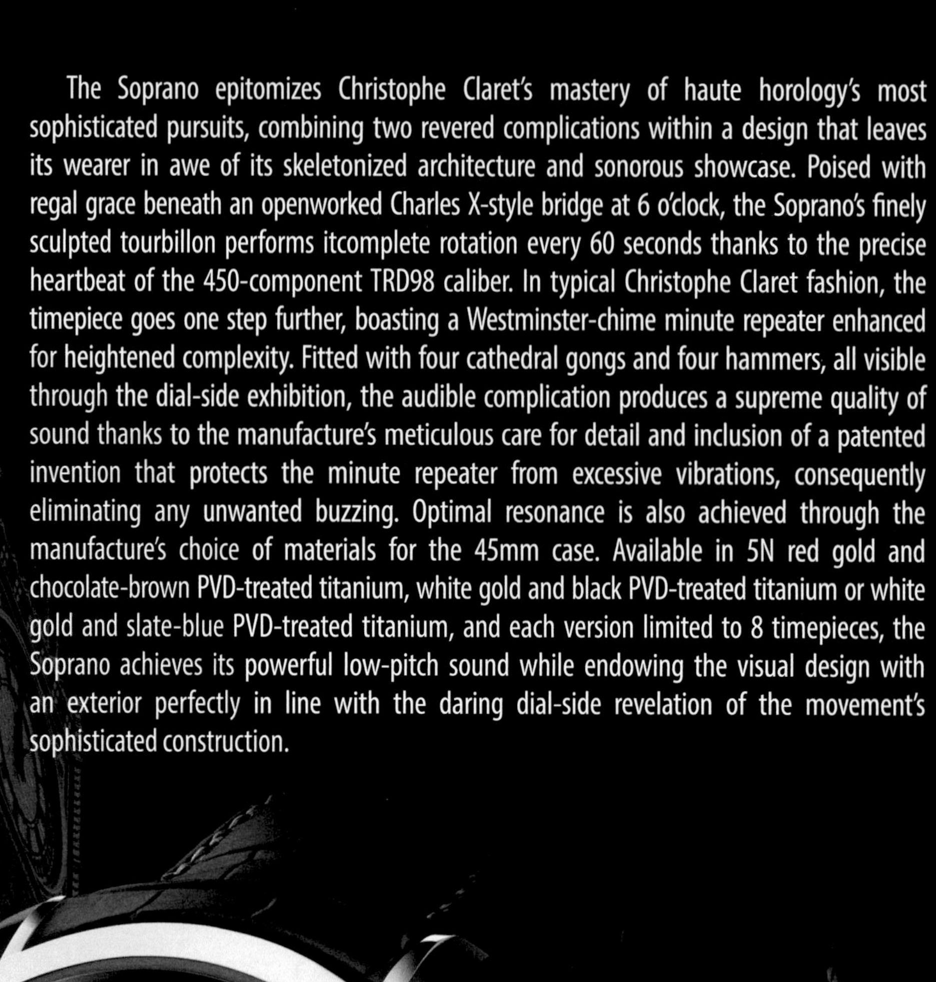

▸ **SOPRANO**

This sophisticated skeletonized timepiece combines a four-gong minute repeater with a 60-second tourbillon.

With the X-TREM-1, Christophe Claret pushes the boundaries of modern haute horology, turning an archenemy of the mechanical art form into a spectacular ally.

While high-end watchmaking has long fought to combat the negative effects of magnetism on mechanical calibers, the Swiss visionary turns foe into friend with an ultra-imaginative retrograde display of the hours and minutes. Positioned to the left and right of the primary structure, two steel spheres, contained within sapphire tubes and with no mechanical connection to the movement, travel as if magically up and down their enclosures, controlled by high-precision magnets moved by cables within the 419-component hand-wound FLY11 caliber. On the lower portion of the structure, Christophe Claret integrates a generously sized tourbillon, inclined at 30° for excellent visibility and endowed with double ceramic bearings for optimal resistance to shocks. By crafting the case in two 8-piece limited edition versions of white or 5N red gold and damascened steel, the Swiss manufacture reaches more than 4,500 years into the past in its quest for avant-garde haute horology. Long regarded as the finest material in the construction of extremely sharp blades, the high-end alloy now bestows its exceptional properties and strength onto a timepiece of ultimate distinction and sophistication.

▲ **X-TREM-1**

Housed in a case made of damascened steel and white gold, this transcendent timepiece uses high-precision magnetic fields to control a fascinating retrograde display of the hours and minutes.

BRIDGE TO EVERYWHERE

Corum **SHOWCASES ITS ARCHITECTURAL VIRTUOSITY** with two stunning and imaginative interpretations of the watchmaker's celebrated in-line mechanical movement.

The Golden Bridge Round wears its inspiration with unmistakable pride. A brilliant play on the brand's iconic Golden Bridge baguette movement, the timepiece complements its centerpiece with a stunning interpretation of one of the Seven Wonders of the Modern World. A masterful 18-karat-gold miniaturization of San Francisco's Golden Gate Bridge, on the left and right side of the openworked dial, creates a striking visual passageway around the timepiece's movement. The symbolic fusion of large- and small-scale architecture would of course not be possible without Corum's micro-mechanical chef d'oeuvre. Aligned vertically on the dial's central axis, the CO113 caliber provides a unique and breathtaking 360º view of its finely finished gears and components. Corum honors its muse with a round case whose colorful warmth evokes the famous hue of San Francisco's emblematic suspended bridge. Crafted in 18-karat rose gold, the timepiece's 43mm case offers a vibrant contrast to the decisive linear framework of the dial. The hand-wound 28,800 vph movement, which drives a central display of the hours and minutes via two faceted yellow-gold hands, ensures excellent reliability thanks to its integration of a variable-inertia balance and barrel with slipping spring. The Golden Bridge Round, created with celebrated designer Dino Modolo, is worn on an alligator leather strap with 18-karat rose-gold buckle.

One hundred and six round diamonds complement the 76 precious stones adorning the bezel and lugs for an enchanting spectacle of light that shines from all angles onto the resplendent Lady Golden Bridge Round.

In unveiling its Lady Golden Bridge Round 39mm, Corum adorns the feminine wrist with an enthralling play on contrasting shapes, colors and precious materials. The 18-karat rose-gold wristwatch begins its narrative with the brilliant revelation of the manufacture's in-line CO113 caliber. By turning it on its side, Corum endows the movement with a new, energetic voice. Atop and beneath the hand-wound caliber, two semi-circles in precious resin bring radiant vigor to the design while their tasteful apertures, used to display two Roman numerals and four hour markers, subtly play off the superb transparency of their central mechanical companion. Scintillating luxury also takes the stage: set onto the movement's two horizontal borders and onto the flange of the dial, 106 round diamonds complement the 76 precious stones adorning the bezel and lugs for an enchanting spectacle of light that shines from all angles onto the resplendent, multi-faceted design. Housed in a 39mm round case that lends aesthetic complexity to the movement's horizontal architecture, the Lady Golden Bridge Round is worn on an eggplant-colored alligator leather strap that brings yet another touch of contrast to the exquisite Art Deco creation.

▲ **LADY GOLDEN BRIDGE ROUND 39MM**
Precious resin, rose gold and diamonds come together to embellish the brilliant interplay of geometric shapes of this timepiece's round case and horizontally aligned caliber.

◄ **GOLDEN BRIDGE ROUND**
This 18-karat rose-gold timepiece complements the captivating architecture of its in-line caliber with a miniature sculpture of the Golden Gate Bridge.

ADMIRAL'S CUP LEGEND 47 WORLDTIMER REF. A637/02743-637.101.05/F371AN01

Movement: automatic-winding CO637 caliber; 16 ¼ lines; 48-hour power reserve; 31 jewels; 28,800 vph.
Functions: hours, minutes, seconds; second time zone; city indicator.
Case: grade 2 titanium; Ø 47mm, thickness: 17.2mm; 5N 18K rose-gold bezel; antireflective sapphire crystal; sapphire crystal caseback with city indication for each time zone; water resistant to 10atm.
Dial: smoky sapphire crystal; brass openworked dauphine-shaped hands with Super-LumiNova.
Strap: black vulcanized rubber; stainless steel triple-blade folding clasp.
Suggested price: $15,800

ADMIRAL 32 REF. A400/02902-400.100.29/V200 PN13

Movement: automatic-winding CO 400 caliber; 9 lines; 40-hour power reserve; 18 jewels; 28,800 vph.
Functions: hours, minutes.
Case: stainless steel; Ø 32mm, thickness: 8.9mm; 5N 18K red-gold bezel set with 52 round diamonds (0.78 carat); 5N 18K red-gold crown; antireflective sapphire crystal; water resistant to 5atm.
Dial: white mother-of-pearl; set with 12 diamond indexes; 5N red-gold-coated dauphine-shaped hour and minute hands.
Bracelet: stainless steel and 5N 18K red gold; stainless steel triple-folding clasp.
Suggested price: $13,900

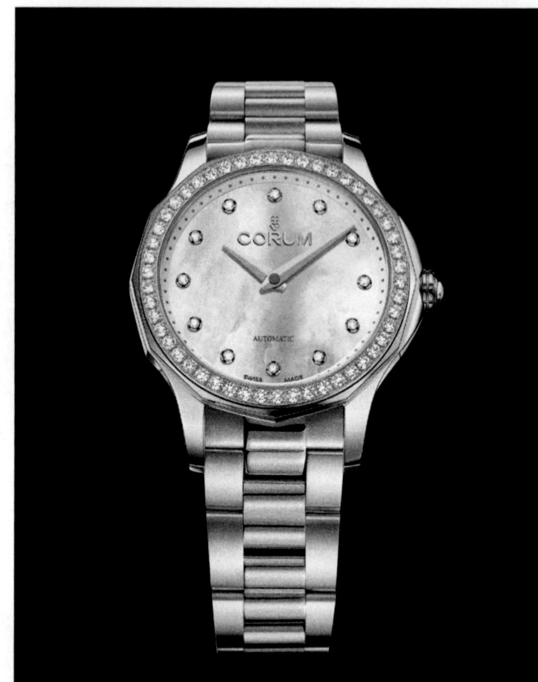

BUBBLE ROULETTE REF. L082/02958-082.310.20/0371 CA01

Movement: automatic-winding CO 082 caliber; 11 ½ lines; 42-hour power reserve; 21 jewels; 28,800 vph.
Functions: hours, minutes, seconds.
Case: stainless steel; Ø 47mm, thickness: 18.5mm; antireflective sapphire crystal; antireflective sapphire crystal caseback; water resistant to 10atm.
Dial: brass; roulette wheel outer ring; brass skeletonized rhodium-finished hands.
Strap: black rubber.
Note: limited edition of 288 pieces.
Suggested price: $5,000

BUBBLE JOKER REF. L082/03037-082.310.20/0371J001

Movement: automatic-winding CO 082 caliber; 11 ½ lines; 42-hour power reserve; 21 jewels; 28,800 vph.
Functions: hours, minutes, seconds.
Case: stainless steel; Ø 47mm, thickness: 18.5mm; antireflective sapphire crystal; antireflective sapphire crystal caseback; water resistant to 10atm.
Dial: white brass; brass openworked leaf-shaped hands with black varnish.
Strap: black rubber; stainless steel pin buckle.
Note: limited edition of 88 pieces.

Suggested price: $4,500

BUBBLE SUPERLUMINOVA REF. L082/03025-082.310.98/0371 BR01

Movement: automatic-winding CO 082 caliber; 11 ½ lines; 42-hour power reserve; 21 jewels; 28,800 vph.
Functions: hours, minutes, seconds.
Case: stainless steel with black PVD treatment; Ø 47mm, thickness: 18.5mm; antireflective sapphire crystal; stainless steel caseback with antireflective sapphire crystal; water resistant to 10atm.
Dial: black brass; black leaf-shaped hands with red SuperLumiNova.
Strap: black vulcanized rubber; stainless steel tongue buckle with black PVD treatment.
Note: limited edition of 88 pieces.
Suggested price: $3,800

BUBBLE MOTHER-OF-PEARL REF. L295/03051-295.100.29/0088 DN36

Movement: automatic-winding CO 295 caliber; 11 ½ lines; 72-hour power reserve; 30 jewels; 21,600 vph.
Functions: hours, minutes; small seconds at 6.
Case: stainless steel; Ø 42mm, thickness: 16.5mm; 5N 18K red-gold bezel set with 50 round diamonds (4.47 carats); 5N 18K red-gold crown; antireflective sapphire crystal; stainless steel caseback with antireflective sapphire crystal; water resistant to 10atm.
Dial: pink mother-of-pearl; 5N red-gold indexes.
Strap: pink alligator leather; stainless steel ardillon buckle.
Suggested price: $15,700

DIPHYLLEIA REF. Z055/03045-055.100.85/0009 0000

Movement: manual-winding CO 055 caliber; 9 lines; 40-hour power reserve; 18 jewels; 21,600 vph.
Functions: hours, minutes.
Case: 5N 18K pink gold; Ø 34mm, thickness: 7.3mm; bezel set with 22 diamonds (5.3 carats); crown set with a diamond (0.03 carat); antireflective sapphire crystal; antireflective sapphire crystal caseback; water resistant to 1atm.
Dial: skeletonized; black-coated brass leaf-shaped hands.
Strap: white alligator leather; 5N 18K pink-gold buckle.
Note: limited edition of 8 pieces.
Suggested price: $64,800

COIN REF. C082/02481-082.645.56/0001 MU52

Movement: automatic-winding CO 082 caliber; 11 ½ lines; 42-hour power reserve; 21 jewels; 28,800 vph.
Functions: hours, minutes.
Case: 3N 18K yellow gold; Ø 36mm, thickness: 7.1mm; crown set with 1 round diamond (0.17 carat); antireflective sapphire crystal; 3N 22K yellow-gold coin caseback; water resistant to 3atm.
Dial: 3N 22K yellow-gold coin; US $50 coin minted in 2014; black baton-shaped hands.
Strap: black alligator leather; 3N 18K yellow-gold tongue buckle with engraved Corum logo.
Note: limited edition of 100 pieces.
Suggested price: $20,800

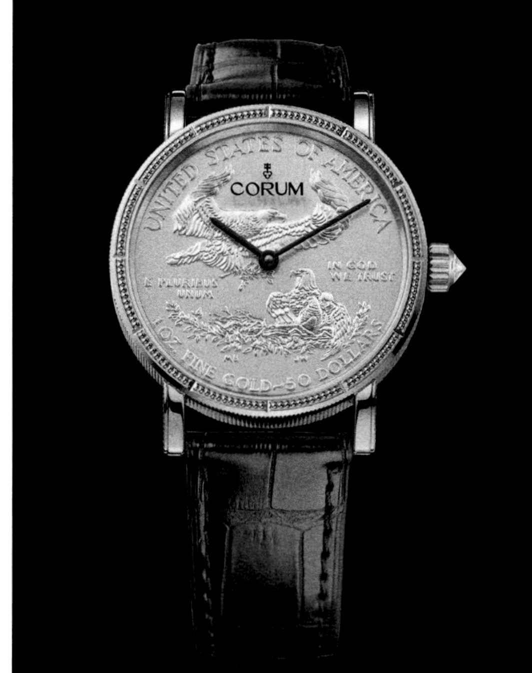

THE RENAISSANCE OF GLAMOUR

In partnering with Samsung, ceaseless innovator de GRISOGONO **FORMS AN UNLIKELY HAUTE HOROLOGY ALLIANCE AND FINDS PERFECTION BY FUSING TWO PIONEERING VISIONS**.

The result is as breathtaking as it is functional, dressed for timeless elegance yet fit for the most modern of lifestyles. The Samsung Gear S2 adorns its owner's wrist with a luxurious femininity that is unmistakably de GRISOGONO. Rotating freely around the dial, the timepiece's rose-gold bezel brings vivacious dynamism to a design full of contrast and intense richness of tones. A setting of 56 white diamonds accentuates every motion, reflecting light for a mesmerizing spectacle. Naturally, de GRISOGONO's incomparable visionary Fawaz Gruosi adorns the 41mm wristwatch with the stunning jewel that has become an unmistakable emblem of his career: the black diamond. Set onto the case as well as on two black DLC-coated arches at 6 and 2 o'clock, 71 black diamonds complement the bezel's scintillating stones by way of harmonious opposition, warm and cool tones working together to give luxury a new dimension of visual texture. Another trademark of de GRISOGONO, the galuchat strap blends in seamlessly with the gem-set case, lending its rugged elegance to a perfectly balanced aesthetic. Beneath its irresistible design, the Samsung Gear S2 by de GRISOGONO represents a leap into the future. From smart fitness and health functions to streamlined mobile payments, round-the-clock connectivity and notifications, to name a few, the timepiece decisively showcases the innovative, high-tech genius of Samsung. The union of these two industry leaders allows the modern woman to live her life to the fullest without compromise. The Samsung Gear S2 becomes her indispensable companion throughout the day, the perfect meeting of form and function.

Two digital-dial variants, both available in white or black, provide an extra sense of flexibility and individuality. The first, displaying the hours and minutes via two central hands, indicates the day and date at 6 o'clock, secondary time zone with day/night indicator at 3 o'clock and small seconds via a subdial at 9 o'clock. The second, which complements its exhibition of the hours and minutes with a central seconds indicator, invigorates its design with a power reserve display at 4 o'clock and radiant moonphase at 8 o'clock. Both dial choices represent the bold DNA of the partnership, presenting an haute horology personality through a state-of-the-art digital medium. The wearer effortlessly transitions from a traditional yet distinctive watch face to the timepiece's numerous smart functions, travelling from the past to the future at the press of a button.

▸ **SAMSUNG GEAR S2**

This high-tech timepiece, adorned with a combination of white and black diamonds, unites de GRISOGONO's brilliant aesthetic vision with Samsung's state-of-the-art interpretation of the smart watch concept.

Beneath its irresistible design, the Samsung Gear S2 represents a leap into the future.

Fawaz Gruosi pays homage to his roots in the world of high jewelry with a one-of-a-kind timepiece of spellbinding brilliance. A sparkling sea of precious stones, the New Retro epitomizes the audacity and gem-setting virtuosity of the celebrated watchmaker. The self-winding wristwatch fluidly plays with shapes and lines, combining graceful curves and straight lines for a stunning multi-faceted geometric effect. The dial, adorned with a full invisible setting of 172 baguette-cut diamonds, counters the rectangular shape of its frame with a gentle curvature, before opposing the shape of its stones with a circular central subdial upon which the hours and minutes are told by way of two dauphine hands. Adorning its multi-layered white-gold structure, 228 white baguette-cut diamonds accentuate every ray of light. Worn on a black crocodile bracelet whose white-gold triple-folding clasp boasts an additional 26 white diamonds, the New Retro, once turned over, grants its wearer a different type of luxury as a sapphire crystal caseback allows for a captivating view of the caliber's mechanical construction.

Guided by the inimitable vision of Fawaz Gruosi, whose Florentine upbringing permeates the DNA of his daring creations, de GRISOGONO makes of haute horology and decadent jewelry a showcase for its limitless imagination and contemporary baroque style. The brand translates its passion, attention to detail and courageous rejection of convention into works of art that defy possibility. Whether adorned with astonishing and masterful gem settings or driven by calibers that reinvent the concept of timekeeping, de GRISOGONO creations represent the magnificent meeting point of uncompromising glamour and modern values. The Vortice jewelry collection is no exception. Every ring, bracelet and pair of earrings hypnotizes the eye with delicate spirals that swirl and interlace. Enchanting diamonds, set to perfection, bring each curve to life, harmoniously complementing without ever overwhelming the elegant design.

▲ **NEW RETRO**

This one-of-a-kind piece boasts 400 baguette-cut diamonds in its case and dial for a breathtaking total of more than 15 carats of precious stones.

Glamour, of course, is a strong focus in—and around—this unique brand. Jeweler to the world's biggest stars, de GRISOGONO is no stranger to the most luxurious of settings, hosting red-carpet events attended by a sparkling guest list in magnificent locales. Just ask 2016 GQ Model of the Year, Bella Hadid, whose presence at the brand's 2016 Cannes event proved the legitimacy of her countless accolades. A believer in beauty and creative individuality, de GRISOGONO is passion. de GRISOGONO is glamour. de GRISOGONO is uncompromising audacity.

▸ **BELLA HADID**
2016 GQ Model of the Year shares the spotlight with gorgeous high jewelry creations at de GRISOGONO's red-carpet event in Cannes.

ALLEGRA

Movement: quartz; 4 jewels.
Functions: hours, minutes.
Case: pink gold; set with 177 white diamonds (5.3 carats); crown set with 1 black diamond (0.1 carat); water resistant to 3atm.
Dial: pink gold; snow-set with 136 white diamonds (2.31 carats); dauphine hands.
Strap: white leather cords and 3 pink-gold cords; set with 144 white diamonds (6.18 carats); pink-gold magnetic clasp set with 74 white diamonds (2.5 carats).
Price: available upon request.

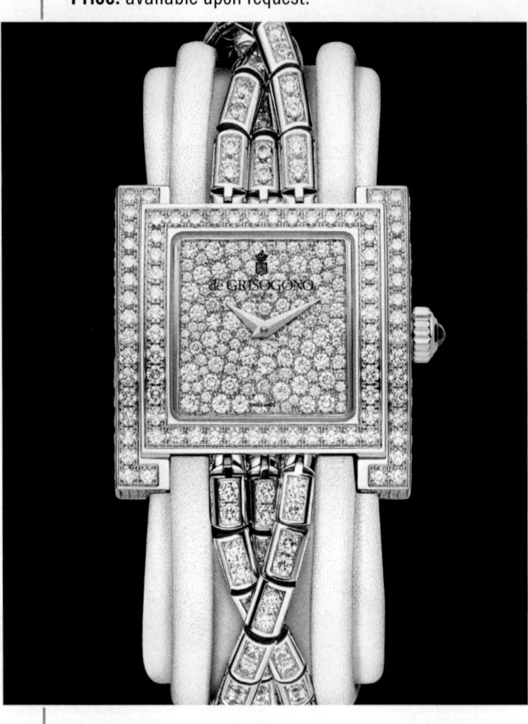

ALLEGRA

Movement: quartz; 4 jewels.
Functions: hours, minutes.
Case: pink gold; set with 80 white diamonds (2.62 carats); crown set with 1 black diamond (0.1 carat); water resistant to 3atm.
Dial: pink gold; snow-set with 136 white diamonds (2.31 carats); dauphine hands.
Strap: white leather cords and 1 pink-gold cord; set with 48 white diamonds (2.06 carats); pink-gold magnetic clasp set with 40 white diamonds (1.3 carats).
Price: available upon request.

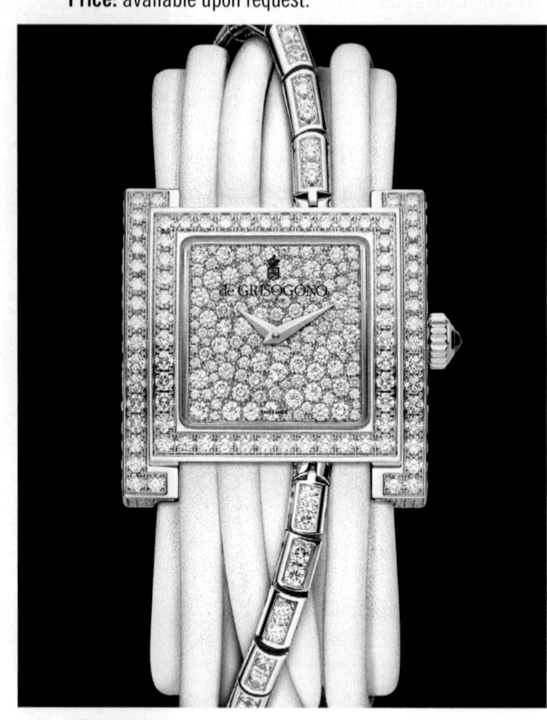

ALLEGRA

Movement: quartz; 4 jewels.
Functions: hours, minutes.
Case: white gold; set with 146 baguette-cut white diamonds (10.8 carats); crown set with 1 black diamond (0.1 carat); water resistant to 3atm.
Dial: white gold; set with 60 baguette-cut white diamonds (4.8 carats).
Strap: Santa Claus red leather and white-gold cords; set with 270 baguette-cut white diamonds (10.10 carats); white-gold set with 74 brilliant-cut white diamonds (2.65 carats).
Price: available upon request.

INSTRUMENTINO

Movement: automatic-winding; 20 jewels.
Functions: hours, minutes; dual time zone.
Case: polished 18K white gold; entirely set with 405 white diamonds (6.48 carats); crown set with 1 black diamond; sapphire crystal caseback; water resistant to 3atm.
Dial: polished 18K white gold; entirely set with 312 white diamonds (0.77 carat); rhodium-applied Arabic numerals and ring.
Strap: white galuchat; polished 18K white-gold de GRISOGONO folding clasp set with 88 white diamonds (0.60 carat).
Price: available upon request.

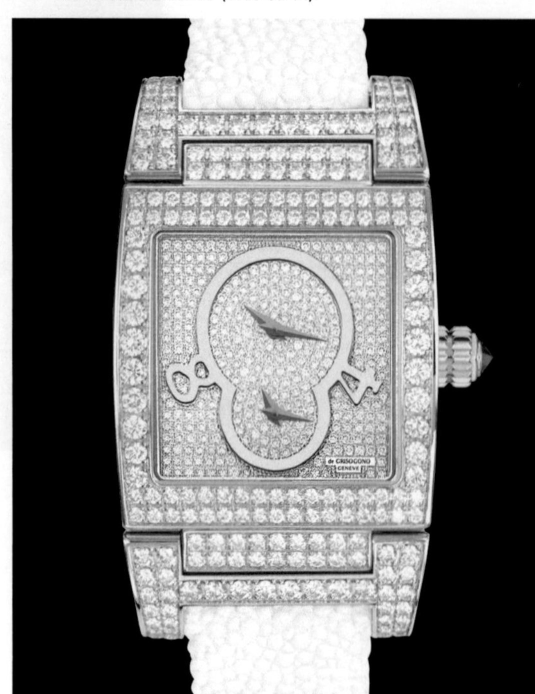

TONDO BY NIGHT

Movement: automatic-winding SF 30-89 caliber; 42-hour power reserve; 24 jewels.
Functions: hours, minutes.
Case: black photoluminescent composite fiberglass; 49x43mm, thickness: 12mm; black PVD-coated steel bezel set with 48 white diamonds (1.37 carats); photoluminescent composite fiberglass crown set with 1 black diamond (0.1 carat); water resistant to 3atm.
Dial: blackened reverse oscillating weight; set with 60 white diamonds (0.26 carat); white hands with SuperLumiNova.
Strap: black galuchat; black photoluminescent composite fiberglass and black PVD-coated steel triple-folding clasp.
Price: available upon request.

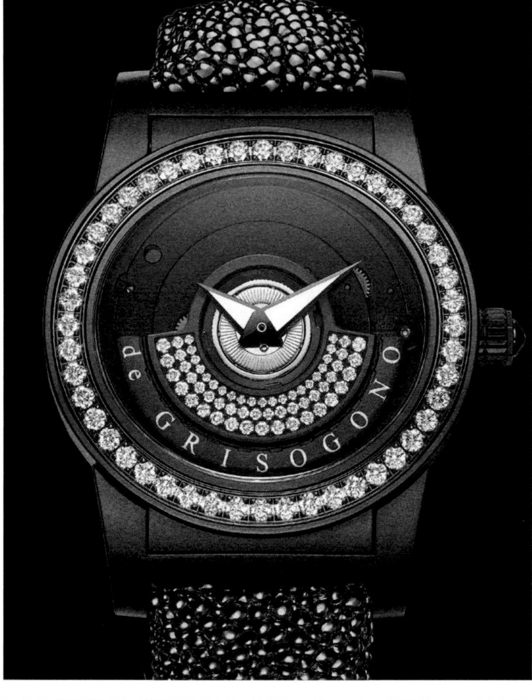

TONDO BY NIGHT

Movement: automatic-winding.
Functions: hours, minutes.
Case: black pearly photoluminescent composite fiberglass with white-gold braces; white-gold bezel set with 48 white diamonds (1.35 carats); white-gold crown set with 1 black diamond (0.1 carat); water resistant to 3atm.
Dial: blackened reverse oscillating weight set with 60 white diamonds (0.25 carat); dauphine hands with black SuperLumiNova.
Strap: black galuchat; steel triple-folding clasp with black PVD coating; white-gold cuffs.
Price: available upon request.

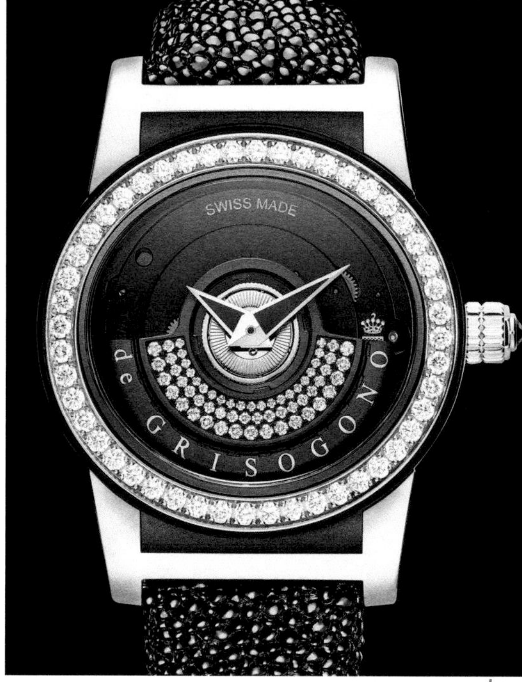

TONDO BY NIGHT

Movement: automatic-winding.
Functions: hours, minutes.
Case: black pearly photoluminescent composite fiberglass with pink-gold braces; pink-gold bezel set with 48 white diamonds (1.35 carats); pink-gold crown set with 1 black diamond (0.1 carat); water resistant to 3atm.
Dial: blackened reverse oscillating weight set with 60 white diamonds (0.25 carat); dauphine hands with black SuperLumiNova.
Strap: black galuchat; steel triple-folding clasp with black PVD coating; pink-gold cuffs.
Price: available upon request.

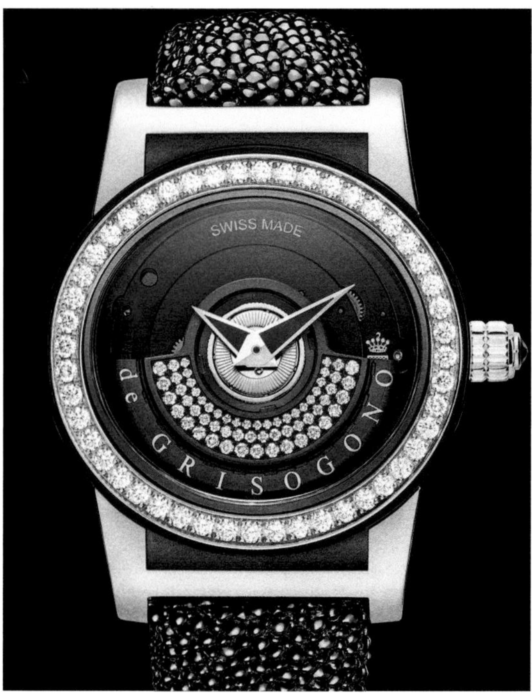

SAMSUNG GEAR S2 BY DE GRISOGONO

Movement: 2-3 day battery life.
Functions: hours, minutes; small seconds at 9; dual time display and day/night indicator at 3; day and date at 6; second face: hours, minutes, seconds; power reserve indicator at 4, moonphase at 8.
Case: rose gold; Ø 41mm; set with 56 white diamonds (approx. 1.2 carats); black DLC-coated stainless steel set with 71 black diamonds (approx. 1.8 carats).
Dial: black; rose-gold dauphine hands.
Strap: black galuchat; black DLC-coated stainless steel triple-folding clasp.
Price: available upon request.

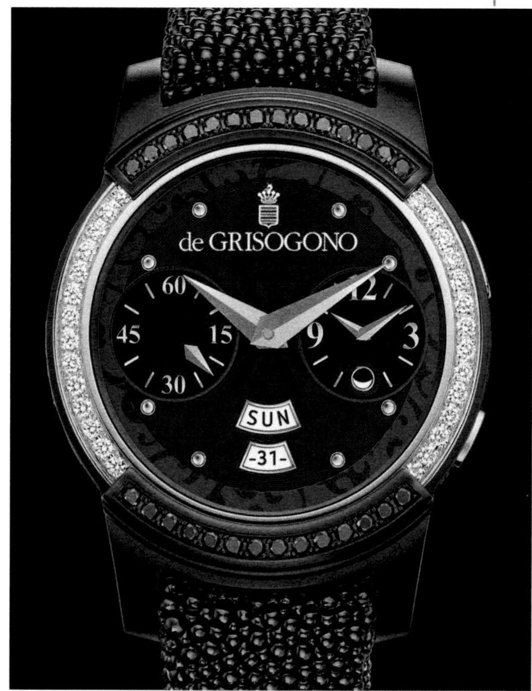

GRAPPOLI

Movement: quartz; 4 jewels.
Functions: hours, minutes.
Case: 18K white gold; set with white diamonds; water resistant to 3atm.
Dial: fully snow-set with white diamonds; 18K white-gold hands.
Strap: icy white galuchat; 18K white-gold clasp set with white diamonds.
Note: set with 70 briolette-cut white diamonds (approx. 63 carats) and 980 brilliant-cut white diamonds (approx. 11 carats).
Price: available upon request.

GRAPPOLI

Movement: quartz; 4 jewels.
Functions: hours, minutes.
Case: pink gold; set with orange sapphires; water resistant to 3atm.
Dial: fully snow-set with orange sapphires; pink-gold hands.
Strap: galuchat; pink-gold clasp set with orange sapphires.
Note: set with 70 briolette-cut orange sapphires (approx. 58 carats) and 960 brilliant-cut orange sapphires (approx. 12 carats).
Price: available upon request.

GRAPPOLI

Movement: quartz.
Functions: hours, minutes.
Case: white gold; full snow-set with 525 tsavorites (4 carats) and 62 briolette-cut peridots (approx. 35 carats); black rhodium grains; water resistant to 3atm.
Dial: white gold; snow-set with 226 tsavorites (1.74 carats); black rhodium grains; white-gold dauphine hands.
Strap: emerald galuchat; white-gold triple-folding clasp set with 68 tsavorites (0.96 carat); black rhodium grains.
Price: available upon request.

GRAPPOLI

Movement: quartz.
Functions: hours, minutes.
Case: white gold; full snow-set with 525 blue sapphires (4.67 carats) and 62 briolette-cut aquamarines (approx. 25 carats); black rhodium grains; water resistant to 3atm.
Dial: white gold; snow-set with 226 blue sapphires (2.02 carats); black rhodium grains; white-gold dauphine hands.
Strap: rich blue galuchat; white-gold triple-folding clasp set with 68 blue sapphires (1.05 carats); black rhodium grains.
Price: available upon request.

LOVIVI

Movement: quartz.
Functions: hours, minutes.
Case: polished white gold; half-set with 96 emeralds (1.95 carats); black rhodium treatment on set grains; water resistant to 3 atm.
Dial: mother-of-pearl; set with 39 emeralds (1.05 carats); ruthenium-treated hands.
Bracelet: turquoise double bangle; opening system by pushbuttons at 6; polished white-gold cylinder with 77 emeralds (1.35 carats); black rhodium treatment on set grains.
Price: available upon request.

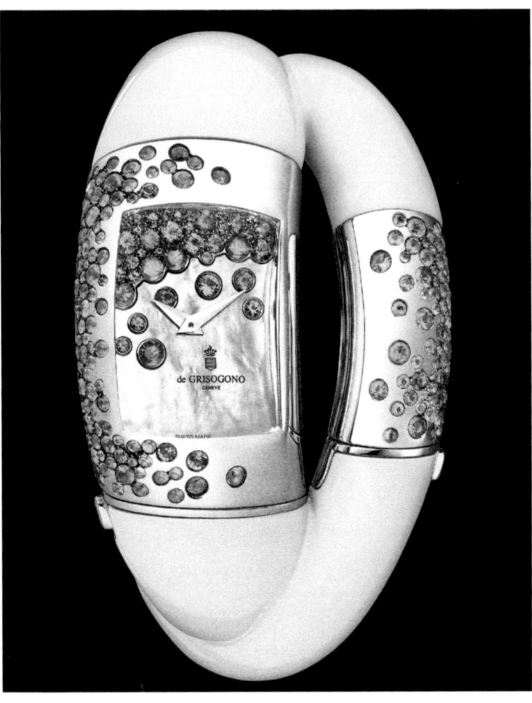

LOVIVI

Movement: quartz.
Functions: hours, minutes.
Case: polished pink gold; half-set with 96 brown diamonds (2.7 carats); water resistant to 3atm.
Dial: pink mother-of-pearl; pink 5N Arabic numerals; pink-gold hands.
Bracelet: amber double bangle; opening system by pushbuttons at 6; polished pink-gold cylinder set with 77 brown diamonds (1.65 carats).
Price: available upon request.

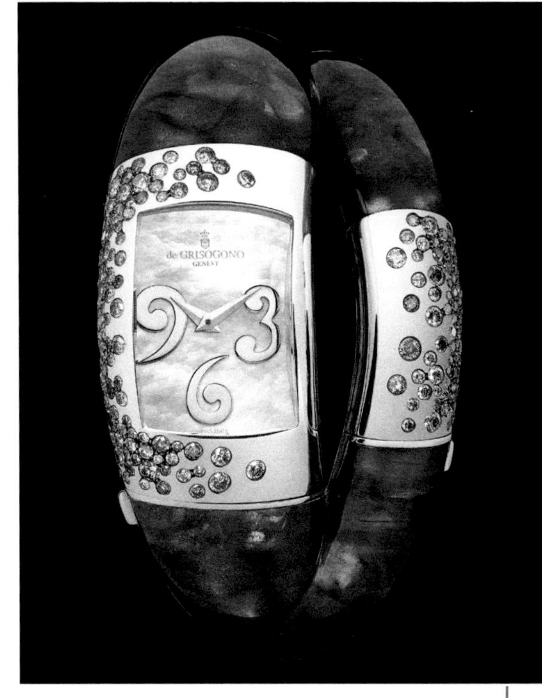

LOVIVI

Movement: quartz.
Functions: hours, minutes.
Case: polished white gold; full-set with 299 white diamonds (6.9 carats); water resistant to 3atm.
Dial: white gold; full-set with 125 white diamonds (3.25 carats); ruthenium-coated hands.
Bracelet: lacquered jet double bangle; opening system by pushbuttons at 6; white-gold cylinder full-set with 170 white diamonds (3.75 carats).
Price: available upon request.

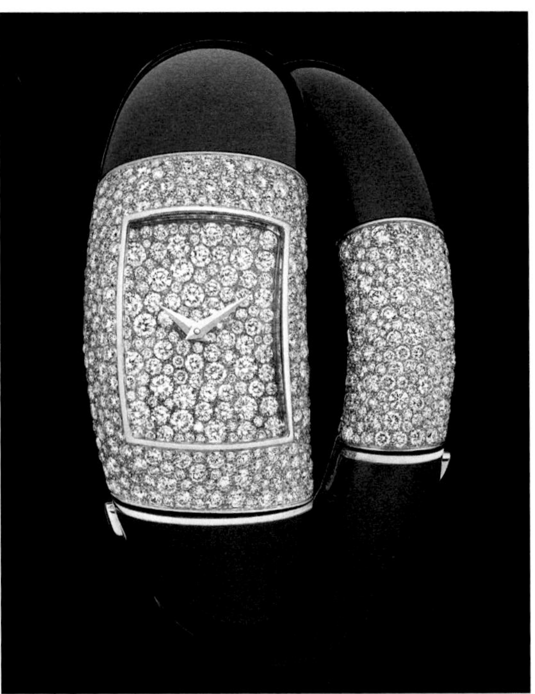

LOVIVI

Movement: quartz.
Functions: hours, minutes.
Case: polished pink gold; full-set with 299 white diamonds (6.9 carats); water resistant to 3atm.
Dial: pink gold; full-set with 125 white diamonds (3.25 carats); pink-gold hands.
Bracelet: fossilized mammoth ivory double bangle; opening system by pushbuttons at 6; polished pink-gold cylinder full-set with 170 white diamonds (3.75 carats).
Price: available upon request.

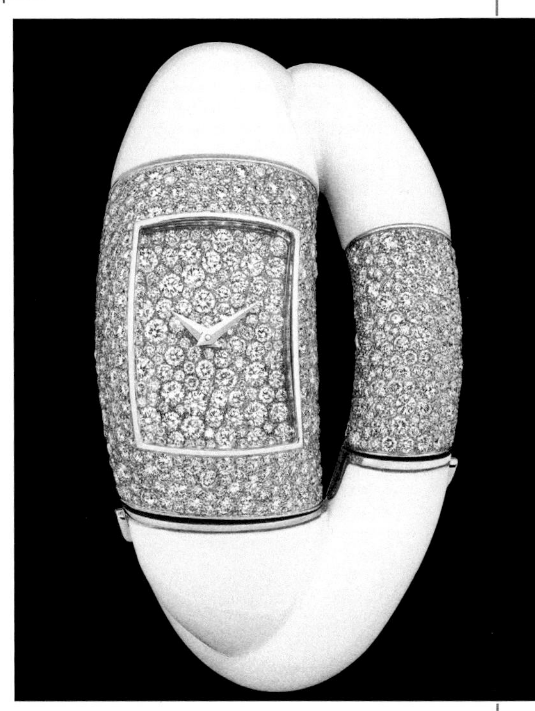

NEW RETRO

Movement: automatic-winding DG 10-91 caliber; 42-hour power reserve; 28,800 vph.
Functions: hours, minutes.
Case: rose gold; set with 303 white diamonds (approx. 3.95 carats); crown featuring the de GRISOGONO coat-of-arms at 12; water resistant to 3atm.
Dial: off-white; set with 94 white diamonds (approx. 0.9 carat); golden Arabic numerals.
Strap: white galuchat; rose-gold triple-folding clasp set with 112 diamonds (approx. 0.65 carat).
Price: available upon request.

NEW RETRO

Movement: automatic-winding DG 10-91 caliber; 42-hour power reserve; 28,800 vph.
Functions: hours, minutes.
Case: rose gold; set with 303 rubies (approx. 4.5 carats); crown featuring the de GRISOGONO coat-of-arms at 12; black rhodium on set grains; water resistant to 3atm.
Dial: off-white; fuchsia SuperLumiNova Arabic numerals.
Strap: ruby galuchat; rose-gold triple-folding clasp set with 112 rubies (approx. 0.8 carat).
Price: available upon request.

NEW RETRO

Movement: automatic-winding DG 10-91 caliber; 42-hour power reserve; 28,800 vph.
Functions: hours, minutes.
Case: white gold; set with 303 blue sapphires (approx. 4.6 carats); crown featuring the de GRISOGONO coat-of-arms at 12; black rhodium on set grains; water resistant to 3atm.
Dial: off-white; blue SuperLumiNova Arabic numerals.
Strap: rich blue galuchat; white-gold triple-folding clasp set with 112 blue sapphires (approx. 0.85 carat).
Price: available upon request.

NEW RETRO

Movement: automatic-winding DG 10-91 caliber; 42-hour power reserve; 28,800 vph.
Functions: hours, minutes.
Case: white gold; set with 303 emeralds (approx. 3.75 carats); crown featuring the de GRISOGONO coat-of-arms at 12; black rhodium on set grains; water resistant to 3atm.
Dial: off-white; green SuperLumiNova Arabic numerals.
Strap: emerald galuchat; white-gold triple-folding clasp set with 112 emeralds (approx. 0.6 carat).
Price: available upon request.

NEW RETRO

Movement: automatic-winding.
Functions: hours, minutes.
Case: white gold; set with 35 emeralds (1.16 carats); crown with de GRISOGONO coat-of-arms at 12; black rhodium grains; sapphire crystal caseback; water resistant to 3atm.
Dial: off-white; set with 12 emeralds (0.1 carat); green Arabic numerals with Super-LumiNova; dauphine hands.
Strap: emerald galuchat; white-gold triple-folding clasp.
Price: available upon request.

NEW RETRO

Movement: automatic-winding.
Functions: hours, minutes.
Case: white gold; set with 70 baguette-cut blue sapphires (8.2 carats); crown with de GRISOGONO coat-of-arms at 12; sapphire crystal caseback.
Dial: off-white; set with 60 baguette-cut blue sapphires (2.2 carats); blue Arabic numerals with SuperLumiNova; dauphine hands.
Strap: rich blue galuchat; white-gold triple-folding clasp set with 112 blue sapphires (0.85 carat); black rhodium grains.
Price: available upon request.

NEW RETRO

Movement: automatic-winding.
Functions: hours, minutes.
Case: pink gold; set with 70 baguette-cut white diamonds (3.41 carats); crown with de GRISOGONO coat-of-arms at 12; sapphire crystal caseback; water resistant to 3atm.
Dial: off-white; set with 60 baguette-cut white diamonds (1.84 carats); golden Arabic numerals; dauphine hands.
Strap: white galuchat; pink-gold triple-folding clasp set with 112 white diamonds (0.65 carat).
Price: available upon request.

NEW RETRO

Movement: automatic-winding.
Functions: hours, minutes.
Case: pink gold; set with 90 baguette-cut diamonds (5.35 carats); crown with de GRISOGONO coat-of-arms at 12; sapphire crystal caseback; water resistant to 3atm.
Dial: black lacquer; set with 28 baguette-cut diamonds (1.6 carats); white Arabic numerals with SuperLumiNova; dauphine hands.
Strap: glossy black genuine alligator leather; pink-gold triple-folding clasp set with 138 diamonds (1.34 carats).
Price: available upon request.

NEW RETRO

Movement: automatic-winding DG 10-01 caliber; 42-hour power reserve; 28,800 vph.
Functions: hours, minutes.
Case: rose gold; 50x44mm, thickness: 12mm; black lacquered gold crown featuring the de GRISOGONO coat-of-arms at 12; water resistant to 3atm.
Dial: graded shades of green; blue Arabic numerals; rose-gold hands.
Strap: black alligator leather; rose-gold triple-folding clasp.
Price: available upon request.

NEW RETRO

Movement: automatic-winding DG 10-01 caliber; 42-hour power reserve; 28,800 vph.
Functions: hours, minutes.
Case: rose gold; 50x44mm, thickness: 12mm; black lacquered gold crown featuring the de GRISOGONO coat-of-arms at 12; water resistant to 3atm.
Dial: black; white Arabic numerals; rose-gold hands.
Strap: black alligator leather; rose-gold triple-folding clasp.
Price: available upon request.

NEW RETRO

Movement: automatic-winding DG 10-01 caliber; 42-hour power reserve; 28,800 vph.
Functions: hours, minutes.
Case: black PVD; 50x44mm, thickness: 12mm; black lacquered crown featuring the de GRISOGONO coat-of-arms at 12; water resistant to 3atm.
Dial: black; white Arabic numerals; rhodium-treated hands.
Strap: black alligator leather; black PVD-coated steel triple-folding clasp.
Price: available upon request.

NEW RETRO

Movement: automatic-winding.
Functions: hours, minutes.
Case: pink gold; crown with de GRISOGONO coat-of-arms at 12; sapphire crystal caseback; water resistant to 3atm.
Dial: off-white; brown Arabic numerals with SuperLumiNova; dauphine hands.
Strap: brown galuchat; pink-gold triple-folding clasp.
Price: available upon request.

INSTRUMENTO N° UNO DF 11

Movement: automatic-winding.
Functions: hours, minutes; dual time zone; date between 7 and 8.
Case: polished 18K pink gold; crown set with a black diamond (0.1 carat); sapphire crystal; sapphire crystal caseback.
Dial: black lacquered; 5N applied Arabic numerals; pink-gold hands.
Strap: integrated glossy black alligator leather; 18K pink-gold de GRISOGONO folding clasp.
Price: available upon request.

INSTRUMENTO N° UNO DOPPIO TRE

Movement: automatic-winding; 25 jewels.
Functions: hours, minutes; three time zones; date between 7 and 8.
Case: polished 18K rose gold; reversible case; double crown with de GRISOGONO coat-of-arms; sapphire crystal; sapphire crystal caseback; water resistant to 5atm.
Dial: black guilloché top dial; black lacquered second dial; rose-gold Arabic numerals and indexes.
Strap: black alligator leather; polished 18K rose-gold butterfly buckle.
Price: available upon request.

INSTRUMENTO N° UNO N31

Movement: automatic-winding.
Functions: hours, minutes; dual time zone; date between 7 and 8.
Case: brushed blackened stainless steel; crown set with a black diamond; sapphire crystal; sapphire crystal caseback with special number and engraving; water resistant to 3atm.
Dial: black guilloché; red appliqué Arabic numerals; red and rhodium-treated timer.
Strap: matte black alligator leather and red lining.
Price: available upon request.

MECCANICO DG

Movement: manual-winding; 36-hour power reserve; 651 components; 111 jewels.
Functions: hours, minutes; first watch in the world with a dual analog and mechanical digital display; power reserve indicator on caseback.
Case: polished 18K pink gold and rubber; 55.9x48mm, thickness: 15mm; rubber crown; sapphire crystal; sapphire crystal caseback; water resistant to 3atm.
Dial: 18K pink-gold indexes, dauphine hands and digits.
Strap: black natural vulcanized rubber; polished 18K pink-gold butterfly buckle.
Note: limited edition of 177 pieces.
Price: available upon request.

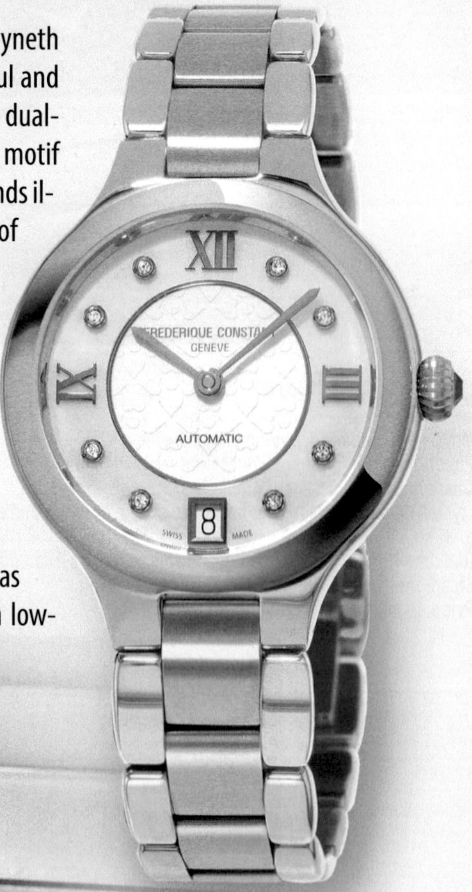

FREDERIQUE CONSTANT
GENEVE

HOROLOGY AND PHILANTHROPY

Frederique Constant partners with a noble philanthropic venture, giving its timepieces **A SENSE OF MEANING BEYOND THEIR OWN FINE CRAFTSMANSHIP AND SOPHISTICATED MECHANICAL CONSTRUCTIONS**.

Presented in collaboration with the brand's global charity ambassador, Oscar winner Gwyneth Paltrow, the Classics Delight Automatic expresses luxurious elegance within a tasteful and delicate design. Crafted in polished stainless steel with a rose-gold-plated bezel, the dual-tone 33mm case frames a meticulously crafted mother-of-pearl dial, whose central guilloché motif lends a textural depth to the watch face. Along the dial's periphery, eight shimmering diamonds illuminate the proceedings, girded by rose-gold-toned settings that reflect the warm palette of the timepiece's case and bracelet. The watch's self-winding FC-306 caliber oscillates at 28,800 vph and boasts a power reserve of 42 hours, giving the date (in a rectangular aperture at 6 o'clock) and central time display a reliable power source. Another model, this one in polished stainless steel, opts for a sleek monochrome look. Eight diamond indexes and a guilloché decoration subtly enhance the silver-colored dial, while an understated blue cabochon on the crown adds a touch of color to the watch.

The elegance of the Classics Delight Automatic goes beyond its visual design and mechanical heartbeat: a portion of its sale proceeds have been devoted to support the DonorsChoose association, which has dedicated its efforts to assisting classrooms in need, mostly from low-income communities and disaster-stricken areas.

▲ **CLASSICS DELIGHT AUTOMATIC**

Elegant decorations, diamonds and golden accents combine to give this self-winding timepiece its graceful personality.

The complex mechanism of the Slimline Manufacture Perpetual Calendar translates to striking legibility on the dial—in the absence of attention-grabbing visual borders, each element of the watch emerges effortlessly from a harmonious, coherent design.

Frederique Constant showcases its impressive skill set with a timepiece of undeniable mechanical sophistication. The Slimline Manufacture Perpetual Calendar endows its chic, classic design with a comprehensive perpetual calendar that needs no adjustments until the year 2100. Powered by the 26-jewel FC-775 manufacture caliber, the 42mm wristwatch complements the hours and minutes with displays of the day at 9 o'clock, date at 3 o'clock, month and leap year at 12 o'clock, and a stunning moonphase module at 6 o'clock. Yet the complex mechanism translates to striking legibility on the silver-colored or navy blue dial. In the absence of attention-grabbing visual borders, each element of the watch emerges effortlessly from a harmonious, coherent design. A transparent caseback completes the picture, providing a view of the movement's perlage and circular Côtes-de-Genève decorations. Housed in a three-part case in stainless steel or rose-gold-plated stainless steel, the Slimline Manufacture Perpetual Calendar dazzles with sophistication and classical refinement.

▲ **SLIMLINE MANUFACTURE PERPETUAL CALENDAR**
This sophisticated wristwatch displays a complete spectrum of calendar indications with excellent clarity and legibility.

MANUFACTURE PERPETUAL CALENDAR — REF. FC-775V4S4

Movement: automatic-winding FC-775 caliber; 38-hour power reserve; 26 jewels; perlage and circular Côtes de Genève decoration.
Functions: hours, minutes; perpetual calendar: date at 3, day at 9, month and leap year at 12; moonphase at 6.
Case: rose gold plated; Ø 42mm; convex sapphire crystal; sapphire crystal caseback; water resistant to 3atm.
Dial: silver; applied rose-gold-plated indexes.
Strap: brown alligator leather.
Note: delivered in a wooden gift box.
Suggested price: $8,995
Also available: rose-gold-plated case, navy blue dial, navy alligator leather strap (ref. FC-775N4S4).

SLIMLINE MOONPHASE MANUFACTURE — REF. FC-710MB4H6

Movement: automatic-winding FC-710 caliber; 42-hour power reserve; 26 jewels; 28,800 vph; perlage and circular Côtes de Genève decoration.
Functions: hours, minutes; date via hand at 6.
Case: polished stainless steel; Ø 42mm; convex sapphire crystal; sapphire crystal caseback; water resistant to 5atm.
Dial: black; white printed Roman numeral indexes; hand-polsihed white hands.
Strap: black alligator leather.
Note: delivered in a wooden gift box.
Suggested price: $2,495
Also available: polished stainless steel case, silver-colored dial, black leather strap (ref. FC-705N4S6B).

HEART BEAT MANUFACTURE — REF. FC-941NS4H6

Movement: automatic-winding FC-941 caliber; 42-hour power reserve; 25 jewels; Perlage and circular Côtes de Genève decoration.
Functions: hours, minutes; date via hand at 12.
Case: polished stainless steel; Ø 42mm; convex sapphire crystal; sapphire crystal caseback; water resistant to 5atm.
Dial: navy; printed Roman numerals; hand-polished white hands.
Strap: navy alligator leather with white stitches.
Note: delivered in a wooden gift box.
Suggested price: $4,795

CLASSIC SLIMLINE — REF. FC-306MR4S6

Movement: automatic-winding FC-306 caliber; 42-hour power reserve; 25 jewels; 28,800 vph.
Functions: hours, minutes; date at 3.
Case: polished stainless steel; Ø 40mm; convex sapphire crystal; sapphire crystal caseback; water resistant to 3atm.
Dial: silver; black printed Roman numeral indexes; hand-polished black hands.
Strap: black leather.
Suggested price: $1,695
Also available: rose-gold-plated case, brown alligator leather strap (ref. FC-306MR4S4).

LADIES AUTOMATIC — REF. FC-310HBAND2P4

Movement: automatic-winding FC-310 caliber; 38-hour power reserve; 26 jewels; colimaçon decoration.
Functions: hours, minutes, seconds.
Case: polished rose-gold-plated stainless steel; Ø 34mm; convex sapphire crystal; sapphire crystal caseback; water resistant to 6atm.
Dial: navy; mother-of-pearl on outer ring; hand-polished rose-gold-plated hands; heartbeat opening at 12.
Strap: blue alligator leather.
Suggested price: $2,650
Also available: polished stainless steel case, blue alligator leather strap (ref. FC-310HBAND2P6).

HOROLOGICAL SMARTWATCH — REF. FC-281WHD3ER6B

Movement: quartz MMT-281 caliber; 4+ years battery life.
Functions: hours, minutes; activity tracking; sleep tracker; sleep cycle alarms; get-active alerts; dynamic coaching; world time; cloud backup and restore.
Case: polished stainless steel; Ø 34mm; convex sapphire crystal; water resistant to 3atm.
Dial: silver-colored with guilloché decoration and mother-of-pearl; applied silver-colored indexes set with 8 diamonds; hand-polished silver-colored hands.
Bracelet: stainless steel.
Suggested price: $950
Also available: stainless steel and rose-gold-plated case, metal bracelet with rose-gold-plated links in center (ref. FC-281WHD3ER2B).

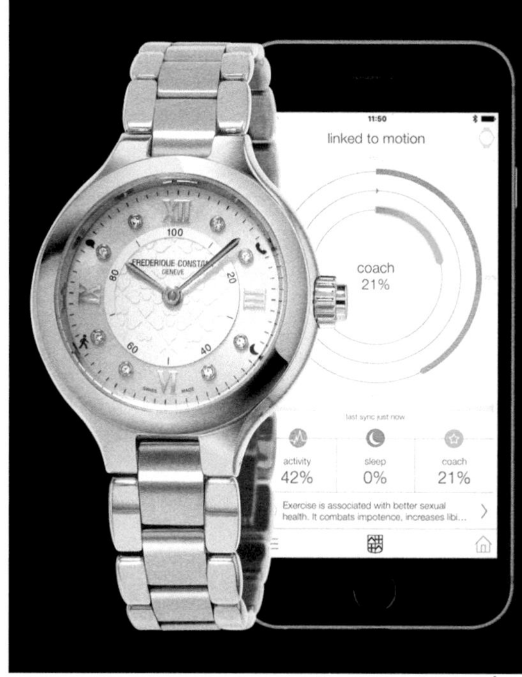

CLASSICS DELIGHT AUTOMATIC — REF. FC-306WHD3ER2B

Movement: automatic-winding FC-306 caliber; 42-hour power reserve; 25 jewels.
Functions: hours, minutes; date at 6.
Case: polished stainless steel; Ø 33mm; convex sapphire crystal; water resistant to 3atm.
Dial: silver; guilloché decoration and mother-of-pearl; applied rose-gold-plated indexes with 8 set diamonds; hand-polished rose-gold-plated hands.
Bracelet: stainless steel and rose-gold-plated.
Suggested price: $1,995
Also available: stainless steel case, silver dial, stainless steel bracelet (ref. FC-306WHD3ER6B).

VINTAGE RALLY — REF. FC-303GBRH5B4

Movement: automatic-winding FC-303 caliber; 38-hour power reserve; 26 jewels.
Functions: hours, minutes, seconds; date at 3.
Case: rose-gold-plated polished stainless steel; Ø 40mm; convex sapphire crystal; water resistant to 5atm.
Dial: gray; burgundy ring and applied rose-gold luminous indexes; hand-polished rose-gold-plated luminous hour and minute hands.
Strap: dark gray leather.
Note: limited edition of 2,888 numbered pieces; comes with a gift box with a Healey NOJ393 car miniature.
Suggested price: $1,895
Also available: polished stainless steel case, silver dial, dark gray ring, dark gray leather strap (ref. FC-303GBRH5B4).

WHAT WAS, IS AND WILL BE

Girard-Perregaux **CELEBRATES MORE THAN TWO AND A QUARTER CENTURIES OF HOROLOGICAL EXCELLENCE** with a pair of timepieces whose roots plunge deep into the glorious history of the manufacture.

The Laureato's immaculate, understated classicism is no accident. The self-winding timepiece pays tribute to the manufacture's iconic 1975 creation of the same name. A bold exploit, the distinguished wristwatch pioneered daring approaches to materials, geometric design and timekeeping calibers with its avant-garde use of steel for the case, octagonal bezel and in-house quartz caliber that set the still-existing standard for the concept at a frequency of 32,768 Hz. The newly presented Laureato celebrates more than four decades of innovation, mechanical excellence and visual elegance with a design that returns to the collection's conception. Housed in a 41mm steel case, the three-hand timepiece harmoniously blends the sharp lines of its eight-sided bezel with the seamless fluidity of a bracelet integrated into the structure. On a blue or silvered dial, the Laureato creates a rich sense of texture and depth behind the time display with a Clous-de-Paris motif. A noble salute to a timepiece that courageously challenged the standards of haute horology more than 40 years ago, the Laureato, limited to 225 pieces, is driven by the in-house 27-jewel GP03300-0030 caliber, which oscillates at a frequency of 28,800 vph and boasts a winding rotor visible through a sapphire crystal caseback.

◂ **LAUREATO**

This 41mm model pays homage to the brand's 1975 timepiece of the same name with an octagonal bezel and steel case that perform a delightful play of geometric contrast.

▸ **ESMERALDA TOURBILLON**

Three hand-decorated gold bridges above this timepiece's barrel, gear train and tourbillon pay a vibrant homage to Girard-Perregaux's 1889 winner of the gold medal at the Universal Exhibition in Paris.

Placed in parallel, the barrel, gear-train and tourbillon bridges are stunningly embellished with hand-decorated double-arrow designs inspired by the Esmeralda Tourbillon's 19th-century ancestor.

Girard-Perregaux continues its celebration of horological history with a timepiece inspired by the manufacture's gold-medal recipient at the 1889 Universal Exhibition in Paris. The Esmeralda Tourbillon, winner of the prestigious Tourbillon Prize at the most recent Grand Prix d'Horlogerie de Genève, breathes new life into the genius of its groundbreaking predecessor with a breathtaking architecture based on the principles of the golden ratio. The 44mm wristwatch echoes its 18-karat pink-gold case with a three-bridge layout (a signature of the manufacture) that highlights the timepiece's trio of dial-side mechanical revelations with a dazzling sense of balance. Perfectly parallel to one another, the barrel, gear-train and tourbillon bridges are stunningly embellished with hand-decorated double-arrow designs inspired by the watch's 19th-century ancestor. The wristwatch's 14.3mm tourbillon carriage, comprised of 80 components and positioned at 6 o'clock, enlivens the design, executing its one-minute rotation under the delighted gaze of the wearer. Atop the balance wheel, the carriage's hand-polished lyre represents another signature of the legendary watchmaker. While the Esmeralda Tourbillon's frontal displays interpret the manufacture's incomparable history, its caseback reveals a further innovation. By placing the 310-component GP09400-0004 caliber's winding rotor concentrically under the barrel and not on the outer edge, Girard-Perregaux makes possible an increase of the barrel drum's diameter and thus allows the timepiece to achieve a generous power reserve of 60 hours. The Esmeralda Tourbillon indicates the hours and minutes via two dauphine hands on the central axis and the small seconds on the tourbillon.

LA ESMERALDA TOURBILLON REF. 99275-52-000-BA6E

Movement: automatic-winding GP09400-0004 caliber; 16 lines; 60-hour power reserve; 310 components; 27 jewels; 21,600 vph.
Functions: hours, minutes; small seconds on tourbillon at 6.
Case: pink gold; Ø 44mm, thickness: 14.55mm; sapphire crystal caseback; water resistant to 3atm.
Strap: black alligator leather; pink-gold triple folding buckle.
Suggested price: $192,000

VINTAGE 1945 TOURBILLON WITH THREE GOLD BRIDGES REF. 99880-53-00B-BA6A

Movement: automatic-winding GP09600-0028 caliber; 13 ¼ x 12 ½ lines; 48-hour power reserve; 249 components; 31 jewels; 21,600 vph.
Functions: hours, minutes; small seconds on tourbillon at 6.
Case: white gold; 36.1x35.25mm, thickness: 11.39mm; satin-finished caseback engraved with the Vintage 1945 anniversary logo; water resistant to 3atm.
Strap: black alligator leather; white-gold folding buckle.
Note: 70th Anniversary edition; limited edition of 18 pieces.
Suggested price: $215,000

CONSTANT ESCAPEMENT L.M. REF. 93505-39-632-BA6I

Movement: manual-winding GP09100-0002 caliber; 17 ½ lines; 6-day power reserve; 280 components; 28 jewels; 21,600 vph.
Functions: off-centered hours and minutes; central seconds; power reserve indicator at 9.
Case: carbon/titanium composite; Ø 46mm, thickness: 14.85mm; sapphire crystal caseback; water resistant to 3atm.
Dial: gray.
Strap: black alligator leather with a rubber effect; titanium/PVD triple folding buckle.
Suggested price: $98,100

NEO-TOURBILLON WITH THREE BRIDGES REF. 99270-21-000-BA6E

Movement: automatic-winding GP09400-0008 caliber; 16 ¼ lines; 60-hour power reserve; 263 components; 27 jewels; 21,600 vph.
Functions: hours, minutes; small seconds on tourbillon at 6.
Case: titanium/DLC; Ø 45mm, thickness: 14.45mm; water resistant to 3atm.
Strap: black alligator leather; titanium/DLC triple folding buckle.
Suggested price: $122,000

TOURBILLON WITH THREE GOLD BRIDGES REF. 99280-52-000-BA6E

Movement: automatic-winding GP09400-0007 caliber; 16 lines; 60-hour power reserve; 263 components; 27 jewels; 21,600 vph.
Functions: hours, minutes; small seconds on tourbillon at 6.
Case: pink gold; Ø 45mm, thickness: 13.78mm; sapphire crystal caseback; water resistant to 3atm.
Strap: black alligator leather; pink-gold triple folding buckle.
Suggested price: $163,000

TOURBILLON WITH THREE GOLD BRIDGES, LADY REF. 99240D52A701-CK7A

Movement: automatic-winding GP09600-0025 caliber; 13 lines; 48-hour power reserve; 233 components; 31 jewels; 21,600 vph.
Functions: hours, minutes; small seconds on tourbillon at 6.
Case: pink gold; Ø 38mm, thickness: 11.16mm; set with 118 brilliant-cut diamonds (approx. 1.8 carats); water resistant to 3atm.
Dial: mother-of-pearl.
Strap: blue alligator leather; pink-gold folding buckle set with 18 brilliant-cut diamonds (approx. 0.2 carat).
Note: an additional black alligator strap is delivered with the timepiece.
Suggested price: $210,000

CAT'S EYE TOURBILLON WITH THREE GOLD BRIDGES REF. 99495D52B00A-CK6A

Movement: manual-winding GP09700-0014 caliber; 12 x 14 ½ lines; 70-hour power reserve; 355 components; 20 jewels; 21,600 vph.
Functions: hours, minutes; small seconds on tourbillon at 6.
Case: pink gold; 37.3x32.3mm, thickness: 11.64mm; set with 54 baguette-cut diamonds (approx. 3.5 carats); crown set with 1 rose-cut diamond (approx. 0.19 carat); water resistant to 3atm.
Dial: set with 178 brilliant-cut diamonds (approx. 0.31 carat).
Strap: blue alligator leather; pink-gold folding buckle set with 14 baguette-cut diamonds (approx. 0.75 carat).
Note: an additional black alligator strap is delivered with the timepiece.
Suggested price: $207,000

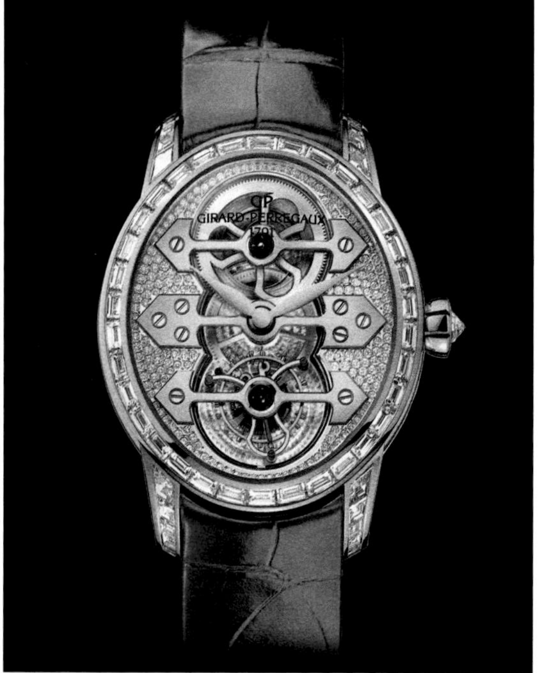

CAT'S EYE TOURBILLON WITH GOLD BRIDGE REF. 99490D52A706-CK6A

Movement: manual-winding GP09700-0013 caliber; 12 x 14 ¼ lines; 70-hour power reserve; 174 components; 20 jewels; 21,600 vph.
Functions: hours, minutes; small seconds on tourbillon at 6.
Case: pink gold; 37.3x32.3mm, thickness: 11.64mm; set with 50 brilliant-cut diamonds (approx. 1.25 carats); water resistant to 3atm.
Dial: hand-engraved mother-of-pearl.
Strap: blue alligator leather; pink-gold folding buckle.
Note: an additional black alligator strap is delivered with the timepiece.
Suggested price: $118,000

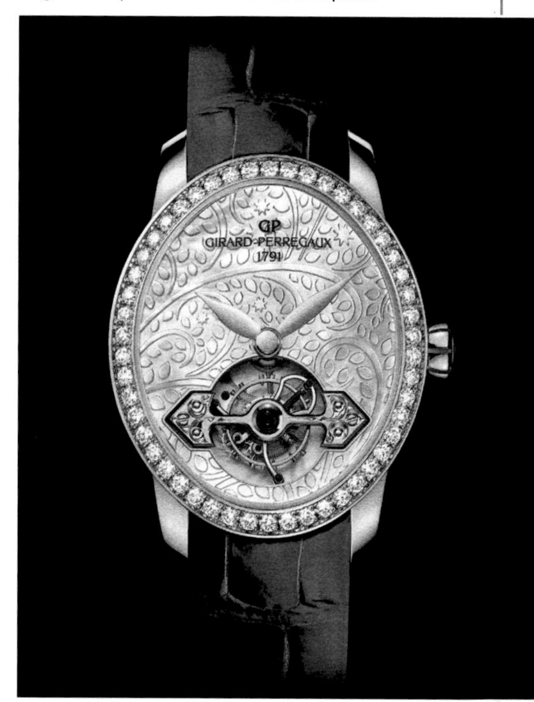

1966 FULL CALENDAR — REF. 49535-11-131-BB60

Movement: automatic-winding GP03300-0118 caliber; 11 ½ lines; 46-hour power reserve; 27 jewels; 28,800 vph.
Functions: hours, minutes, seconds; full calendar: date at 6, day and month at 12; moonphase at 6.
Case: steel; Ø 40mm, thickness: 10.8mm; sapphire crystal caseback; water resistant to 3atm.
Dial: silvered opaline.
Strap: black alligator leather; steel pin buckle.
Suggested price: $10,600

1966 LARGE DATE AND MOON PHASES — REF. 49546-52-131-BB60

Movement: automatic-winding GP03300-0110 caliber; 11 ½ lines; 46-hour power reserve; 32 jewels; 28,800 vph.
Functions: hours, minutes; small seconds on moonphase at 6; large date at 12.
Case: pink gold; Ø 41mm, thickness: 11.22mm; sapphire crystal caseback; water resistant to 3atm.
Dial: opaline.
Strap: black alligator leather; pink-gold pin buckle.
Suggested price: $24,400

1966 44 MM — REF. 49551-53-231-BB60

Movement: automatic-winding GP01800-0009 caliber; 13 ¼ lines; 54-hour power reserve; 28 jewels; 28,800 vph.
Functions: hours, minutes, seconds; date at 3.
Case: white gold; Ø 44mm, thickness: 10.12mm; sapphire crystal caseback; water resistant to 3atm.
Dial: faded slate.
Strap: black alligator leather; white-gold folding buckle.
Suggested price: $19,200

1966 44 MM — REF. 49551-52-231-BB60

Movement: automatic-winding GP01800-0009 caliber; 13 ¼ lines; 54-hour power reserve; 28 jewels; 28,800 vph.
Functions: hours, minutes, seconds; date at 3.
Case: pink gold; Ø 44mm, thickness: 10.12mm; sapphire crystal caseback; water resistant to 3atm.
Dial: faded slate.
Strap: black alligator leather; pink-gold folding buckle.
Suggested price: $18,100

VINTAGE 1945 XXL, SMALL SECOND — REF. 25880-52-721-BB6A

Movement: automatic-winding GP03300-0052 caliber; 11 ½ lines; 46-hour power reserve; 32 jewels; 28,800 vph.
Functions: hours, minutes; small seconds at 6.
Case: pink gold; 36.2x35.25mm, thickness: 10.83mm; sapphire crystal caseback; water resistant to 3atm.
Dial: opaline.
Strap: black alligator leather; pink-gold folding buckle.
Suggested price: $26,800

VINTAGE 1945 XXL, LARGE DATE AND MOON PHASES — REF. 25882-52-222-BB6B

Movement: automatic-winding GP03300-0105 caliber; 11 ½ lines; 46-hour power reserve; 32 jewels; 28,800 vph.
Functions: hours, minutes; small seconds on moonphase at 6; large date at 12.
Case: pink gold; 36.1x35.25mm, thickness: 11.74mm; sapphire crystal caseback; water resistant to 3atm.
Dial: smoked sapphire crystal.
Strap: black alligator leather; pink-gold folding buckle.
Suggested price: $33,800

COMPETIZIONE STRADALE — REF. 49590-11-111-BBBA

Movement: automatic-winding GP03300-0031 caliber; 11 ½ lines; 46-hour power reserve; 63 jewels; 28,800 vph.
Functions: hours, minutes; small seconds at 3; date between 4 and 5; chronograph: central seconds hand, 12-hour counter at 6, 30-minute counter at 9.
Case: steel; Ø 42mm, thickness: 13.99mm; sapphire crystal caseback; water resistant to 3atm.
Dial: silvered.
Strap: brown alligator leather; steel folding buckle.
Suggested price: $9,400

COMPETIZIONE CIRCUITO — REF. 49590-39-612-BB6B

Movement: automatic-winding GP03300-0122 caliber; 11 ½ lines; 46-hour power reserve; 63 jewels; 28,800 vph.
Functions: hours, minutes; small seconds at 3; date between 4 and 5; chronograph: central seconds hand, 12-hour counter at 6, 30-minute counter at 9.
Case: carbon/titanium composite; Ø 42mm, thickness: 13.99mm; sapphire crystal caseback; water resistant to 3atm.
Dial: “honeycomb”.
Strap: carbon-effect calfskin with DLC steel folding buckle.
Suggested price: $13,200

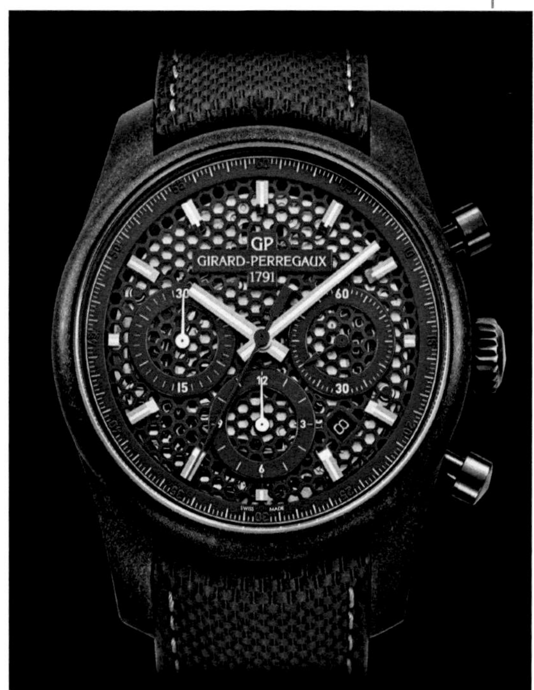

1966 LADY, 30 MM — REF. 49528D11A172-CB6A

Movement: automatic-winding GP03200-0012 caliber; 10 ½ lines; 42-hour power reserve; 26 jewels; 28,800 vph.
Functions: hours, minutes.
Case: steel; Ø 30mm, thickness: 9.15mm; set with 60 brilliant-cut diamonds (approx. 0.55 carat); sapphire crystal caseback; water resistant to 3atm.
Dial: flinqué silver; set with 10 brilliant-cut diamonds.
Strap: black alligator leather; steel pin buckle.
Suggested price: $9,500

1966 LADY MOON PHASES — REF. 49524D11A171-CK6A

Movement: automatic-winding GP03300-0116 caliber; 11 ½ lines; 46-hour power reserve; 32 jewels; 28,800 vph.
Functions: hours, minutes; small seconds on moonphase at 6.
Case: steel; Ø 36mm, thickness: 10.29mm; set with 54 brilliant-cut diamonds (approx. 1.35 carats); sapphire crystal caseback; water resistant to 3atm.
Dial: flinqué silver.
Strap: black alligator leather; steel pin buckle.
Suggested price: $15,300

VINTAGE 1945 LADY — REF. 25860D11A1A1-11A

Movement: automatic-winding GP02700-0003 caliber; 8 ¾ lines; 36-hour power reserve; 26 jewels; 28,800 vph.
Functions: hours, minutes; date at 6.
Case: steel; 28.2x27.86mm, thickness: 10.21mm; set with 30 brilliant-cut diamonds (approx. 0.55 carat); sapphire crystal caseback; water resistant to 3atm.
Dial: white lacquered; set with 42 brilliant-cut diamonds (approx. 0.105 carat).
Bracelet: steel; triple folding buckle.
Suggested price: $14,500

CAT'S EYE POWER RESERVE — REF. 80486D56A162-CK6A

Movement: automatic-winding GP03300-0070 caliber; 11 ½ lines; 46-hour power reserve; 27 jewels; 28,800 vph.
Functions: hours, minutes; small seconds at 9; date at 3; power reserve indicator between 4 and 5.
Case: steel and pink gold; 37.84x32.84mm, thickness: 11.22mm; set with 64 brilliant-cut diamonds (approx. 0.95 carat); sapphire crystal caseback; water resistant to 3atm.
Dial: flinqué silver; set with 8 brilliant-cut diamonds (approx. 0.10 carat).
Strap: black alligator leather; steel folding buckle.
Suggested price: $17,800

CAT'S EYE MAJESTIC — REF. 80493D52A763-52A

Movement: automatic-winding GP03300-0121 caliber; 11 ½ lines; 46-hour power reserve; 27 jewels; 28,800 vph.
Functions: hours, minutes.
Case: pink gold; 40x34.72mm, thickness: 12.57mm; set with 60 brilliant-cut diamonds (approx. 1 carat); sapphire crystal caseback; water resistant to 3atm.
Dial: hand-polished mother-of-pearl with sunray decoration; set with 8 brilliant-cut diamonds (approx. 0.032 carat).
Strap: pink gold; folding buckle.
Suggested price: $39,700

CAT'S EYE SMALL SECOND — REF. 80484D52A763-BK6B

Movement: automatic-winding GP03300-0044 caliber; 11 ½ lines; 46-hour power reserve; 28 jewels; 28,800 vph.
Functions: hours, minutes; small seconds at 9; date at 3.
Case: pink gold; 35.4x30.4mm, thickness: 9.1mm; set with 62 brilliant-cut diamonds (approx. 0.85 carat); sapphire crystal caseback; water resistant to 3atm.
Dial: hand-polished white mother-of-pearl; set with 9 brilliant-cut diamonds (approx. 0.108 carat).
Strap: black alligator leather; pink-gold folding buckle.
Suggested price: $27,500

CAT'S EYE WATER LILY — REF. 80489D53A1B3-CKAA

Movement: automatic-winding GP03300-0101 caliber; 11 ½ lines; 46-hour power reserve; 27 jewels; 28,800 vph.
Functions: hours, minutes.
Case: white gold; 35.4x30.4mm, thickness: 11.3mm; set with 62 brilliant-cut diamonds (approx. 0.8 carat); sapphire crystal caseback; water resistant to 3atm.
Dial: set with 412 brilliant-cut diamonds (approx. 2 carats) and 6 marquise-cut emeralds (approx. 0.15 carat).
Strap: emerald alligator leather; white-gold folding buckle set with 14 brilliant-cut diamonds (approx. 0.118 carat).
Suggested price: $58,100

CAT'S EYE AVENTURINE — REF. 80488D52A451-CK4A

Movement: automatic-winding GP03300-0090 caliber; 11 ½ lines; 46-hour power reserve; 32 jewels; 28,800 vph.
Functions: hours, minutes; small seconds on day/night indicator at 6.
Case: pink gold; 35.4x30.4mm, thickness: 11.29mm; set with 62 brilliant-cut diamonds (approx. 0.8 carat); sapphire crystal caseback; water resistant to 3atm.
Dial: aventurine; set with 18 brilliant-cut diamonds (approx. 0.06 carat).
Strap: blue alligator leather; pink-gold folding buckle.
Suggested price: $31,600

PERFECTLY SIMPLE, SIMPLY PERFECT

Glashütte Original **EPITOMIZES THE CONCEPT OF PURPOSEFUL INNOVATION** with a collection whose models' shared Calibre insists upon timeless values.

The German watchmaker's Senator Excellence collection endows its aesthetic classicism with a new manufacture Calibre that captures the essence of timekeeping. Four key principles guided the Calibre 36's creation: stability, precision, extended running time and flawless finishing. By replacing the more vulnerable components with innovative solutions, such as the integration of a bi-directional-wind reduction gear instead of a conventional winding-system detent click, Glashütte Original ensures a level of sustained performance under the wearer's real-life conditions. In addition, a bayonet mount, settling the movement in the case, provides exceptional impact resistance as well as ease of service. An innovative silicon balance spring, impervious to temperature variations and magnetic fields, optimizes oscillation regularity and thus rate precision. Without compromising the performance of the 28,800 vph movement, and without the need for a second barrel, the manufacture endows the Calibre with 100 hours of autonomy. This impressive feat is achieved by way of an increase in the barrel's diameter and reduction in the dimensions of its arbor, resulting in a longer mainspring with a larger number of winding turns.

Understated yet rich in character, the Senator Excellence, in stainless steel or red gold, uses minimalism to bring attention to the most fundamental details. On a light, silver-grained lacquered dial, laser-cut galvanized indexes gain prominence, along with a railroad-track minute ring, thanks to the presence of only two Roman numerals. Positioned at 12 and 6 o'clock, they allow for an open and spacious dial design, where two slim poire hands (for the hours and minutes) and a filigreed stem (for the seconds), all blued for a vibrant contrast, bring to life the outstanding performance of the timepiece's Calibre. A sapphire crystal caseback grants the wearer a superb view of the Calibre 36's numerous visual delights, from its skeletonized rotor with an elegant stripe finish, to the perlage, polished steel parts and decorative millings on wheels and on the rotor track.

◂ SENATOR EXCELLENCE

This elegant self-winding timepiece is driven by the Calibre 36, a newly designed manufacture movement optimized for stability, precision and real-life use.

Two slim poire hands and a filigreed stem, all blued for a vibrant contrast, bring to life the outstanding performance of the Senator Excellence's Calibre 36.

The Senator Excellence Panorama Date enlivens the collection's refined dial with an exhibition of Glashütte Original's celebrated date display. Two concentric discs, arranged on the same level, allow for both numerals to stand out without the need for a central separation bar. Enriched with a jumping mechanism, the Panorama Date, positioned at 4 o'clock, boasts excellent precision as it transitions to the next day at midnight. Its seamless integration with the dial's background strengthens the timepiece's effect of understated visual continuity.

The Senator Excellence Panorama Date Moon Phase complements its fluid aesthetic with a celebration of the earth's changeable companion. Visible through a softly curved aperture at 10 o'clock, a graphical exhibition of the lunar cycle dazzles upon a galvanic starry blue sky. The sophisticated complication requires only a single-day adjustment every 122 years—yet another expression of the Calibre 36's guiding principles.

▲ **SENATOR EXCELLENCE PANORAMA DATE**

Thanks to two concentric discs, this timepiece displays the date with perfect legibility and precision while affirming the seamless refinement of the overall design.

▶ **SENATOR EXCELLENCE PANORAMA DATE MOON PHASE**

A finely crafted moonphase complication demonstrates the sophistication of this timepiece's self-winding Calibre, while adding a vibrant touch of colorful dynamism to a design of timeless classicism.

PANOLUNAR TOURBILLON — REF. 1-93-02-05-05-05

Movement: automatic-winding 93-02 caliber.
Functions: off-centered hours and minutes; small seconds on tourbillon at 7; panorama date at 3; moonphase at 1.
Case: 18K red gold; crown with double-G logo; sapphire crystal; sapphire crystal caseback; water resistant to 5atm.
Dial: galvanized silver; rose-gold appliques; rose-gold hands with SuperLumiNova.
Strap: nubuck alligator leather; 18K red-gold fold fastener.
Suggested price: $117,400

SENATOR COSMOPOLITE — REF. 1-89-02-01-04-30

Movement: automatic-winding 89-02 caliber.
Functions: hours, minutes; small seconds at 6; panorama date at 4; second time zone at 12; selection of 36 time zones; daylight saving time indicator; power reserve display at 12; day/night indicator at 9.
Case: 18K white gold; crown with double-G logo; sapphire crystal; sapphire crystal caseback; water resistant to 5atm.
Dial: varnished silver-grainé; Roman and Arabic numerals; blued hands.
Strap: blue Louisiana alligator leather; 18K white-gold fold fastener.
Suggested price: $45,300

PANOMATICINVERSE — REF. 1-91-02-02-02-30

Movement: automatic-winding 91-02 caliber.
Functions: off-centered hours and minutes; off-centered small seconds; panorama date at 1.
Case: stainless steel; crown with double-G logo; sapphire crystal; sapphire crystal caseback; water resistant to 5atm.
Dial: galvanized rhodium; blued hands with SuperLumiNova.
Strap: black Louisiana alligator leather; stainless steel fold fastener.
Suggested price: $14,900

SENATOR MOONPHASE MANUAL WINDING SKELETON EDITION — REF. 1-49-13-15-04-30

Movement: manual-winding 49-13 caliber.
Functions: hours, minutes; small seconds at 6; moonphase between 10 and 11; power reserve indicator between 1 and 2.
Case: 18K white gold; crown with double-G logo; sapphire crystal; sapphire crystal caseback; water resistant to 3atm.
Dial: skeletonized galvanized silver; black Roman numerals.
Strap: blue Louisiana alligator leather; white-gold fold fastener.
Suggested price: $45,000

SENATOR CHRONOMETER — REF. 1-58-01-05-34-30

Movement: manual-winding 58-01 caliber.
Functions: hours, minutes; small seconds at 6; panorama date at 3; power reserve indicator and day/night display at 12.
Case: 18K white gold; crown with double-G logo; sapphire crystal; sapphire crystal caseback; water resistant to 5atm.
Dial: varnished blue-grainé; white-gold hands.
Strap: blue Louisiana alligator leather; 18K white-gold fold fastener.
Suggested price: $32,200

SENATOR EXCELLENCE PANORAMA DATE MOON PHASE — REF. 1-36-04-02-05-30

Movement: automatic-winding 36-04 caliber.
Functions: hours, minutes, seconds; panorama date at 4; moonphase between 10 and 11.
Case: 18K red gold; crown with double-G logo; sapphire crystal; sapphire crystal caseback; water resistant to 5atm.
Dial: varnished silver-grainé; laser engraved black hour markers with Roman numerals; red Arabic numerals; blued hands.
Strap: black Louisiana alligator leather; red-gold fold fastener.
Suggested price: $23,900

SEVENTIES CHRONOGRAPH PANORAMA DATE — REF. 1-37-02-03-02-70

Movement: automatic-winding 37-02 caliber.
Functions: hours, minutes; small seconds at 9; panorama date at 6; chronograph: central seconds hand, 12-hour counter at 12, 30-minute counter at 3; power reserve display at 9.
Case: stainless steel; crown with double-G logo; sapphire crystal; sapphire crystal caseback; water resistant to 10atm.
Dial: varnished blue; white-gold appliques; white-gold hands with SuperLumiNova.
Bracelet: stainless steel; stainless steel fold fastener.
Suggested price: $16,400

LADY SERENADE — REF. 1-39-22-18-11-04

Movement: automatic-winding 39-22 caliber.
Functions: hours, minutes, seconds; panorama date at 6.
Case: 18K rose gold; bezel set with 52 diamonds (approx. 1.09 carats); crown set with 1 diamond (approx. 0.1 carat); sapphire crystal; sapphire crystal caseback; water resistant to 5atm.
Dial: galvanized black with sunray decoration; rose-gold appliques; rose-gold hands.
Strap: black Louisiana alligator leather; rose-gold fold fastener.
Suggested price: $22,900

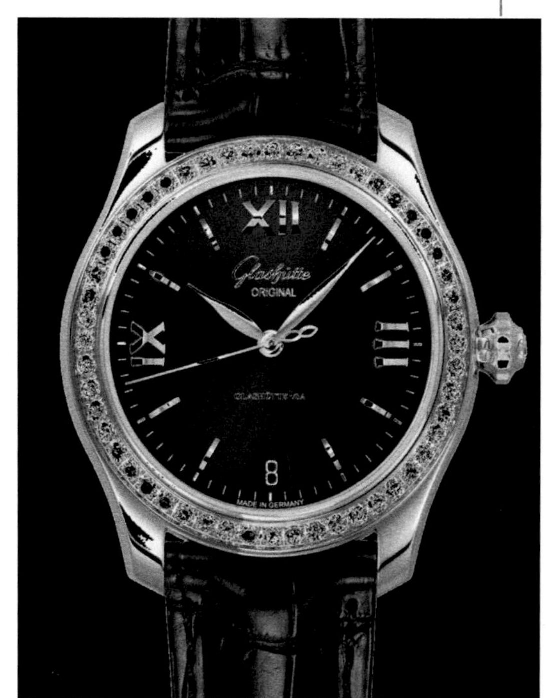

GREUBEL FORSEY

ART INVENTION

THE SOUL OF MASTERY

With six extraordinary creations, Greubel Forsey **CLARIFIES AND EXPANDS ITS UNIQUE HOROLOGICAL VISION**. Combining the highest degree of technical skill with an audacious imagination and philosophical spirit, Greubel Forsey timepieces ceaselessly remap the frontiers of the watchmaking art form.

With the Signature 1, the celebrated Swiss Atelier extends its expertise and horological resources to fellow brilliant watchmaker Didier J.G. Cretin. In doing so, Robert Greubel and Stephen Forsey pass on their unparalleled level of savoir-faire while giving Cretin the freedom necessary to express his unique creativity. In line with the Atelier's standard of excellence, yet imbued with a distinctive vision, the limited edition Signature 1 (housed in a 41.4mm case in white gold, platinum, red gold or steel) boasts a first in the proud history of Greubel Forsey: a manual-winding movement featuring three hands, without a tourbillon. Atop an openworked construction revealing a number of the caliber's exquisitely finished components, two off-centered subdials indicate the hours, minutes and seconds with geometric contrast against the rest of the timepiece. The juxtaposition of traditional display styles and semi-openworked architecture provides the watch with the perfect balance of visual texture and depth. At the heart of the Signature 1 beats a caliber without compromise. From the superb Côtes-de-Genève decoration of its principal dial-side mainplate, to the flawless construction of its 61-component escapement platform, variable-inertia balance wheel and barrel with fixed mainspring bridle, the Signature 1's 190-part caliber earns its prominent showcase with dazzling confidence.

▲ **SIGNATURE 1**

Created by Didier J.G. Cretin and co-signed with Robert Greubel and Stephen Forsey, this semi-openworked timepiece represents the first hand-wound three-hand creation, without a tourbillon, in the Atelier's whis-

A cleverly integrated crystal dome protrudes from the caseback of the Tourbillon 24 Secondes Vision, allowing for the necessary additional volume without enlarging the overall design of the timepiece or interfering with the wearer's comfort.

Building upon the overwhelming success of its predecessor (winner of the prestigious Aiguille d'Or at the 2015 Grand Prix d'Horlogerie de Genève), the Tourbillon 24 Secondes Vision now houses its award-winning caliber in a luxurious platinum case. The 43.5mm hand-wound timepiece represents a valiant refusal to sacrifice mechanical excellence in the quest for aesthetic purity. Instead, thanks to the ingenuity of the Atelier's visionary namesakes, the timepiece successfully fits its 86-part tourbillon cage at a 25º incline while preserving the graceful silhouette of the case. A cleverly integrated crystal dome protrudes from the caseback, allowing for the necessary additional volume without enlarging the overall design of the timepiece or interfering with the wearer's comfort. The tourbillon, which completes its rapid revolution in just 24 seconds, is visible at 9 o'clock via an aperture in the multi-level salmon-colored gold dial. Its two bridges, composed of titanium, are gracefully curved to accommodate its volume. Along with its obvious geometric benefits, the caseback's protruding dome showcases the tourbillon with extraordinary splendor. The Tourbillon 24 Seconds Vision boasts a 72-hour power reserve, visible on the caseback, thanks to its caliber's two series-coupled barrels. Fitted with a variable-inertia balance wheel, the 293-component movement indicates the hours and minutes, as well as the small seconds on a subdial at 4 o'clock.

▲ **TOURBILLON 24 SECONDES VISION**

A protruding dome on the caseback allows for this timepiece to retain its elegant silhouette while housing a breathtaking 24-second tourbillon inclined at 25º.

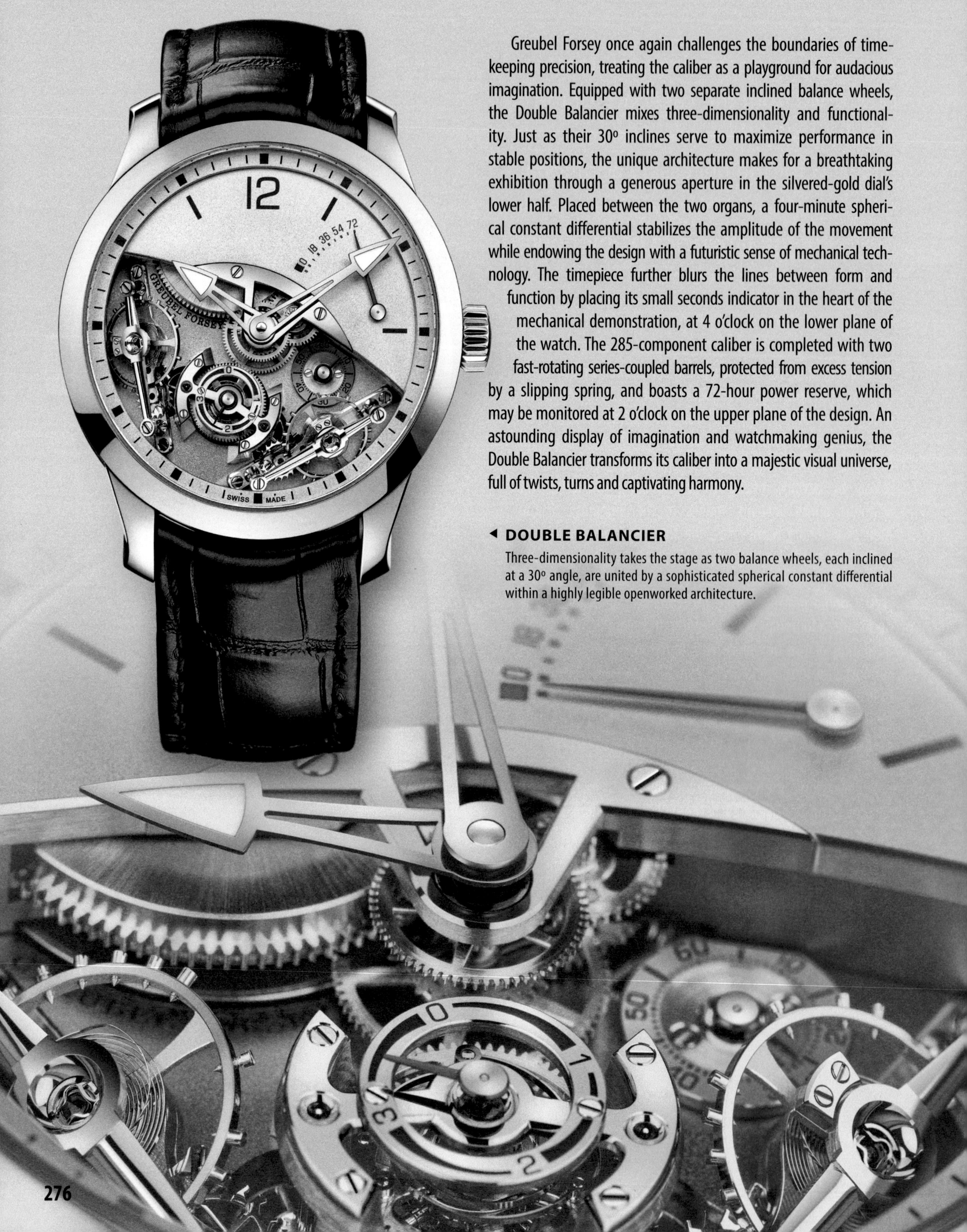

Greubel Forsey once again challenges the boundaries of timekeeping precision, treating the caliber as a playground for audacious imagination. Equipped with two separate inclined balance wheels, the Double Balancier mixes three-dimensionality and functionality. Just as their 30º inclines serve to maximize performance in stable positions, the unique architecture makes for a breathtaking exhibition through a generous aperture in the silvered-gold dial's lower half. Placed between the two organs, a four-minute spherical constant differential stabilizes the amplitude of the movement while endowing the design with a futuristic sense of mechanical technology. The timepiece further blurs the lines between form and function by placing its small seconds indicator in the heart of the mechanical demonstration, at 4 o'clock on the lower plane of the watch. The 285-component caliber is completed with two fast-rotating series-coupled barrels, protected from excess tension by a slipping spring, and boasts a 72-hour power reserve, which may be monitored at 2 o'clock on the upper plane of the design. An astounding display of imagination and watchmaking genius, the Double Balancier transforms its caliber into a majestic visual universe, full of twists, turns and captivating harmony.

◂ **DOUBLE BALANCIER**

Three-dimensionality takes the stage as two balance wheels, each inclined at a 30º angle, are united by a sophisticated spherical constant differential within a highly legible openworked architecture.

The GMT Black brilliantly juxtaposes its dark case and dial with the vibrant tones of its dynamic centerpiece, taking the concept of world time on a fascinating voyage. Dressed in a 43.5mm titanium case treated with vacuum-deposited amorphous diamond-like carbon (ADLC), giving it a high level of hardness, the hand-wound timepiece brings an irresistible visual element to its sophisticated interpretation of multiple time zones. At 7 o'clock on the frosted, black-treated gold dial, an elaborately finished titanium globe orbits around its axis, granting the wearer a spectacular 24-hour overview of the time throughout the planet. In a touch of genius by Greubel Forsey, a transparent sapphire window on the side of the case brings added light to the hemisphere currently experiencing daytime hours. Driven by a 437-component caliber with variable-inertia balance wheel and two coaxial series-coupled barrels, the GMT Black complements its display of the hours, minutes, small seconds at 2 o'clock, power reserve at 3 o'clock and second time zone display at 10 o'clock with a state-of-the-art tourbillon contained within the dial's openworked lower half. The gravity regulator, which executes its full rotation in just 24 seconds, boasts an incline of 25º, maximizing precision and performance while granting the wearer an optimal view of its 86-component construction. Blackened as if to highlight the illuminated Earth orbiting through an infinite night sky, the GMT Black, limited to only 22 pieces, is finished with a black ADLC titanium crown and worn on a black leather strap with hand-stitched rubber.

▼ GMT BLACK

This titanium world-time wristwatch places a detailed orbiting globe within a deep black sky filled with technical sophistication and comprehensive indicators.

The Double Tourbillon 30° Technique Bi-Color offers its owner a breathtaking view of its many components and their dynamic choreography. Housed in a red-gold or platinum case, and adorned with engraved black ADLC-finished titanium plates on the caseband, the 47.5mm timepiece presents the full extent of its extraordinary mechanical complexity within a sophisticated design. Composed of an outer and inner carriage, conducting their revolutions in four minutes and 60 seconds respectively, the timepiece's Double Tourbillon performs a mesmerizing spectacle of multi-dimensional motion. At 3 o'clock, the watch's power reserve indicator, highlighting the impressive 120-hour autonomy made possible by the movement's four coaxial series-coupled barrels at 11 o'clock, is elegantly enhanced by a Greubel Forsey spherical differential at 2 o'clock. The Double Tourbillon 30° Technique Bi-Color, finished with a small seconds subdial at 9 o'clock, extends its graceful mechanical performance to the caseback, where a transparent synthetic sapphire crystal affords the wearer a brilliant view of the caliber's immaculate craftsmanship.

◀ **DOUBLE TOURBILLON 30° TECHNIQUE BI-COLOR**

A spacious multi-dimensional architecture allows this timepiece to reveal the full fascination of its mechanical caliber, including a tourbillon composed of two carriages orbiting on separate axes and at different speeds of rotation.

▶ **ART PIECE 2 – EDITION 1**

Only revealing the hours and minutes when requested to do so, this fusion of philosophy and haute horology complements its inclined Double Tourbillon with a highly detailed nano-engraved sketch, visible thanks to a 23x magnification instrument housed in the case.

The Art Piece 2 – Edition 1 represents a declaration of horological artistry that supersedes the supposed purpose for its existence. In fact, the Art Piece 2 – Edition 1 only tells the time upon request. The press of a pusher activates a bi-stable shutter mechanism that reveals the hours and minutes, but the wristwatch stands complete even in its "timeless" state. At 1 o'clock on the dial, the Art Piece 2 – Edition 1's Double Tourbillon executes its rotations on different axes and at different speeds, the outer carriage revolving in four minutes while the inner carriage, inclined at 30º, completes its rotation in 60 seconds. The spirited exclamation of art and science's meeting point does not end on the dial. An optical instrument, housed in the case, allows the wearer to admire the magnificent details of a nano-engraved sketch of the Double Tourbillon 30° mechanism found on the side of the case. Magnified 23x, the artwork, achieved using a secret process on a sapphire tablet, becomes a spellbinding exhibition in itself, as worthy of attention as its "living" counterpart found in the heart of the timepiece. Challenging the conventions and paradigms of the timekeeping art form, the Art Piece 2 – Edition 1, endowed with two series-coupled barrels, transcends its most fundamental purpose and finds thought-provoking raison d'être deep within its own heartbeat.

DOUBLE TOURBILLON 30° TECHNIQUE

Movement: manual-winding GF02s caliber; Ø 38.4mm, thickness: 12.15mm; 120-hour power reserve; 396 components; 43 jewels; 21,600 vph; Phillips terminal curve balance spring; free sprung variable-inertia balance wheel with white-gold mean-time screws; four coaxial series-couple fast-rotating barrels.
Functions: hours, minutes; small seconds at 9; power reserve indicator at 3; tourbillon at 6.
Case: platinum; Ø 47.5mm, thickness: 16.84mm; platinum crown with engraved and black lacquered GF logo; convex synthetic sapphire crystal; synthetic sapphire crystal caseback; water resistant to 3atm.
Dial: synthetic sapphire crystal hour-dial; gold small seconds dial and power reserve indicator; gold hour and minute hands with SuperLumiNova.
Strap: hand-sewn black alligator leather; platinum folding clasp hand-engraved with the Greubel Forsey logo.
Note: limited edition of 22 pieces.
Price: available upon request.

DOUBLE TOURBILLON ASYMETRIQUE

Movement: manual-winding GF02a2 caliber; Ø 36.4mm, thickness: 9.38mm; 72-hour power reserve; 319 components; 39 jewels; 21,600 vph; Phillips terminal curve balance spring; free sprung variable-inertia balance with white-gold mean-time screws; two series-coupled fast rotating barrels.
Functions: hours, minutes; small seconds at 6; power reserve indicator at 2; tourbillon at 8.
Case: white gold; Ø 43.5mm, thickness: 16.13mm; platinum crown with engraved and black lacquered GF logo; convex synthetic sapphire crystal; convex synthetic sapphire crystal caseback; water resistant to 3atm.
Dial: black oxidized gold; gold hours, small seconds and power reserve indicators; applied gold Greubel Forsey logo; polished gold hour and minute hands with SuperLumiNova.
Strap: hand-sewn black alligator leather; platinum folding clasp hand-engraved with the Greubel Forsey logo.
Note: unique edition of 11 pieces.
Price: available upon request.

QUADRUPLE TOURBILLON SECRET

Movement: manual-winding GF03j caliber; Ø 36.4mm, thickness: 9.85mm; 50-hour power reserve; 509 components; 63 jewels; 21,600 vph; Phillips terminal curve balance spring; free sprung variable-inertia balance wheel with white-gold mean-time screws; rapid rotating twin barrels.
Functions: hours, minutes; small seconds at 2; power reserve indicator at 2; tourbillon at 5.
Case: platinum 950; Ø 43.5mm, thickness: 16.11mm; polished bezel; platinum crown with engraved and black lacquered GF logo; asymmetrical convex synthetic sapphire crystal; asymmetrical convex synthetic sapphire crystal caseback; water resistant to 3atm.
Dial: silver-colored gold; gold hour makers; gold display sectors; applied gold Greubel Forsey logo.
Strap: hand-sewn black alligator leather; platinum 950 folding clasp hand-engraved with the Greubel Forsey logo.
Note: unique edition of 8 pieces.
Price: available upon request.

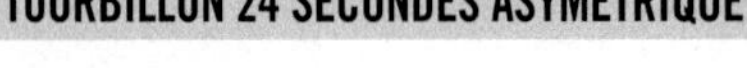

TOURBILLON 24 SECONDES ASYMETRIQUE

Movement: manual-winding GF01 caliber; Ø 36.4mm, thickness: 9.35mm; 72-hour power reserve; 275 components; 36 jewels; 21,600 vph; Phillips terminal curve balance spring; free sprung variable-inertia balance wheel with gold mean-time screws; two series-coupled fast rotating barrels.
Functions: hours, minutes; small seconds between 4 and 5; 24-second tourbillon rotation indicator.
Case: 5N red gold; Ø 43.5mm, thickness: 16.11mm; polished bezel; 5N red-gold crown with engraved and black lacquered GF logo; convex synthetic sapphire crystal; convex synthetic sapphire crystal case back; water resistant to 3atm.
Dial: silver-colored gold; gold hour markers; gold display sectors; applied gold Greubel Forsey logo; polished gold hands.
Strap: hand-sewn black alligator leather; 18K white-gold tang buckle hand-engraved with the Greubel Forsey logo.
Price: available upon request.

TOURBILLON 24 SECONDES CONTEMPORAIN

Movement: manual-winding GF01c caliber; Ø 36.4mm, thickness: 10.85mm; 72-hour power reserve; 365 components; 40 jewels; 21,600 vph; Phillips terminal curve balance spring; free sprung variable-inertia balance wheel with gold mean-time screws; two coaxial series-coupled fast rotating barrels.
Functions: hours, minutes; small seconds at 9; power reserve indicator at 4; tourbillon cage inclined at 25° angle, 24-second rotation.
Case: 18K 5N red gold; Ø 44.5mm, thickness: 15.2mm; 5N red-gold crown with engraved and black lacquered GF logo; convex synthetic sapphire crystal; synthetic sapphire crystal caseback; water resistant to 3atm.
Dial: blue oxidized; synthetic sapphire crystal hour-ring; gold small seconds dial and power reserve indicator; polished gold hour and minute hands with SuperLumiNova.
Strap: hand-sewn dark blue alligator leather; 5N red-gold folding clasp hand-engraved with the Greubel Forsey logo.
Note: limited edition of 33 pieces.
Price: available upon request.

TOURBILLON 24 SECONDES CONTEMPORAIN

Movement: manual-winding GF01c caliber; Ø 36.4mm, thickness: 10.85mm; 72-hour power reserve; 362 components; 40 jewels; 21,600 vph; Phillips terminal curve balance spring; free sprung variable-inertia balance wheel with gold mean-time screws; two coaxial series-coupled fast rotating barrels.
Functions: hours, minutes; small seconds at 9; power reserve indicator at 4; tourbillon between 7 and 8.
Case: white gold; Ø 44.5mm, thickness: 15.2mm; bezel set with 60 baguette diamonds (2.71 carats); white-gold crown with engraved and black lacquered GF logo; convex synthetic sapphire crystal; synthetic sapphire crystal caseback; water resistant to 3atm.
Dial: blue oxidized; white-gold upper plate set with 78 baguette diamonds (3.51 carats); synthetic sapphire crystal hour-ring; lugs set with 80 baguette diamonds (2.74 carats); gold small seconds dial and power reserve indicator; polished gold hour and minute hands.
Strap: hand-sewn dark blue alligator leather; white-gold folding clasp set with 54 baguette diamonds (0.75 carat), hand-engraved with the Greubel Forsey logo.
Price: available upon request.

GMT ASYMETRIQUE

Movement: manual-winding GF05 caliber; Ø 36.4mm, thickness: 9.8mm; 72-hour power reserve; 437 components; 50 jewels; 21,600 vph; Phillips terminal curve; free sprung variable-inertia balance with gold mean-time screws; two coaxial series-coupled fast-rotating barrels.
Functions: hours, minutes; small seconds at 2; power reserve indicator at 3; 2nd time zone GMT indicator at 10; 24 time zone worldtime display on caseback; rotating titanium globe with universal time display; tourbillon inclined at 25° angle, 24-second rotation.
Case: black ADLC titanium; Ø 43.5mm, thickness: 16.14mm; polished bezel; black ADLC titanium crown with engraved GF logo; convex synthetic sapphire crystal; asymmetrical convex synthetic sapphire crystal caseback; water resistant to 3atm.
Dial: gold frosted hour-minute dial with black chrome treatment; gold power reserve sector; gold small seconds dial; gold GMT indicator; applied gold Greubel Forsey logo; polished gold hour and minute hands with SuperLumiNova; polished gold small seconds and power reserve indicators; red triangle 2nd time zone GMT indicator.
Strap: hand-sewn black rubber strap; black ADLC titanium folding clasp hand-engraved with the Greubel Forsey logo.
Note: limited edition of 22 pieces.
Price: available upon request.

GMT ASYMETRIQUE

Movement: manual-winding GF05 caliber; Ø 36.4mm, thickness: 9.8mm; 72-hour power reserve; 437 components; 50 jewels; 21,600 vph; Phillips terminal curve balance spring; free sprung variable-inertia balance wheel with gold mean-time screws; two coaxial series-coupled fast-rotating barrels.
Functions: hours, minutes; small seconds at 2; power reserve indicator at 3; 2nd time zone GMT indicator at 10; 24 time zone worldtime display on caseback; rotating titanium globe with universal time display; tourbillon inclined at 25° angle, 24-second rotation.
Case: platinum; Ø 43.5mm, thickness: 16.14mm; polished bezel; platinum crown with engraved and black lacquered GF logo; asymmetrical convex synthetic sapphire crystal; asymmetrical convex synthetic sapphire crystal caseback; water resistant to 3atm.
Dial: gold frosted hour-minute dial with black chrome treatment; gold power reserve indicator; gold small seconds dial; gold GMT indicator; applied gold Greubel Forsey logo; polished gold hour and minute hands with SuperLumiNova; blued steel small seconds and power reserve hands; red triangle 2nd time zone GMT indicator.
Strap: hand-sewn black alligator leather; platinum folding clasp hand-engraved with the Greubel Forsey logo.
Note: limited edition of 22 pieces.
Price: available upon request.

GUY ELLIA

CIRCLE OF LIGHT

Guy Ellia dresses the feminine **WRIST WITH EFFORTLESS ELEGANCE, PRESENTING A CONVEX TIMEPIECE THAT ELEVATES ITS VIBRANT DESIGN WITH A GENEROUS SETTING OF PRECIOUS STONES.**

▲▶ **CIRCLE "LA PETITE"**

Available in three case choices and with a variety of dial personalities and gem settings, this convex ladies' wristwatch showcases its unique personality at every turn.

The snow-set variation of the Circle "La Petite" reflects the bold individuality of its wearer with sumptuous elegance.

The watchmaker's Circle "La Petite" finds striking beauty in the purity of geometric simplicity. Housed in a convex 45mm case that perfectly follows the curves of the wrist, the timepiece com-plements its elegant shape with a variety of tones and gem settings to match the distinctive personality of its elegant wearer. Whether dressed in white, yellow or rose gold, the Circle "La Petite" enlivens the elegance of its captivating curvature with 105 brilliant-cut diamonds on the bezel that affirm the luxurious refinement of the design. Its thickness, of only 6mm, contrasts with the otherwise imposing dimensions to maintain a seamless tone of unassuming grace. On the dial, 12 elongated indexes, with or without 192 additional brilliant-cut stones, mark the hours and appear to emanate radiantly from a small central circle where the hours and minutes are told via two dauphine hands of just 6 and 7.5mm. The Circle "La Petite" also expresses itself with a wide variety of dial colors. From brilliant black to opal, night blue, polished or matte "rose" and polished or matte yellow, the timepiece allows its owner to make an uncompromising aesthetic statement. The watch may thus range from a single-tone demonstration of nuanced subtleties to a high-contrast creation full of bold combinations and shimmering accents.

The Circle "La Petite" has yet another shimmering trick up its sleeve. A full-snow-set model replaces its colorful dial and converging rays with an incredible 1,044 brilliant-cut diamonds, totalling 4.88 carats. Gracing its riveting convex disposition with boundless light and intriguing texture, this snow-set variation reflects the bold individuality of its wearer with sumptuous opulence.

The Circle "La Petite" is finished with a 2.8mm diamond on the crown and is secured to the wrist by way of a curved bracelet perfectly integrated into the structure of the timepiece.

ELYPSE

Movement: quartz; Blancpain caliber PGE 820; Ø 18.8mm, thickness: 1.95mm; rhodiumed and "Côtes de Genève"-decorated cage.
Functions: hours, minutes.
Case: 18K white gold (53.38g); 52x35mm, thickness: 5.6mm; bezel set with 80 diamonds; crown set with one diamond (Ø 2.5mm); sapphire glass with thermal counter-shock marking; mirror-polished caseback set with one diamond on the "I" of ELLIA (Ø 0.95mm) and deep mechanical engraving; water resistant to 3atm.
Dial: shiny gold black painted; Roman numerals; gold dauphine-shaped hands.

Strap: black alligator leather; 18K white-gold pin buckle set with nine diamonds (Ø 1.5mm); pin set with one diamond (Ø 0.9mm) (0.12 carat).
Also available: case: pink and yellow gold; dial: Roman numeral versions: matte black, matte chocolate, brilliant gold, matte khaki, brilliant Burgundy, matte Burgundy, brilliant blue, matte orange, matte lilac, pink salmon, matte beige; dial: mirror or polished gold (white, pink and yellow), brilliant black, black matte, pearly white, light brown matte, navy pearly, light blue matte, opal.

ELYPSE

Movement: quartz; Blancpain caliber PGE 820; Ø 18.8mm, thickness: 1.95mm; rhodiumed and "Côtes de Genève"-decorated cage.
Functions: hours, minutes.
Case: white gold (53.38g); 52x35mm, thickness: 5.6mm; bezel set with 80 diamonds; crown set with one diamond (Ø 2.5mm); sapphire glass with thermal counter-shock marking; mirror-polished caseback set with one diamond on the "I" of ELLIA (Ø 0.9mm) and deep mechanical engraving; water resistant to 3atm.
Dial: microblasted white gold; blue painted Roman numerals; gold dauphine-shaped hands.

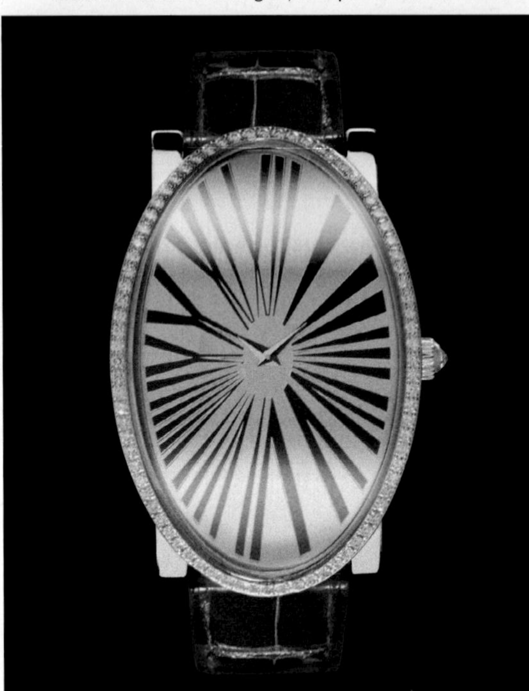

Strap: blue alligator leather; 18K white-gold buckle set with nine diamonds (Ø 1.5mm); pin set with one diamond (Ø 0.9mm) (0.12 carat).
Also available: case: pink and yellow gold; dial: Roman numeral versions: matte black, matte chocolate, brilliant gold, matte khaki, brilliant Burgundy, matte Burgundy, matte orange, matte lilac, pink salmon, matte beige; dial: mirror or polished gold (white, pink and yellow); brilliant black, black matte, light brown matte, navy pearly, light blue matte, opal.

QUEEN

Movement: quartz; Blancpain caliber PGE 820; Ø 18.8mm, thickness: 1.95mm; rhodiumed and "Côtes de Genève"-decorated cage.
Functions: hours, minutes.
Case: white gold (63.13g); 52x38.5mm, thickness: 7.2mm; bezel set with 96 diamonds (0.89 carat); crown set with one diamond (0.08 carat); sapphire glass with thermal counter-shock marking; mirror-polished caseback set with one diamond on the "I" of ELLIA (Ø 0.95mm) and deep mechanical engraving; water resistant to 3atm.
Dial: navy mother-of-pearl; white-gold Roman numerals.

Strap: black alligator leather; solid 18K white-gold pin buckle (4.32g) set with 81 diamonds (0.37 carat).
Also available: case: pink gold, yellow gold; mother-of-pearl dial with Roman numerals or mirror-polished dial with indexes set with 116 brillant-cut diamonds (0.35 carat)

QUEEN

Movement: quartz; Blancpain caliber PGE 820; Ø 18.8mm, thickness: 1.95mm; rhodiumed and "Côtes de Genève"-decorated cage.
Functions: hours, minutes.
Case: 18K pink gold (59.34g); 52x38.5mm, thickness: 7.2mm; fully set with 409 diamonds (3.05 carats); crown set with one diamond (0.08 carat); sapphire glass with thermal counter-shock marking; mirror-polished caseback set with one diamond on the "I" of ELLIA (Ø 0.95mm) and deep mechanical engraving; water resistant to 3atm.
Dial: pink gold; fully set with 450 diamonds (2.19 carats).

Strap: brown alligator leather; solid 18K pink-gold buckle and pin (3.84g) set with 81 diamonds (0.37 carat).
Also available: case: pink gold, yellow gold; mother-of-pearl dial with Roman numals or mirror-polished dial with indexes set with 116 brillant-cut diamonds (0.35 carat)

JUMBO CHRONO

Movement: automatic-winding Blancpain caliber PGE 1185; Ø 25.6mm, thickness: 5.5mm; 45-hour power reserve; chronograph with column wheel; Côtes de Genève finished bridges with rhodium plating; "GUY ELLIA" engraved on rotor with rhodium plating.
Functions: hours, minutes at 12; small seconds at 6; date at 2; column-wheel chronograph: 12-hour counter at 8, 30-minute counter at 4, central sweep seconds hand.
Case: 18K pink gold (85.75g); Ø 50mm, thickness: 11.5mm; sapphire crystal with thermal antireflective coating; water resistant to 3atm.
Strap: brown alligator leather; 18K pink-gold folding buckle (11.90g).
Also available: black gold; set black-gold bezel; full-set black gold; white gold; set white-gold bezel; full-set white gold; set pink-gold bezel; full-set pink gold.

JUMBO CHRONO

Movement: automatic-winding Blancpain caliber PGE 1185; Ø 25.6mm, thickness: 5.5mm; 45-hour power reserve; chronograph with column wheel; Côtes de Genève finished bridges with rhodium plating; "GUY ELLIA" engraved on rotor with rhodium plating.
Functions: hours, minutes at 12; small seconds at 6; date at 2; column-wheel chronograph: 12-hour counter at 8, 30-minute counter at 4, central sweep seconds hand.
Case: microblasted 18K white gold (90.14g); Ø 50mm, thickness: 11.5mm; bezel full set with 323 diamonds (7.93 carats); sapphire crystal with antireflective coating; water resistant to 3atm.
Strap: gray alligator leather; 18K white-gold folding buckle; set with 35 diamonds (0.35 carat).
Also available: black gold; set black-gold bezel; full-set black gold; white gold; set white-gold bezel; pink gold; set pink-gold bezel; full-set pink gold.

JUMBO HEURE UNIVERSELLE

Movement: automatic-winding Blancpain caliber PGE 1150; Ø 36.2mm, thickness: 6.24mm; 72-hour power reserve; 37 jewels; five-position adjustment; blue sapphire disc; Côtes de Genève-finished bridges with rhodium plating; "GUY ELLIA" engraved on rotor with rhodium plating.
Functions: hours, minutes; 24-hour time zone indicator; large date; day/night indicator.
Case: microblasted 18K gray gold (82.9g); Ø 50mm, thickness: 11mm; sapphire crystal with antireflective coating; openwork caseback with sapphire crystal; water resistant to 3atm.
Strap: gray alligator leather; 18K gray-gold folding buckle (16g).
Also available: white gold; black gold.

JUMBO HEURE UNIVERSELLE

Movement: automatic-winding Blancpain caliber PGE 1150; Ø 36.2mm, thickness: 6.24mm; 72-hour power reserve; 37 jewels; five-position adjustment; blue sapphire disc; Côtes de Genève-finished bridges with rhodium plating; "GUY ELLIA" engraved on rotor with rhodium plating.
Functions: hours, minutes; 24-hour time zone indicator; large date; day/night indicator.
Case: microblasted 18K black gold (82.9g); Ø 50mm, thickness: 11mm; sapphire crystal with antireflective coating; openwork caseback with sapphire glass; water resistant to 3atm.
Strap: black alligator leather; 18K black-gold folding buckle (16g).
Also available: white gold; pink gold.

TOURBILLON ZEPHYR

Movement: manual-winding Christophe Claret caliber GES 97; 37x37mm, thickness: 6.21mm; 110-hour power reserve; 233 components; 17 jewels; 21,600 vph; winding ring set with 36 baguette-cut diamonds (1.04 carats) or engine turning; entirely hand-chamfered cage; bottom plate and bridges in blue sapphire; five-position adjustment.
Functions: hours, minutes; tourbillon.
Case: white sapphire case with platinum sides (54.9g); 54x45.3mm, thickness: 15.4mm; crown set with one diamond (Ø 1mm); water resistant to 3atm.
Strap: alligator leather; white-gold folding buckle (15.64g).

Note: limited edition of 12 number pieces.
Also available: pink gold; bottom plate and bridges sapphire: white, smokey.

REPETITION MINUTE ZEPHYR

Movement: manual-winding Christophe Claret GEC 88 caliber; 41.2x38.2mm, thickness: 9.41mm; 48-hour power reserve; 720 components; 72 jewels; 18,000 vph; gear wheels with different platings; five-position adjustment.
Functions: hours, minutes; power reserve indicator; minute repeater; five time zones with day/night indicators.
Case: sapphire crystal block and titanium; 53.6x43.7mm, thickness: 14.8mm; sapphire and titanium crown set with a diamond (Ø 2.2mm); water resistant to 3atm.
Strap: black rubber with titanium and white-gold folding buckle (17.27g).

Note: limited edition of 20 numbered pieces.
Also available: pink gold and white gold; alligator leather strap.

TOURBILLON MAGISTERE

Movement: manual-winding Christophe Claret caliber PGE 97; 37.4x29.9mm, thickness: 5.4mm; 110-hour power reserve; 20 jewels; 21,600 vph; flat balance-spring; mysterious winding; skeletonized barrel and ratchet wheel; entirely hand-chamfered cage; white-gold bottom plate and bridges.
Functions: hours, minutes; tourbillon.
Case: pink gold (73.09g); 43.5x36mm, thickness: 10.9mm; sapphire glass with antireflective coating; water resistant to 3atm.
Strap: brown alligator leather; 18K pink-gold folding buckle (14.61g).

Also available: white gold; titanium; platinum; bezel set with 52 baguette diamonds (2.15 carats); full set with 172 baguette diamonds (19.56 carats); full set with 535 brilliant-cut diamonds (8.25 carats).

TOURBILLON MAGISTERE II

Movement: manual-winding Christophe Claret caliber MGE 97; 38.4x30.9mm, thickness: 5.71mm; 90-hour power reserve; 266 components; 33 jewels; 21,600 vph; flat balance-spring; mysterious winding; skeletonized ratchet and wheels with curved arms and wolf-teeth; entirely hand-chamfered cage; 18K white-gold tourbillon and barrel bridges.
Functions: hours, minutes; tourbillon.
Case: white gold (125g); 44x36.7mm, thickness: 15mm; antireflective sapphire glass; transparent caseback; water resistant to 3atm.

Strap: black alligator leather; solid 18K white-gold folding buckle (18.77g).
Note: limited edition of 12 numbered pieces.
Also available: red gold.

TIME SPACE

Movement: manual-winding Blancpain caliber PGE 15; Ø 35.64mm, thickness: 1.9mm; 43-hour power reserve; 20 jewels; 21,600 vph; five position adjustment; Côtes de Genève finished bridges with black PVD treatment; "GE" engraved on stippled plate with black PVD treatment.
Functions: hours, minutes.
Case: 18K full-set black gold (33.73g); Ø 46.8mm, thickness: 4.9mm; bezel set with 234 diamonds (1.83 carats); bottom plate set with 366 diamonds (1.03 carats); sapphire crystal with antireflective coating; water resistant to 3atm.
Strap: black alligator leather; 18K black-gold pin buckle (4.82g) set with 31 diamonds (0.41 carat).
Also available: white gold; set-bezel white gold; full-set white gold; pink gold; set-bezel pink gold; full-set pink gold; black gold; set-bezel black gold.

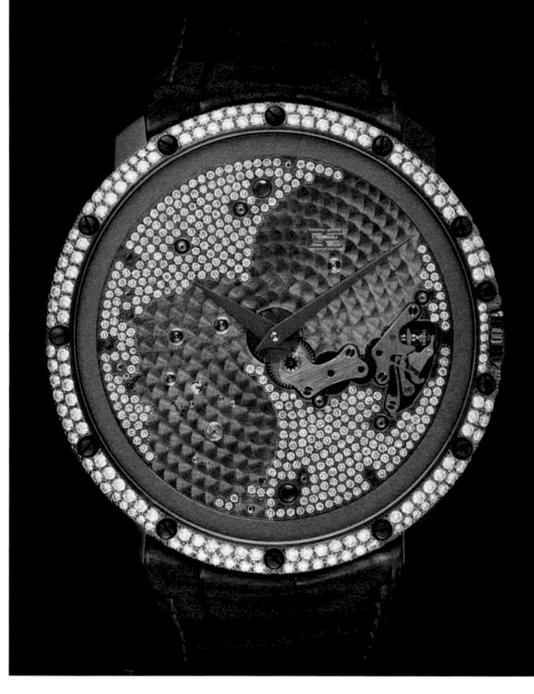

TIME SPACE

Movement: manual-winding Blancpain caliber PGE 15; Ø 35.64mm, thickness: 1.9mm; 43-hour power reserve; 20 jewels; 21,600 vph; five position adjustment; Côtes de Genève finished bridges with black PVD treatment; "GE" engraved on stippled plate with black PVD treatment.
Functions: hours, minutes.
Case: 18K pink gold (31.42g); Ø 46.8mm, thickness: 4.9mm; sapphire glass with antireflective coating; water resistant to 3atm.
Strap: brown alligator leather; gold pin buckle (4.28g).
Also available: white gold; set-bezel white gold; full-set white gold; set-bezel pink gold; full-set pink gold; black gold; set-bezel black gold; full-set black gold.

TIME SPACE QUANTIEME PERPETUEL

Movement: manual-winding Blancpain PGE 5615 D caliber; Ø 35.64mm, thickness: 4.7mm; 43-hour power reserve; 20 jewels; 21,600 vph; five-position adjustment; Côtes de Genève-finished bridges with black PVD treatment; GUY ELLIA logo engraved on stippled plate with black PVD treatment; watch box with an integrated specific automatic winder.
Functions: hours, minutes; perpetual calendar: day, date, month, leap-year cycle; moonphase.
Case: black gold (32.61g); Ø 46.8mm, thickness: 7.75mm; crown set with one brilliant-cut diamond (Ø 1.3mm); sapphire middle ring; sapphire crystal with antireflective coating; water resistant to 3atm.
Strap: black alligator leather; 18K black-gold pin buckle (4.82g).
Also available: black-gold bezel set, full-set black gold; white gold, white-gold bezel set, full-set white gold; pink gold, pink-gold bezel set, full-set pink gold.

TIME SPACE QUANTIEME PERPETUEL

Movement: manual-winding Blancpain caliber PGE 15; Ø 35.64mm, thickness: 4.7mm; 43-hour power reserve; 20 jewels; 21,600 vph; five-position adjustment; Côtes de Genève finished bridges with black PVD treatment; "GE" engraved on stippled plate with black PVD treatment; watch box with an integrated specific automatic winder.
Functions: hours, minutes; perpetual calendar: day, date, month, leap-year cycle; moonphase.
Case: white gold (32.61g); Ø 46.8mm, thickness: 7.75mm; crown set with one diamond (Ø 1.3mm); sapphire middle ring; sapphire crystal with antireflective coating; water resistant to 3atm.
Strap: black alligator leather; 18K white-gold pin buckle (4.82g).
Also available: set-bezel white gold; full-set white gold; pink gold; set-bezel pink gold; full-set pink gold; black gold; set-bezel black gold; full-set black gold.

DOUZE

Movement: quartz; Blancpain caliber PGE 820; Ø 18.8mm, thickness: 1.95mm; rhodiumed and "Côtes de Genève"-decorated cage.
Functions: hours, minutes.
Case: 18K pink gold (74.44g); 52.5x35.5mm, thickness: 5.8mm; bezel set with 82 diamonds (Ø 2mm); crown set with one diamond (Ø 2.3mm); sapphire glass with thermal counter-shock marking; mirror-polished caseback set with one diamond on the "I" of ELLIA (Ø 0.95mm) and deep mechanical engraving; water resistant to 3atm.
Strap: navy alligator leather; 18K pink-gold pin buckle set with 13 diamonds (Ø 2mm); pin set with one diamond (Ø 0.9mm).
Also available: case and pin buckle: yellow gold, white gold; dial: opal, gray, black, chocolate, burgundy; markers: mirror-polished gold (yellow, white).

DOUZE

Movement: quartz; Blancpain caliber PGE 820; Ø 18.8mm, thickness: 1.95mm; rhodiumed and "Côtes de Genève"-decorated cage.
Functions: hours, minutes.
Case: 18K pink gold (74.44g); 52.5x35.5mm, thickness: 5.8mm; bezel set with 82 diamonds (Ø 2.5mm); crown set with one diamond (Ø 2.3mm); sapphire glass with thermal counter-shock marking; mirror-polished caseback set with one diamond on the "I" of ELLIA (Ø 0.95mm) and deep mechanical engraving; water resistant to 3atm.
Strap: light brown alligator leather; 18K pink-gold pin buckle set with 13 diamonds (Ø 2mm); pin set with one diamond (Ø 0.9mm).
Also available: case and pin buckle: yellow gold, white gold; dial: navy, gray, black, chocolate, burgundy; markers: mirror-polished gold (yellow, white).

CONVEX

Movement: quartz; Blancpain caliber PGE 820; Ø 18.8mm, thickness: 1.95mm; rhodiumed and "Côtes de Genève"-decorated cage.
Functions: hours, minutes.
Case: 18K white gold (59.17g); 41x41mm, thickness: 7.1mm; bezel set with 100 diamonds (Ø 1.5mm); crown set with one diamond (Ø 2.3mm) (1.25 carats); sapphire glass with thermal counter-shock marking; mirror-polished caseback set with one diamond on the "I" of ELLIA (Ø 0.95mm) and deep mechanical engraving; water resistant to 3atm.
Dial: 18K white gold (25.35g); fully set with 558 diamonds (2.28 carats); four gold Arabic numerals; 18K white-gold dauphine-shaped hands.
Strap: black alligator leather; 18K white-gold pin buckle set with 40 diamonds (Ø 1.5mm); pin set with one diamond (Ø 0.9mm) (0.49 carat).
Also available: case: yellow gold, pink gold; dial: solid 18K gold (white, yellow, pink), mother-of-pearl (navy, jeans, pink beige); markers: diamond set with 204 diamonds (0.79 carat), gold (white, yellow, pink), outlined.

CONVEX

Movement: quartz; Blancpain caliber PGE 820; Ø 18.8mm, thickness: 1.95mm; rhodiumed and "Côtes de Genève"-decorated cage.
Functions: hours, minutes.
Case: 18K pink gold (55.4g); 41x41mm, thickness: 7.1mm; bezel set with 100 diamonds (Ø 1.5mm); crown set with one diamond (Ø 2.3mm); sapphire glass with thermal counter-shock marking; mirror-polished caseback set with one diamond on the "I" of ELLIA (Ø 0.95mm) and deep mechanical engraving; water resistant to 3atm.
Dial: mother-of-pearl with four Arabic numerals; 18K gold dauphine-shaped hands.
Strap: dark blue alligator leather; 18K pink-gold pin buckle set with 40 diamonds (Ø 1.5mm); pin set with one diamond (Ø 0.9mm) (0.49 carat).
Also available: case: yellow gold, white gold; dial: fully set 18K gold (white, yellow, pink), mother-of-pearl: navy, jeans, pink beige; markers: diamond set with 204 diamonds (0.79 carat), gold (white, yellow, pink), outlined.

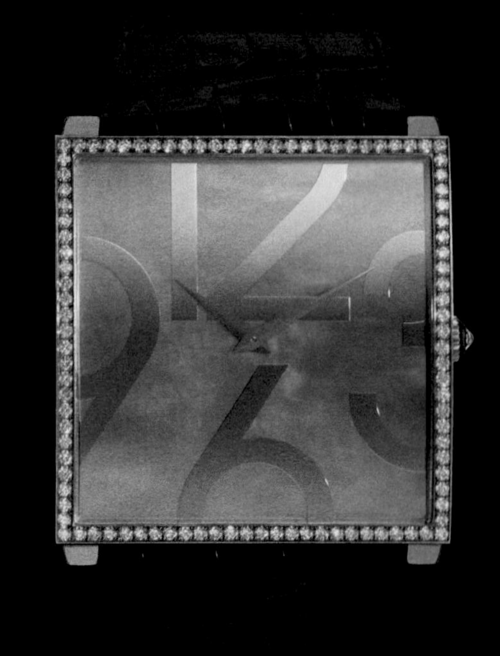

CIRCLE "LA PETITE"

Movement: quartz; Blancpain caliber PGE 820; Ø 18.8mm, thickness: 1.95mm.
Functions: hours, minutes.
Case: polished white gold (41g); Ø 45mm, thickness: 6mm; bezel set with 105 diamonds (0.71 carat); crown set with one diamond (Ø 2.8mm) (0.08 carat); sapphire crystal with thermal counter-shock marking; caseback set with one diamond on the "I" of ELLIA (Ø 0.95mm) (0.003 carat); water resistant to 3atm.
Dial: mirror white; hour markers set with 192 brilliant-cut diamonds (0.58 carat); 18K white-gold dauphine-shaped hands.
Bracelet: solid 18K white gold (115.1g).
Also available: case: pink gold, yellow gold; dial: shiny black, opal or navy, mirror or matte gold white, pink and yellow; markers: mirror-polished gold, diamond set; strap: alligator leather with 18K solid gold pin buckle set with one diamond (Ø 0.9mm).

CIRCLE "LA PETITE"

Movement: quartz; Blancpain caliber PGE 820; Ø 18.8mm, thickness: 1.95mm.
Functions: hours, minutes.
Case: pink gold (37g); Ø 45mm, thickness: 6mm; bezel set with 105 diamonds (0.71 carat); crown set with one diamond (Ø 2.8mm); sapphire crystal with thermal counter-shock marking; caseback set with one diamond on the "I" of ELLIA (Ø 0.95mm) (0.003 carat); water resistant to 3atm.
Dial: black; pink-gold mirror-polished hour markers; 18K pink-gold dauphine-shaped hands.
Bracelet: pink gold (104.2g).
Also available: case: pink gold, yellow gold, white gold; dial: opal, navy, matte gold, full set; markers: mirror-polished gold, diamond set; strap: alligator leather with 18K solid gold pin buckle set with one diamond (Ø 0.9mm).

CIRCLE

Movement: quartz; Blancpain caliber PGE 820; Ø 18.8mm, thickness: 1.95mm.
Functions: hours, minutes.
Case: pink gold (80.13g); Ø 52mm, thickness: 7mm; bezel set with 124 diamonds (Ø 1.15mm); crown set with one diamond (Ø 2.8mm); sapphire crystal with thermal counter-shock marking; mirror-polished caseback set with one diamond on the "I" of ELLIA (Ø 0.95mm); water resistant to 3atm.
Dial: opal; pink-gold hour markers; 18K pink-gold dauphine-shaped hands.
Strap: alligator leather; solid 18K pink-gold pin buckle set with 86 diamonds (0.384 carat); pin set with one diamond (Ø 0.9mm).
Also available: case: black gold, yellow gold, white gold; dial: opal, mirror or matte gold (white, pink, yellow), full set; markers: diamond set, full set.

CIRCLE

Movement: quartz; Blancpain caliber PGE 820; Ø 18.8mm, thickness: 1.95mm.
Functions: hours, minutes.
Case: black gold (83.86g); Ø 52mm, thickness: 7mm; bezel set with 124 diamonds (0.743 carat); crown set with one diamond (Ø 2.8mm); sapphire crystal with thermal counter-shock marking; caseback set with one diamond on the "I" of ELLIA (Ø 0.95mm); water resistant to 3atm.
Dial: matte black; hour markers set with 168 brilliant-cut diamonds (1.0025 carats); 18K white-gold dauphine-shaped hands.
Strap: alligator leather; solid 18K black-gold pin buckle set with 86 diamonds (0.384 carat); pin set with one diamond (Ø 0.9mm).
Also available: case: pink gold, yellow gold, white gold; dial: opal, mirror or matte gold (black, white, pink, yellow), full set; markers: gold, full set.

HARRY WINSTON
TIMEPIECES

CELESTIAL COMPLICATION

Harry Winston **CAPTURES THE TIMELESS FASCINATION OF THE MOON**, unveiling timepieces that grace the celestial object with a stunning stage.

The Midnight Date Moon Phase Automatic 36mm honors the Earth's nightly companion with a design of joyful luxury. Housed in a 36mm case in 18-karat rose gold, the self-winding ladies' timepiece begins its celestial tale with a radiant backdrop in white mother-of-pearl that evokes the dreamy enchantment of pearlescent white clouds. A subdial at 1 o'clock brings scintillating contrast to the composition as an 18-karat rose-gold border, set with 43 brilliant-cut diamonds, frames its indication of the hours and minutes. At 7 o'clock, gently intersecting the principal time ring, the timepiece's hand-guided date counter gestures at both numerals and dots, achieving a striking balance of luxury and legibility. At 4 o'clock, the wristwatch makes its most exquisite declaration. Breaking through the lustrous clouds by way of a crescent-shaped aperture, the HW3205 caliber's picturesque complication depicts the moon's cycle as it orbits the Earth over the course of 29.5 days. From full to new moon, the 18-karat rose-gold-plated satellite glows irresistibly in a galvanized blue midnight sky, bringing vibrant contrast to the rest of the dial. The Midnight Date Moon Phase Automatic 36mm illuminates its exhibition with a sparkling setting of 83 brilliant-cut diamonds on the bezel and lugs, including three larger stones at 3 o'clock—a sly visual reference to the arched doorway of Harry Winston's flagship New York boutique.

◂ **MIDNIGHT DATE MOON PHASE AUTOMATIC 36MM**

This self-winding, diamond-studded ladies' timepiece depicts the moon's 29.5-day cycle amidst a deep blue sky that emerges from the soft clouds of a mother-of-pearl dial.

At 4 o'clock, the Midnight Date Moon Phase Automatic 42mm's recessed scale turns into an overlapping layer, seamlessly merging with an aperture depicting the moon amidst a textured sky in intense midnight blue.

A demonstration of interweaving layers and subtle multi-dimensionality, the Midnight Date Moon Phase Automatic 42mm transforms the moon's cycle into a sophisticated affair. A 42mm case in 18-karat white or rose gold, with or without a gleaming row of brilliant-cut diamonds on the bezel, elegantly frames Harry Winston's distinctive interpretation of horological geometry. Driven by the 279-component HW3203 caliber oscillating at a frequency of 28,800 vph and endowed with a flat silicon balance spring, the timepiece finds an effortless harmony of shapes and elements as three circular subsections weave into one another. At 7 o'clock on the silver-toned sunburst dial, a slender gold stem indicates the date against a gently recessed numbered ring. The latter then intersects an hours-and-minutes subdial framed by a thin gold border at 1 o'clock. At 4 o'clock, the recessed scale turns into an overlapping layer, seamlessly merging with an aperture depicting the moon amidst a textured sky in intense midnight blue. On the caseback, the wearer is treated to a captivating view of the timepiece's caliber, including its delicate Côtes-de-Genève decoration and 18-karat-gold openworked oscillating weight.

▲ ▶ **MIDNIGHT DATE MOON PHASE AUTOMATIC 42MM**

Design components intersect with effortless grace, setting a captivating multi-layered stage for the caliber's splendid moonphase complication.

PREMIER MOON PHASE 36MM — REF. PRNQMP36RR001

Movement: quartz.
Functions: hours, minutes; date at 6; moonphase.
Case: 18K rose gold; Ø 36mm; bezel set with diamonds.
Dial: white beaded mother-of-pearl; blue mother-of-pearl moonphase disc and 18K rose-gold moon; diamond indexes; pavé brilliant-cut diamonds at 6.
Strap: white alligator leather.
Suggested price: $28,800

PREMIER MOON PHASE 36MM — REF. PRNQMP36WW002

Movement: quartz.
Functions: hours, minutes; date at 6; moonphase.
Case: 18K white gold; Ø 36mm; bezel set with diamonds.
Dial: blue beaded mother-of-pearl; blue mother-of-pearl moonphase disc and 18K white-gold moon; diamond indexes; pavé brilliant-cut diamonds at 6.
Strap: blue alligator leather.
Suggested price: $29,900

PREMIER PEARLY LACE AUTOMATIC 36MM — REF. PRNAHM36RR014

Movement: automatic-winding.
Functions: hours, minutes.
Case: 18K rose gold; Ø 36mm; bezel set with diamonds.
Dial: burgundy beaded mother-of-pearl; Tahitian mother-of-pearl lacework.
Strap: burgundy alligator leather.
Suggested price: $31,400

PREMIER PEARLY LACE AUTOMATIC 36MM — REF. PRNAHM36WW010

Movement: automatic-winding.
Functions: hours, minutes.
Case: 18K white gold; Ø 36mm; bezel set with diamonds.
Dial: blue beaded mother-of-pearl; white beaded mother-of-pearl lacework.
Bracelet: 18K white gold.
Suggested price: $52,000

AVENUE DIAMOND DROPS — REF. AVEQHM21RR120

Movement: quartz.
Functions: hours, minutes.
Case: 18K rose gold; bezel set with diamonds.
Dial: grained brown; snow-set with 129 brilliant-cut diamonds.
Bracelet: 18K rose gold.
Suggested price: $53,200

AVENUE C™ MINI — REF. AVCQHM16RR045

Movement: quartz.
Functions: hours, minutes.
Case: 18K rose gold; bezel set with diamonds.
Dial: white mother-of-pearl; central elliptic motif set with 114 brilliant-cut diamonds; 18K gold indexes.
Strap: black alligator leather.
Suggested price: $23,700

AVENUE C™ MINI — REF. AVCQHM16WW054

Movement: quartz.
Functions: hours, minutes.
Case: 18K white gold; bezel set with diamonds.
Dial: white mother-of-pearl; central elliptic motif set with 114 brilliant-cut diamonds; 18K gold indexes.
Bracelet: 18K white gold; set with 212 brilliant-cut diamonds.
Suggested price: $58,000

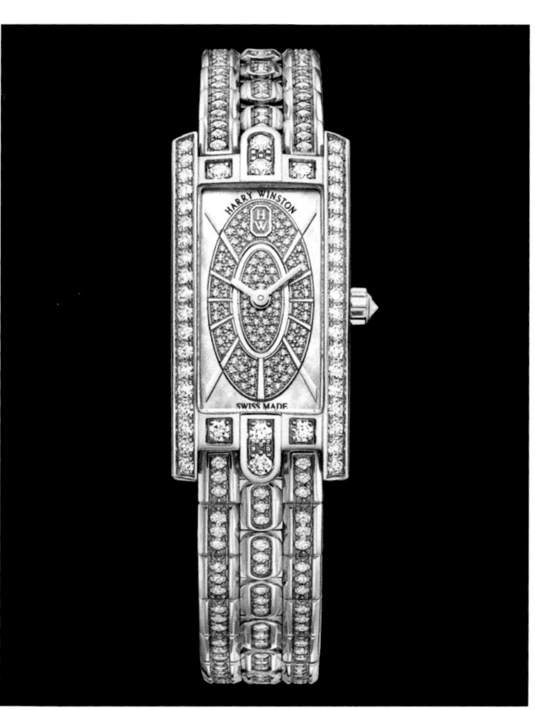

ROSEBUD HEART BY HARRY WINSTON — REF. HJTQHM26WW003

Movement: quartz.
Functions: hours, minutes.
Case: 18K white gold; bezel set with diamonds.
Dial: white beaded mother-of-pearl; diamond-set arrow with 7 brilliant-cut diamonds.
Strap: black satin; 18K white-gold chain.
Suggested price: $29,100

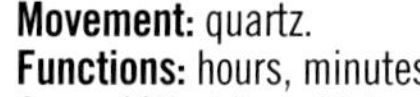

MIDNIGHT DIAMOND DROPS 39MM — REF. MIDQMP39WW004

Movement: quartz.
Functions: hours, minutes; date at 6; moonphase.
Case: 18K white gold; Ø 39mm; bezel set with diamonds.
Dial: blue-toned with sunray satin-brushed finish; snow-set with 214 brilliant-cut diamonds; index at 9 with 3 brilliant-cut diamonds; central moonphase with 18K white-gold-plated moon.
Strap: blue alligator leather.
Suggested price: $30,100

MIDNIGHT DIAMOND STALACTITES AUTOMATIC 36MM — REF. MIDAHM36RR001

Movement: automatic-winding.
Functions: hours, minutes.
Case: 18K rose gold; Ø 36mm; bezel set with diamonds.
Dial: gray mother-of-pearl with stalactites décor; set with 161 brilliant-cut diamonds.
Strap: taupe alligator leather.
Suggested price: $34,400

HARRY WINSTON EMERALD — REF. EMEQHM18RR002

Movement: quartz.
Functions: hours, minutes.
Case: 18K rose gold; bezel set with diamonds.
Dial: white satin sunburst; indexes at 3, 6 and 9 set with 3 brilliant-cut diamonds; hand-applied 18K gold Emerald logo at 12.
Bracelet: 18K rose gold; Milanese; set with 36 brilliant-cut diamonds.
Suggested price: $21,000

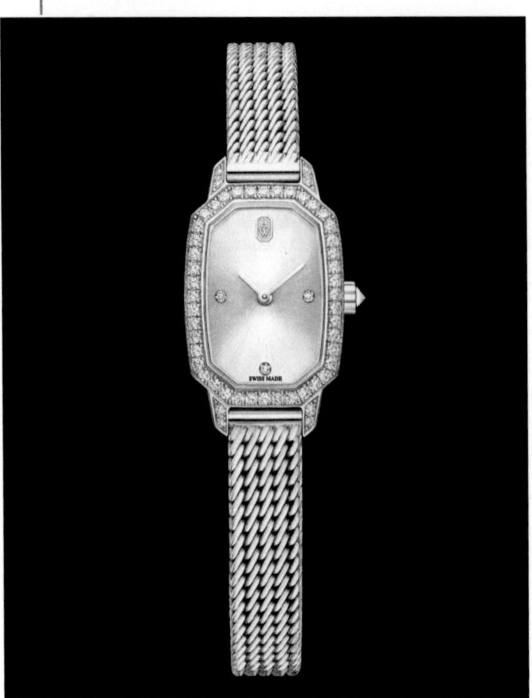

HARRY WINSTON EMERALD — REF. EMEQHM18WW001

Movement: quartz.
Functions: hours, minutes.
Case: 18K white gold; bezel set with diamonds.
Dial: blue satin sunburst; indexes at 3, 6 and 9 set with 3 brilliant-cut diamonds; hand-applied 18K gold Emerald logo at 12.
Strap: blue satin double tour.
Suggested price: $12,000

OCEAN BIRETROGRADE 36MM REF. OCEABI36WW051

Movement: automatic-winding.
Functions: hours, minutes; date at 6; retrograde seconds at 8; retrograde day at 4.
Case: 18K white gold; Ø 36mm; bezel set with diamonds.
Dial: multi-level white pearled mother-of-pearl with blue varnish; set with 180 brilliant-cut diamonds.
Bracelet: 18K white gold; set with 424 brilliant-cut diamonds.
Suggested price: $140,800

OCEAN MOON PHASE 36MM REF. OCEQMP36RR027

Movement: quartz.
Functions: hours, minutes; date at 6; moonphase.
Case: 18K rose gold; Ø 36mm; bezel set with diamonds.
Dial: beaded mother-of-pearl with black varnish; central moonphase covered with an openworked grid; moonphase ring and mother-of-pearl set with 58 brilliant-cut diamonds.
Bracelet: 18K rose gold.
Suggested price: $67,900

OCEAN CHRONOGRAPH AUTOMATIC 44MM REF. OCEACH44RR001

Movement: automatic-winding.
Functions: hours, minutes; shuriken small seconds and date at 6; 5Hz chronograph: central seconds hand, 30-minute counter at 3, 12-hour counter at 9.
Case: 18K rose gold.
Dial: openworked gold and galvanic black base; circular Côtes de Genève; circular graining; openworked date disk; blue SuperLumiNova on hands, indexes and underneath date.
Strap: black alligator leather.
Suggested price: $40,500

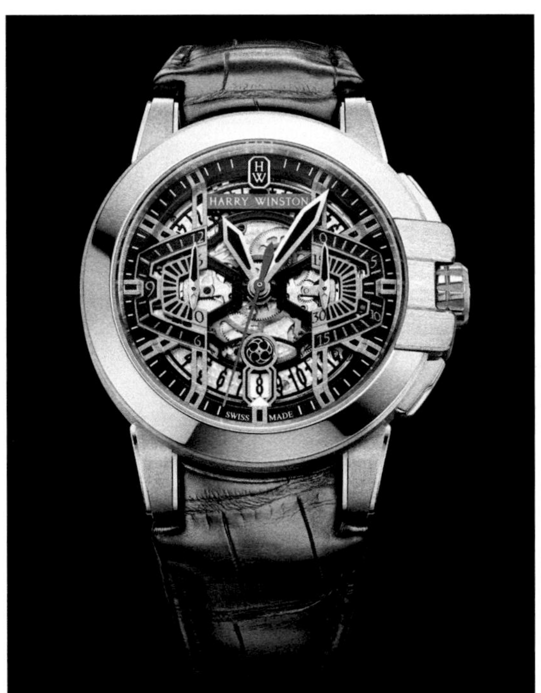

PROJECT Z10 REF. OCEABI42ZZ001

Movement: automatic-winding.
Functions: hours, minutes; date at 6; retrograde seconds at 8; retrograde day at 4.
Case: Zalium™.
Dial: blue anodized skeleton; galvanic black circular satin-finished chapter ring; white and blue SuperLumiNova on indexes; blue SuperLumiNova with blue emission on hands; red lacquered arrow on top of the date; red lacquered hands on second and day counters.
Strap: blue alligator leather on rubber.
Suggested price: $22,100

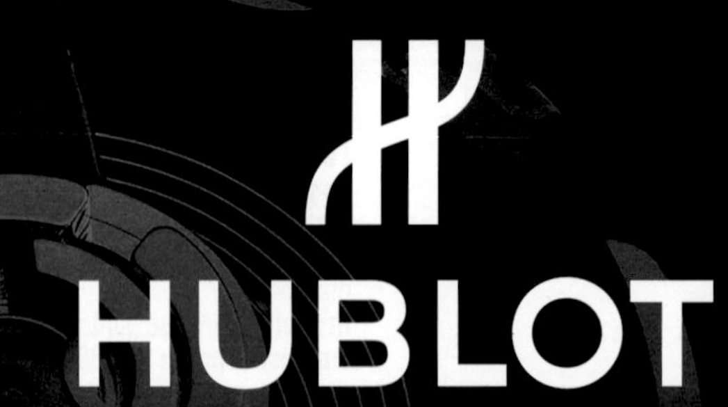

LIGHT, COLOR & DARKNESS

From transparent sapphire cases to dials in Berluti leather or hand-woven linen, Hublot **SHOWCASES ITS INIMITABLE COMBINATION OF ELEGANCE AND INNOVATION** with six timepieces that rewrite the rules of style.

Inspired by nostalgia for mechanical toys that opened up infinite construction possibilities to their owners, the Big Bang MECA-10 vividly captures the world of micro-mechanical architecture. Its 45mm case, in micro-blasted titanium or polished and micro-blasted black ceramic, presents a rugged masculine frame for the dial's multi-dimensional playground. The in-house HUB1201 caliber, composed of 223 parts, is strikingly revealed thanks to an uninhibited, skeletonized design. At 12 o'clock, a captivating two-rack system slides on a horizontal axis to express the timepiece's mechanical soul. Two separate power reserve indicators at 3 and 6 o'clock illustrate the Big Bang MECA-10's impressive 10-day power reserve, made possible by a visible dual-barrel construction. The limited edition wristwatch evokes childhood's insatiable curiosity and adult sophistication, revealing its regulating organ at 7 o'clock and boasting an immaculate finish on its numerous bridges, gears and demonstrative ratchet wheels.

◂ BIG BANG MECA-10

This skeletonized black ceramic timepiece reveals a detailed mechanical construction inspired by the world of engineering.

The Big Bang Unico Sapphire's spectacular transparency comes at no cost to durability, as sapphire is nearly as hard as diamond.

Skeletonization reveals much more than watch enthusiasts are used to seeing, but Hublot takes visibility to the next level: complete transparency. The Big Bang Unico Sapphire, in a limited edition of 500 pieces, houses its sophisticated, openworked caliber in a case composed of transparent, polished sapphire crystal. The 45mm timepiece proudly showcases every detail of its self-winding HUB 1242 UNICO caliber: column wheel, flyback chronograph, dial-side double clutch and date aperture. The movement also boasts a power reserve of 72 hours. The model's spectacular transparency comes at no cost to strength and durability—sapphire is nearly as hard, and as scratch-resistant, as diamond! Even the strap echoes the theme of the case and transparent resin dial, extending visibility all the way around the wrist.

Hublot celebrates the ten-year anniversary of its trendsetting "All Black" concept with a transcendent fusion of materials. With its Big Bang Unico Sapphire All Black, the brand stays true to an all-black monochrome aesthetic while creating a timepiece of stunning transparency. The remarkable interplay of darkness, light and visibility is achieved with a pioneering case crafted from blocks of smoked sapphire crystal and machined with masterful precision into Hublot's signature Big Bang form. The dial, made of black transparent composite resin, reveals the elegant inner workings of the HUB 1242 UNICO caliber, complete with flyback chronograph, column wheel, date and visible double clutch. A seemingly star-crossed tale of opposites attracting, the 45mm self-winding timepiece exemplifies Hublot's ambitious pursuit of innovation in all facets of haute horology.

▲ **BIG BANG UNICO SAPPHIRE**

Boasting a completely transparent case in polished sapphire crystal, this 45mm timepiece with flyback chronograph provides a stunning level of transparency.

▶ **BIG BANG UNICO SAPPHIRE ALL BLACK**

This 45mm self-winding timepiece combines the transparency of sapphire with elegant black monochrome for spectacular visual balance.

Hublot challenges horological convention with a daring combination of materials, collaborating with legendary Parisian leather virtuoso Berluti. Housed in a 45mm 18-karat King Gold case, the Classic Fusion Berluti Scritto is secured to the wrist via a tobacco-colored Venezia Scritto Berluti leather strap embellished with a rich patina and adorned with expertly carved calligraphy. This blend of traditional and novel materials is just the beginning of the piece's commitment to fusion. The limited edition timepiece's dial is itself crafted from Venezia leather thanks to a delicate and demanding process that neutralizes the unique material. Three gold-toned hands animate the hours, minutes and seconds of the self-winding HUB1100 caliber, which oscillates at a frequency of 28,800 vph.

◂ **CLASSIC FUSION BERLUTI**

Even the dial of this collaborative timepiece is crafted in Berluti leather.

Building on the MP-05 "LaFerrari," an ultra-sophisticated tribute to one of motor sports' most high-performance supercars, the MP-05 "LaFerrari" Sapphire shields its breathtaking caliber in a transparent sapphire case for a stunning weightless effect. The caliber in question, the HUB9005.H1.PN.1, composed of no fewer than 637 parts, is the magnificent result of 600 hours of work on a case middle machined from seven individual blocks of sapphire. To the right of the movement's 11 central series-coupled barrels, the 108-jewel timepiece reveals the hours and minutes via two transparent cylinders, while the power reserve is indicated in identical fashion on the opposite side of the face. At the bottom of the creative composition, the wearer may read the running seconds on a third transparent cylinder, this time affixed to the timepiece's suspended vertical tourbillon. The MP-05 "LaFerrari" Sapphire completes its dramatic demonstration with a transparent strap that reflects the watch's innovative case.

▸ **MP-05 "LAFERRARI" SAPPHIRE**

A transparent sapphire case machined from seven sapphire blocks grants the wearer an unobstructed view of this timepiece's ultra-sophisticated caliber.

▼ **BIG BANG LINEN**

Hublot gives linen a new luxurious treatment with a case, dial and strap hand-woven from the age-old textile.

A summery burst of vibrant colors brings one of the world's oldest textiles to the forefront of haute horology in Hublot's Big Bang Linen. The collection, presented in four radiant hues (ocean blue, turquoise, orange and purple), does not merely use linen for its colorful strap, but also displays Hublot's innovative drive by incorporating the fiber into its central construction. Both the dial and 41mm case of the timepiece are composed of fully natural fibers, hand-woven by artisans to achieve a carbon-fiber-like strength with a lighter weight and a dazzling palette. Driven by the self-winding HUB4300 caliber with chronograph and date aperture, the Big Bang Linen illuminates its ingenious organic demonstration with a luxurious setting of sapphires, topazes or amethysts on the polished steel bezel. Each of the four Big Bang Linen models is limited to 200 pieces.

BIG BANG ALARM REPEATER — REF. 403.CI.0140.RX

Movement: manual-winding HUB5003 caliber; 72-hour power reserve; 356 components; 49 jewels; 28,800 vph; Swiss lever escapement.
Functions: hours, minutes, seconds; GMT display at 11; local time indicator at 1; alarm indicator at 7.
Case: micro-blasted and polished black ceramic; Ø 45mm; micro-blasted and polished black ceramic bezel; antireflective sapphire crystal; micro-blasted black ceramic caseback with sapphire crystal; water resistant to 3atm.
Dial: multilayered sapphire and matte black.
Strap: black structured lined rubber; black-plated titanium deployant buckle clasp.
Note: limited edition of 100 pieces.
Suggested price: $44,200

BIG BANG BRODERIE SUGAR SKULL — REF. 343.CS.6599.NR.1213

Movement: automatic-winding HUB1110 caliber; 42-hour power reserve; 63 components.
Functions: hours, minutes, seconds.
Case: black polished ceramic; Ø 41mm; bezel with black treatment set with 36 red spinels; antireflective sapphire crystal; water resistant to 10atm.
Dial: carbon fiber and embroidery on organza silk; index of 11 red spinels; hands with black treatment.
Strap: black rubber and Sugar Skull-colored embroidery on silk satin.
Note: limited edition of 200 pieces.
Suggested price: $15,700

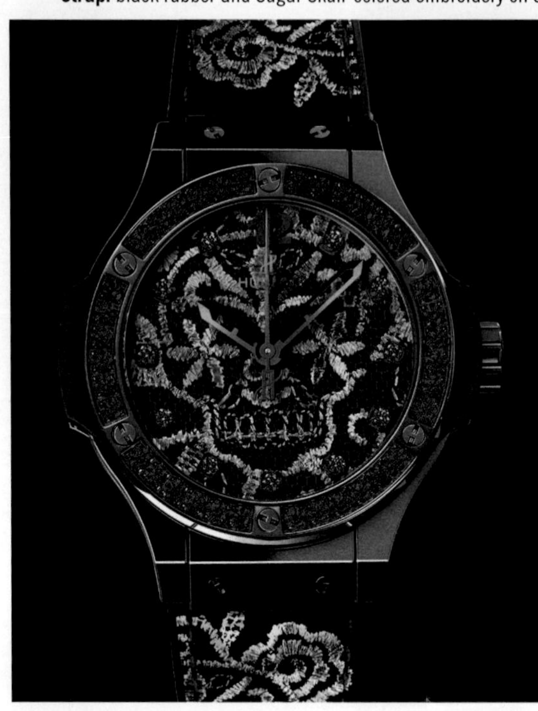

BIG BANG JEANS — REF. 301.QX.2740.NR.JEANS16

Movement: automatic-winding HUB4100 caliber; 42-hour power reserve; 252 components; 27 jewels; 28,800 vph; openworked rotor oscillating weight; Swiss lever escapement.
Functions: hours, minutes; small seconds at 9; date at 4:30; chronograph: central seconds hand, 30-minute counter at 3, 12-hour counter at 6.
Case: matte carbon fiber; Ø 44mm, thickness: 14.6mm; matte carbon fiber bezel with 6 H-shaped black-plated titanium screws; antireflective sapphire crystal; matte carbon fiber caseback with sapphire crystal; water resistant to 10atm.
Dial: genuine blue jeans; black subdials.
Strap: black rubber and genuine blue jeans with black stitching; black-plated stainless steel deployant buckle clasp.
Note: limited edition of 250 pieces.
Suggested price: $22,500
Also available: satin-finished stainless steel case, $14,600 (ref. 301.SX.2770.NR.JEANS16); satin-finished stainless steel case, bezel set with 36 diamonds (1.80 carats), dial set with 8 diamonds (0.14 carat), $18,300 (ref. 341.SX.2770.NR.1204.JEANS); satin-finished black ceramic case, bezel set with 36 black diamonds (1.80 carats), dial set with 8 black diamonds (0.14 carat), $21,500 (ref. 341.CX.2740.NR.1200.JEANS).

BIG BANG MECA-10 — REF. 414.NI.1123.RX

Movement: manual-winding HUB1201 caliber; 10-day power reserve; 223 components; 24 jewels.
Functions: hours, minutes; small seconds at 9; power reserve indicator at 6.
Case: micro-blasted titanium; Ø 45mm; micro-blasted titanium bezel; titanium and rubber crown; antireflective sapphire crystal; micro-blasted titanium caseback with sapphire crystal; water resistant to 10atm.
Dial: matte black; skeleton.
Strap: structured ribbed black rubber; titanium folding buckle.
Suggested price: $19,900
Also available: polished and micro-blasted black ceramic case, limited edition of 500 pieces, $22,000 (ref. 414.CI.1110.RX).

BIG BANG ONE CLICK REF. 465.SX.1170.RX.1204

Movement: automatic-winding HUB1710 caliber; 50-hour power reserve; 185 components; 27 jewels; 28,800 vph; tungsten openworked rotor oscillating weight; Swiss lever escapement.
Functions: hours, minutes, seconds; date at 3.
Case: satin-finished and polished stainless steel; Ø 39mm, thickness: 12.55mm; polished stainless steel bezel set with 42 diamonds (1 carat); antireflective sapphire crystal; satin-finished stainless steel caseback with sapphire crystal; water resistant to 10atm.
Dial: matte black.
Strap: black structured lined rubber; stainless steel deployant buckle clasp.
Suggested price: $14,600
Also available: matte white dial, white structured lined rubber strap (ref. 465. SE.2010.RW.1204); 18K King Gold case (ref. 465. OX.1180.RX.1204); 18K King Gold case, matte white dial, white structured lined rubber strap (ref. 465. OE.2080.RW.1204); case set with 118 diamonds (0.84 carat), $20,900 (ref. 465.SX.1170.RX.1604); 18K King Gold case set with 118 diamonds. $32,500 (0.84 carat) (ref. 465. OX.1180.RX.1604); case set with 118 diamonds (0.84 carat), matte white dial, white structured lined rubber strap, $20,900 (ref. 465.SE.2010.RW.1604); 18K King Gold case set with 118 diamonds (0.84 carat), matte white dial, white structured lined rubber strap, $32,500 (ref. 465. OE.2080.RW.1604).

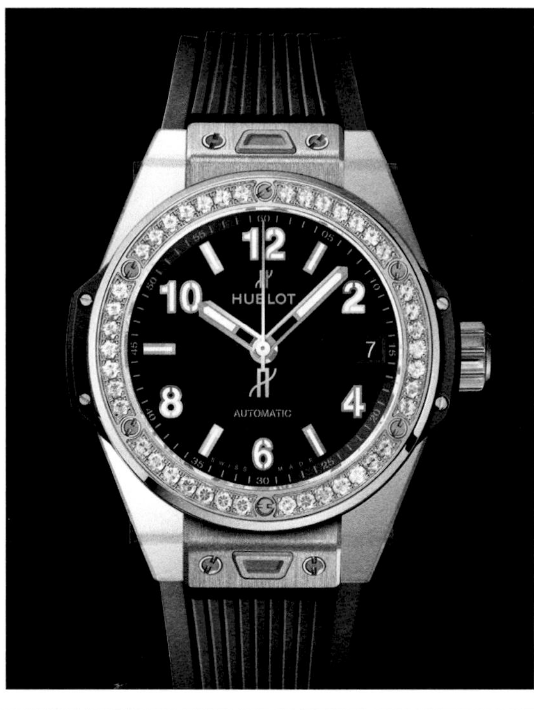

BIG BANG TOURBILLON CHRONOGRAPH CATHEDRAL MINUTE REPEATER REF. 404.MX.0138.RX

Movement: manual-winding HUB8110 caliber; 85-hour power reserve; 427 components; 38 jewels; 21,600 vph; anthracite gray-coated bridges; polished rhodium-plated balance; tourbillon cage escapement.
Functions: hours, minutes; chronograph: 60-second counter between 1 and 2, 30-minute counter at 10; tourbillon at 6; minute repeater.
Case: polished Magic Gold; Ø 45mm, thickness: 16.8mm; polished Magic Gold bezel; antireflective sapphire crystal; micro-blasted black-plated titanium caseback with sapphire crystal; water resistant to 3atm.
Dial: sapphire.
Strap: black structured lined rubber; black-plated titanium deployant buckle clasp.
Note: limited edition of 20 pieces.
Suggested price: $295,000
Also available: micro-blasted black ceramic case, $274,000 (ref. 404.CI.0110.RX).

BIG BANG UNICO ITALIA INDEPENDENT REF. 411.YL.5190.NR.ITI16

Movement: automatic-winding HUB 1242 caliber; 72-hour power reserve.
Functions: hours, minutes; small seconds at 9; date at 3; chronograph: central seconds hand, 60-minute counter at 3.
Case: blue carbon fiber and Texalium®; Ø 45mm; blue carbon fiber bezel and Texalium® pattern; black PVD-treated titanium and black rubber crown; antireflective sapphire crystal; antireflective sapphire crystal caseback; water resistant to 10atm.
Dial: varnished and skeletonized in matte black and blue.
Strap: black rubber with blue chino; black-coated titanium deployant buckle.
Note: limited edition of 500 pieces.
Suggested price: $26,200
Also available: green carbon fiber and Texalium® case, matte black and golden yellow dial, black rubber strap with green chino, limited edition of 250 pieces, $29,400 (ref. 411. YG.1198.NR.ITI16); black carbon fiber and Texalium® case, matte black and King Gold color dial, black rubber strap with black chino, limited edition of 250 pieces, $29,400 (ref. 411. YT.1198.NR.ITI16).

BIG BANG UNICO USAIN BOLT REF. 411.VX.1189.VR.USB16

Movement: automatic-winding HUB1242 caliber; 72-hour power reserve; 330 components; 38 jewels; 28,800 vph; black-coated main plate and bridges; black-coated tungsten oscillating weight with micro-blasted and satin-finished surface; Swiss lever escapement.
Functions: hours, minutes; small seconds at 9; date at 3; chronograph: central seconds hand, 60-minute counter at 3.
Case: satin-finished and polished 18K yellow gold; Ø 45mm, thickness: 15.45mm; satin-finished and polished 18K yellow-gold bezel; antireflective sapphire crystal; polished 18K yellow-gold caseback with sapphire crystal; water resistant to 10atm.
Dial: matte black skeleton; lightning bolt chronograph hand.
Strap: black rubber and gold shiny calf leather; embossed Jamaican flag; black-plated titanium deployant buckle clasp.
Note: limited edition of 100 pieces.
Suggested price: $42,000
Also available: satin-finished and polished black ceramic case, black rubber and schedoni leather strap with embossed Jamaican flag, limited edition of 250 pieces, $22,000 (ref. 411.CX.1189.VR.USB16).

BIG BANG UNICO SAPPHIRE REF. 411.JX.4802.RT

Movement: automatic-winding HUB 1242 caliber; 72-hour power reserve.
Functions: hours, minutes; small seconds at 9; date at 3; chronograph: central seconds hand, 60-minute counter at 3.
Case: polished sapphire crystal; Ø 45mm; polished sapphire crystal bezel; transparent silicon and satin-finished titanium crown; antireflective sapphire crystal; polished sapphire crystal caseback; water resistant to 5atm.
Dial: polished transparent composite resin skeleton; white luminescent appliqués and hands.
Strap: transparent; structured and lined; titanium deployant buckle.
Note: limited edition of 500 pieces.
Suggested price: $57,900

BIG BANG LINEN REF. 341.XL.2770.NR.1201

Movement: automatic-winding HUB4300 caliber; 42-hour power reserve.
Functions: hours, minutes; small seconds at 3; date at 4:30; chronograph: central seconds hand, 12-hour counter at 6, 30-minute counter at 9.
Case: ocean blue natural linen; Ø 41mm; polished steel bezel set with blue sapphires; satin-finished and polished titanium crown; antireflective sapphire crystal; satin-finished titanium caseback with antireflective sapphire crystal; water resistant to 10atm.
Dial: ocean blue linen.
Strap: blue; sewn onto matching rubber; titanium deployant buckle.
Note: limited edition of 200 pieces for each version.
Suggested price: $16,700
Also available: turquoise linen case, bezel set with topazes, turquoise strap, $15,700 (ref. 341.XL.2770.NR.1237); orange linen case, bezel set with orange sapphires, orange strap, $16,700 (ref. 341.XO.2770.NR.1206); purple linen case, bezel set with amethysts, purple strap, $15,700 (ref. 341.XP.2770.NR.1205).

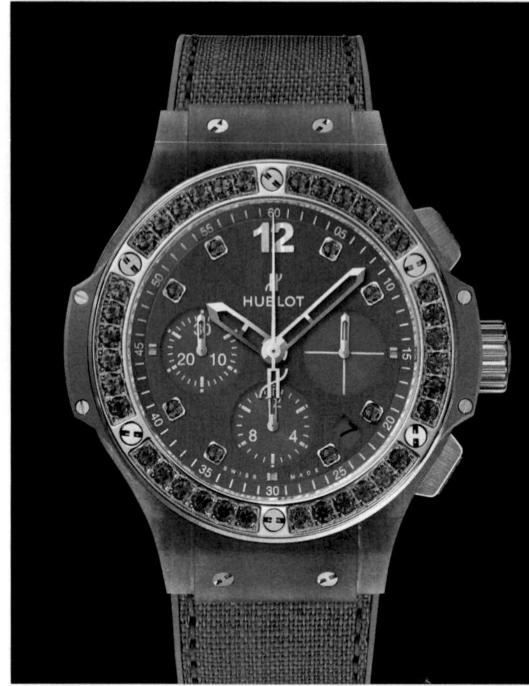

CLASSIC FUSION AEROFUSION MOONPHASE REF. 517.NX.0170.LR.1104

Movement: automatic-winding HUB1131 caliber; 42-hour power reserve; 134 components; 25 jewels; 28,800 vph; openworked rotor oscillating weight; Swiss lever escapement.
Functions: hours, minutes, seconds; day and month at 12; date by hand at 6; moonphase at 6.
Case: satin-finished and polished titanium; Ø 45mm, thickness: 11.90mm; polished titanium bezel set with 126 diamonds (1.41 carats); antireflective sapphire crystal; satin-finished titanium caseback with sapphire crystal; water resistant to 5atm.
Dial: sapphire.
Strap: black rubber and alligator leather; stainless steel deployant buckle clasp.
Suggested price: $20,300
Also available: case set with 284 diamonds (1.38 carats), $28,900 (ref. 517.NX.0170.LR.1704); satin-finished and polished 18K King Gold case, $32,900 (ref. 517.OX.0180.LR.1104); polished 18K King Gold case set with 284 diamonds, $40,800 (1.38 carats) (ref. 517.OX.0180.LR.1704).

CLASSIC FUSION BRACELET REF. 510.NX.1170.NX

Movement: automatic-winding HUB1112 caliber; 42-hour power reserve; 63 components; 21 jewels; 28,800 vph; openworked rotor oscillating weight; Swiss lever escapement.
Functions: hours, minutes; date at 3.
Case: satin-finished and polished titanium; Ø 45mm, thickness: 10.95mm; satin-finished and polished titanium bezel; antireflective sapphire crystal; satin-finished titanium caseback with sapphire crystal; water resistant to 5atm.
Dial: matte black.
Bracelet: satin-finished and polished titanium; titanium deployant buckle clasp.
Suggested price: $8,800
Also available: satin-finished and polished 18K King Gold case, 18K King Gold bracelet, $37,400 (ref. 510.OX.1180.OX).

CLASSIC FUSION CHRONOGRAPH BRACELET REF. 520.NX.1170.NX

Movement: automatic-winding HUB1143 caliber; 42-hour power reserve; 280 components; 59 jewels; 28,800 vph; openworked rotor oscillating weight; Swiss lever escapement.
Functions: hours, minutes; small seconds at 3; date at 6; chronograph: central seconds hand, 30-minute counter at 9.
Case: satin-finished and polished titanium; Ø 45mm, thickness: 13.05mm; satin-finished and polished titanium bezel; antireflective sapphire crystal; satin-finished titanium caseback with sapphire crystal; water resistant to 5atm.
Dial: matte black.
Bracelet: satin-finished and polished titanium; titanium deployant buckle clasp.
Suggested price: $12,000
Also available: satin-finished and polished 18K King Gold case, 18K King Gold bracelet, $44,100 (ref. 520.OX.1180.OX).

CLASSIC FUSION RACING GREY REF. 521.NX.7071.LR

Movement: automatic-winding HUB1143 caliber; 42-hour power reserve.
Functions: hours, minutes; small seconds at 3; date at 6; chronograph: central seconds hand, 30-minute counter at 9.
Case: satin-finished and polished titanium; Ø 45mm; satin-finished and polished titanium bezel; antireflective sapphire crystal; titanium caseback satin-finished with antireflective sapphire crystal; water resistant to 5atm.
Dial: satin-finished gray sunburst.
Strap: gray alligator leather and black rubber; steel deployant buckle.
Suggested price: $10,800
Also available: 18K King Gold case, $30,800 (ref. 521.OX.7081.LR); without chronograph (ref. 511.NX.7071.LR); 18K King Gold case, without chronograph (ref. 511.OX.7081.LR); Ø 42mm, without chronograph (ref. 542.NX.7071.LR); 18K King Gold case, Ø 42mm, without chronograph (ref. 542.OX.7081.LR); Ø 38mm, without chronograph (ref. 565.NX.7071.LR); 18K King Gold, Ø 38mm, without chronograph (ref. 565.OX.7081.LR); Ø 33mm, without chronograph (ref. 581.NX.7071.LR); 18K King Gold case, Ø 33mm, without chronograph (ref. 581.OX.7081.LR).

MP-07 42 DAYS POWER RESERVE REF. 907.ND.0001.RX

Movement: manual-winding HUB9007.H1.PN caliber; 42-day power reserve; 487 components; 62 jewels; 21,600 vph; black-coated bridge; vertical tourbillon cage escapement.
Functions: hours, minutes, seconds; power reserve indicator.
Case: microblasted and polished black-plated titanium; 51x42.95mm, thickness: 24mm; antireflective sapphire crystal; microblasted black-plated titanium caseback with sapphire crystal; water resistant to 3atm.
Strap: black smooth rubber; carbon fiber and black-plated titanium deployant buckle clasp.
Note: limited edition of 50 pieces.
Suggested price: $276,000

SPIRIT OF BIG BANG BRUCE LEE BE WATER REF. 601.CI.1190.LR.BLF16

Movement: automatic-winding HUB4700 caliber; 50-hour power reserve.
Functions: hours, minutes; small seconds at 9; date between 4 and 5; chronograph: central seconds hand, 30-minute counter at 3, 12-hour counter at 6.
Case: microblasted black ceramic; 47.7x56.3mm; microblasted black ceramic bezel; antireflective sapphire crystal; microblasted black ceramic caseback engraved with "SPECIAL EDITION"; water resistant to 10atm.
Dial: skeletonized.
Strap: black rubber and blue alligator leather with blue stitching.
Note: limited edition of 100 pieces.
Suggested price: $30,300

THE SKY IS NOT THE LIMIT

Encapsulating the wonders of the universe, mastering the nostalgia of travel or combining sights and sounds in one breathtaking horological performance, Jacob & Co. demonstrates **A VISION OF WATCHMAKING WHOSE EXUBERANT AUDACITY IS MATCHED ONLY BY AN ASTOUNDING DEGREE OF TECHNICAL SAVOIR-FAIRE**.

▲ **ASTRONOMIA FLAWLESS**

A fully transparent sapphire case allows this timepiece's multi-axial rotating caliber to shine without the slightest visual obstruction.

▶ **ASTRONOMIA SKY**

This timepiece transforms the backdrop of its rotating four-arm caliber into an interpretation of the Earth's rotations and revolutions.

With the Astronomia Flawless, the adventurous horological visionary continues its exploration of the timekeeping concept it pioneered. A timepiece of endless fascination, the Astronomia Flawless honors its mesmerizing mechanical choreography with an unparalleled level of transparency. Composed of a single piece of sapphire crystal, the watch's case joins the dome and caseback in achieving the fully transparent construction that the Astronomia Flawless's caliber merits. Even the barrel bridge, dial and buckle do their part to ensure a total lack of obstruction to the admiration of the architecture. And what an architecture it is! Four arms, each with its own function, orbit the center of the dial every 20 minutes. During this shared revolution, each independent satellite takes the concept one step further, rotating on its own axis as well. A first module indicates the hours and minutes on an openworked subdial that maintains its relative orientation, with the 12-o'clock marker always at the top, thanks to an ingenious differential-gear system. A second arm, on the opposite side of the movement, presents the caliber's breathtaking Gravitational Triple Axis Tourbillon with spectacular visibility thanks to the watch's sapphire crystal construction. Joining its 20-minute revolution around the dial, the complication conducts rotations of 60 seconds and five minutes around two additional axes for an unforgettable degree of dynamic multidimensionality. The stunning demonstration is finished with rotating depictions of the Earth, via a detailed titanium sphere, and the Moon, by way of a 288-facet Jacob-cut diamond that reflects the abundance of incoming light in every imaginable direction.

The Astronomia Sky establishes its unique personality with a blued titanium dial, decorated with the Zodiac, that conducts its own rotation around the timepiece in one sidereal year.

Jacob & Co. captures a bit of the spellbinding grandeur of the universe with the Astronomia Sky. Measuring intervals ranging from mere seconds all the way to a sidereal year, the 18-karat rose-gold timepiece places its Gravitational Triple Axis Tourbillon within a fantastic window into the vastness of the heavens. The brand's now iconic four-arm display, orbiting the center of the dial every 20 minutes and sitting atop a rotating backdrop, astounds with its captivating design. Joining the caliber's hours-and-minutes subdial, fitted with a differential-gear system for constant vertical orientation, a tourbillon module conducts three independent revolutions, of one, five and 20 minutes, on three separate axes for a magnificent effect of free-flowing motion. While an additional arm depicts a radiant red moon via a 288-facet sphere of orange sapphire, a final satellite, made up of an openworked titanium wheel, indicates the seconds with excellent precision. Beneath the seemingly floating masterpiece, the Astronomia Sky establishes its unique personality: a blued titanium dial, decorated with the signs of the Zodiac, conducts its own rotation around the timepiece in one sidereal year, accurately mirroring the time required for the Earth to orbit the Sun. Atop this celestial dial, an oval sky indicator showcases the stars visible from the Northern Hemisphere, while completing its full rotation in one sidereal day, the actual time required for the Earth to rotate fully on its own axis. Poetically, the vibrant hand-wound timepiece is finished with a rotating Earth in its very center, composed of a hand-engraved lacquered titanium globe that revolves around its own axis inside a tinted half-dome, symbolizing the day/night status.

Scintillating stones, like shooting stars across the sky, illuminate the Astronomia Meteorite for a daring combination of mechanical sophistication and magnificent luxury. Set throughout the timepiece, 356 "architecture-cut" diamonds, expertly shaped into shimmering triangles, provide this unique piece with an irresistible amount of light. The radiant display, totaling more than 35 carats, sets the stage for the timepiece's other interpretation of visual energy—one based on infinite motion. Revolving from the center of the dial every 20 minutes, the Astronomia Meteorite's four-satellite module showcases Jacob & Co.'s Gravitational Triple Axis Tourbillon, with its three axes and speeds of rotation, alongside an indication of the hours and minutes that always maintains its vertical orientation using an exclusive differential-gear system. The final two arms take a more figurative approach to the theme with exquisite designs: a Jacob-cut blue sapphire with 288 facets rotates over 60 seconds while reflecting rays of light in every direction, and a lacquered, hand-painted magnesium sphere depicts an Earth revolving on its axis against a precious sky of blinding beauty.

◂ **ASTRONOMIA METEORITE**

This inventive and sophisticated wristwatch, inspired by the universe's countless orbits, is adorned with more than 35 carats of triangular-cut diamonds for an astounding level of luxurious light.

The Epic SF24 Tourbillon Baguette enriches its riveting time display with a design of equal parts shimmering luxury and mechanical sophistication. Inspired by vintage information boards in airports and train stations, the wristwatch's secondary-time-zone display, located at 12 o'clock, employs a groundbreaking system of miniaturized flaps to execute a highly legible showcase of the time in any of 24 chosen cities. Jacob & Co. thereby imbues the traveler's concept with an irresistibly nostalgic charm. Enabling the demonstration, the 528-component JCAA03 caliber further showcases its state-of-the-art personality with a dial-side display of its meticulous one-minute flying tourbillon. In genuine Jacob & Co. fashion, mechanical excellence deserves a home of extraordinary visual distinction. Housed in a case in 18-karat rose gold, the Epic SF24 Tourbillon Baguette plays off the rich darkness of its lacquered black dial with a scintillating setting of 25 baguette diamonds around the tourbillon and principal hours-and-minutes indicator while 79 additional baguette-cut stones bring dazzling energy to the case's unique geometry. A transcendent display of imagination and technical expertise, the Epic SF24 Tourbillon Baguette, oscillating at a frequency of 28,800 vph and endowed with a glucydur balance wheel, takes its wearer on a trip around the world, back in time, and into the exciting future of haute horology.

▸ **EPIC SF24 TOURBILLON BAGUETTE**

This flying-tourbillon timepiece evokes the nostalgic charm of vintage train station information boards within a setting of 104 baguette-cut diamonds.

Jacob & Co.'s Opera represents a journey far beyond time—a voyage into sound, space and harmony of motion. Activated by a pusher at 2 o'clock, the breathtaking creation performs a rich and complex melody while keeping no secrets from its astounded audience. Two steel combs brush against the studded pins of two rotating cylinders to produce a vibrant 120-note interpretation of Andrew Lloyd Webber's "Memory" from the musical *Cats*. As the entire display revolves around the dial's central axis throughout the performance, the 30-second melody finds additional beauty in the visual realm. Jacob & Co. accentuates this balance of sound and movement with its integration of a triple-axis tourbillon, composed of three cages that rotate on independent axes over 40 seconds, three minutes and eight minutes respectively, for a mesmerizing sense of graceful weightlessness. Even the time display enters the choreography: an hours-and-minutes subdial orbits the center of the dial, aided by a differential-gear system that ensures a constant upright orientation. Housed in a 47mm case, the Opera delights multiple senses, complementing its sonorous spectacle with a multi-axial display of motion that gives timekeeping an irresistible new dimension.

Jacob & Co. takes on two revered horological complications with a bold statement of contemporary audacity. Housed in a uniquely shaped case in 5N 18K rose gold, the Twin Turbo expresses a modern sporty personality, while honoring the rich traditions of haute horology. Revealing its 572-component JCFM01 caliber through a skeletonized dial architecture, the hand-wound timepiece dazzles with its integration of two triple-axis tourbillons at 5 and 7 o'clock. The twin gravity regulators, composed of three cages that rotate around their respective axes in 40 seconds, 8 minutes and 3 minutes, are united by a regulator to give the timepiece an added level of precision. Jacob & Co. then turns to the Queen of Complications, the minute repeater, and adds a modern twist. The Twin Turbo's "on-demand time strike" foregoes the traditional 15-minute interval, opting instead for a more intuitive composition of hours, 10-minute increments and minutes. Chimed by way of two hammers at 12 o'clock, the Twin Turbo's Cathedral Gong brings timeless refinement to the timepiece's contemporary design. The hyper-sophisticated wristwatch, limited to 18 pieces, is worn on a black leather strap with an 18K rose-gold deployment buckle.

◂ **OPERA**

This breathtaking timepiece performs a complex and enchanting 120-note melody during a ballet of motion epitomized by the enthralling rotations of its triple-axis tourbillon.

▾ **TWIN TURBO**

Combining a minute repeater with two triple-axis tourbillons, this sophisticated timepiece celebrates the rich history of haute horology in the contemporary language of Jacob & Co.

ASTRONOMIA SKY — REF. AT110.40.AA.SD.A

Movement: exclusive manual-winding Jacob&Co. JCAM11 caliber; Ø 40mm, thickness: 17.15mm; 60-hour power reserve; 395 components; 42 jewels; 21,600 vph; triple-axis gravitational tourbillon; plate and bridges: hand-angled and polished, flank-drawn, circular-graining, polished sink; polished screws.
Functions: hours, minutes; sidereal time display: celestial panorama, oval sky indicator, month indicator; legal time display: day and night indicator; triple-axis gravitational tourbillon: rotating on 3 axes in 60 seconds, 5 minutes and on the central axis; orbital second indicator: rotating on 2 axes in 60 seconds and on the central axis, openworked titanium wheel and hand indicating seconds; faceted orange sapphire Jacob Cut red moon rotating on 2 axes in 60 seconds and on the central axis (1 carat, 288 facets).

Case: 18K rose gold; Ø 47mm, thickness: 25mm; unique domed antireflective sapphire crystal; sapphire crystal apertures on sides; winding and time-setting via 18K rose-gold lift-out rotating "bows" on caseback; 18 rose-gold caseback; water resistant to 3atm.
Dial: blue grade-5 titanium; 18K gold hand-engraved and applied stars and constellation; titanium hours and minutes subdial: hand-angled and polished, lacquered indexes, finished blue hands.
Strap: alligator leather; 18K rose-gold folding buckle.
Note: limited edition of 18 pieces.
Suggested price: $580,000

ASTRONOMIA TOURBILLON BLACK GOLD — REF. AT100.31.AC.SD.A

Movement: exclusive manual-winding Jacob&Co. JCAM10 caliber; Ø 40mm, thickness: 17.15mm; 60-hour power reserve; 365 components; 42 jewels; 21,600 vph; triple-axis gravitational tourbillon; plate and bridges: hand-angled and polished, flank-drawn, circular-graining, polished sink; hand-polished screws; circular-graining barrel; pinions: conical, 4 mechanical ball bearing devices; flat balance spring.
Functions: hours, minutes; dial rotating in 20 minutes on the central axis; differential gears system; magnesium lacquered globe rotating on 2 axes in 60 seconds and on the central axis; gravitational tourbillon cage rotating on 3 axes in 60 seconds, 5 minutes and on the central axis; faceted diamond Jacob Cut red moon rotating on 2 axes in 60 seconds and on the central axis (1 carat, 288 facets).

Case: 18K white gold with black DLC treatment; Ø 50m, thickness: 25mm; unique domed antireflective sapphire crystal; winding and time setting via 18K white-gold lift-out rotating "bows" with black DLC treatment on caseback; 18K white-gold caseback with black DLC treatment; water resistant to 3atm.
Dial: hand-polished and angled titanium; lacquered indexes; hand-finished blue.
Strap: alligator leather; 18K black-gold folding buckle.
Note: limited edition of 18 pieces.
Suggested price: $540,000
Also available: 18K white-gold case; 18K rose-gold case.

TWIN TURBO — REF. TT100.21.NS.MK.A

Movement: exclusive manual-winding Jacob&Co. JCFM01 caliber; Ø 34.43mm, thickness: 13.2mm; 72-hour power reserve; 572 components; 49 jewels; 21,600 vph; twin triple-axis tourbillon with decimal minute repeater; plate and bridges: hand-angled and polished, flank-drawn, circular-graining; circular barrel and plate; polished screws; pinions: conical, 4 mechanical ball bearing devices; 2 screw balances.
Functions: hours, minutes; decimal minute repeater; cathedral gong; twin triple-axis tourbillon: 40 seconds, 8 minutes and 3 minutes; regulator between the two triple-axis tourbillon carriages.

Case: grade-5 titanium and carbon fiber; 57.3x51mm, thickness: 16.9mm; domed sapphire crystal; domed sapphire crystal caseback; water resistant to 3atm.
Dial: smoked sapphire crystal with applied "Jacob&Co." logo; red neoralithe inner ring with second graduation; black skeletonized hands with SuperLumiNova coating.
Strap: black leather; grade-5 titanium deployment buckle.
Note: limited edition of 18 pieces.
Suggested price: $360,000
Also available: carbon and rose-gold case; carbon and grade-5 titanium case with black DLC treatment.

EPIC SF24 TOURBILLON — REF. ES102.40.NS.LC.A

Movement: exclusive automatic-winding Jacob&Co. JCAA03 caliber; 35.5x42.1mm, thickness: 12.2mm; 48-hour power reserve; 528 components; 36 jewels; 28,800 vph; glucydur balance wheel system; anti-shock; high-end finishing.
Functions: hours, minutes; small seconds on tourbillon at 10; 24-hour world time indicator at 12.
Case: 18K rose gold; Ø 45mm, thickness: 13.65mm at the center, 16.7mm at the world time display; satin-finished, micro-blasted and polished; antireflective sapphire crystal; water resistant to 3atm.

Dial: anthracite opaline; gold skeletonized central hands with white SuperLumiNova coating.
Strap: alligator leather; 18K rose-gold folding buckle.
Note: limited edition of 101 pieces.
Suggested price: $190,000
Also available: set with baguette diamonds.

ASTRONOMIA TOURBILLON RUBY & DIAMONDS REF. AT800.40.BD.BR.A

Movement: exclusive manual-winding Jacob&Co. JCAM10 caliber; Ø 40mm, thickness: 17.15mm; 60-hour power reserve; 42 jewels; 365 components; 21,600 vph; triple-axis gravitational tourbillon; plate and bridges: hand-angled and polished, flank-drawn, circular graining, polished sink; hand-polished screws; circular-graining barrel; conical pinions, 4 mechanical ball bearing devices; flat balance spring.
Functions: hours, minutes; dial rotating in 20 minutes on the central axis; differential gears system; magnesium lacquered globe rotating on 2 axes in 60 seconds and on the central axis; gravitational tourbillon cage rotating on 3 axes in 60 seconds, 5 minutes and on the central axis; Jacob Cut diamond moon rotating on 2 axes in 60 seconds and on the central axis (1 carat, 288 facets).
Case: 18K rose gold; Ø 50mm, thickness: 25mm; antireflective sapphire crystal; ruby layer front case: 18K rose gold invisibly set with 257 rubies (approx. 10.4 carats); lugs invisibly set with 80 baguette white diamonds (approx. 6.1 carats); winding and time setting via 18K rose-gold lift-out rotating "bows" on caseback; 18K rose-gold caseback; water resistant to 3atm.
Dial: hand-polished and angled titanium; lacquered indexes; hand-finished blue hands.
Strap: green alligator leather; 18K rose-gold folding buckle invisibly set with 22 baguette white diamonds (approx. 1.4 carats).
Note: limited edition of 9 pieces.
Suggested price: $1,000,000
Also available: set with blue sapphires and diamonds.

CAVIAR TOURBILLON DIAMONDS BRACELET REF. CV201.30.BD.BD.A30BA

Movement: exclusive manual-winding Jacob&Co. JCBM05 caliber; Ø 30.4mm, thickness: 9.1mm; 100-hour power reserve; 19 jewels; 169 components; 21,600 vph; titanium balance with gold timing screw; anti-shock.
Functions: hours, minutes; one-minute flying tourbillon at 6.
Case: 216 baguette white diamonds (approx. 24 carats); Ø 47mm, thickness: 15.85mm; crown set with 16 baguette-cut diamonds and one rose-cut white diamond (approx. 1.13 carats); antireflective sapphire crystal; water resistant to 3atm.
Dial: invisibly set with 138 baguette white diamonds (approx. 13 carats); skeletonized hands.
Bracelet: 18K white gold; set with 464 baguette white diamonds (approx. 49.24 carats).
Note: limited edition of 18 pieces.
Suggested price: $1,600,000

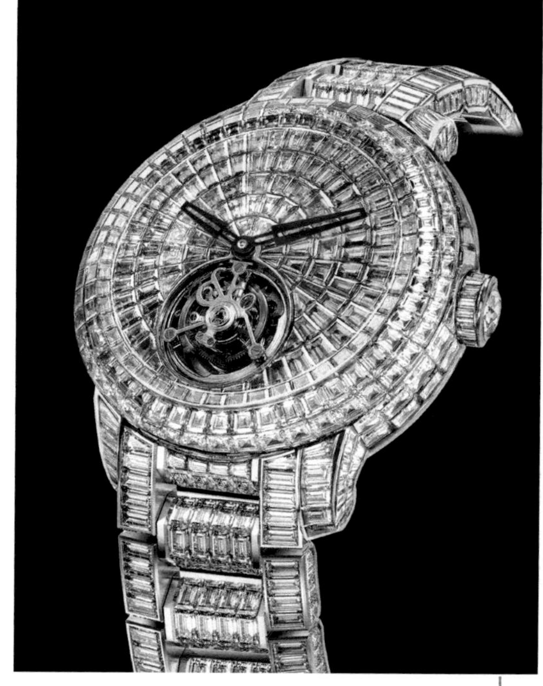

EPIC X TOURBILLON BAGUETTE REF. EX500.30.BD.BR.A

Movement: exclusive manual-winding Jacob&Co. JCAM03 caliber; Ø 34mm, thickness: 5.9mm; 72-hour power reserve; 19 jewels; 21,600 vph; barrel and tourbillon balance wheel vertically aligned; anti-shock; Jacob & Co. upper bridge; sand-blasted, chamfered and drawn-finished bridges; mirror-polished finishing screws; circular-grained bridges on the caseback.
Functions: hours, minutes; small seconds on tourbillon at 6; time-setting spring with three functions: ratchet, level and setting lever.
Case: 18K white gold; Ø 44mm, thickness: 12.3mm; set with 36 baguette diamonds (approx. 6.78 carats) and 24 baguette rubies (approx. 3.81 carats); bezel set with 26 baguette white diamonds (approx. 4.6 carats); crown set with 10 baguette rubies (approx. 0.42 carat) and one rose-cut white diamond; microblasted and satin-finished; Jacob & Co. letters in the inner ring; antireflective sapphire crystal; sapphire crystal caseback; visible time-setting mechanism; water resistant to 5atm.
Dial: skeletonized hands.
Strap: alligator leather; 18K white-gold tang buckle set with 11 baguette white diamonds (approx. 7.07 carats).
Note: limited edition of 6 pieces.
Suggested price: $540,000
Also available: set with blue sapphires; set in full white diamonds.

CALIGULA TOURBILLON BAGUETTE REF. CL801.30.BD.BD.A

Movement: exclusive manual-winding Jacob&Co. JCAM08 caliber; Ø 35mm; 48-hour power reserve; 236 components; 25 jewels; glucydur balance system; anti-shock; front: circular-grained, Côtes de Genève, sand-blasted, tourbillon upper bridge; back: hand-engraving, polished, hand-angled, drawn flank, Côtes de Genève.
Functions: hours, minutes; tourbillon at 12; manually-wound automaton scene.
Case: polished 18K white gold; Ø 46mm, thickness: 16.45mm; pierced rounded fishnet design set with baguette triangle diamonds as follows: case set with 150 baguette triangle white diamonds (approx. 13.36 carats), bezel set with 60 baguette triangle white diamonds (approx. 7.51 carats), two crowns each set with 32 baguette triangle white diamonds (approx. 2.92 carats); antireflective sapphire crystal; antireflective colored sapphire crystal caseback; water resistant to 3atm.
Dial: 18K white gold; set with 91 baguette triangle diamonds (approx. 4.9 carats); Côtes de Genève and hand-engraved graining; inner dial ring with hour markers; covered aperture that opens to reveal the concealed erotic scene at 6, hand-painted by miniature artist André Martinez; scene is revealed by turning the crown at 4 and is activated by the crown at 3; Jacob & Co. logo at 12; skeletonized 18K gold hands with blue PVD treatment.
Strap: alligator leather; 18K white-gold tang buckle set with 26 baguette triangle white diamonds (approx. 1.36 carats).
Note: unique piece.
Suggested price: $1,350,000

PALATIAL FLYING TOURBILLON MINUTE REPEATER REF. PT500.40.NS.OG.A

Movement: manual-winding Jacob&Co. JCMB03 caliber; Ø 30mm, thickness: 6.1mm; 90-hour power reserve; 308 components; 29 jewels; 21,600 vph; anti-shock; titanium balance with gold timing screw; tourbillon carriage: circular satin-brushed upper bridge, black finish, Jacob & Co. lettering; bridges: Côtes de Genève, hand-polished angles, finely drawn-finished edges.
Functions: hours, minutes; minute repeater; tourbillon at 6.
Case: 18K rose gold; Ø 43mm, thickness: 12.3mm; circular satin-finished; bezel with polished gadroon; polished crown and outer lugs; antireflective sapphire crystal; circular satin-finished caseback with polished gadroon; water resistant to 3atm.
Dial: green mineral crystal; applied 18K rose-gold brushed G Clef and Jacob & Co. logo; skeletonized hands.
Strap: alligator leather; 18K rose-gold tang buckle.
Note: limited edition of 12 pieces.
Suggested price: $265,000
Also available: black, red or blue mineral crystal dial.

PALATIAL FLYING TOURBILLON HOURS & MINUTES REF. PT520.40.NS.QR.A

Movement: manual-winding Jacob&Co. JCMB01 caliber; Ø 34.1mm, thickness: 6mm; 100-hour power reserve; 194 components; 29 jewels; 21,600 vph; titanium balance with gold timing screw; anti-shock; tourbillon carriage: circular satin-brushed Jacob & Co. upper bridges; satin-finished bridges, hand-polished angles, drawn-finished flanks; black-finish bridges on the caseback: mirror-polished ornamental plate with circular satin-finished black-gold disc with engraved and white-lacquered Jacob & Co. logo.
Functions: hours, minutes; tourbillon at 6; power reserve indicator.
Case: 18K rose gold; Ø 43mm, thickness: 12.7mm; circular satin-finished; bezel with polished gadroon; 18K rose-gold polished crown; polished outer lugs; antireflective sapphire crystal; circular satin-finished caseback with polished gadroon; water resistant to 3atm.
Dial: red mineral crystal; 18K rose-gold-applied polished Jacob & Co. logo and Roman hour numerals; gilt Jacob & Co. and Swiss Made lettering; skeletonized hands.
Strap: alligator leather; 18K rose-gold tang buckle.
Note: limited edition of 36 pieces.
Suggested price: $115,000
Also available: blue or green mineral crystal dial.

PALATIAL FLYING TOURBILLON JUMPING HOURS RETROGRADE MINUTES REF. PT510.24.NS.PB.A

Movement: manual-winding Jacob&Co. JCMB02 caliber; Ø 34.1mm, thickness: 8.8mm; 100-hour power reserve; 251 components; 31 jewels; 21,600 vph; titanium balance with gold timing screw; anti-shock; tourbillon carriage: circular satin-brushed Jacob & Co upper bridge; satin-finished bridges, hand-polished angles and drawn-finished flanks; black-finish bridges on the caseback: circular satin-finished mirror-polished ornamental plate; disc with black finish and engraved white-lacquered Jacob & Co. logo.
Functions: jumping hours at 10; retrograde minutes between 12 and 3; tourbillon at 6; power reserve indicator.

Case: titanium; Ø 43mm, thickness: 12.7mm; circular satin-finished; bezel with polished gadroon; 18K rose-gold polished crown; polished outer lugs; antireflective sapphire crystal; circular satin-finished caseback with polished gadroon; water resistant to 3atm.
Dial: blue mineral crystal; 18K rose-gold-applied polished Jacob & Co. logo; gilt Jacob & Co., tourbillon and Swiss Made lettering; skeletonized hands.
Strap: alligator leather; titanium tang buckle.
Note: limited edition of 36 pieces.
Suggested price: $120,000
Also available: red mineral crystal dial; 18K rose-gold case.

EPIC SF24 RACING REF. ES101.20.NS.YR.A

Movement: exclusive self-winding Jacob&Co. JCAA02 caliber; 35.5x42.1mm, thickness: 12.2mm; 48-hour power reserve; 34 jewels; 473 components; 28,800 vph; balance with screw system; anti-shock; hand finishing: Côtes de Genève engraving, circular graining.
Functions: hours, minutes, seconds; 24-hour world time indicator.
Case: grade 5 titanium; Ø 45mm, thickness: 13.65mm at the center, 16.7mm at the world time display; case sides, pusher and crown: inserts of red honeycomb pattern rubber; high-end Côtes de Genève and circular-graining finishes; polished screw; antireflective sapphire crystal; sapphire crystal and metalized caseback with Jacob&Co. decoration; water resistant to 3atm.
Dial: anthracite opaline; digital and vertical GMT display; applied Roman numerals coated with red SuperLumiNova; skeletonized central hands with red SuperLumiNova.
Strap: black alligator leather; grade-5 titanium deployment buckle.
Note: limited edition of 101 pieces.
Suggested price: $69,000
Also available: black, blue and green detailing.

EPIC X CHRONO — REF. EX300.24.AA.BB.A

Movement: automatic-winding Jacob & Co. JCAA05 caliber; Ø 30.4mm; 48-hour power reserve; 27 jewels; 28,800 vph; column-wheel balance screws system; anti-shock; high-end finishing.
Functions: hours, minutes; small seconds at 9; chronograph: central seconds hand, 30-minute counter at 3.
Case: titanium and 18K rose gold; Ø 47mm; antireflective sapphire crystal; sapphire crystal caseback; water resistant to 5atm.
Dial: skeletonized hands.
Strap: openworked honeycomb rubber; titanium tang buckle.
Note: limited edition and individually numbered pieces.
Price: available upon request.
Also available: titanium or black DLC titanium case.

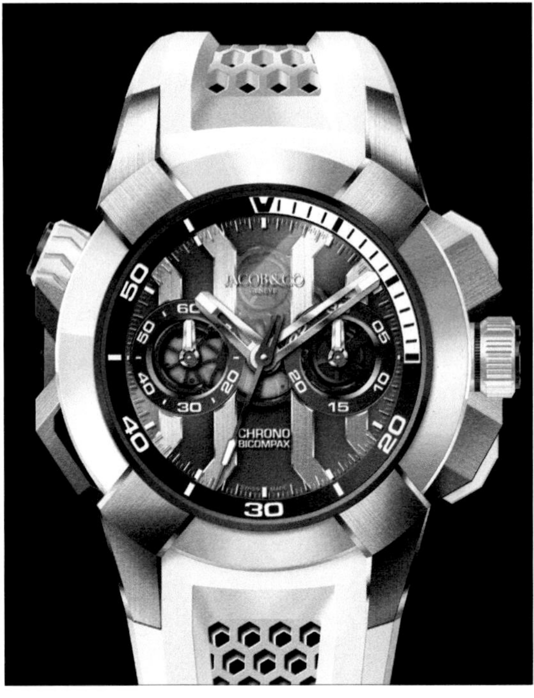

EPIC X ROSE GOLD — REF. EX100.40.PS.OP.A

Movement: exclusive manual-winding Jacob & Co. JCAM02 caliber; Ø 14.25mm, thickness: 5.9mm; 48-hour power reserve; 158 components; 21 jewels; 28,800 vph; barrel and balance wheel vertically aligned; barrel with sliding clamp system; balance screws visible on the front side; time-setting spring with three functions: ratchet, level and setting lever; anti-shock; Jacob & Co. upper bridge; sand-blasted, angled and drawn-finished bridges; anthracite and red lacquered "EPIC X" engraving on the right-side bridge; mirror-polished finishing screws; circular-grained bridges on caseback.
Functions: hours, minutes.
Case: 18K rose gold; Ø 44mm, thickness: 12.3mm; satin-finished and polished edges; engraving in the inner ring; antireflective sapphire crystal; sapphire crystal caseback; water resistant to 3atm.
Dial: skeletonized hands.
Strap: openworked honeycomb rubber; 18K rose-gold tang buckle.
Note: limited edition and individually numbered pieces.
Suggested price: $39,000
Also available: titanium or black DLC case.

EPIC X — REF. EX100.21.PS.RW.A

Movement: exclusive manual-winding skeleton Jacob&Co. JCAM02 caliber; Ø 14.25mm, thickness: 5.9mm; barrel and balance wheel vertically aligned; 48-hour power reserve; 21 jewels; 158 components; 28,800 vph; barrel with sliding clamp system; balance screws visible on the front side; time setting spring with three functions: ratchet, level and setting lever; anti-shock; "Jacob&Co." upper bridge; sand-blasted, angled and drawn-finished bridges; anthracite and red lacquered "EPIC X": engraving on the right-side bridge; mirror-polished finishing screws; circular-grained bridges on caseback.
Functions: hours, minutes.
Case: black DLC grade-5 titanium; Ø 44mm, thickness: 12.3mm; satin-finished and polished edges; engraving in the inner ring; antireflective sapphire crystal; sapphire crystal caseback; water resistant to 5atm.
Dial: red neoralithe inner ring; skeletonized hands.
Strap: openworked honeycomb rubber; adjustable deployment clasp.
Suggested price: $18,000
Also available: grade-5 titanium case; alligator leather strap.

PALATIAL CLASSIC MANUAL BIG DATE — REF. PC.400.40.NS.NB.A

Movement: manual-winding Jacob&Co. JCCM01 caliber; Ø 30.4mm, thickness: 5.8mm; 50-hour power reserve; 18 jewels; 28,800 vph; anti-shock; glucydur balance wheel system; Côtes de Genève, circular graining and vertical satin-finished; Jacob & Co. logo and lettering.
Functions: hours, minutes; date at 12; power reserve indicator at 6.
Case: polished 18K rose gold; Ø 42mm, thickness: 13.5mm; crown with engraved and microblasted Jacob & Co. logo; antireflective sapphire crystal; water resistant to 5atm.
Dial: rose with guilloché pattern; polished applied Jacob & Co. logo and hour markers; satin-finished and polished minute and power reserve rings; polished dauphine hands.
Strap: alligator leather; polished 18K rose-gold tang buckle.
Suggested price: $22,500
Also available: steel case.

BRILLIANT FLYING TOURBILLON ARLEQUINO TUTTI FRUTTI REF. BT543.40.HX.HX.B

Movement: manual-winding Jacob&Co. JCBM01 caliber; Ø 34.1mm, thickness: 6mm; 100-hour power reserve; 206 components; 29 jewels; 21,600 vph; titanium balance system with gold timing screw; anti-shock; circular satin-brushed Jacob & Co. upper bridge of the tourbillon cage; satin-finished hand-polished angles, drawn-finished flanks; bridges set with 346 brilliant-cut white diamonds (approx. 1.5 carats); power reserve indicator set with 8 multi-colored brilliant-cut sapphires (approx. 0.05 carat).
Functions: hours, minutes; tourbillon at 6; power reserve indicator.
Case: 18K rose gold; Ø 47mm, thickness: 14.65mm; invisibly set with 94 baguette multi-colored sapphires (approx. 10.8 carats) and 76 baguette white diamonds (approx. 7.21 carats); crown set with 14 baguette multi-colored sapphires (approx. 0.6 carat) and 1 rose-cut blue sapphire (approx. 0.56 carat); antireflective sapphire crystal; circular satin-finished sapphire crystal caseback with polished gadroon; water resistant to 5atm.
Dial: invisibly set with 78 baguette multi-colored sapphires (approx. 7.25 carats) and 68 baguette white diamonds (approx. 4.8 carats); leaf-shaped hands.
Strap: alligator leather; 18K rose-gold tang buckle set with 14 baguette multi-colored sapphires (approx. 1.2 carats) and 7 baguette white diamonds (approx. 0.5 carat).
Note: unique piece.
Suggested price: $770,000

BRILLIANT FULL BAGUETTE RAINBOW REF. BQ532.40.HR.HR.A

Movement: Swiss quartz; Jacob & Co. JCGQ01 caliber; 7 jewels.
Functions: hours, minutes.
Case: 18K rose gold; Ø 44mm, thickness: 12mm; invisibly set with 226 baguette multi-colored sapphires (approx. 16.38 carats); crown set with 13 baguette multi-colored sapphires and one rose-cut sapphire (approx. 0.14 carat); antireflective sapphire crystal; circular satin-finished and engraved caseback; water resistant to 3atm.
Dial: invisibly set with 187 baguette multi-colored sapphires (approx. 12.06 carats); leaf-shaped hands.
Strap: alligator leather; 18K rose-gold tang buckle set with 21 multi-colored sapphires (approx. 1.43 carats).
Note: limited edition of 18 pieces.
Suggested price: $500,000

BRILLIANT ART DECO ARLEQUINO REF. BT545.40.HX.BD.A

Movement: exclusive manual-winding Jacob&Co. JCAM05 caliber; Ø 32.6mm, thickness: 6mm; 72-hour power reserve; 172 components; 19 jewels; 21,600 vph; openworked movement with sapphire plates and finely diamond-set bridges: 177 brilliant-cut multi-colored sapphires (approx. 1.92 carats) and one brilliant-cut diamond (approx. 0.1 carat); hand-polished angles.
Functions: hours, minutes; tourbillon at 6.
Case: 18K rose gold; Ø 47mm, thickness: 14.35mm; polished and invisibly set with 127 baguette multi-colored sapphires (approx. 12.86 carats) and 78 baguette white diamonds (approx. 2.11 carats); inside upper bezel set with 48 baguette white diamonds (approx. 2.11 carats); crown set with 11 baguette multi-colored sapphires (approx. 0.56 carat), 3 baguette white diamonds (approx. 0.22 carat) and one rose-cut yellow sapphire (approx. 0.53 carat); antireflective sapphire crystal; water resistant to 3atm.
Dial: skeletonized; gun-blue leaf-shaped hands.
Strap: alligator leather; 18K rose-gold tang buckle set with 15 baguette multi-colored sapphires (approx. 1.13 carats) and 6 baguette diamonds (approx. 0.44 carat).
Note: unique piece.
Suggested price: $770,000

BRILLIANT RAINBOW REF. BA537.40.GR.KW.A

Movement: exclusive automatic-winding Jacob & Co. JCAA04 caliber; Ø 25.6mm; 21 jewels; 28,800 vph.
Functions: hours, minutes, seconds.
Case: polished 18K rose gold; Ø 44mm, thickness: 11.7mm; set with 48 multi-colored rainbow baguette sapphires (approx. 5.76 carats); crown set with 31 brilliant-cut white diamonds (approx. 0.39 carat); antireflective sapphire crystal; circular satin-finished and engraved caseback; water resistant to 3atm.
Dial: white mother-of-pearl; set with 11 multi-colored sapphire hour markers (approx. 0.88 carat); center pavé dial set with 50 brilliant-cut diamonds (approx. 0.96 carat); leaf-shaped hands.
Strap: alligator leather; 18K rose-gold buckle set with 42 brilliant-cut diamonds (approx. 0.72 carat).
Note: limited edition of 101 pieces.
Suggested price: $69,000
Also available: 18K white-gold case.

BRILLIANT SKELETON NORTHERN LIGHTS REF. BS431.40.RD.QR.A

Movement: exclusive manual-winding Jacob&Co. JCAM01 caliber; Ø 32mm, thickness: 5.8mm; 46-hour power reserve; 21 jewels; openworked anthracite movement with rhodium-plated gears.
Functions: hours, minutes.
Case: 18K rose gold; Ø 44mm; case polished and pavé set with 251 round white diamonds (approx. 9.25 carats); crown set with 33 round white diamonds (approx. 0.2 carat); antireflective sapphire crystal; engraved edge caseback; water resistant to 3atm.
Dial: red mineral crystal; leaf-shaped hands.
Strap: alligator leather; 18K rose-gold tang buckle set with 42 round white diamonds (approx. 0.54 carat).
Note: limited edition of 101 pieces.
Suggested price: $79,000
Also available: blue or green mineral crystal dial.

BRILLIANT SKELETON JEWELRY REF. BS431.40.RD.CB.A

Movement: exclusive manual-winding Jacob&Co. JCAM01 caliber; Ø 32mm, thickness: 5.8mm; 46-hour power reserve; 150 components; 21 jewels; openworked anthracite movement with rose-gold-finished Jacob & Co. logo, bridges and gears.
Functions: hours, minutes.
Case: 18K rose gold; Ø 44mm; polished and pavé set with 294 round diamonds (approx. 8.88 carats); crown set with 31 round white diamonds (approx. 0.39 carat); antireflective sapphire crystal; engraved edge caseback; water resistant to 3atm.
Dial: skeletonized; leaf-shaped hands.
Strap: satin; 18K rose-gold tang buckle set with 42 round white diamonds (approx. 0.72 carat).
Note: limited edition of 101 pieces.
Suggested price: $79,000
Also available: 18K white-gold case.

BRILLIANT MYSTERY PAVE DIAMONDS REF. BM556.40.RD.RD.A

Movement: Swiss quartz; Jacob&Co. JCGQ063 caliber; Ø 11mm; 5 jewels.
Functions: hours, minutes.
Case: polished 18K rose gold; Ø 44mm, thickness: 10.15mm; invisibly set with 298 round white diamonds (approx. 9.22 carats); inner ring set with 89 round diamonds (approx. 1.16 carats); antireflective sapphire crystal; time setting by a corrector; water resistant to 3atm.
Dial: invisibly set center with 56 round white diamonds (approx. 0.84 carat); two floating black triangle hands.
Strap: satin; 18K rose-gold tang buckle set with 33 round white diamonds (approx. 0.54 carat).
Note: limited edition and individually numbered pieces.
Suggested price: $84,000
Also available: 18K white-gold case.

BRILLIANT REF. BQ030.10.RH.KR.A

Movement: Swiss quartz; Jacob&Co. JCGQ01 caliber; Ø 24mm; 7 jewels.
Functions: hours, minutes.
Case: polished stainless steel; Ø 44mm, thickness: 11.6mm; crown set with 408 round diamonds (approx. 5.22 carats); antireflective sapphire crystal; circular satin-finished and engraved caseback; water resistant to 3atm.
Dial: white mother-of-pearl; set with 11 multicolored sapphire hour markers (approx. 0.88 carat); leaf-shaped hands.
Strap: satin; polished stainless steel tang buckle; set with 76 round diamonds (approx. 0.61 carat).
Suggested price: $36,500
Also available: set with ruby, tsavorite, blue sapphire or pink sapphire hour markers.

JAEGER-LECOULTRE

DOUBLE AGENTS

Jaeger-LeCoultre celebrates the rich history of its Reverso line of timepieces with three creations bearing dual identities. Each driven by a single caliber, **THE WATCHES POSSESS TWICE THE TIMEKEEPING ELEGANCE AT THE TURN OF A DIAL**.

With the Reverso Tribute Gyrotourbillon, the Swiss manufacture demonstrates a breathtaking command of multi-dimensional design. Combining transparency and gyroscopic motion with spectacular engravings and meticulous craftsmanship, the hand-wound platinum masterpiece celebrates the Reverso collection's heralded history, which began in 1931. At 6 o'clock on both the front and rear faces of the limited edition wristwatch, the Calibre 179's Gyrotourbillon seems to float in space as it conducts its independent bi-axial revolutions. The module cycles through its external rotation every 60 seconds, and its internal carriage completes its cycle in 12.6 seconds. As the timepiece executes its choreography, the wearer witnesses the movement's hemispherical, handcrafted balance spring in all its dynamism. The front dial complements its hours, minutes and day/night indicator with an ingenious seconds display featuring a rotating graduated disc around the tourbillon's carriages. The Reverso Tribute Gyrotourbillon contrasts its front dial's grained white appearance with an exquisite, openworked architecture on the second face, accessed by a simple swivel of the case. The "reverse" face enhances its skeletonized artwork with a two-tone, 24-hour mode at 2 o'clock and small seconds driven directly by the Gyrotourbillon's external carriage.

▲ **REVERSO TRIBUTE GYROTOURBILLON**

This platinum wristwatch, limited to 75 pieces, boasts a bi-axial tourbillon that executes full revolutions lasting 60 and 12.6 seconds, respectively, on two independent axes.

Housed in an 18-karat pink-gold case, the Reverso Tribute Calendar uses its front dial to present a calendar complete with day and month, via two apertures at 12 o'clock, as well as date and moonphase.

▲ **REVERSO ONE DUETTO MOON**

While the front side of this feminine wristwatch devotes itself to hours and minutes on an intricately crafted backdrop, a turn of the diamond-adorned case reveals a radiant moonphase complication amidst a scintillating night sky.

◄ **REVERSO TRIBUTE CALENDAR**

With a comprehensive calendar on one side and dynamic day/night display on the other, this pink-gold timepiece creates harmony through contrasting colors and textures.

The Reverso Tribute Calendar plays with contrasting tones and textures to add a captivating day/night narrative to its sophisticated mechanical construction.

Housed in an 18-karat pink-gold case, the hand-wound timepiece uses its front dial, in silver-toned grained opaline, to present a calendar complete with day and month via two apertures at 12 o'clock, as well as date and moonphase using a dual-function subdial on the lower half of the face. The date, indicated by a crescent-tipped stem, thus surrounds a finely crafted depiction of the moon's cycle. The elegant display sets the stage for the back dial's dark, textured anthracite. Atop a Clous-de-Paris guilloché motif, a generously sized day/night subdial intersects the principal time display, rotating throughout the day to align its display with a white, triangular indicator. The Reverso Tribute Calendar is driven by the 283-component Calibre 853 and boasts a power reserve of 45 hours.

The Reverso One Duetto Moon introduces itself with an understated indication of the hours and minutes on a vibrant backdrop. Decorated with a sunburst guilloché motif, the front dial invites the eye to dive toward a seemingly infinite focal point in the center of the design. A simple rotation of the watch's stainless steel case reveals a scintillating, profound night sky, composed of paillonné blue enamel, upon which a mother-of-pearl moonphase display reigns as the undeniable queen. On the lunar side of the case, 28 diamonds frame the striking exhibition, lighting a wondrous night sky. The Calibre 842, which powers both sides of the Reverso One Duetto Moon, boasts 129 components, 19 jewels and a power reserve of 38 hours.

REVERSO TRIBUTE GYROTOURBILLON — REF. 3946420

Movement: manual-winding 179 caliber.
Functions: hours, minutes; seconds around tourbillon at 6; day/night indicator at 11.
Case: platinum; 51.1x31mm, thickness: 12.4mm; sapphire crystal caseback; water resistant to 3atm.
Dial: front: finely-grained white, blued steel dauphine-type hands; back: skeletonized.
Strap: black leather.
Note: limited edition of 75 pieces.
Suggested price: 270,000 Euros (excluding VAT)

REVERSO TRIBUTE CALENDAR — REF. 3912420

Movement: manual-winding 853 caliber; thickness: 5.15mm; 280 components; 19 jewels; 21,600 vph.
Functions: hours, minutes; date via hand at 6; day and month at 12; moonphase at 6; second time zone and day/night indicator on caseback.
Case: pink gold; 49.7x29.9mm, thickness: 10.9mm; water resistant to 3atm.
Dial: front: silvered, grained, appliquéd hour markers; back: charcoal gray, Clous de Paris guilloché, appliquéd hour markers.
Strap: brown leather.
Suggested price: $25,200

REVERSO TRIBUTE DUOFACE — REF. 3908420

Movement: manual-winding 854A/2 caliber; 17.2x22mm, thickness: 3.8mm; 45-hour power reserve; 180 components; 21 jewels; 21,600 vph.
Functions: front: hours, minutes, small seconds at 6; back: second time zone, 24-hour day/night indicator at 6.
Case: stainless steel; 42.8x25.5mm, thickness: 9.15mm; water resistant to 3atm.
Dial: front: finely grained opaline, blue hour markers, blued dauphine-type hands; back: blue with Clous de Paris hobnail guilloché pattern, silver-toned hour markers, silver-toned dauphine-type hands.
Strap: dark blue alligator leather; stainless steel folding clasp.
Suggested price: $12,200

REVERSO CLASSIC LARGE — REF. 3828420

Movement: automatic-winding 965 caliber; Ø 20mm, thickness: 4.02mm; 38-hour power reserve; 197 components; 30 jewels; 28,800 vph.
Functions: hours, minutes.
Case: stainless steel; 45.6x27.4mm, thickness: 9.7mm; water resistant to 3atm.
Dial: silver-toned; vertical brushed and guilloché; transferred numerals; blued baton-type hands.
Strap: black alligator leather; stainless steel folding clasp.
Suggested price: $8,850

REVERSO CLASSIC LARGE DUOFACE REF. 3832420

Movement: automatic-winding 969 caliber; Ø 20mm, thickness: 4.77mm; 38-hour power reserve; 229 components; 30 jewels; 28,800 vph.
Functions: hours, minutes; 24-hour day/night indicator at 6; second time zone on caseback.
Case: 18K pink gold; 47x28.3mm, thickness: 11.6mm; water resistant to 3atm.
Dial: front: silver-toned, vertical brushed and guilloché, black transferred numerals, blued hands; back: black with Clous de Paris hobnail guilloché pattern, white hour markers, dauphine-type hour and minute hands.
Strap: black alligator leather; stainless steel folding clasp.
Suggested price: $22,400
Also available: stainless steel case, $12,200 (ref. Q3838420).

REVERSO CLASSIC MEDIUM DUETTO REF. 2572420

Movement: automatic-winding 968A caliber; thickness: 4.27mm; 207 components; 30 jewels; 28,800 vph.
Functions: hours, minutes; hours, minutes on caseback.
Case: pink gold; 40.1x24.4mm, thickness: 9.6mm; water resistant to 3atm.
Dial: front: silvered, guilloché, vertically brushed, black transferred numerals; back: black, guilloché and sunray-brushed, frosted minute scale.
Strap: black leather; pin buckle.
Suggested price: $22,900
Also available: stainless steel case, stainless steel bracelet, $12,000 (ref. 2578120); pink-gold bracelet, $37,800 (ref. 2572120); stainless steel case, $10,900 (ref. 2578420).

REVERSO ONE CORDONNET REF. 3264420

Movement: quartz 657 caliber; thickness: 2.15mm; 43 components; 4 jewels.
Functions: hours, minutes.
Case: 18K pink gold and stainless steel; 33.8x16.3mm, thickness: 7mm; water resistant to 3atm.
Dial: silvered, guilloché and sunray-brushed; Arabic numerals.
Strap: black leather.
Suggested price: $7,600

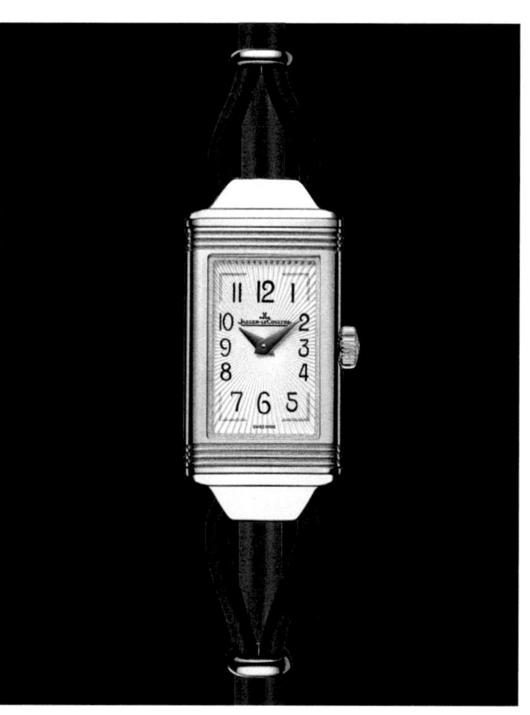

REVERSO ONE REEDITION REF. 3258470

Movement: quartz 657 caliber; thickness: 2.15mm; 43 components; 4 jewels.
Functions: hours, minutes.
Case: stainless steel; 32.5x16.3mm, thickness: 7mm; water resistant to 3atm.
Dial: black opaline; Arabic numerals.
Strap: black leather.
Suggested price: $4,900

REVERSO ONE DUETTO MOON — REF. 3358420

Movement: manual-winding 842 caliber; thickness: 4.19mm; 129 components; 18 jewels; 21,600 vph.
Functions: hours, minutes; hours, minutes, moonphase on caseback.
Case: stainless steel; 40.1x20mm, thickness: 10mm; water resistant to 3atm.
Dial: front: silvered, guilloché and sunray-brushed, Arabic numerals; back: midnight blue, powdered silvered hour markers.
Strap: blue leather.
Suggested price: $11,500

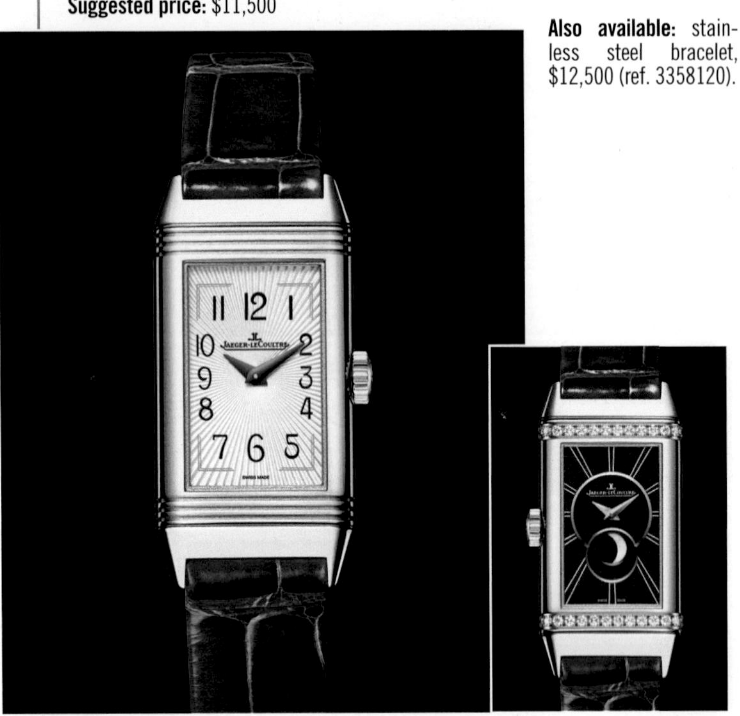

Also available: stainless steel bracelet, $12,500 (ref. 3358120).

REVERSO ONE DUETTO MOON — REF. 3352120

Movement: manual-winding 842 caliber; thickness: 4.19mm; 129 components; 18 jewels; 21,600 vph.
Functions: hours, minutes; hours, minutes, moonphase on caseback.
Case: pink gold; 40.1x20mm, thickness: 10mm; water resistant to 3atm.
Dial: front: silvered, guilloché and sunray-brushed, Arabic numerals; back: brown, gilt hour markers.
Bracelet: pink gold.
Suggested price: $38,200

Also available: red leather strap, $23,800 (ref. 3352420).

RENDEZ-VOUS NIGHT & DAY — REF. 3442450

Movement: automatic-winding 898A/1 caliber; thickness: 3.3mm; 204 components; 30 jewels; 28,800 vph.
Functions: hours, minutes, seconds; day/night indicator at 6.
Case: pink gold; Ø 34mm, thickness: 12.4mm; water resistant to 3atm.
Dial: slate; sunray-brushed; Arabic numerals.
Strap: gray leather.
Suggested price: $22,400

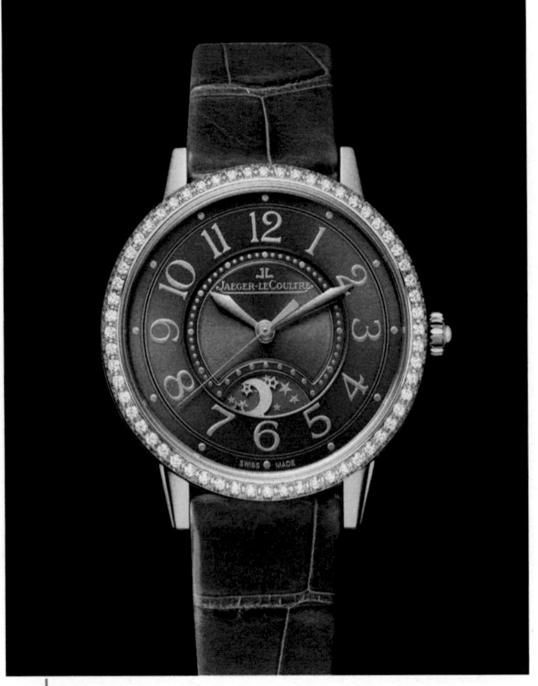

RENDEZ-VOUS MOON — REF. 3532490

Movement: automatic-winding 935 caliber; thickness: 4.63mm; 265 components; 41 jewels; 28,800 vph.
Functions: hours, minutes; Rendez-Vous indicator; moonphase at 6.
Case: pink gold; Ø 39mm, thickness: 10.77mm; bezel set with 192 diamonds (approx. 2.62 carats); water resistant to 5atm.
Dial: burgundy; aventurine; appliquéd numerals.
Strap: burgundy leather.
Suggested price: $51,500

Also available: white-gold case, blue dial, blue satin strap, $54,000 (ref. 3533490); white-gold case, blue dial with leaf pattern, blue satin strap, $67,500 (ref. 35334E1); white-gold case, mother-of-pearl dial, blue satin strap, $44,100 (ref. 3523490); white-gold case, white gem-set dial, blue satin strap, price on demand (ref. 3533401).

GEOPHYSIC TRUE SECOND — REF. 8012520

Movement: automatic-winding 770 caliber; thickness: 6.57mm; 275 components; 36 jewels; 28,800 vph.
Functions: hours, minutes, true seconds; date at 3.
Case: pink gold; Ø 39.6mm, thickness: 11.81mm; water resistant to 5atm.
Dial: silvered; grained; appliquéd hour markers.
Strap: brown leather.
Suggested price: $17,500
Also available: stainless steel, black leather strap, $9,050 (ref. 8018420).

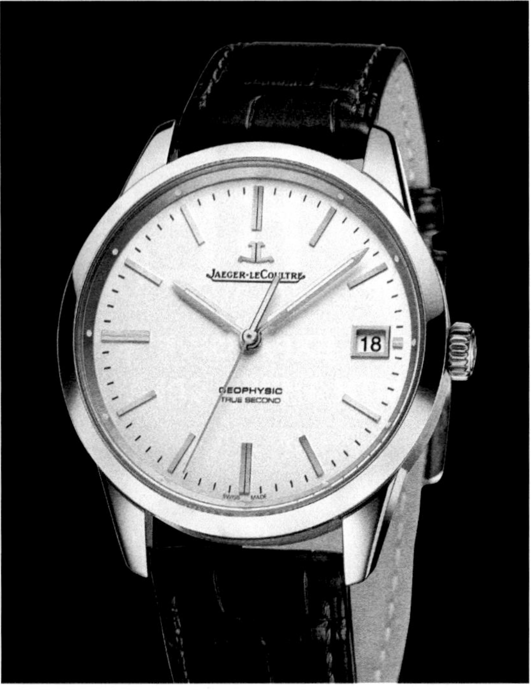

GEOPHYSIC UNIVERSAL TIME — REF. 8108420

Movement: automatic-winding 772 caliber; thickness: 7.13mm; 274 components; 36 jewels; 28,800 vph.
Functions: hours, minutes, true seconds; world time.
Case: stainless steel; Ø 41.6mm, thickness: 11.84mm; water resistant to 5atm.
Dial: blue; lacquered; appliquéd hour markers.
Strap: black leather.
Suggested price: $15,000
Also available: pink-gold case, brown leather strap, $25,000 (ref. 8102520).

DUOMETRE QUANTIEME LUNAIRE — REF. 6043420

Movement: manual-winding 381 caliber; thickness: 7.25mm; 374 components; 40 jewels; 21,600 vph.
Functions: hours, minutes off-set at 2; central seconds; date and moonphase at 10; power reserve indicator at 6.
Case: white gold; Ø 40.5mm, thickness: 13.5mm; water resistant to 5atm.
Dial: silvered; opaline; baton hour markers.
Strap: black leather.
Suggested price: $43,000
Also available: white dial, blue leather strap, $57,000 (ref. 60435E1).

MASTER COMPRESSOR CHRONOGRAPH CERAMIC — REF. 205C571

Movement: automatic-winding 757 caliber; thickness: 6.26mm; 300 components; 45 jewels; 28,800 vph.
Functions: hours, minutes; small seconds at 6; date between 4 and 5; chronograph: central seconds hand, 30-minute counter at 3, 12-hour counter at 9; second time zone; day/night indicator.
Case: ceramic; Ø 46mm, thickness: 14.3mm; water resistant to 10atm.
Dial: charchoal gray; opaline; blue numerals and hands.
Strap: blue Trieste cloth.
Suggested price: $13,900
Also available: black dial, $14,000 (ref. 205C570).

J⁂D

JAQUET DROZ

NATURAL BEAUTY

Jaquet Droz **DEMONSTRATES THE EXPANSIVE BREADTH OF ITS IMAGINATION AND EXPERTISE WITH THREE CREATIONS** that affirm a vision of haute horology as a vast artistic playground.

The Grande Seconde Off-Centered celebrates the history of the Swiss watchmaker within a vibrantly modern design. On a dial composed of an expertly cut onyx disc, the timepiece finds a striking balance of minimalist refinement and bold geometric themes. However, the visual understatement marks a tribute to Pierre Jaquet-Droz's groundbreaking 18th-century innovation of an overlapping, off-centered subdial indicating only the running seconds. With the Grande Seconde Off-Centered, the manufacture turns the spotlight to the fundamental unit of haute horology. Forming the lower section of the brand's iconic "figure 8" on the rich blackness of the dial, the timepiece's small seconds display smoothly intersects an hours-and-minutes subdial above it. Their shimmering rings, in 18-karat white gold, add a stunning play of light to the depth of the backdrop. By carving the indexes directly into the precious metal, Jaquet Droz achieves excellent legibility without compromising the sober elegance of the design. The watchmaker even extends the off-centered theme of the timepiece to the 43mm stainless steel case, where the crown, cleverly positioned at 4 o'clock, confirms the harmonious diagonal positioning of the dial-side architecture. Subtle yet unmistakable, the aesthetic element gives the overall design a pleasing sense of geometric balance.

◂ **GRANDE SECONDE OFF-CENTERED**

Atop a precisely cut onyx dial, two intersecting subdials epitomize Jaquet Droz's powerful minimalism.

▸ **PETITE HEURE MINUTE THOUSAND YEAR LIGHTS** *(top)*

This timepiece reawakens an ancestral Korean art form to adorn the feminine wrist with a vibrant bouquet of flowers.

▸ **CHARMING BIRD** *(bottom)*

An innovative mechanical triumph gives the Charming Bird's centerpiece its unparalleled singing voice as it serenades its owner atop a Swiss landscape in mother-of-pearl.

Combining miniature painting with meticulous engraving, Jaquet Droz brings the Petite Heure Minute Thousand Year Lights' flowers to life atop their lustrous stage.

With the Petite Heure Minute Thousand Year Lights, Jaquet Droz presents a breathtaking floral tableau that revives one of the noblest ancestral Korean artistic techniques. A tribute to the millennium-old "Najeon Chilgi" method, the 35mm or 39mm timepiece adorns its mother-of-pearl lacquer dial with a magnificent wildflower décor. By combining miniature painting with meticulous engraving, Jaquet Droz achieves layers of light, color and texture, bringing the flowers to life atop their lustrous stage. The visual masterpiece then gently wraps itself around the contour of an off-centered subdial, where the hours and minutes are indicated via two golden hands. A generous setting of diamonds, on the red- or white-gold case, lights the vivid bouquet to perfection. The enchanting timepiece, available with or without precious stones, is limited to 28 pieces for each model and is endowed with a 68-hour power reserve and a transparent caseback. Playful, luxurious and full of magnificent details, the Petite Heure Minute Thousand Year Lights captures the timeless beauty of flowers and ancient craftsmanship.

A celebrated master of the automaton, Jaquet Droz presents an innovative timepiece whose enchanting visual display is matched only by its ability to serenade its wearer. The Charming Bird, housed in a 47mm case composed of red or white gold, epitomizes the comprehensive nature of the watchmaker's technical mastery and endless imagination. A miniaturized sculpture, at 6 o'clock, depicts a highly detailed bird atop a revelation of the watch's sophisticated hand-decorated caliber. Thanks to an impressive feat of inventive engineering, the Charming Bird performs its song by way of air compression, and not vibration, as is traditionally the case. Jaquet Droz employs three small sapphire crystal tubes, allowing the air to enter the first, be stored in the second and finally pushed into the third to produce a perfect melody regulated by the volume of air and the speed of the piston. Jaquet Droz finds a home for its musical star amidst a Swiss countryside landscape hand-painted and engraved on precious mother-of-pearl. The hours and minutes are told on a subdial at 12 o'clock that subtly combines with the songbird's enclosure to complete the manufacture's famous "figure 8."

PETITE HEURE MINUTE MOTHER-OF-PEARL — REF. J005003572

Movement: automatic-winding 2653.P caliber; 68-hour power reserve; 28 jewels; 28,800 vph; silicon balance spring and pallet horns; double barrel; 18K red-gold oscillating weight.
Functions: off-centered hours and minutes.
Case: 18K red gold; Ø 35mm, thickness: 10.8mm; set with 232 diamonds (1.22 carats); individual limited serial number engraved on caseback; water resistant to 3atm.
Dial: white mother-of-pearl; 18K red-gold hands; 18K red-gold applied ring.
Strap: rolled-edge handmade brown satin; 18K red-gold ardillon buckle.
Suggested price: $30,600

PETITE HEURE MINUTE THOUSAND YEAR LIGHTS — REF. J005004201

Movement: automatic-winding 2653.P caliber; 68-hour power reserve; 28 jewels; 28,800 vph; silicon balance spring and pallet horns; double barrel; 18K white-gold oscillating weight.
Functions: off-centered hours and minutes.
Case: 18K white gold; Ø 35mm, thickness: 10.8mm; set with 232 diamonds (1.22 carats); individual limited serial number engraved on caseback; water resistant to 3atm.
Dial: 18K white gold with black lacquer and hand-engraved and hand-painted white mother-of-pearl; 18K white-gold applied ring; white mother-of-pearl subdial; blued steel hands.
Strap: rolled-edge handmade blue alligator leather; 18K white-gold ardillon buckle.
Note: limited edition of 28 pieces.
Suggested price: $49,400

PETITE HEURE MINUTE RELIEF SEASONS — REF. J005024575

Movement: automatic-winding 2653 caliber; 68-hour power reserve; 28 jewels; 28,800 vph; double barrel; 18K white-gold oscillating weight.
Functions: off-centered hours and minutes.
Case: 18K white gold; Ø 41mm, thickness: 13.77mm; bezel and lugs set with 272 diamonds (1.04 carats); individual limited serial number engraved on caseback; water resistant to 3atm.
Dial: hand-engraved and hand-painted white mother-of-pearl; rhodium-plated and hand-painted 18K red-gold bird appliqué; blued steel hands.
Strap: rolled-edge handmade gray satin; 18K white-gold ardillon buckle set with 24 diamonds (0.15 carat).
Note: limited edition of 88 pieces.
Suggested price: $71,400

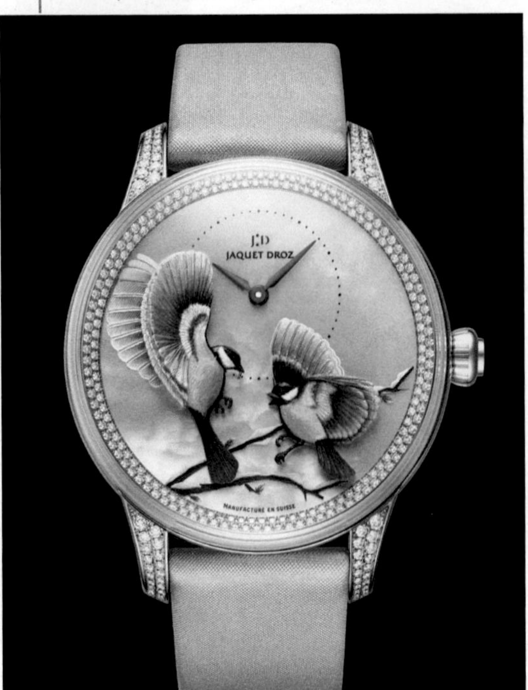

GRANDE SECOND OFF CENTERED ONYX — REF. J006030270

Movement: automatic-winding 2663A.P caliber; 68-hour power reserve; 30 jewels; 28,800 vph; silicon balance spring and pallet horns; double barrel; heavy metal oscillating weight.
Functions: off-centered hours and minutes; large seconds subdial.
Case: stainless steel; Ø 43mm, thickness: 12mm; individual serial number engraved on caseback; water resistant to 3atm.
Dial: black onyx; rhodium-treated hands; 18K white-gold ring.
Strap: rolled-edge handmade black alligator leather; stainless steel folding clasp.
Suggested price: $10,700

GRANDE SECONDE QUANTIEME IVORY ENAMEL — REF. J007013200

Movement: automatic-winding 2660Q2.P caliber; 68-hour power reserve; 30 jewels; 28,800 vph; silicon balance; double barrel; red-gold oscillating weight.
Functions: off-centered hours and minutes; large seconds subdial; date via hand at 6.
Case: 18K red gold; Ø 39mm, thickness: 12.13mm; individual serial number engraved on caseback; water resistant to 3atm.
Dial: ivory Grand Feu enamel; 18K red-gold hands; date hand with red varnished tip.
Strap: rolled-edge handmade black alligator leather; red-gold ardillon buckle.
Suggested price: $19,400

GRANDE SECOND QUANTIEME SILVER — REF. J007030242

Movement: automatic-winding 2660Q2 caliber; 68-hour power reserve; 30 jewels; 28,800 vph; double barrel; heavy metal oscillating weight.
Functions: off-centered hours and minutes; large seconds subdial; date via hand at 6.
Case: stainless steel; Ø 43mm, thickness: 11.63mm; individual serial number engraved on caseback; water resistant to 3atm.
Dial: silvery opaline; blued steel hands; date with red varnished tip; silver applied ring.
Strap: rolled-edge handmade black alligator leather; stainless steel folding clasp.
Suggested price: $9,100

GRANDE SECOND DEADBEAT BLACK ENAMEL — REF. J008033201

Movement: automatic-winding 2695SMR caliber; 38-hour power reserve; 34 jewels; 21,600 vph; silicon balance spring and pallet horns; 18K red-gold oscillating weight.
Functions: off-centered hours and minutes; large deadbeat seconds; retrograde date via hand at 6.
Case: 18K red gold; Ø 43mm, thickness: 13.79mm; individual limited serial number engraved on caseback; water resistant to 3atm.
Dial: black Grand Feu enamel; individual limited serial number indicated on dial; 18K red-gold hands; date hand with red varnished tip; seconds hand with red-gold treatment.
Strap: rolled-edge handmade black alligator leather; 18K red-gold ardillon buckle.
Note: limited edition of 88 pieces.
Suggested price: $30,500

ECLIPSE ONYX — REF. J012630270

Movement: automatic-winding 6553L2 caliber; 68-hour power reserve; 28 jewels; 28,800 vph; double barrel; heavy metal oscillating weight.
Functions: hours, minutes; date via central hand; day and month at 12; moonphase at 6.
Case: stainless steel; Ø 43mm, thickness: 12.44mm; individual serial number engraved on caseback; water resistant to 3atm.
Dial: black onyx; 8 star and 1 moon appliqués with rhodium treatment; rhodium-treated hands; black onyx moonphase.
Strap: rolled-edge handmade black alligator leather; stainless steel ardillon buckle.
Suggested price: $17,900

GRANDE SECONDE TOURBILLON PAILLONNEE REF. J013033242

Movement: automatic-winding 25JD caliber; 7-day power reserve; 31 jewels; 21,600 vph; 18K red-gold oscillating weight with lapis lazuli appliqué.
Functions: hours and minutes at 6; seconds on tourbillon at 12.
Case: 18K red gold; Ø 43mm, thickness: 13.1mm; individual limited serial number engraved on caseback; water resistant to 3atm.
Dial: paillonné in blue Grand Feu enamel; silvery opaline hours and minutes subdial; blued stainless steel hands; 18K red-gold ring.
Strap: rolled-edge handmade dark blue alligator leather; 18K red-gold folding clasp.
Note: limited edition of 8 pieces.
Suggested price: $119,200

LADY 8 AVENTURINE REF. J014500270

Movement: automatic-winding 1153 caliber; 68-hour power reserve; 28 jewels; 28,800 vph; double barrel; 22K white-gold oscillating weight.
Functions: hours, minutes.
Case: stainless steel; Ø 35mm; set with 48 diamonds (0.53 carat); ball bearing and aventurine cabochon at 12; individual serial number engraved on caseback; water resistant to 3atm.
Dial: aventurine; cambered 18K white-gold hands.
Strap: handmade blue alligator leather; stainless steel folding clasp.
Suggested price: $15,600

GRANDE SECONDE DUAL TIME IVORY ENAMEL REF. J016033200

Movement: automatic-winding 2663H24 caliber; 65-hour power reserve; 42 jewels; 28,800 vph; silicon balance spring and pallet horns; double barrel; 18K red-gold oscillating weight.
Functions: off-centered hours and minutes; large seconds subdial; date via hand at 6; 24-hour second time zone at 6.
Case: 18K red gold; Ø 43mm, thickness: 13.13mm; individual serial number engraved on caseback; water resistant to 3atm.
Dial: ivory Grand Feu enamel; 18K red-gold hands; date with red varnished tip; blued steel second time zone hand.
Strap: rolled-edge handmade black alligator leather; 18K red-gold ardillon buckle.
Suggested price: $26,800

GRANDE SECONDE SW RED GOLD REF. J029033401

Movement: automatic-winding 2663A-S caliber; 68-hour power reserve; 30 jewels; 28,800 vph; double barrel; 18K white-gold oscillating weight with black PVD treatment.
Functions: off-centered hours and minutes; large seconds subdial.
Case: 18K red gold; Ø 45mm, thickness: 11.93mm; crown with rubber cast; individual serial number engraved on caseback; water resistant to 5atm.
Dial: black with rubber treatment; indexes in white SuperLumiNova; hands with red-gold treatment and white SuperLumiNova tips; 18K applied ring and plates with red-gold treatment.
Strap: natural black rubber; 18K red-gold folding clasp; stainless steel folding system with black PVD finish.
Suggested price: $27,300

BIRD REPEATER FALL OF THE RHINE — REF. J031033206

Movement: manual-winding RMA88 caliber; 48-hour power reserve; 69 jewels; 18,000 vph; single barrel.
Functions: off-centered hours and minutes; minute repeater.
Case: 18K red gold; Ø 47.5mm, thickness: 18.93mm; individual limited serial number engraved on caseback.
Dial: 18K red gold; hand-engraved and hand-painted mother-of-pearl subdial; hand-engraved and hand-painted 18K gold birds; 18K red-gold hands.
Strap: rolled-edge handmade brown alligator leather; 18K red-gold folding buckle.
Note: limited edition of 8 pieces.
Suggested price: $472,500

CHARMING BIRD — REF. J031534200

Movement: automatic-winding 615 caliber; 38-hour power reserve; 29 jewels; 21,600 vph; silicon balance spring and pallet horns; platinum oscillating weight.
Functions: off-centered hours and minutes; singing bird automaton at 6.
Case: 18K white gold; Ø 47mm, thickness 1: 15.75mm, thickness 2: 22.85mm; individual limited serial number engraved on caseback.
Dial: hand-engraved and hand-painted white mother-of-pearl; 18K white-gold hands; 18K white-gold ring; onyx hours and minutes subdial.
Strap: rolled-edge handmade black alligator leather with black alligator leather lining; 18K white-gold prestige folding clasp.
Suggested price: $430,500

LADY 8 FLOWER — REF. J032003270

Movement: automatic-winding 615 caliber; 38-hour power reserve; 29 jewels; 21,600 vph; silicon balance spring and pallet horns; platinum oscillating weight.
Functions: hours, minutes; flower automaton at 12.
Case: 18K red gold; Ø 35mm, thickness 1: 12.76mm, thickness 2: 17.6mm; individual serial number engraved on caseback; set with 114 diamonds (1.4 carats); water resistant to 3atm.
Dial: white mother-of-pearl; 18K red-gold hands with curved contours; 18K red-gold ring with studded motif.
Strap: rolled-edge handmade brown alligator leather; 18K red-gold folding clasp.
Note: limited edition of 8 pieces.
Suggested price: $136,500

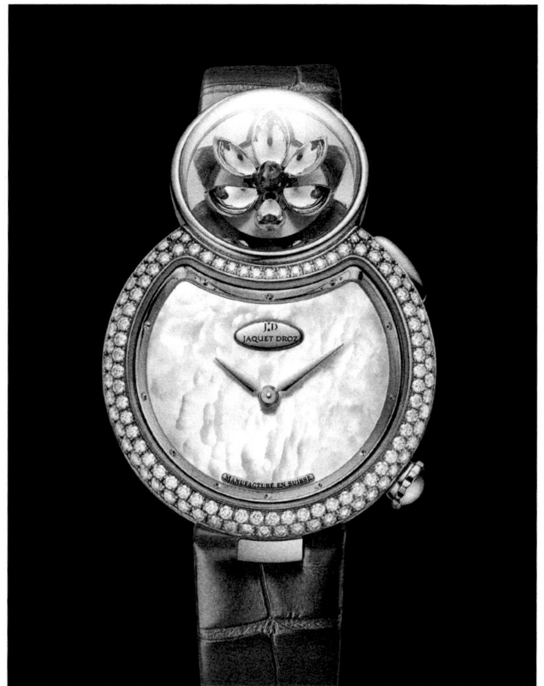

POCKET WATCH PAILLONNEE — REF. J080033046

Movement: manual-winding 2615 caliber; 40-hour power reserve; 20 jewels; 21,600 vph.
Functions: off-centered hours and minutes; large seconds subdial.
Case: 18K red gold; Ø 50mm, thickness: 12.07mm; individual limited serial number engraved on caseback.
Dial: paillonné in red Grand Feu enamel; silvery opaline subdials; blued stainless steel hands; 18K red-gold ring.
Chain: 18K red gold.
Suggested price: $47,300

LONGINES
Flagship
AUTOMATIC
SWISS MADE
3
6
9
12

FLAGSHIP HERITAGE

60TH ANNIVERSARY 1957-2017: AN EXCEPTIONAL ANNIVERSARY TIMEPIECE

Saint-Imier (Switzerland), January 2017 – Longines celebrates this year the 60th anniversary of its first Flagship collection. For this occasion, the watchmaking brand introduces the Flagship Heritage – 60th Anniversary 1957-2017. This timepiece was inspired by a Flagship model kept in the Swiss watchmaker's headquarters, favored by Longines's Ambassador of Elegance, Kate Winslet. Available in steel, yellow gold or rose gold, these numbered and limited edition models display a flagship on the back, as did the original pieces.

Longines sold its first Flagship in 1957, and ever since, the collection has met with lasting success. This timeless watch, with its white dial, thin profile and fine fasteners, quickly won over Longines's clients. A perfect blend of technical mastery and subdued elegance, the Flagship owes its name to the ship upon which the flag of the fleet's commander in chief snaps in the wind. A symbol of Longines's wishes for this new collection, this caravel is stamped on the back of Flagship watches. Today, the Swiss watchmaking brand celebrates 60 years of this iconic collection, a symbol of quality, high precision and distinction, by launching the Flagship Heritage – 60th Anniversary 1957-2017. It was Longines's Ambassador of Elegance herself, Kate Winslet, who chose the face of this anniversary timepiece. During a visit to the brand's headquarters in Switzerland, the British actress fell in love with a model from the Swiss watchmaker. This is the timepiece from which Longines drew inspiration for the subdued and chic dial of this anniversary edition. Available in steel, yellow gold or rose gold, the numbered timekeepers house an L609 mechanical caliber in their 38.5mm case. Exclusive timepieces, the gold versions are limited to 60 watches while the steel versions are limited to 1,957 watches. The brushed silvery dial is adorned with eight indexes and four Arabic numerals, in yellow-gold or rose-gold colors. As with the original timepieces, the back of these commemorative watches bears a stamped caravel—the flagship. A brown leather watch strap completes this exceptional timepiece.

THE LONGINES EQUESTRIAN COLLECTION

THE LONGINES EQUESTRIAN COLLECTION ADDS NEW MODELS INSPIRED BY THE BRAND'S PASSION FOR THE EQUESTRIAN WORLD

As a token of its long-running passion for equestrian sports and its commitment to its lady customers, Longines expands The Longines Equestrian Collection with the creation of new models inspired by the rectangular buckle on the show bridle of the only Swiss horse breed, the Franches-Montagnes. While remaining true to the elegance that characterizes the winged hourglass brand, these models have been created as an allegory to the equestrian world.

Longines's history and the history of equestrian sports have been intertwined for over a century. It was therefore natural for the brand to dedicate a collection to this passion. The various models of The Longines Equestrian Collection are linked by their references to the equine world. Shapes and materials derive their inspiration from symbolic elements of this environment, like a sublime echo of the world of horse lovers. Longines thus celebrates the elegance of riders and their mounts. Today, Longines is expanding this collection and proposing new variations that repeat the lines of the rectangular buckle found on the show bridle of the only Swiss horse breed, the Franches-Montagnes. In addition, this horse is native to the historical Swiss Jura area, a region that is dear to the winged hourglass brand, since it is also the region where Longines was founded and earned its place within the inner circle of great watchmakers. These new models mirror the overall distinctive attributes of The Longines Equestrian Collection, and are dedicated to female equestrian sports lovers. On their wrist, the hands waltz to the rhythm of time and merge with the pace of the horses. With The Longines Equestrian Collection, Longines offers a genuine allegory of the equestrian world in tribute to the deep bonds the brand has forged with it. Available in four sizes, these new steel models house a quartz movement. The polished black-lacquered, white mother-of-pearl and silver-colored checkerboard pattern dials are all decorated with diamond indexes, while the silver-colored "flinqué" dial is decorated with blue Roman numerals and the matte white dial is adorned with black Arabic numerals. The elegance of these timepieces is sometimes elevated by a ribbon of diamonds that enhances the harmonious curves of the case. These models are fitted with steel bracelets or leather straps, the latter stitched to match the outfits of female riders.

LONGINES
10
20
30
40
50
60
SWISS MADE

LONGINES
AUTOMATIC
JAN
MON

THE LONGINES MASTER COLLECTION

A DAZZLING DISPLAY OF THE BRAND'S WATCHMAKING KNOW-HOW

As a traditional watchmaking company, Longines has been producing exceptional timepieces since the very beginning. Today, The Longines Master Collection is the perfect illustration of this corporate ethos, as can be seen from the success enjoyed by this range since it was launched in 2005. All fitted with self-winding movements, the various models in this collection offer various sophistications. The Longines Master Collection brings together the classical elegance and excellent quality that never cease to delight those who appreciate exceptional timepieces.

In 2005, Longines launched the line that would become its "best-selling" product: The Longines Master Collection. Right from the start, this range has enjoyed a level of success that has never waned, making it an emblem of the brand's watchmaking know-how. Over the years, new sizes and sophistications have been added, while the timeless classicism that is the brand's essential characteristic, and that has played a major role in its success worldwide, has always been maintained. In addition to the traditional models with three hands, The Longines Master Collection offers a wide range of sophistications. Businessman one day, sportsman the next and at times a jet-setter, today's man is many-sided and always on the move. And his entire range of requirements can all be satisfied by the choice of displays offered by the models in The Longines Master Collection: chronograph functions, indication of time in all 24 time zones worldwide, power reserve indicator, phases of the moon or retrograde functions. The sophisticated models in The Longines Master Collection are available in various diameter sizes (38.5mm, 40mm, 41mm, 42mm, 44mm) in order to provide the ideal watch to suit every wrist. All models are fitted with self-winding movements. The cases are available in steel, steel and yellow gold or 18-karat rose gold. The black or silver dials are decorated with a barleycorn design that enhances the rhodium-plated or blued steel hands. Water resistant to 3 bar, these models also have a transparent caseback through which the proud owner can admire the fascinating working of the movement. Each timepiece is mounted on a steel and yellow-gold or a steel bracelet, or on a black or dark brown alligator strap, all having a folding safety clasp.

LONGINES DOLCEVITA — REF. L5.512.5.79.7

Movement: quartz caliber L176.
Functions: hours, minutes; small seconds at 6.
Case: stainless steel; 23x37mm rectangular; set with 46 Top Wesselton VVS diamonds (0.552 carat); solid rose-gold crown; sapphire crystal; water resistant to 3atm.
Dial: silver "flinqué"; painted Roman numerals; blued steel hands.
Bracelet: stainless steel and rose-gold cap with butterfly clasp.

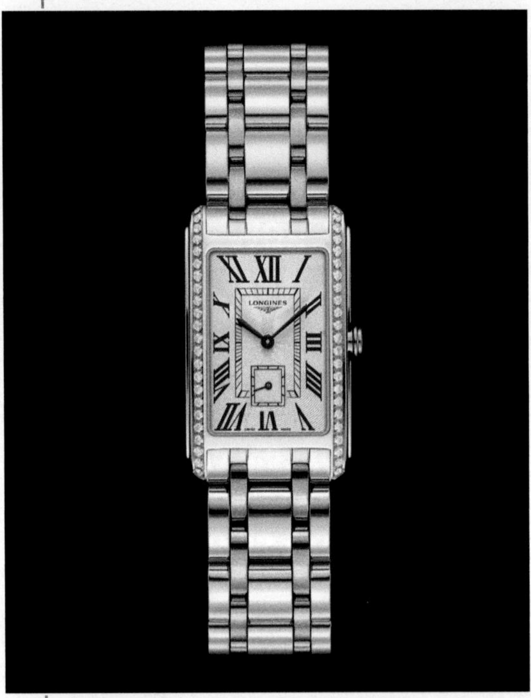

LONGINES SYMPHONETTE — REF. L2.305.0.83.6

Movement: quartz caliber L963.2.
Functions: hours, minutes.
Case: stainless steel; 18.9x29.4mm oval; set with 56 Top Wesselton VVS diamonds (0.280 carat); antireflective sapphire crystal; water resistant to 3atm.
Dial: white mother-of-pearl; 12 Arabic numerals; blued steel hands.
Bracelet: stainless steel with butterfly clasp.

LA GRANDE CLASSIQUE DE LONGINES — REF. L4.513.0.11.2

Movement: quartz caliber L420.
Functions: hours, minutes.
Case: stainless steel; Ø 29mm; set with 56 Top Wesselton VVS diamonds (0.470 carat); scratch-resistant sapphire crystal; water resistant to 3atm.
Dial: white dial; 12 Roman black-painted numerals; blackened steel hands.
Strap: black alligator with buckle.

THE LONGINES ELEGANT COLLECTION — REF. L4.309.5.88.7

Movement: automatic-winding caliber L595; 8¾ lines; 40-hour power reserve; 20 jewels; 28,800 vph.
Functions: hours, minutes, seconds; date at 3.
Case: stainless steel and rose gold; Ø 25.5mm; set with 52 Top Wesselton VVS diamonds (0.353 carat); scratch-resistant sapphire crystal; sapphire crystal caseback; water resistant to 3atm.
Dial: white mother-of-pearl; 12 diamond hour markers; black hands.
Bracelet: stainless steel and rose-gold cap; triple-folding safety clasp and pushpieces.

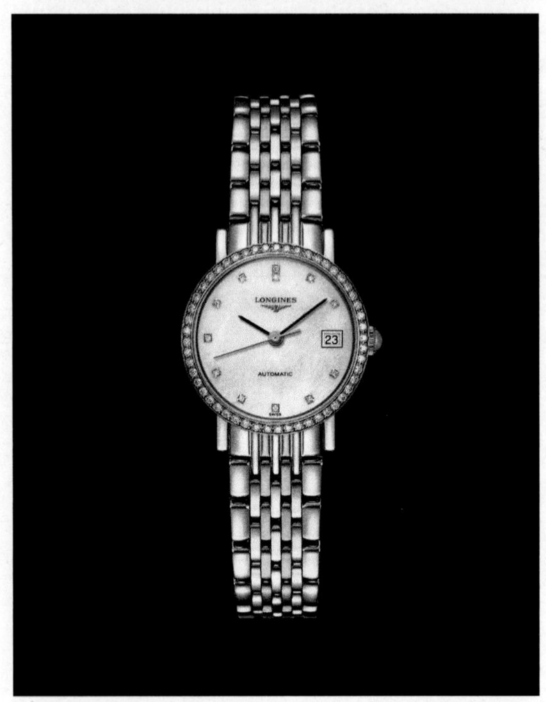

THE LONGINES MASTER COLLECTION REF. L2.673.4.78.3

Movement: automatic-winding caliber L678; 13¼ lines; 48-hour power reserve; 25 jewels; 28,800 vph.
Functions: hours, minutes; small seconds and 24-hour indicator at 9; date; day and month at 12; moonphase at 6; chronograph: 12-hour counter at 6, 30-minute counter at 12, central seconds hand.
Case: stainless steel; Ø 40mm; antireflective sapphire crystal; sapphire crystal caseback; water resistant to 3atm.
Dial: silver-finished stamped "barleycorn"; nine Arabic numerals; blued-steel hands; black-painted minute track, 31-day calendar.
Strap: dark brown alligator leather; triple-folding safety clasp.

LONGINES EVIDENZA REF. L2.643.4.73.4

Movement: automatic-winding caliber L650; 12½ lines; 42-hour power reserve; 37 jewels; 28,800 vph.
Functions: hours, minutes; small seconds at 3; date at 6; chronograph: 12-hour counter at 6, 30-minute counter at 9, central seconds hand.
Case: stainless steel; 34.9x40mm; antireflective sapphire crystal; water resistant to 3atm.
Dial: silvered "flinqué"; 10 blue-painted Arabic numerals; blued-steel hands.
Strap: dark brown alligator leather; triple-folding safety clasp.

CONQUEST CLASSIC REF. L2.285.5.88.7

Movement: automatic-winding caliber L595.2; 8¾ lines; 40-hour power reserve; 20 jewels; 28,800 vph.
Functions: hours, minutes, seconds; date at 3.
Case: stainless steel and rose gold; Ø 29.5mm; set with 30 Top Wesselton VVS diamonds (0.501 carat); scratch-resistant sapphire crystal with several layers of antireflective coating; screw-down sapphir crystal caseback; water resistant to 5atm.
Dial: white mother-of-pearl; 12 diamond hour markers; rose-gold polished hands with SuperLumiNova.
Bracelet: stainless steel and rose-gold cap; triple-folding safety clasp and pushpieces.

CONQUEST CLASSIC REF. L2.786.8.56.3

Movement: automatic-winding caliber L688; 13¼ lines; 54-hour power reserve; 27 jewels; 28,800 vph.
Functions: hours, minutes; small seconds at 9, date between 4 and 5.
chronograph: 12-hour counter at 6, 30-minute counter at 3, central sweep seconds.
Case: 18K rose gold; Ø 41mm; scratch-resistant sapphire crystal with several layers of antireflective coating; sapphire crystal caseback; water resistant to 5atm.
Dial: black; 1 applied Arabic numeral and 11 applied indexes with SuperLumiNova; rose-polished hands with SuperLumiNova.
Strap: black alligator; triple-folding safety clasp and pushpiece opening mechanism.

THE LONGINES EQUESTRIAN COLLECTION — REF. L6.141.4.77.6

Movement: quartz caliber L178.
Functions: hours, minutes; small seconds at 6.
Case: stainless steel; 22x32mm rectangular; antireflective sapphire crystal; water resistant to 3atm.
Dial: silvered-colored "checkerboard"; 12 diamond indexes; blued steel hands.
Bracelet: stainless steel with folding clasp.

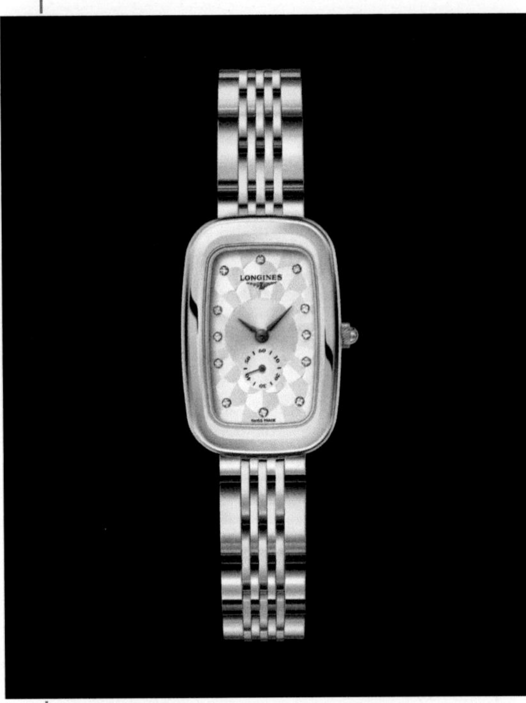

CONQUEST — REF. L3.677.4.58.6

Movement: automatic-winding caliber L633; 11½ lines; 38-hour power reserve; 25 jewels; 28,800 vph.
Functions: hours, minutes, seconds; date at 3.
Case: stainless steel; Ø 41mm; scratch-resistant sapphire crystal with several layers of antireflective coating on the underside; screw-down caseback and screw-down crown with protective shoulder; water resistant to 30atm.
Dial: black dial; 2 applied Arabic numerals and 10 applied hour markers with SuperLumiNova; rhodium-plated hands with SuperLumiNova.
Bracelet: stainless steel; triple-folding safety clasp and pushpieces.

CONQUEST ROLAND GARROS — REF. L3.379.4.79.6

Movement: quartz chronograph caliber L538.
Functions: hours, minutes; small seconds at 6; date at 4; chronograph: 30-minute counter at 10, 1/10th of a second counter at 2.
Case: stainless steel; Ø 36mm; scratch-resistant sapphire crystal with several layers of antireflective coating; screw-down caseback and screw-down crown with protective shoulder; commemorative "Roland Garros Paris" engraving on the caseback; water resistant to 30atm.
Dial: anthracite; 1 applied Arabic numeral and 11 applied indexes with SuperLumiNova; rhodium-plated hands; orange chronograph hands.
Bracelet: stainless steel; triple-folding safety clasp and pushpieces.

CONQUEST JUMPING — REF. L3.701.4.76.6

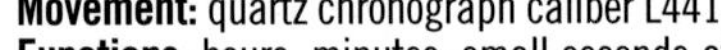

Movement: quartz chronograph caliber L441.
Functions: hours, minutes; small seconds at 6; date at 4; tables and second timing counter at 2; pts/sec penalties counter at 10; chronograph: central 1/100th of second.
Case: stainless steel; Ø 41mm; scratch-resistant sapphire crystal with several layers of antireflective coating on the underside; screw-down caseback and screw-down crown with protective shoulder; water resistant to 5atm.
Dial: silvered; 1 applied Arabic numeral and 11 applied hour markers with SuperLumiNova; rhodium-plated hands; red 1/100th of seconds and counter hands.

Bracelet: stainless steel; triple-folding safety clasp and pushpieces.

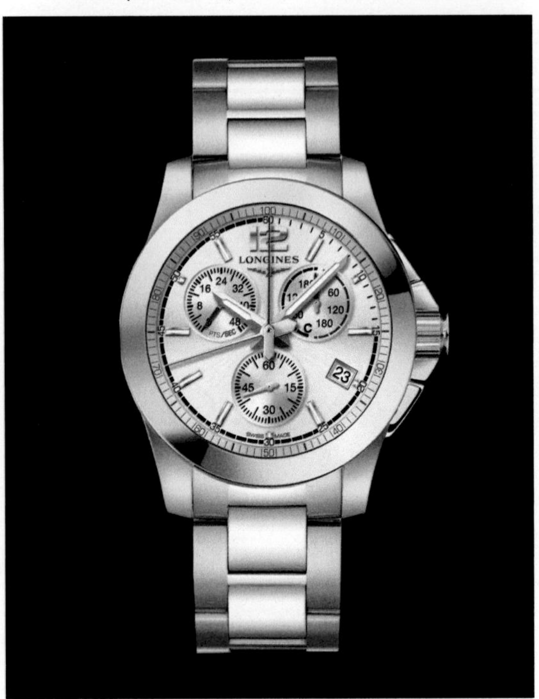

FLAGSHIP HERITAGE – 60TH ANNIVERSARY 1957-2017 REF. L4.817.4.76.2

Movement: automatic-winding caliber L609; 11½ lines; 42-hour power reserve; 27 jewels; 28,800 vph.
Functions: hours, minutes, seconds.
Case: stainless steel; Ø 38.5mm; sapphire crystal with several layers of anti-reflective coating; Flagship stamped on the caseback; limited numbered edition; water resistant to 3atm.
Dial: brushed silver, 2 zones; 4 Arabic numerals and 8 applied index in pink; pink dauphine hands; hour and minute hands coated with SuperLumiNova.
Strap: brown alligator with buckle.

THE LONGINES AVIGATION WATCH TYPE A-7 1935 REF. L2.812.4.23.2

Movement: automatic-winding caliber with a single pushpiece and column-wheel chronograph mechanism L788.2; 13¼ lines; 54-hour power reserve; 27 jewels; 28,800 vph.
Functions: hours, minutes; small seconds and date at 6; chronograph: central seconds hand; 30-minute counter at 12.
Case: stainless steel; Ø 41mm; sapphire crystal with several layers of antireflective coating; single pushpiece integrated into the crown; water resistant to 3atm.
Dial: white lacquered polished; angled at 40° to the right; 12 honey-colored Arabic numerals; blued steel hands with honey-colored varnish (hours, minutes).
Strap: brown alligator with buckle.

THE LONGINES HERITAGE 1918 REF. L2.309.0.23.2

Movement: automatic-winding caliber L615; 11½ lines; 42-hour power reserve; 27 jewels; 28,800 vph.
Functions: hours, minutes; small seconds and date at 6.
Case: stainless steel; Ø 38.5mm; set with 60 diamonds (1 carat); sapphire crystal with several layers of antireflective coating; water resistant to 3atm.
Dial: white-lacquered polished; 12 honey-colored Arabic numerals; blued steel hands with honey-colored varnish (hours, minutes).
Strap: honey-colored alligator with buckle.

THE LONGINES RAILROAD REF. L2.803.4.23.0

Movement: automatic-winding caliber L888; 11½ lines; 64-hour power reserve; 21 jewels; 25,200 vph.
Functions: hours, minutes, seconds.
Case: stainless steel; Ø 40mm; sapphire crystal with several layers of antireflective coating; screwed caseback; engraving on the caseback; water resistant to 3atm.
Dial: off-white polished; 24 black painted Arabic numerals; shiny lacquer black hands.
Strap: black alligator with buckle.

A WORLD OF POSSIBILITIES

WITH PASSIONATE ARTISTRY AND SEEMINGLY LIMITLESS IMAGINATION, Louis Vuitton takes horological enthusiasts on a fascinating voyage into the heart of the timepiece and to the corners of the world.

The Flying Tourbillon "Poinçon de Genève" celebrates the brand's exclusive certification with a bold interpretation of watchmaking geometry and transparency.

Its case, neither cushion nor oval shaped, combines the smooth curves of a circle with the sharp symmetry of a square for a unique and stunning effect. Meanwhile, the luxurious sheen of its 950 platinum smoothly leads the eye toward an interior design that adeptly plays with negative space. Off-centered at 12 o'clock, the timepiece's gray metalized-sapphire subdial indicates the hours and minutes while providing a captivating view of the movement's construction beneath, namely the barrel responsible for its 80-hour power reserve. The sapphire cunningly attracts attention to the revelation below thanks to a smoky effect that distinguishes it from the perfect transparency of the rest of the dial. At 6 o'clock on the face, the timepiece presents its greatest performance: solely supported from beneath for a brilliant air of weightlessness, the LV104 caliber's flying one-minute tourbillon dazzles the wearer and reveals the micro-mechanical artistry of the brand. As the tourbillon completes each revolution, the V from its carriage perfectly overlaps the complication's identically shaped lower bridge, forming a powerful three-dimensional display of the letter and imbuing the timepiece with a bold touch of Louis Vuitton's iconic DNA. Radically contemporary in its aesthetic personality, yet demonstrating tremendous respect for the fine traditions of Swiss haute horology, the Flying Tourbillon "Poinçon de Genève" stands out for its brilliant, minimalist approach to watchmaking design.

The timepiece marks a remarkable milestone for Louis Vuitton, becoming the first of the brand's timepieces to earn the prestigious "Poinçon de Genève." The honor, bestowed upon only the finest timekeeping creations and regulated by the laws of the Geneva canton, demands an extraordinary degree of execution throughout the entire watch. Every component, from the power reserve to the case, is subjected to expert scrutiny, both from a design and technical standpoint, demanding the highest level of craftsmanship and timekeeping reliability. The Flying Tourbillon "Poinçon de Genève" completes its riveting look into the heart of its movement with a transparent caseback and is worn on a navy blue alligator strap with 18-karat white-gold folding buckle.

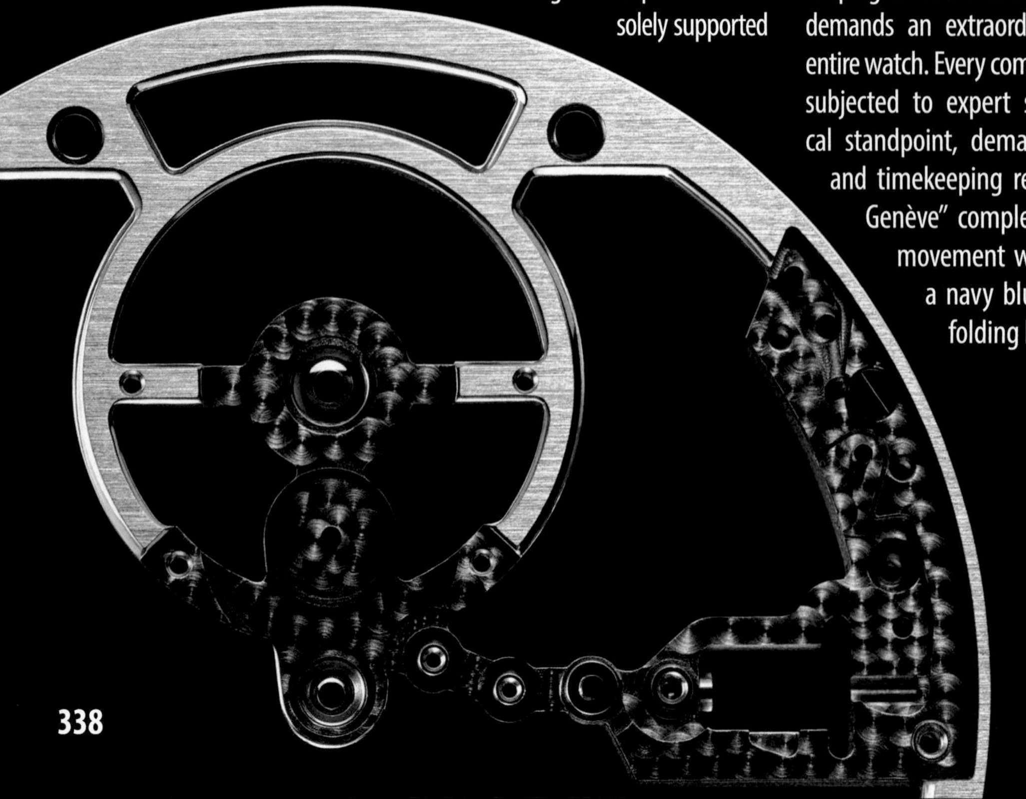

▶ **FLYING TOURBILLON "POINÇON DE GENÈVE"**

This masterful display of transparency reveals the brilliant depth of its flying tourbillon and is certified with the prestigious Seal of Geneva.

Radically contemporary, yet demonstrating tremendous respect for fine horological tradition, the Flying Tourbillon "Poinçon de Genève" stands out for its minimalist approach to watchmaking design.

La Fabrique du Temps Louis Vuitton dresses the global traveler with a timepiece of masculine sophistication and elegant modernity. Imbued with the Maison's distinguished design codes, the Voyager GMT takes on the dual-time concept with extraordinary readability thanks to an ingenious combination of display types. While two luminous hands indicate the primary hours and minutes in a traditional style, Louis Vuitton presents the secondary time zone by way of a rotating disc on the lower half of the face. Calibrated as a 24-hour display that adds a second touch of differentiation from the primary hours and minutes, the disc boasts two distinct colors for an unambiguous clarification of the day/night status of the chosen location. Decisively Louis Vuitton, a commanding V in the center of the dial turns form into function as its base serves as the pointer for the GMT complication. The letter then spreads across the width of the design, transforming into a bridge that vibrantly frames the watch's GMT semi-circle. A smaller V, at 12 o'clock, acts as an hour marker and completes the design, leading the eye toward the captivating center of the timepiece. The 41.5mm self-winding wristwatch presents its masculine demeanor in a variety of styles, fitting the distinctive personality of its wearer.

A stainless steel model contrasts the silver tone of its dial with an anthracite V bridge brushed and polished for a superb finish. A second variation places the tasteful darkness of its anthracite dial against a silver-toned V bridge that echoes the hue of its case. The stainless steel Voyager GMT honors Louis Vuitton's rich tradition of exquisite leather craftsmanship with a supple strap in the house's slightly grained calfskin leather. The timepiece may also be worn on a stainless steel bracelet composed of links alternating between polished and satin finishes, gracefully reiterating the two-tone design of the dial.

A third interpretation adorns the charismatic timepiece with a luxurious balance of materials and accents. Matching the rich warmth of its 18-karat pink-gold case, this Voyager GMT complements the deep blue personality of its dial with a bold pink-gold finish on its hands, hour markers and central V bridge. Its strap joins in on the colorful theme, composed of navy blue alligator leather to perfectly reinforce the tonal blend of the overall design.

▸ VOYAGER GMT

A 24-hour rotating disc allows for an exciting and intuitive reading of the time in a secondary location on the timepiece imbued with Louis Vuitton's proud DNA.

LOUIS VUITTON
AUTOMATIQUE
14 15 16 17 18 19 20 21 22 23 24
GMT
SWISS MADE

With the Escale collection, Louis Vuitton unleashes its immense creativity and audacious vision of watchmaking, turning the world-time concept into a celebration of color, shapes and unique time displays. Each timepiece, embellished with a cornucopia of lively motifs, pays homage to the brand's passionate history of personalized travel trunks, each telling the unique story of its owner's fascinating voyages.

The Escale Spin Time eschews convention to boldly highlight the brand's rich artistic prowess. By transforming twelve cubes, each rendered by hand to display a unique combination of flags, into the very indicators of time, the wristwatch puts visual delight at the forefront of functionality. Boasting two geometric flags as well as two numerals, two cubes rotate at the beginning of every hour thanks to the sophisticated LV77 caliber. At the turn of 10 o'clock, for example, the cube in the 9 o'clock position rotates to conceal its numeral (9 or 21 depending on the day or night status), while the cube at 10 o'clock turns its flag into the appropriate current hour. The ingenious system turns the dial into a constantly transforming medley of colors and shapes, painting a brand new tableau 24 times a day. The minutes are read more traditionally via a short hand against a graduated inner ring. Housed in a 41mm titanium case with 18-karat white- or pink-gold bezel, horns and crown, the Escale Spin Time speaks of world time in a language of joy, color and unbridled artistic creativity.

◂ **ESCALE SPIN TIME**

An ingenious system of rotating cubes displays the time with immense creativity while transforming the finely crafted colorful composition of its dial throughout the day.

The Escale Time Zone, housed in a stainless steel case with 18-karat pink-gold bezel, horns and crown, presents a world-time display as functionally intuitive as it is visually captivating. An outer disc, adjustable via the crown to place the desired reference city at 12 o'clock, displays 24 time zones, each with its own colorful pictogram. A second disc, two-toned for day/night status, boasts the 24 hours of the day and revolves to place the appropriate numeral next to each city on the outer ring. The result is an instantaneous reading of the time throughout the globe. In the center of the watch, two hands indicate the hours and minutes, allowing for a conventional indication of local time and providing a lively contrast between contemporary artistry and timekeeping tradition.

▸ **ESCALE TIME ZONE**

The Escale Time Zone combines its simultaneous display of the time in 24 time zones with a traditional indication of local time within a vivaciously decorated design.

The Escale Worldtime Blue tells the time simultaneously in 24 different cities through an ingenious, intuitive, hands-free complication. Thanks to a combination of three rotating discs and a single fixed element in the center, the timepiece allows a simple glance to take in the hour throughout the world with exceptional ease. The outer disc, composed of 24 city initials and 24 magnificent hand-painted flags, is rotated on demand to place a reference city at 12 o'clock, or anywhere the wearer desires. A middle disc, adorned with two colors to distinguish day from night in each location, rotates without interruption to continuously place the appropriate hour next to each city indicator. The third disc, placed in the center of the navy blue dial, indicates the minutes against a fixed yellow arrow that sits atop a pyramid in the middle of the design. Masterfully crafted using 38 vibrant colors, the Escale Worldtime Blue is housed in a 41mm brushed titanium case with 18-karat white-gold bezel, horns and crown, and is animated by the self-winding LV106 caliber.

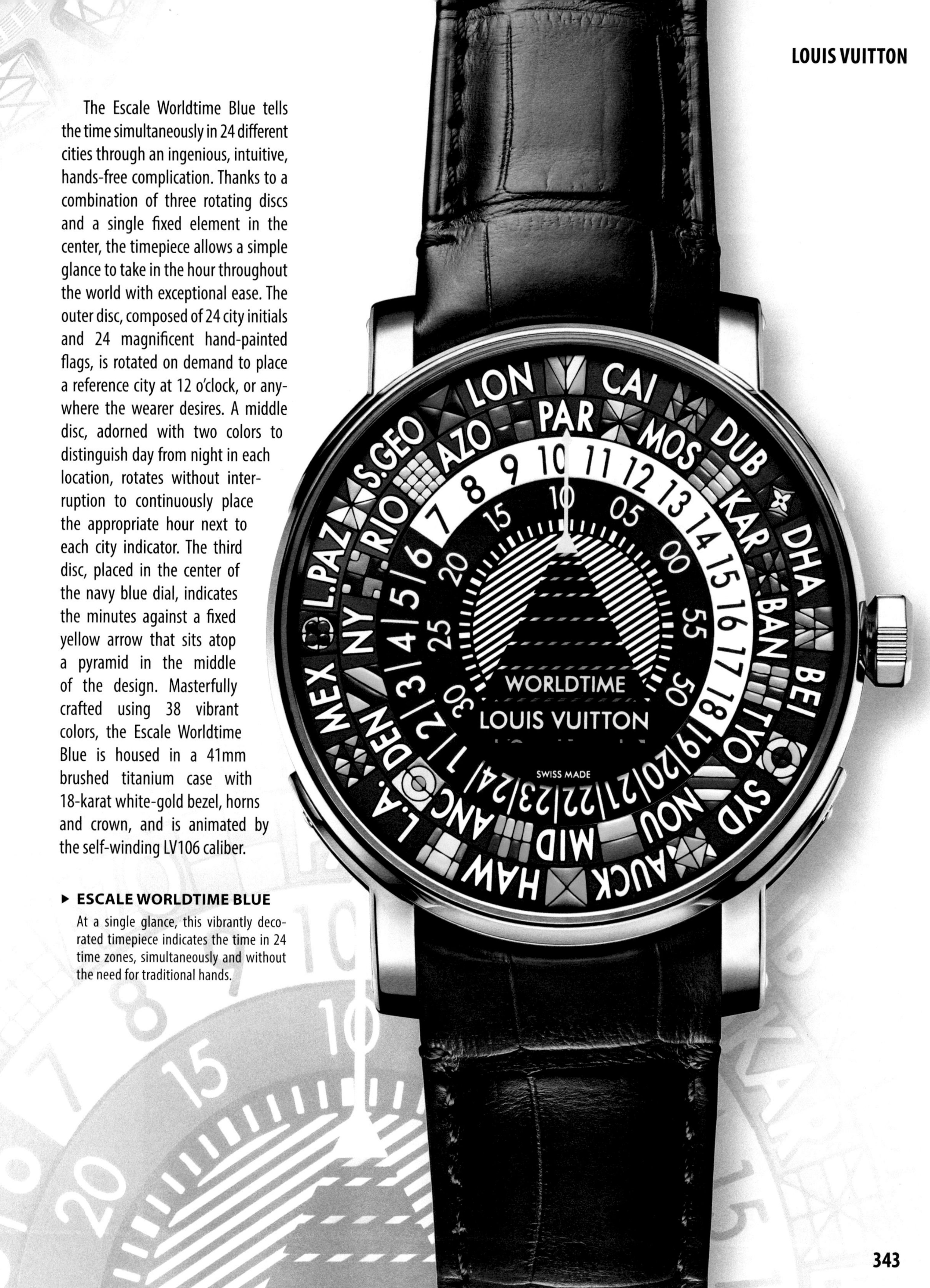

▸ ESCALE WORLDTIME BLUE

At a single glance, this vibrantly decorated timepiece indicates the time in 24 time zones, simultaneously and without the need for traditional hands.

ESCALE TIME ZONE — REF. Q5D200

Movement: automatic-winding; 42-hour power reserve; 21 jewels; 28,800 vph.
Functions: hours, minutes; 24 time zones.
Case: stainless steel; Ø 39mm, thickness: 8.4mm; sapphire metallized caseback with LV signature; water resistant to 5atm.
Dial: 24 flags.
Strap: gray alligator leather; yellow leather lining; stainless steel deployant buckle.
Price: available upon request.

TAMBOUR BLUE CHRONOGRAPH — REF. Q102V0

Movement: automatic-winding; Ø 28mm, thickness: 6.1mm; 42-hour power reserve; 37 jewels; 28,800 vph.
Functions: hours, minutes; small seconds at 3; date between 4 and 5; chronograph: central seconds hand, 12-hour counter at 6, 30-minute counter at 9.
Case: stainless steel; Ø 44mm; steel crown with black rubber; antireflective sapphire crystal; stainless steel caseback engraved with Louis Vuitton logo; water resistant to 10atm.
Dial: blue; black V signature and "Clous de Paris" black counters; half-skeleted indexes and hands with SuperLumiNova.
Strap: black alligator and calfskin leather with blue seams; stainless steel ardillon buckle.
Price: available upon request.

TAMBOUR ESSENTIEL BRUN GMT — REF. Q11550

Movement: automatic-winding; Ø 26.2mm, thickness: 4.25mm; 42-hour power reserve; 21 jewels; 28,800 vph.
Functions: hours, minutes, seconds; date at 3; GMT.
Case: stainless steel; Ø 41.5mm; stainless steel caseback with Louis Vuitton logo; water resistant to 10atm.
Dial: brown sunray; black lacquer flange and yellow GMT marks; half-skeleted hands with SuperLumiNova.
Strap: brown Damier infini calfskin leather.
Price: available upon request.

TAMBOUR DAMIER GRAPHITE — REF. Q1D070

Movement: quartz; 7 jewels.
Functions: hours, minutes, seconds; date between 4 and 5.
Case: stainless steel; Ø 39mm, thickness: 7.94mm; satin-finished bezel; antireflective sapphire crystal; stainless steel caseback engraved with Louis Vuitton logo; water resistant to 5atm.
Dial: stamped and embossed Damier pattern; polished indexes and nails.
Strap: Damier graphite canvas; stainless steel ardillon buckle.
Price: available upon request.

TAMBOUR SLIM COLOR BLOSSOM — REF. Q1H010

Movement: automatic-winding; 21 jewels.
Functions: hours, minutes.
Case: 18K pink gold; Ø 35mm, thickness: 8.65mm; bezel set with 52 diamonds (1.12 carats); antireflective sapphire crystal; caseback engraved with monogram canvas; water resistant to 5atm.
Dial: snow-set with 404 diamonds (0.81 carat); decorated with a monogram flower in sculpted mother-of-pearl enhanced with pink shading.
Strap: shiny raspberry alligator leather; 18K pink-gold ardillon buckle.
Price: available upon request.

TAMBOUR PALLAS — REF. Q12200

Movement: quartz; 6 jewels.
Functions: hours, minutes, seconds; date at 3.
Case: steel; Ø 28mm, thickness: 8.45mm; antireflective sapphire crystal; caseback engraved with monogram canvas; water resistant to 10atm.
Dial: brown lacquer; red seconds hand.
Strap: Nano monogram canvas; V-shaped red calfskin leather nailed by a nail; steel ardillon buckle.
Price: available upon request.

TAMBOUR SLIM DIGITAL BLUE — REF. Q13MJH

Movement: quartz; 7 jewels.
Functions: hours, minutes.
Case: stainless steel; Ø 33mm, thickness: 8.65mm; antireflective sapphire crystal; caseback engraved with monogram canvas; water resistant to 5atm.
Dial: silver opalescent; monogram flowers and mirror-polished lozine; 8 monogram flower indexes with nails in their centers and Arabic numerals at 3, 6 and 9.
Strap: monogram digital blue canvas.
Price: available upon request.

TAMBOUR SPIN TIME COLOR BLOSSOM — REF. Q1EG20

Movement: automatic-winding; Ø 30.8mm, thickness: 7.85mm; 40-hour power reserve; 21 jewels; 28,800 vph.
Functions: hours via a spin time display; minutes.
Case: 18K white gold; Ø 39.5mm, thickness: 11.9mm; set with 336 diamonds (4.42 carats); transparent caseback; water resistant to 10atm
Dial: snow-set with 656 diamonds (1.71 carats); decorated with a monogram flower in sculpted mother-of-pearl enhanced with blue shading; flange paved with 48 blue sapphires (0.68 carat) and 12 diamond indexes; 18K white-gold and black lacquer hands.
Strap: shiny blue alligator leather; 18K white-gold ardillon buckle full-set with 159 diamonds (1.45 carats).
Price: available upon request.

FREE THINKING

Nearly two and a half centuries after Voltaire's founding of Manufacture Royale, the Swiss watchmaker continues to embody the pioneering principles of the French philosopher. **ALWAYS ACHIEVING A UNIQUE VOICE THROUGH MECHANICAL INGENUITY AND BOLD DESIGNS**, the horologer presents four timepieces that represent the harmonious coexistence of contrasting ideas.

▲ **1770 HAUTE VOLTIGE**

Armed with a second time zone, this self-winding wristwatch exposes the elegant intricacies of its mechanical construction thanks to a dial-side exhibition of its escapement and 14mm lightweight balance wheel.

The 1770 Haute Voltige tells a transcendent story of freedom inspired by Voltaire's own words: "Man is free at the instant he wants to be." From the visual weightlessness of its exposed components to the integration of a second time zone tailored to worldwide travels, the 45mm self-winding wristwatch takes flight with grace and personality. On the upper left quadrant of the black sunray dial, the timepiece reveals the captivating precision of the MR07 caliber's lightweight balance wheel and escapement. Elevated from the surface by a slender bridge, the harmonious construction presents the heartbeat of the watch to its owner, uncluttered and with stunning clarity. At 5 o'clock, the 1770 Haute Voltige takes on a different kind of flight. A secondary time zone, highlighted by a central quilted motif and polished rim, grants the wearer the freedom to view the hours and minutes and any chosen location, forging a seamless connection with the rest of the world. By openworking the principal hour and minute hands, Manufacture Royale ensures an unobstructed view of the fascinating architecture while preserving the sleek, modern design codes of the timepiece. The MR07 caliber, entirely hand decorated and finished to perfection with Côtes de Genève, boasts a 40-hour power reserve and is housed in a stainless steel case whose transparent caseback allows for a vibrant view of the movement's dynamic interior.

Two flying tourbillons, exposed at 5 and 7 o'clock, evoke Voltaire's tale of relativity, as they work toward a harmonious common goal while oscillating at vastly different speeds.

Named after the mythical 120,000-foot-tall Voltarian hero, the 1770 Micromegas achieves its exemplary precision through a dialogue between large and small. Two flying tourbillons, exposed at 5 and 7 o'clock, conduct their choreography while evoking Voltaire's tale of relativity, working toward a harmonious common goal yet oscillating at vastly different speeds. While the cage at 5 o'clock completes its revolution in the traditional 60 seconds, its partner achieves its journey in one tenth of the time, every six seconds. Their rates are then averaged by a double-torque stabilizer for an optimal degree of timekeeping precision. This triumph of innovation and ingenuity, performed by the in-house self-winding MR04 caliber, is housed within a 45mm case in rose gold with black Côtes de Genève that contrasts the titanium dial's rubber-effect black-lacquer finish and Titalyte treatment. Bold yet refined, the 1770 Micromegas relates a story of harmonious opposites. Warm, luxurious tones combine with the cool modernity of the dial and its racing-inspired tourbillon cages, just as the horological tradition of the tourbillon is brought to new heights by the watchmaker's ambitious pursuit of absolute precision. The 1770 Micromegas boasts a transparent caseback and is worn on a hand-stitched alligator strap.

▲ **1770 MICROMEGAS**

Micro and Mega unite for a greater good in the form of two flying tourbillons, oscillating at highly different rates and averaged by a sophisticated torque stabilizer, in this timepiece of formidable precision.

The Voltige Black Feather (Plume Noire) pays homage to the spirited rivalry between two of the Enlightenment's finest minds: Voltaire and Rousseau. Filled with intensity and passionate contrasts of colors and forms, the 45mm timepiece honors the power of eloquence and rhetorical wit with a design that reveals everything that it must without wasting a single breath. Risen from the bold aesthetic of a black dial with Côtes de Genève, the MR05 caliber's escapement and enhanced 14mm titanium balance wheel express to the wearer the exquisite refinement of mechanical haute horology. Yet the rest of the movement remains concealed as to not obstruct the perfection of the poignant narrative. The deep blue of the hour and minute hands, screws and balance wheel is echoed at 6 o'clock via a stem that indicates the running seconds against a sieve-like backdrop that separates it from the principal construction. The avant-garde Voltige Black Feather extends its commanding design to the case, where a black-PVD treatment gives the stainless steel its formidable tone. The timepiece is worn on a hand-stitched alligator strap, oscillates at a frequency of 21,600 vph and is limited to 38 pieces: a tribute to Voltaire's age at the beginning of his battle of the pen with his intellectual rival.

▸ **VOLTIGE BLACK FEATHER**

This tribute to the historic feud between Voltaire and Rousseau uses striking contrast to prominently showcase the exquisite construction of its escapement and balance wheel on the dial side.

What would a philosopher as progressive and audacious as Voltaire wear if he were alive today? Manufacture Royale's Androgyne "Royale" answers the question with uncompromising individuality. Housed in a steampunk-inspired 52-part stainless steel case, the hand-wound timepiece makes the wearer privy to its internal monologue, revealing the entirety of its 167-component caliber. The skeletonized design, punctuated by the vivid "Royale Blue" finishes of the MR06 caliber and contrasting openworked hands, brings motion and dynamism to the forefront. Finesse, however, remains at the heart of the construction, exemplified by a flying tourbillon with silicon escape wheel and ceramic ball bearing. The Androgyne "Royale" thus blends the refinement of horological tradition with a fearless interpretation of contemporary art, capturing the intellectual curiosity of Voltaire's 18th-century epoch in a frame bursting with 21st-century personality. Hand-finished to perfection for flawless viewing pleasure, the 43mm timepiece is worn on an alligator strap with hand-rolled edges.

▸ ANDROGYNE "ROYALE"

A hyper-contemporary steampunk-inspired case provides a robust home for this timepiece's entirely skeletonized caliber with flying tourbillon.

OMEGA

SOARING HIGH, DIVING DEEP

Whether diving far beneath the surface, **TRANSFORMING MECHANICAL SOPHISTICATION INTO A GRACEFULLY UNDERSTATED AFFAIR, OR OFFERING A GLIMPSE OF THE VASTNESS OF THE UNIVERSE**, Omega shows off its unique vision of haute horology with three timepieces immune to limitations.

The watchmaker explores the boundaries of its daring identity with the state-of-the-art Seamaster Planet Ocean "Deep Black." The timepiece, available in four distinct yet equally bold variations, boasts a rugged construction capable of withstanding depths of up to 600m… while being made entirely from ceramic. Along with its numerous advantageous properties in the field of authentic sporting watches, the high-tech material gives the timepiece a commanding visual identity. Crafted from a single (polished or brushed) block of ceramic, the watch's 45mm case complements its unidirectional rotating diver's bezel with a helium escape valve that facilitates the most challenging of underwater journeys. Emphasizing clarity, the Seamaster Planet Ocean "Deep Black" takes on the darkness of the ocean with potent luminescent enhancements, using a vibrant blue SuperLumiNova coating for the hour, seconds and GMT hands, with bright green to distinguish the two most crucial indicators for a diver: the minutes hand and 12 o'clock dot on the bezel. Available in red, blue, black or 18-karat Sedna gold, the self-winding timepiece is driven by the 8906 Chronometer caliber with hand-guided secondary-time-zone function, co-axial escapement and silicon balance spring.

◂ **SEAMASTER PLANET OCEAN "DEEP BLACK"**

This genuine diver's timepiece challenges the darkness of the ocean's depths with its use of two distinct luminescent hues on the hands, dial and unidirectional rotating bezel.

By transforming the space between each hour marker, the periphery of the Globemaster Omega Master Chronometer Annual Calendar does double duty as an annual-calendar display.

The Globemaster Omega Co-Axial Master Chronometer Annual Calendar makes clever use of its dial's geometry to present a sophisticated caliber with graceful subtlety. By converting the space between each hour marker into labeled month increments with a dedicated hand to match, the timepiece's periphery does double duty as an uncluttered, 12-sided annual-calendar display. The date, indicated through an aperture at 6 o'clock, completes the impressive complication while preserving the design's elegant simplicity. The gray dial is finished with 12 hour markers whose red accents echo those of the hour and minute hands and effortlessly differentiate the time display from the rest of the design. Housed in a 41mm platinum case, the limited edition wristwatch is driven by the self-winding Omega 8923 caliber, endowed with a co-axial escapement, silicon balance spring, two series-mounted barrels and special luxury finish in 18-karat Sedna gold.

Omega takes haute horology into outer space—or rather, brings outer space into haute horology—with a timepiece of extra-terrestrial distinction. Housed in a 44.25mm case in gray ceramic with plasma treatment, the Speedmaster Moonwatch Meteorite Omega Co-Axial Chronograph sports a dial composed of a solid piece of gray meteorite, acid-etched to accentuate its stunning nuances. Upon this journey beyond our stratosphere, the Omega 9300 caliber, endowed with a column-wheel mechanism and co-axial escapement, drives a display of the hours, minutes, date and small seconds accompanied by a chronograph with a dual-purpose 60-minute/12-hour counter at 3 o'clock. By combining the chronograph's two subdials into one, Omega avoids any clutter that might detract from the majestic visual impact of the meteorite. The spectacular timepiece is finished with an 18-karat Sedna-gold bezel with tachometer scale.

▲ **GLOBEMASTER OMEGA CO-AXIAL MASTER CHRONOMETER ANNUAL CALENDAR**

This platinum timepiece makes clever use of the space between its hour markers to present its annual calendar within a unique and highly legible design.

▶ **SPEEDMASTER MOONWATCH METEORITE OMEGA CO-AXIAL CHRONOGRAPH**

A solid piece of meteorite turns this timepiece's dial into an unforgettable voyage into outer space.

CONSTELLATION GLOBEMASTER OMEGA CO-AXIAL MASTER CHRONOMETER ANNUAL CALENDAR REF. 130.33.41.22.06.001

Movement: automatic-winding Omega 8922 caliber; 55-hour power reserve; free-sprung balance with silicon balance spring; rhodium-plated rotor and bridges with Geneva waves in arabesque.
Functions: hours, minutes, seconds; annual calendar: date at 6, month via central hand.
Case: steel; Ø 41mm; scratch-resistant antireflective sapphire crystal; sapphire crystal caseback; water resistant to 10atm.
Dial: gray.
Strap: blue leather.

CONSTELLATION GLOBEMASTER OMEGA CO-AXIAL MASTER CHRONOMETER ANNUAL CALENDAR REF. 130.23.41.22.06.001

Movement: automatic-winding Omega 8922 caliber; 55-hour power reserve; free-sprung balance with silicon balance spring; rhodium-plated rotor and bridges with Geneva waves in arabesque.
Functions: hours, minutes, seconds; annual calendar: date at 6, month via central hand.
Case: steel and Sedna gold; Ø 41mm; scratch-resistant antireflective sapphire crystal; sapphire crystal caseback; water resistant to 10atm.
Dial: gray.
Strap: brown leather.

SEAMASTER PLANET OCEAN CO-AXIAL MASTER CHRONOMETER GMT REF. 215.92.46.22.01.002

Movement: automatic-winding Omega 8906 caliber; 60-hour power reserve; free-sprung balance with silicon balance spring; rhodium-plated rotor and bridges with Geneva waves in arabesque.
Functions: hours, minutes, seconds; date at 3; 24-hour GMT.
Case: black ceramic; Ø 45.5mm; unidirectional rotating bezel; screw-down crown; scratch-resistant antireflective sapphire crystal; sapphire crystal caseback; water resistant to 60atm.
Dial: black.
Strap: rubber.

SEAMASTER PLANET OCEAN CO-AXIAL MASTER CHRONOMETER GMT REF. 215.92.46.22.01.001

Movement: automatic-winding Omega 8906 caliber; 60-hour power reserve; free-sprung balance with silicon balance spring; rhodium-plated rotor and bridges with Geneva waves in arabesque.
Functions: hours, minutes, seconds; date at 3; 24-hour GMT.
Case: black ceramic; Ø 45.5mm; unidirectional rotating bezel; screw-down crown; scratch-resistant antireflective sapphire crystal; sapphire crystal caseback; water resistant to 60atm.
Dial: black.
Strap: rubber.

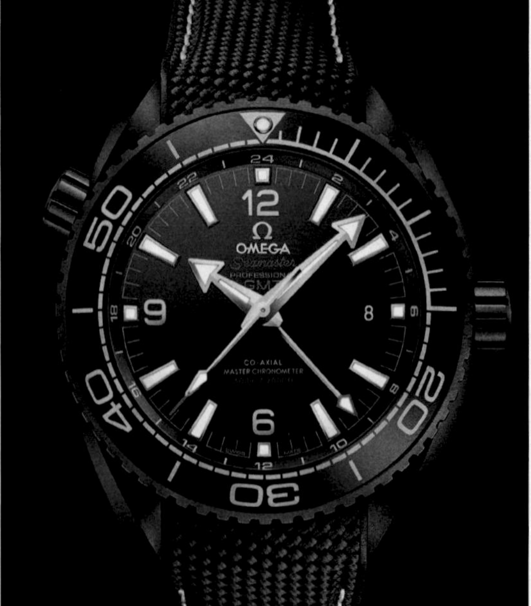

SEAMASTER PLANET OCEAN 600M CO-AXIAL MASTER CHRONOMETER CHRONOGRAPH REF. 215.92.46.51.99.001

Movement: automatic-winding Omega 9900 caliber; 60-hour power reserve; free-sprung balance with silicon balance spring; rhodium-plated finish with Geneva waves in arabesque.
Functions: hours, minutes; small seconds at 9; date at 6; chronograph: central seconds hand, 12-hour counter at 3.
Case: titanium; Ø 45.5mm; unidirectional rotating bezel; screw-down crown; scratch-resistant antireflective sapphire crystal; sapphire crystal caseback; water resistant to 60atm.
Dial: gray.
Strap: gray rubber.

SEAMASTER PLANET OCEAN 600M CO-AXIAL MASTER CHRONOMETER CHRONOGRAPH REF. 215.23.46.51.03.001

Movement: automatic-winding Omega 9900 caliber; 60-hour power reserve; free-sprung balance with silicon balance spring; rhodium-plated finish with Geneva waves in arabesque.
Functions: hours, minutes; small seconds at 9; date at 6; chronograph: central seconds hand, 12-hour counter at 3.
Case: steel and Sedna gold; Ø 45.5mm; unidirectional rotating bezel; screw-down crown; scratch-resistant antireflective sapphire crystal; sapphire crystal caseback; water resistant to 60atm.
Dial: blue.
Strap: blue leather with rubber lining.

SEAMASTER PLANET OCEAN 600M CO-AXIAL MASTER CHRONOMETER REF. 215.30.44.21.01.001

Movement: automatic-winding Omega 8900 caliber; 60-hour power reserve; free-sprung balance with silicon balance spring; rhodium-plated rotor and bridges with Geneva waves in arabesque.
Functions: hours, minutes, seconds; date at 3.
Case: steel; Ø 43.5mm; unidirectional rotating bezel; screw-down crown; scratch-resistant antireflective sapphire crystal; sapphire crystal caseback; water resistant to 60atm.
Dial: black.
Bracelet: steel.

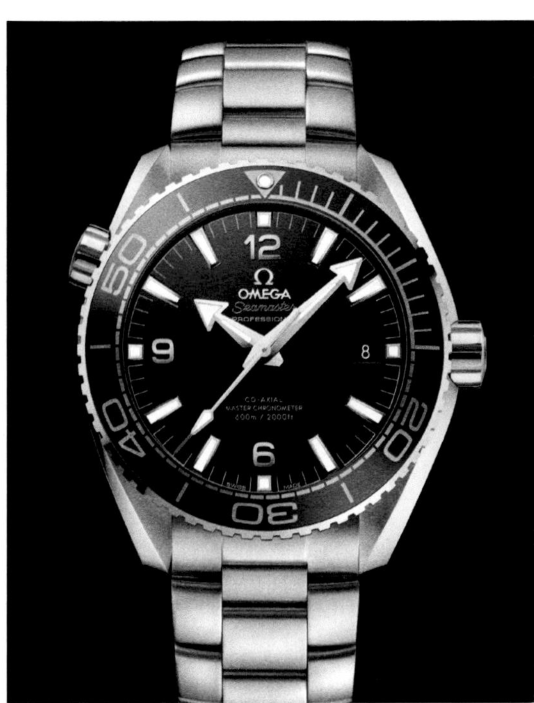

SEAMASTER PLANET OCEAN 600M CO-AXIAL MASTER CHRONOMETER GMT REF. 215.30.44.22.01.001

Movement: automatic-winding 8906 caliber; 60-hour power reserve; free-sprung balance with silicon balance spring; rhodium-plated rotor and bridges with Geneva waves in arabesque.
Functions: hours, minutes, seconds; date at 3; GMT.
Case: stainless steel; Ø 43.5mm, thickness: 17.04mm; bi-directional rotating black/white ceramic bezel; screw-down crown; scratch-resistant antireflective sapphire crystal; sapphire crystal caseback engraved with "Planet Ocean" and "600 m / 2000 ft"; water resistant to 60atm.
Dial: black ceramic; applied rhodium-plated indexes with white SuperLumiNova; new applied Arabic numerals at 12, 6 and 9; polished faceted rhodium-plated hands with white SuperLumiNova.
Bracelet: stainless steel; stainless steel clasp.
Also available: black leather strap with rubber lining.

SPEEDMASTER MOONWATCH CO-AXIAL MASTER CHRONOMETER MOONPHASE CHRONOGRAPH REF. 304.33.44.52.03.001

Movement: automatic-winding Omega 9904 caliber; 60-hour power reserve; free-sprung balance with silicon balance spring; rhodium-plated finish with Geneva waves in arabesque.
Functions: hours, minutes; small seconds at 3; date via hand at 9; moonphase at 6; chronograph: central seconds hand, 12-hour counter at 3, 60-minute counter at 9; tachometer scale.
Case: steel; Ø 44.25mm; scratch-resistant antireflective sapphire crystal; sapphire crystal caseback; water resistant to 10atm.
Dial: blue.
Strap: blue leather.

SPEEDMASTER MOONWATCH CO-AXIAL MASTER CHRONOMETER MOONPHASE CHRONOGRAPH REF. 304.23.44.52.13.001

Movement: automatic-winding Omega 9904 caliber; 60-hour power reserve; free-sprung balance with silicon balance spring; rhodium-plated finish with Geneva waves in arabesque.
Functions: hours, minutes; small seconds at 3; date via hand at 9; moonphase at 6; chronograph: central seconds hand, 12-hour counter at 3, 60-minute counter at 9; tachometer scale.
Case: steel and Sedna gold; Ø 44.25mm; scratch-resistant antireflective sapphire crystal; sapphire crystal caseback; water resistant to 10atm.
Dial: brown.
Strap: brown leather.

DE VILLE PRESTIGE CO-AXIAL REF. 424.13.40.20.03.003

Movement: automatic-winding Omega 2500 caliber; 48-hour power reserve; rhodium-plated finish.
Functions: hours, minutes, seconds; date at 3.
Case: steel; Ø 39.5mm; scratch-resistant antireflective sapphire crystal; water resistant to 3atm.
Dial: blue with teddy bear pattern.
Strap: blue leather.

DE VILLE PRESTIGE CO-AXIAL POWER RESERVE REF. 424.23.40.21.13.001

Movement: automatic-winding Omega 2627 caliber; 48-hour power reserve; rhodium-plated finish.
Functions: hours, minutes; small seconds at 9; date at 3; power reserve indicator at 6.
Case: steel and red gold; Ø 39.5mm; scratch-resistant antireflective sapphire crystal; water resistant to 3atm.
Dial: brown.
Strap: brown leather.

DE VILLE PRESTIGE CO-AXIAL — REF. 424.57.37.20.55.003

Movement: automatic-winding Omega 2500 caliber; 48-hour power reserve; rhodium-plated finish.
Functions: hours, minutes, seconds; date at 6.
Case: red gold; Ø 36.8mm; scratch-resistant antireflective sapphire crystal; water resistant to 3atm.
Dial: white; 9 diamond indexes; butterfly motif.
Strap: white leather.

DE VILLE LADYMATIC CO-AXIAL — REF. 425.65.34.20.55.008

Movement: automatic-winding Omega 8521 caliber; 50-hour power reserve; free-sprung balance with silicon balance spring; 18K red-gold oscillating weight and balance bridge; finish with exclusive Geneva waves in arabesque.
Functions: hours, minutes, seconds; date at 3.
Case: Sedna gold; Ø 34mm; bezel set with diamonds; scratch-resistant antireflective sapphire crystal; sapphire crystal caseback; water resistant to 10atm.
Dial: white; 11 diamond indexes.
Strap: Sedna gold; set with diamonds.

CONSTELLATION CO-AXIAL MASTER CHRONOMETER SMALL SECONDS — REF. 127.25.27.20.55.001

Movement: automatic-winding Omega 8704 caliber; 50-hour power reserve; free-sprung balance with silicon balance spring; rhodium-plated finish with Geneva waves in arabesque.
Functions: hours, minutes; small seconds at 9; date at 6.
Case: steel and red gold; Ø 27mm; bezel set with diamonds; scratch-resistant antireflective sapphire crystal; sapphire crystal caseback; water resistant to 10atm.
Dial: white; 10 diamond indexes.
Strap: steel and red gold.

CONSTELLATION CO-AXIAL — REF. 123.20.38.21.03.001

Movement: automatic-winding Omega 8500 caliber; 60-hour power reserve; free-sprung balance; bridges and oscillating weight decorated with exclusive Geneva waves in arabesque.
Functions: hours, minutes, seconds; date at 3.
Case: steel and red gold; Ø 38mm; scratch-resistant antireflective sapphire crystal; sapphire crystal caseback; water resistant to 10atm.
Dial: blue.
Bracelet: steel and red gold.

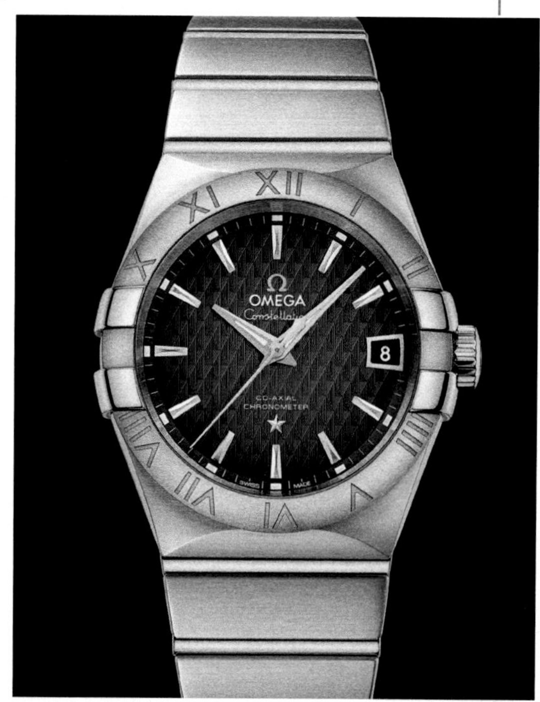

PATEK PHILIPPE
GENEVE

UNCOMPROMISING LUXURY

Patek Philippe strikes **A MASTERFUL EQUILIBRIUM BETWEEN VISUAL ELEGANCE AND MICRO-MECHANICAL EXCELLENCE** with its presentation of a vivacious ultra-thin ladies' timepiece and a men's wristwatch fit for a modern globetrotting lifestyle.

The Swiss watchmaker demonstrates a distinctive blend of artistic finesse and technical sophistication with a timepiece that travels with unmistakable elegance to all corners of the world. The self-winding World Time Chronograph Ref. 5930G-001 houses its 343-component CH 28-520 HU caliber in a 39.5mm white-gold case, animating a dynamic display of the planet's 24 principal time zones on a blue opaline dial with intricate hand-guilloché motif. The time in each location is seamlessly noted against a rotating 24-hour inner ring whose two-tone design shows the day/night distinction at a glance. Sharing the stage, a slender stem, centrally located, joins an instantaneous 30-minute counter at 6 o'clock in executing the movement's precise chronograph mechanism. By expertly combining textures, colors, luminous enhancements and geometric forms, Patek Philippe achieves a brilliant level of separation and subsequent clarity throughout the entire display—a feat in itself, given the wealth of dial-side indications.

◂ **WORLD TIME CHRONOGRAPH REF. 5930G-001**

A chronograph with instantaneous 30-minute counter elegantly complements the world-time function of this self-winding white-gold timepiece.

Adorned with 142 diamonds, the 34.6mm rose-gold case of the Ladies' Calatrava illuminates its understated dial.

The timepiece's caseback also exhibits to the manufacture's intricate perfectionism and technical skill, showcasing the vibrant details of the movement as well as its exquisite finishes. Oscillating at a frequency of 28,800 vph and equipped with a Spiromax spiral, the 5930G-001 is worn on a hand-stitched, matte, navy blue alligator strap with square scales.

With its presentation of the Ladies' Calatrava Ref. 7200/200R-001, Patek Philippe proves that shimmering luxury, mechanical excellence and feminine refinement can coexist splendidly in the world of haute horology. Adorned with 142 "Flamme"-set diamonds, the 34.6mm rose-gold case illuminates an understated dial. Two graceful hands indicate the hours and minutes against 12 gold numerals whose supple curvature complements the warmth of the silvery grained surface. At the heart of the timepiece, the self-winding ultra-thin 240 caliber preserves the refined dimensions of the piece, putting technical expertise at the service of aesthetic delicacy. Composed of 161 parts, 27 jewels and a 22-karat gold off-centered mini-rotor, the 2.53mm-tall movement may be admired through the caseback. A hand-stitched royal-purple alligator strap plays off the sober dial to add a touch of extravagant vivacity while its buckle, set with 26 additional diamonds, underscores the piece's luxurious personality.

▲ **LADIES CALATRAVA REF. 7200/200R-001**

This self-winding ladies' wristwatch complements its impressive ultra-thin caliber with a 22-karat off-centered micro-rotor and 142 diamonds set into its rose-gold case.

MENS AQUANAUT — REF. 5164R-001

Movement: automatic-winding 324 S C FUS caliber; Ø 31mm, thickness: 4.82mm; min. 35-hour power reserve; 294 components; 29 jewels; 28,800 vph.
Functions: hours, minutes, seconds; dual time zone; day/night indicator via aperture for local and home time; date via hand at 6.
Case: rose gold; Ø 40.8mm; screw-down crown; sapphire crystal caseback; water resistant to 12atm.
Dial: brown embossed; gold applied numerals with luminescent coating.
Strap: "tropical" composite; aquanaut fold-over clasp.
Suggested price: $51,030

MENS COMPLICATIONS — REF. 5170R-010

Movement: manual-winding CH 29-535 PS caliber; Ø 29.6mm, thickness: 5.35mm; min. 65-hour power reserve; 269 components; 33 jewels; 28,800 vph.
Functions: hours, minutes; small seconds at 9; chronograph: central seconds hand, 30-minute counter at 3.
Case: rose gold; Ø 39.4mm; sapphire crystal caseback; water resistant to 3atm.
Dial: ebony black opaline; gold applied Breguet numerals.
Strap: black alligator leather; fold-over clasp.
Suggested price: $81,010

MENS COMPLICATIONS — REF. 5170R-001

Movement: manual-winding CH 29-535 PS caliber; Ø 29.6mm, thickness: 5.35mm; min. 65-hour power reserve; 269 components; 33 jewels; 28,800 vph.
Functions: hours, minutes; small seconds at 9; chronograph: central seconds hand, 30-minute counter at 3.
Case: rose gold; Ø 39.4mm; sapphire crystal caseback; water resistant to 3atm.
Dial: silvery opaline; gold applied Breguet numerals.
Strap: chocolate brown alligator leather; fold-over clasp.
Suggested price: $81,080

MENS COMPLICATIONS — REF. 5230G-001

Movement: automatic-winding 240 HU caliber; Ø 27mm, thickness: 3.88mm; min. 48-hour power reserve; 239 components; 33 jewels; 21,600 vph.
Functions: hours; minutes; world time.
Case: white gold; Ø 38.5mm; sapphire crystal caseback; water resistant to 3atm.
Dial: charcoal gray lacquered; hand-guilloché; gold applied hour markers.
Strap: black alligator leather; fold-over clasp.
Suggested price: $47,630

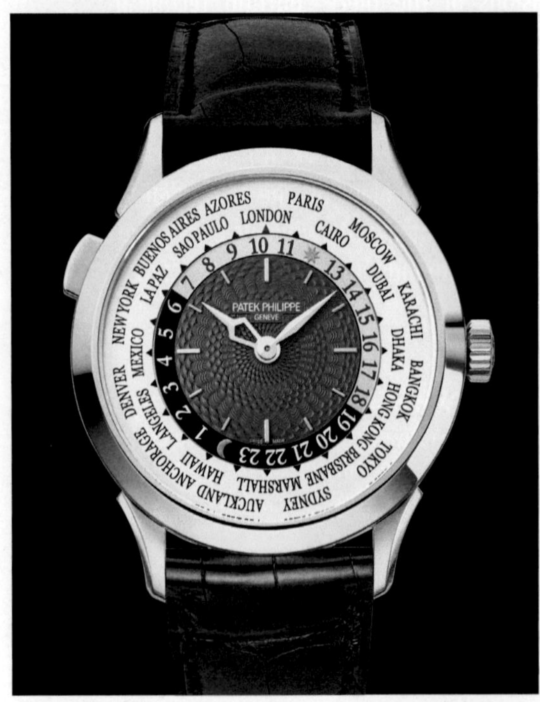

MENS COMPLICATIONS — REF. 5230R-001

Movement: automatic-winding 240 HU caliber; Ø 27.5mm, thickness: 3.88mm; min. 48-hour power reserve; 239 components; 21,600 vph.
Functions: hours, minutes; world time.
Case: rose gold; Ø 38.5mm; sapphire crystal caseback; water resistant to 3atm.
Dial: charcoal gray lacquered; hand-guilloché; gold applied hour markers.
Strap: chocolate brown alligator leather; fold-over clasp.
Suggested price: $47,630

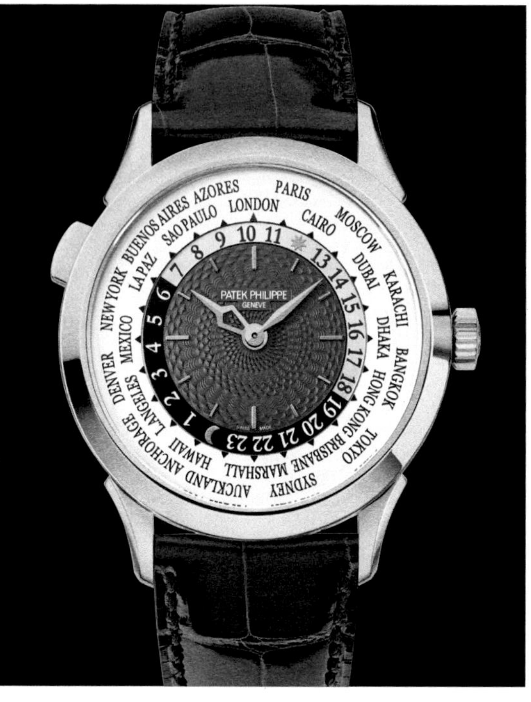

MENS COMPLICATIONS — REF. 5396G-014

Movement: automatic-winding 324 S QA LU 24H/303 caliber; Ø 33.3mm, thickness: 5.78mm; min. 35-hour power reserve; 347 components; 34 jewels; 28,800 vph.
Functions: hours, minutes, seconds; 24-hour display and moonphase at 6; annual calendar: day and month at 12, date at 6.
Case: white gold; Ø 38.5mm; sapphire crystal caseback; water resistant to 3atm.
Dial: charcoal gray sunburst; gold applied Breguet numerals.
Strap: matte black alligator leather; fold-over clasp.
Suggested price: $47,970

MENS COMPLICATIONS — REF. 5396R-012

Movement: automatic-winding 324 S QA LU 24H/303 caliber; Ø 33.3mm, thickness: 5.78mm; min. 35-hour power reserve; 347 components; 34 jewels; 28,800 vph.
Functions: hours, minutes, seconds; 24-hour display and moonphase at 6; annual calendar: day and month at 12, date at 6.
Case: rose gold; Ø 38.5mm; sapphire crystal caseback; water resistant to 3atm.
Dial: silvery opaline; gold applied Breguet numerals.
Strap: chocolate brown alligator leather.
Suggested price: $47,970

MENS GRAND COMPLICATIONS — REF. 5140P-017

Movement: automatic-winding 240 Q caliber; Ø 27.5mm, thickness: 3.88mm; min. 38-hour power reserve; 275 components; 27 jewels; 21,600 vph.
Functions: hours, minutes; moonphase at 6; perpetual calendar: month and leap year at 3, date at 6, day at 9; 24-hour indicator via hand at 9.
Case: platinum; Ø 37.2mm; interchangeable full back and sapphire crystal caseback; water resistant to 3atm.
Dial: charcoal gray sunburst; gold applied hour markers.
Strap: black alligator leather; fold-over clasp.
Suggested price: $105,920

MENS GRAND COMPLICATIONS — REF. 5160/500G-001

Movement: automatic-winding 324 S QR caliber; Ø 28mm, thickness: 5.35mm; min. 35-hour power reserve; 361 components; 30 jewels; 28,800 vph.
Functions: hours, minutes, seconds; moonphase at 6; perpetual calendar: month at 3, day at 9, date via retrograde hand.
Case: white gold; Ø 38mm; sapphire crystal caseback protected by a hand-engraved hinged dust cover; water resistant to 3atm.
Dial: silvery opaline; hand-engraved center; gold applied Breguet numerals.
Strap: matte black alligator leather; hand-engraved fold-over clasp.

Suggested price: $170,100

MENS GRAND COMPLICATIONS — REF. 5204R-001

Movement: manual-winding CHR 29-535 PS Q caliber; Ø 32mm, thickness: 8.7mm; min. 55-hour power reserve; 496 components; 34 jewels; 28,800 vph.
Functions: hours, minutes; small seconds at 9; moonphase at 6; perpetual calendar: day and month at 12, date via hand at 6; chronograph: central split-seconds hand, 30-minute counter at 3.
Case: rose gold; Ø 40mm; interchangeable full back and sapphire crystal caseback; water resistant to 3atm.
Dial: silvery opaline; gold applied hour markers with luminescent coating.
Strap: chocolate brown alligator leather.

Suggested price: $283,500

MENS GRAND COMPLICATIONS — REF. 5327G-001

Movement: automatic-winding 240 Q caliber; Ø 27.5mm, thickness: 3.88mm; min. 38-hour power reserve; 275 components; 27 jewels; 21,600 vph.
Functions: hours, minutes; moonphase at 6; perpetual calendar: month and leap year at 3, date at 6, day at 9; 24-hour indicator at 9.
Case: white gold; Ø 39mm; interchangeable full back and sapphire crystal caseback; water resistant to 3atm.
Dial: royal blue sunburst; gold applied Breguet numerals.
Strap: navy blue alligator leather; fold-over clasp.

Suggested price: $85,050

MENS GRAND COMPLICATIONS — REF. 5327J-001

Movement: automatic-winding 240 Q caliber; Ø 27.5mm, thickness: 3.88mm; min. 38-hour power reserve; 275 components; 27 jewels; 21,600 vph.
Functions: hours, minutes; moonphase at 6; perpetual calendar: month and leap year at 3, date at 6, day at 9; 24-hour indicator at 9.
Case: yellow gold; Ø 39mm; interchangeable full back and sapphire crystal caseback; water resistant to 3atm.
Dial: ivory lacquered; gold applied Breguet numerals.
Strap: chocolate brown alligator leather; fold-over clasp.

Suggested price: $82,780

MENS GRAND COMPLICATIONS — REF. 5327R-001

Movement: automatic-winding 240Q caliber; Ø 27.5mm, thickness: 3.88mm; min. 38-hour power reserve; 275 components; 27 jewels; 21,600 vph.
Functions: hours, minutes; moonphase at 6; perpetual calendar: month and leap year at 3, date at 6, day at 9; 24-hour indicator at 9.
Case: rose gold; Ø 39mm; interchangeable full back and sapphire crystal caseback; water resistant to 3atm.
Dial: ivory lacquered; gold applied Breguet numerals.
Strap: dark chestnut alligator leather.
Suggested price: $84,050

MENS GRAND COMPLICATIONS — REF. 5374P-001

Movement: automatic-winding R 27 Q caliber; thickness: 6.9mm; min. 38-hour power reserve; 467 components; 39 jewels; 21,600 vph.
Functions: hours, minutes; moonphase at 6; perpetual calendar: month and leap year at 3, date at 6, day and 24-hour indicator at 9; minute repeater.
Case: platinum; Ø 42mm; interchangeable full back and sapphire crystal caseback.
Dial: black enamel; gold applied Breguet numerals.
Strap: black alligator leather; fold-over clasp.
Price: available upon request.

MENS GRAND COMPLICATIONS — REF. 5496P-015

Movement: automatic-winding 324 S QR caliber; Ø 28mm, thickness: 5.35mm; min. 35-hour power reserve; 361 components; 30 jewels; 28,800 vph.
Functions: hours, minutes, seconds; moonphase at 6; perpetual calendar: day at 9, date via retrograde hand, month at 3, leap year at 12.
Case: platinum; Ø 39.5mm; interchangeable full back and sapphire crystal caseback; water resistant to 3atm.
Dial: silvery; vertical satin-finished; gold applied hour markers.
Strap: chocolate brown alligator leather; fold-over clasp.
Suggested price: $107,730

MENS GRAND COMPLICATIONS — REF. 5539G-010

Movement: manual-winding R TO 27 PS caliber; Ø 28mm, thickness: 6.58mm; min. 40-hour power reserve; 336 components; 28 jewels; 21,600 vph.
Functions: hours, minutes; small seconds at 6; minute repeater; tourbillon.
Case: white gold; Ø 37mm; interchangeable full back and sapphire crystal caseback; humidity and dust protected.
Dial: blue enamel; gold applied Breguet numerals.
Strap: dusk blue alligator leather; fold-over clasp.
Price: available upon request.

MENS GRAND COMPLICATIONS — REF. 5950R-001

Movement: manual-winding CHR 27 525 PS caliber; thickness: 5.25mm; min. 48-hour power reserve; 332 components; 31 jewels; 21,600 vph.
Functions: hours, minutes; small seconds at 9; chronograph: central split-seconds counter, 60-minute counter at 3.
Case: rose gold; 37x44.6mm; interchangeable full back and sapphire crystal caseback; water resistant to 3atm.
Dial: silvery grained; vertical satin-finished with decorative blackened engravings; gold applied Breguet numerals.
Strap: chocolate brown alligator leather; engraved prong buckle.
Price: available upon request.

MENS GRAND COMPLICATIONS — REF. 5950R-010

Movement: manual-winding CHR 27 525 PS caliber; thickness: 5.25mm; min. 48-hour power reserve; 332 components; 31 jewels; 21,600 vph.
Functions: hours, minutes; small seconds at 9; chronograph: central split-seconds counter, 60-minute counter at 3.
Case: rose gold; 37x44.6mm; interchangeable full back and sapphire crystal caseback; water resistant to 3atm.
Dial: rose gold; vertical satin-finished with decorative blackened engravings.
Strap: chocolate brown alligator leather; engraved prong buckle.
Price: available upon request.

LADIES CALATRAVA — REF. 4897/300G-001

Movement: manual-winding 215 caliber; Ø 21.9mm, thickness: 2.55mm; min. 44-hour power reserve; 130 components; 18 jewels; 28,800 vph.
Functions: hours, minutes.
Case: white gold; Ø 33mm; bezel set with 48 baguette diamonds (~1.21 carats); sapphire crystal caseback; water resistant to 3atm.
Dial: guillochéd night blue; powdered white-gold hour markers.
Strap: midnight blue brushed satin; prong buckle set with 6 baguette diamonds (~0.19 carat).
Suggested price: $43,090

LADIES CALATRAVA — REF. 7122/200G-001

Movement: manual-winding 215 PS caliber; thickness: 2.55mm; 18 jewels; 28,800 vph.
Functions: hours, minutes; small seconds at 6.
Case: white gold; Ø 33mm; bezel set with 44 diamonds (~0.47 carat); sapphire crystal caseback; water resistant to 3atm.
Dial: white lacquered; gold applied hobnail-patterned hour markers.
Strap: matte pearly white alligator leather; prong buckle.
Suggested price: $27,220

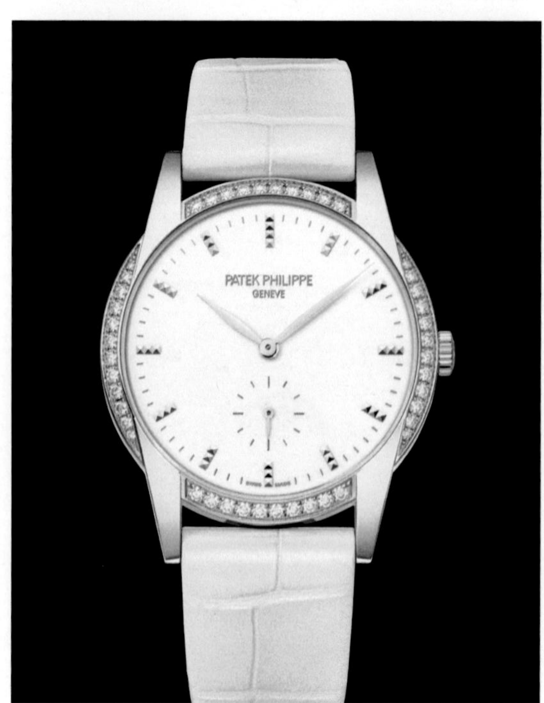

LADIES CALATRAVA — REF. 7122/200R-001

Movement: manual-winding 215 PS caliber; thickness: 2.55mm; 18 jewels; 28,800 vph.
Functions: hours, minutes; small seconds at 6.
Case: rose gold; Ø 33mm; bezel set with 44 diamonds (~0.47 carat); sapphire crystal caseback; water resistant to 3atm.
Dial: white lacquered; gold applied hobnail-patterned hour markers.
Strap: matte pearly white alligator leather; prong buckle.
Suggested price: $27,220

LADIES AQUANAUT — REF. 5067A-024

Movement: quartz E23 250 S C caliber; Ø 23.9mm, thickness: 2.5mm; 80 components; 8 jewels.
Functions: hours, minutes, seconds; date at 3.
Case: stainless steel; Ø 35.6mm; bezel set with 46 diamonds (~1 carat); screw-down crown; water resistant to 12atm.
Dial: embossed; gold applied numerals.
Strap: "tropical" composite; aquanaut fold-over clasp.
Suggested price: $16,220

LADIES COMPLICATIONS — REF. 4968/400R-001

Movement: manual-winding 215 PS LU caliber; Ø 21.9mm, thickness: 3mm; min. 39-hour power reserve; 157 components; 18 jewels; 28,800 vph.
Functions: hours, minutes; small seconds and moonphase at 6.
Case: rose gold; Ø 33.3mm; sapphire crystal caseback; water resistant to 3atm.
Dial: fully set with diamonds; 12 rubies for the hour markers (~0.11 carat); lugs set with 48 diamonds (~0.17 carat).
Strap: cherry red alligator leather; prong buckle set with 32 diamonds (~0.25 carat).
Note: bezel and dial set 587 graduated size diamonds in a spiral (~3.02 carats).
Suggested price: $68,040

MENS GRAND COMPLICATIONS — REF. 6002G-010

Movement: manual-winding R TO 27 QR SID LU CL caliber; Ø 38mm, thickness: 12.61mm; 48-hour power reserve; 705 components; 55 jewels; 21,600 vph.
Functions: hours, minutes; tourbillon; moonphase at 6; perpetual calendar: day at 9, date via retrograde hand, month at 3, leap year at 12; minute repeater; reverse side: sidereal time, sky chart, phases and orbit of the moon.
Case: white gold; Ø 44mm; humidity- and dust-protected.
Dial: black enamel in champlevé and cloisonné; gold applied Roman numerals.
Strap: black alligator leather; hand-engraved fold-over clasp.
Price: available upon request.

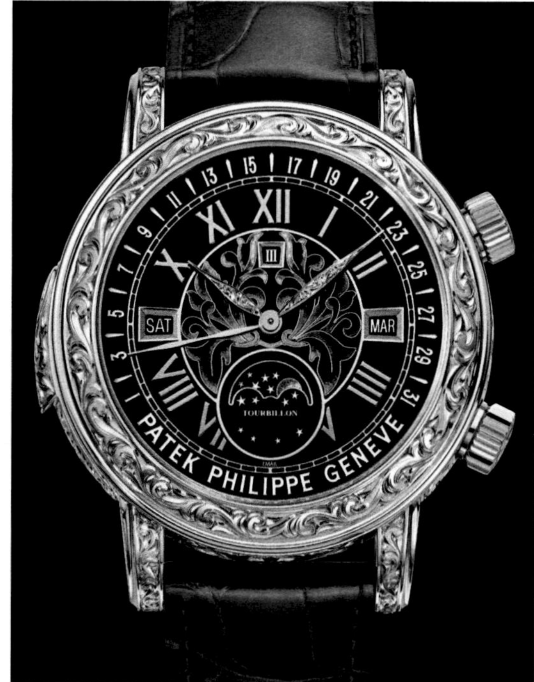

PERRELET
1777

A POWERFUL CREATIVITY AND A BOUNDLESS SPIRIT OF INNOVATION

Perrelet energizes four new timepieces thanks to **ITS AUDACIOUS USE OF TRANSPARENCY AND HIGH-SPEED ROTATING COMPONENTS ON THE FRONT SIDE OF THE WATCH**.

Transforming the dial into a highly dynamic display of mechanical motion, the LAB treats its owner to a glimpse into the heart of its movement's perpetual energy. The Swiss watchmaker shines the spotlight on an often-unsung hero, the oscillating weight, thanks to a dial architecture that strikes a perfect balance of legibility and revealing transparency. By fixing the winding rotor to a toothed wheel on the outer rim of the P-411 caliber, Perrelet allows for a stunning exhibition of the former, exquisitely decorated with a slanted-line motif, through a peripheral aperture on the face. The unique mechanical display does not obstruct the time display. Two central hands, enhanced with SuperLumiNova for optimal nighttime visibility, indicate the hours and minutes against 12 cut-out hour markers, also luminous, that appear to float in midair thanks to their application on a sapphire crystal ring. Embellished with a vertical decoration, the timepiece's anthracite, black or silver-toned dial is finished with a date window at 6 o'clock and central seconds stem whose journey around the dial makes for a vibrant effect when combined with the exhilarating movements of the caliber's winding rotor, which oscillates at 28,800 vph. Housed in a 42mm stainless steel case that complements the curves of its cushion shape with an octagonal bezel, the LAB boasts a see-through caseback through which the wearer may admire the intricacies of the watch's Côtes-de-Genève-decorated caliber.

◂ **LAB**

This casual-chic stainless steel timepiece reveals its oscillating weight on the dial

A map of the world, meticulously engraved on the Turbine GMT's under-dial, adds a splendid touch of imagery to a timepiece with a jet-setting raison d'être.

The Turbine, with its 10 or 12 anodized aluminum blades, features 5 tungsten counterweights enabling it to turn freely and return to its original location with a simple movement of the wrist. This is a highly complex technical element requiring intricate mastery of the assembly process so that all the components are perfectly balanced and operate optimally.

The Turbine GMT takes Perrelet's iconic dial design on a trip around the world. The 44mm timepiece's turbine responds to every movement of the wrist, spinning to the point of near transparency to reveal Perrelet's imagination and extensive artistic mastery. A map of the world, meticulously engraved on a Côtes-de-Genève-adorned under-dial, adds a splendid touch of imagery to a timepiece with a decisive jet-setting raison d'être. Driven by the self-winding P-401 caliber, the Turbine GMT complements its display of the hours, minutes and seconds with a fourth central hand, indicating the time in a second location against a two-tone 24-hour scale that clearly delineates the city's day or night status.

The Turbine Pilot pays homage to the world of aviation with a technical design that brings spectacular meaning to the brand's emblematic, dynamic dial. Housed in a 48mm stainless steel case, the timepiece's stunning turbine, spins with each action of the wrist, seemingly disappearing to expose an under-dial decorated with black and yellow stripes evocative of the high-speed aviation world. The Turbine Pilot is powered by the self-winding P-331 caliber and indicates the hours, minutes and seconds by way of three luminous hands.

Designed in collaboration with action movie star Sung Kang, the Turbine Sung Kang goes full throttle with a design inspired by the actor's passion for high-speed racing automobiles. Ingeniously offset to optimize readability while at the wheel, the black-PVD-coated stainless steel timepiece features its 12 o'clock marker at 2 o'clock on the watch face to counteract the shirtsleeve's tendency to conceal part of the dial while driving. Activated by the movement of the wrist, 10 anodized aluminum blades then spin around the dial to create an effect of high-speed transparency that reveals an under-dial featuring minutes markers and a yellow and red scale that evokes the tones of high-powered racecars. The Turbine Sung Kang is powered by the 28,800 vph P-331 caliber and features the actor's initials at 4 o'clock on the offset dial.

▲ **TURBINE GMT** *(top left)*
This dual-time-zone timepiece reveals a meticulously engraved world map beneath 10 fast-moving blades activated by the movement of the wrist.

▲ **TURBINE PILOT** *(top right)*
The Turbine Pilot showcases its decisive high-flying personality with 12 spinning titanium blades on a dial equipped with a bi-directional rotating ring and aviation slide rule.

◂ **TURBINE SUNG KANG**
This racing-inspired wristwatch equipped with a spinning turbine boasts an offset design for optimal readability while driving.

LAB — REF. A1100/1

Movement: automatic-winding P-411 caliber; 42-hour power reserve.
Functions: hours, minutes, seconds; date at 6.
Case: stainless steel; Ø 42mm, thickness: 13.25mm; antireflective sapphire crystal; sapphire crystal caseback; water resistant to 5atm.
Dial: silver; central stamped vertical lines; sapphire ring with applied luminous hour markers; oscillating mass visible on dial side.
Strap: black alligator leather; stainless steel buckle.
Suggested price: $4,950

FIRST CLASS — REF. A1073/6

Movement: automatic-winding P-321 caliber; 42-hour power reserve.
Functions: hours, minutes, seconds; date at 6.
Case: stainless steel; Ø 42.5mm, thickness: 10.7mm; antireflective sapphire crystal; sapphire crystal caseback; water resistant to 5atm.
Dial: grained guilloché champagne; applied hour markers.
Strap: brown alligator leather; stainless steel folding buckle.
Suggested price: $2,580

FIRST CLASS OPEN HEART — REF. A1087/9

Movement: automatic-winding P-391 caliber; 42-hour power reserve.
Functions: hours, minutes, seconds.
Case: stainless steel; Ø 42.5mm, thickness: 10.7mm; antireflective sapphire crystal; sapphire crystal caseback; water resistant to 5atm.
Dial: grained silver guilloché; applied hour markers; transparent balance wheel on Côtes de Genève background.
Strap: black alligator leather; stainless steel folding clasp.
Suggested price: $2,850

FIRST CLASS DOUBLE ROTOR SKELETON — REF. A1091/6

Movement: automatic-winding P-481-20Y caliber; 42-hour power reserve.
Functions: hours, minutes, seconds.
Case: stainless steel; Ø 42.5mm, thickness: 10.7mm; antireflective sapphire crystal; sapphire crystal caseback; water resistant to 5atm.
Dial: skeletonized center; blue hours ring with vertical guilloché motif; applied hour markers; openworked double rotor with Côtes de Genève decoration.
Bracelet: stainless steel; folding clasp.
Suggested price: $5,080

TURBINE REF. A1047/2

Movement: automatic-winding P-331 caliber; 42-hour power reserve.
Functions: hours, minutes, seconds.
Case: stainless steel with black PVD coating; Ø 44mm, thickness: 13mm; antireflective sapphire crystal; sapphire crystal caseback; water resistant to 5atm.
Dial: black turbine; luminous Arabic numerals, hour markers and hands.
Strap: black rubber; steel buckle with black PVD coating.
Suggested price: $4,470

TURBINE CHRONO REF. A3036/1

Movement: automatic-winding P-361 caliber; 42-hour power reserve.
Functions: hours, minutes; date at 6; chronograph: central seconds hand, sapphire crystal central 60-minute counter.
Case: stainless steel with black PVD coating; Ø 47mm, thickness: 16mm; 4N rose-gold bezel ring; antireflective sapphire crystal; sapphire crystal caseback; water resistant to 5atm.
Dial: black turbine; 4N rose-gold top rotor ring; black dial ring; luminous Arabic numerals, hour markers and hands.
Strap: black rubber; steel buckle with black PVD coating.
Suggested price: $7,980

DIAMOND FLOWER AMYTIS REF. A2066/8

Movement: automatic-winding P-181-H caliber; 42-hour power reserve.
Functions: hours, minutes, seconds.
Case: stainless steel; Ø 36.5mm, thickness: 12.3mm; bezel set with 64 diamonds (0.96 carat); antireflective sapphire crystal; sapphire crystal caseback; water resistant to 5atm.
Dial: champagne; Roman numerals; mother-of-pearl double rotor.
Bracelet: stainless steel; folding clasp.
Suggested price: $8,680

DIAMOND FLOWER AMYTIS REF. A2066/4

Movement: automatic-winding P-181-H caliber; 42-hour power reserve.
Functions: hours, minutes, seconds.
Case: stainless steel; Ø 36.5mm, thickness: 12.3mm; bezel set with diamonds; antireflective sapphire crystal; sapphire crystal caseback; water resistant to 5atm.
Dial: anthracite and white engraved mother-of-pearl; Roman numerals; petal-shaped double rotor in diamond-set mother-of-pearl.
Strap: black alligator leather; stainess steel folding clasp.
Note: set with 80 diamonds (1.02 carats).
Suggested price: $9,960

PIAGET

TRANSCENDING THE TIMES

With the spirited revival of two of its most iconic collections, Piaget **CELEBRATES ITS PIONEERING PAST WHILE CAPTURING THE ESSENCE OF MODERN HAUTE HOROLOGY**.

The Swiss watchmaker honors the 60th anniversary of its groundbreaking ultra-thin icon with a limited edition Piaget Altiplano collection that perfectly encapsulates the refined understatement of its historic predecessor. The first model, a self-winding wristwatch housed in a 43mm 18-karat white-gold case, drives its indication of the hours and minutes by way of the 1200P caliber. Measuring a mere 2.3mm in thickness, the 180-component movement allows the timepiece to achieve its breathtaking slenderness while performing with excellent precision. The dial then plays off the extraordinary luster of the case with a rich sunburst Piaget-blue finish that brings a contemporary feel to the vintage personality of the timepiece. On the face, twelve white-gold hour markers subtly echo the shape of the watch's two slim baton hands, confirming the stunning geometric harmony of the minimalist wristwatch.

A second variation, this one endowed with the hand-wound 430P caliber, pays homage to Piaget's exceptional history within even slighter dimensions. The 18-karat white-gold timepiece, housed in a case measuring 38mm in diameter, again contrasts the sheen of its precious metal with a deep blue hue on the dial that expresses its decisive personality. Finished with Côtes de Genève and circular graining, the 131-component caliber boasts a thickness of only 2.1mm and drives the hours and minutes via two baton-shaped stems. Worthy heirs to the Maison's 1957 creation, the Piaget Altiplano collection's two ultra-thin timepieces prove that aesthetic and mechanical sophistication transcends all generations.

Distinguished by Piaget's iconic shape-within-a-shape design, the Piaget Polo S wristwatches speak the language of modernity and sporty refinement.

The legendary horologer invigorates its 1979-born Piaget Polo collection with five timepieces imbued with the brand's unmistakable DNA. Framed by 42mm stainless steel cases and distinguished by Piaget's iconic shape-within-a-shape design, the Piaget Polo S wristwatches speak of modernity and sporty refinement with exquisite character, the harmonious contrast of their round cases and cushion-shaped dials giving them a sense of multi-dimensionality perfectly in line with their contemporary narrative.

The Piaget Polo S, driven by the 110P caliber, showcases a display of the hours, minutes and sweeping seconds on a silvered, blue or slate-gray dial complemented by a discreet date aperture at 6 o'clock. A sapphire crystal caseback treats the owner to an exhibition of the movement's meticulous construction. Two Piaget Polo S Chronograph variations bring lively movement and increased technical complexity to the collection. Animated on a silvered or Piaget-blue dial, the 1160P caliber drives a demonstration of the hours, minutes, central chronograph seconds, and date at 6 o'clock, as well as a pair of counters at 3 and 9 o'clock for the stopwatch's 30-minute and 12-hour counters. Like the Piaget Polo S, the chronograph variant gives its wearer a fascinating glimpse into the movement's inner workings via a transparent sapphire crystal on the back of the watch.

▸ **PIAGET POLO S**

Distinguished by its integration of a cushion-shaped dial within a round case, this set of five self-winding wristwatches exudes an air of timeless modernity.

◂ **PIAGET ALTIPLANO**

This homage to the Maison's revolutionary 1957 ultra-thin achievement celebrates its ancestry with a pair of exquisitely slender timepieces available with self-winding or hand-wound calibers.

PIAGET POLO S — REF. G0A41003

Movement: automatic-winding 1110P caliber; slate gray oscillating weight.
Functions: hours, minutes, seconds; date at 6.
Case: steel; Ø 42mm, thickness: 9.4mm; sapphire crystal caseback; water resistant to 10atm.
Dial: slate gray; silvered appliqué indexes with SuperLumiNova.
Bracelet: steel; integrated folding clasp.
Suggested price: $9,350

PIAGET POLO S — REF. G0A41002

Movement: automatic-winding 1110P caliber; slate gray oscillating weight.
Functions: hours, minutes, seconds; date at 6.
Case: steel; Ø 42mm, thickness: 9.4mm; sapphire crystal caseback; water resistant to 10atm.
Dial: blue; silvered appliqué indexes with SuperLumiNova.
Bracelet: steel; integrated folding clasp.
Suggested price: $9,350

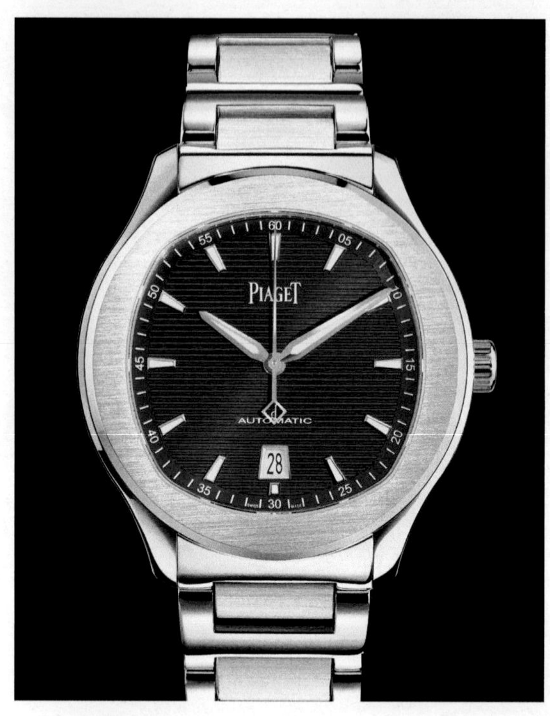

PIAGET POLO S — REF. G0A41004

Movement: automatic-winding 1160P caliber.
Functions: hours, minutes; date at 6; chronograph: central seconds hand, 30-minute counter at 3, 12-hour counter at 9.
Case: steel; Ø 42mm, thickness: 11.2mm; sapphire crystal caseback; water resistant to 10atm.
Dial: silvered; slate gray appliqué indexes with SuperLumiNova.
Bracelet: steel; integrated folding clasp.
Suggested price: $12,400

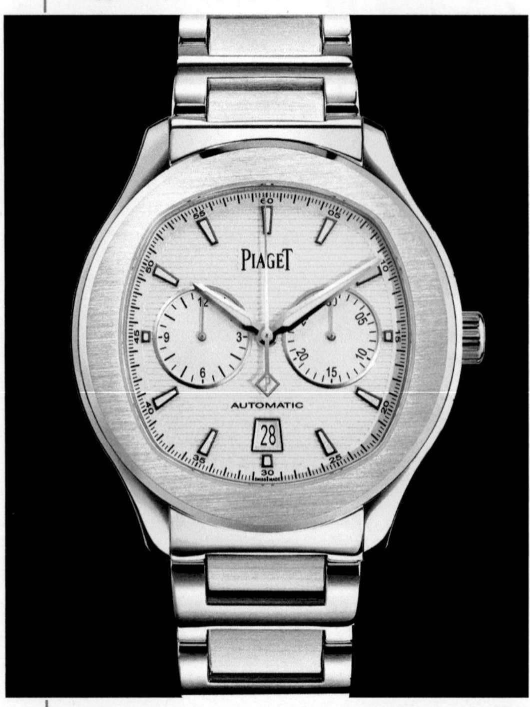

PIAGET POLO S — REF. G0A41006

Movement: automatic-winding 1160P caliber.
Functions: hours, minutes; date at 6; chronograph: central seconds hand, 30-minute counter at 3, 12-hour counter at 9.
Case: steel; Ø 42mm, thickness: 11.2mm; sapphire crystal caseback; water resistant to 10atm.
Dial: blue; silvered appliqué indexes with SuperLumiNova.
Bracelet: steel; integrated folding clasp.
Suggested price: $12,400

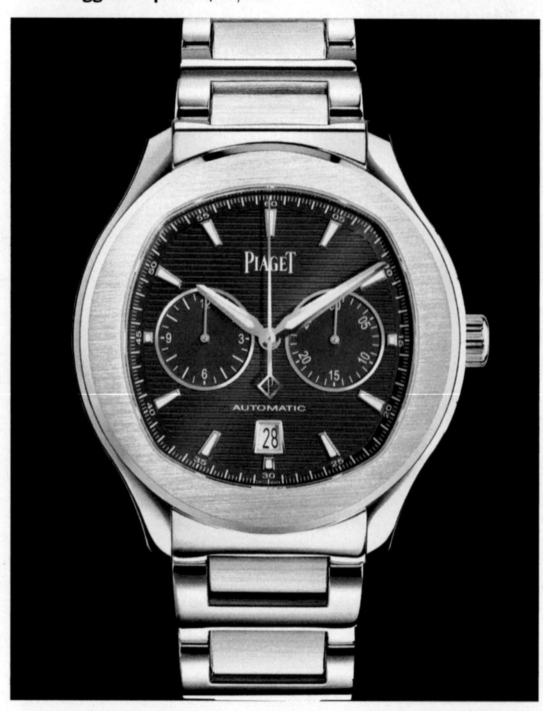

PIAGET ALTIPLANO 900P — REF. G0A39111

Movement: manual-winding 900P caliber; 48-hour power reserve; 145 components; 20 jewels; 21,600 vph; finishing: black sunburst satin-brushed bridges, beveled bridges, sunburst or circular satin-brushed wheels.
Functions: offset hours and minutes at 10.
Case: 18K white gold; Ø 38mm, thickness: 3.65mm; satin-brushed caseback.
Dial: 18K white gold; black baton indexes.
Strap: black alligator leather; 18K white-gold pin buckle.
Suggested price: $26,500

PIAGET ALTIPLANO — REF. G0A41011

Movement: manual-winding 900P caliber; 48-hour power reserve; 145 components; 20 jewels; 21,600 vph; finishing: black sunburst satin-brushed bridges, beveled bridges, sunburst or circular satin-brushed wheels.
Functions: offset hours and minutes at 10.
Case: 18K pink gold; Ø 38mm, thickness: 3.65mm.
Dial: 18K pink gold; black baton indexes.
Strap: black alligator leather; 18K pink-gold ardillon buckle.
Suggested price: $24,900

PIAGET ALTIPLANO 900P — REF. G0A39112

Movement: manual-winding 900P caliber; 48-hour power reserve; 145 components; 20 jewels; 21,600 vph; finishing: sunburst satin-brushed bridges, beveled bridges, sunburst or circular satin-brushed wheels.
Functions: offset hours and minutes at 10.
Case: 18K white gold; Ø 38mm, thickness: 3.65mm; set with 78 brilliant-cut diamonds (approx. 0.71 carat); satin-brushed caseback.
Dial: black; 18K white-gold baton indexes.
Strap: black alligator leather; 18K white-gold pin buckle.
Suggested price: $31,100

PIAGET ALTIPLANO 900P HIGH JEWELLERY — REF. G0A39120

Movement: manual-winding 900P caliber; 48-hour power reserve; 145 components; 20 jewels; 21,600 vph; finishing: black sunburst satin-brushed bridges, beveled bridges, sunburst or circular satin-brushed wheels.
Functions: offset hours and minutes at 10.
Case: 18K white gold; Ø 38mm, thickness: 5.65mm; set with 38 baguette-cut diamonds (approx. 1.36 carats) and 267 brilliant-cut diamonds (approx. 1.86 carats); satin-brushed caseback.
Dial: set with 33 baguette-cut diamonds (approx. 1.41 carats).
Strap: black alligator leather; triple folding clasp set with 23 brilliant-cut diamonds (approx. 0.05 carat).
Suggested price: $162,000

PIAGET ALTIPLANO CHRONOGRAPH — REF. G0A41035

Movement: manual-winding 883P caliber.
Functions: hours, minutes; small seconds at 9; chronograph: central seconds hand, 30-minute counter at 3; second time zone at 9.
Case: 18K white gold; Ø 41mm; sapphire crystal caseback.
Dial: white; black baton indexes.
Strap: black alligator leather; 18K white-gold ardillon buckle.
Suggested price: $28,600

PIAGET ALTIPLANO CHRONOGRAPH — REF. G0A40030

Movement: manual-winding 883P caliber; Ø 27mm, thickness: 4.65mm; 50-hour power reserve; 30 jewels; 28,800 vph; finishing: circular Côtes de Genève, circular-grained mainplate, beveled bridges.
Functions: hours, minutes; small seconds at 6; chronograph: central seconds hand, 30-minute counter at 3; second time zone at 9.
Case: 18K pink gold; Ø 41mm; sapphire crystal caseback.
Dial: silvered; black baton indexes.
Strap: black alligator leather; 18K pink-gold ardillon buckle.
Suggested price: $28,600

PIAGET ALTIPLANO — REF. G0A31114

Movement: manual-winding 430P caliber; Ø 20.5mm, thickness: 2.1mm; 43-hour power reserve; 18 jewels; 21,600 vph; finishing: circular Côtes de Genève, circular-grained mainplate and bridges, beveled bridges.
Functions: hours, minutes.
Case: 18K red gold; Ø 38mm.
Dial: silvered; black baton indexes.
Strap: black alligator leather; 18K red-gold ardillon buckle.
Suggested price: $15,200

PIAGET ALTIPLANO 40MM BRACELET — REF. G0A38131

Movement: automatic-winding 1205P caliber; pink-gold oscillating weight.
Functions: hours, minutes; small seconds at 5; date at 9.
Case: 18K red gold; Ø 40mm; sapphire crystal caseback.
Dial: silvered; black baton indexes.
Strap: brown alligator leather.
Suggested price: $23,800

PIAGET ALTIPLANO SKELETON REF. G0A37132

Movement: automatic-winding 1200S caliber; thickness: 2.4mm; 44-hour power reserve; 26 jewels; 21,600 vph; finishing: sunburst satin-brushed plate and bridges, hand-drawn and hand-beveled bridges and mainplate, black platinum oscillating weight.
Functions: hours, minutes.
Case: 18K white gold; Ø 38mm; sapphire crystal caseback.
Dial: skeletonized.
Strap: black alligator leather; 18K white-gold ardillon buckle.
Suggested price: $57,000

PIAGET ALTIPLANO AUTOMATIC GEM-SET SKELETON REF. G0A38125

Movement: automatic-winding 1200D caliber; 44-hour power reserve; 26 jewels; 21,600vph; set with 259 brilliant-cut diamonds (approx. 0.8 carat) and 11 black sapphire cabochons (approx. 0.1 carat); finishing: 14K gold mainplate and bridges gem-set on the upper part, sunray satin-brushed bridges.
Functions: hours, minutes.
Case: 18K white gold; Ø 40mm; bezel set with 40 baguette-cut diamonds; case, crown, lugs and sapphire crystal caseback set with 347 brilliant-cut diamonds (approx. 1.4 carats)
Dial: skeletonized.
Strap: black alligator leather; 18K white-gold triple folding clasp with 24 brilliant-cut diamonds (approx. 0.06 carat).
Suggested price: $181,000

PIAGET ALTIPLANO HIGH JEWELLERY REF. G0A41122

Movement: manual-winding 900P caliber.
Functions: hours, minutes.
Case: 18K white gold.
Dial: set with diamonds.
Strap: black alligator leather.
Note: set with 656 brilliant-cut diamonds (approx. 3.06 carats), 1 diamond (approx. 0.03 carat), and 76 baguette-cut diamonds (approx. 2.73 carats).
Suggested price: $165,000

PIAGET ALTIPLANO REF. G0A37128

Movement: automatic-winding 1200P caliber; thickness: 2.35mm; 44-hour power reserve; 180 components; 25 jewels; 21,600 vph; finishing: beveled bridges, platinum oscillating weight, circular-grained mainplate, circular Côtes de Genève.
Functions: hours, minutes.
Case: 18K white gold; Ø 41mm; set with 313 brilliant-cut diamonds (approx. 1.7 carats) and 48 baguette-cut diamonds (approx. 2.5 carats); sapphire crystal caseback.
Dial: set with 155 brilliant-cut diamonds (approx. 1.8 carats) and 36 baguette-cut diamonds (approx. 0.1 carat).
Strap: black alligator leather; buckle set with 24 brilliant-cut diamonds (approx. 0.06 carat).
Suggested price: $218,000

PIAGET ALTIPLANO — REF. GOA40109

Movement: automatic-winding 534P caliber; 42-hour power reserve; 25 jewels; 21,600 vph.
Functions: hours, minutes.
Case: 18K white gold; Ø 34mm; bezel set with 68 brilliant-cut diamonds (approx. 0.6 carat).
Dial: white; slate gray hour markers.
Bracelet: 18K white gold; folding clasp.
Suggested price: $22,000

PIAGET ALTIPLANO — REF. GOA40105

Movement: automatic-winding 534P caliber; 42-hour power reserve; 25 jewels; 21,600 vph.
Functions: hours, minutes.
Case: 18K pink gold; Ø 34mm.
Dial: white; slate gray hour markers.
Bracelet: 18K pink gold; folding clasp.
Suggested price: $28,700

PIAGET ALTIPLANO — REF. GOA40112

Movement: automatic-winding 534P caliber; 42-hour power reserve; 25 jewels; 21,600 vph; finishing: circular Côtes de Genève, circular-grained mainplate, beveled bridges.
Functions: hours, minutes.
Case: 18K white gold; Ø 38mm; bezel set with 78 brilliant-cut diamonds (approx. 0.7 carat).
Dial: white; slate gray baton-shaped hour markers.
Bracelet: 18K white gold; folding clasp.
Suggested price: $40,700

PIAGET ALTIPLANO — REF. GOA40114

Movement: automatic-winding 534P caliber; 42-hour power reserve; 25 jewels; 21,600 vph; finishing: circular Côtes de Genève, circular-grained mainplate, beveled bridges.
Functions: hours, minutes.
Case: 18K pink gold; Ø 38mm; bezel set with 78 brilliant-cut diamonds (approx. 0.7 carat).
Dial: white; slate gray baton-shaped hour markers.
Bracelet: 18K pink gold; Ø 38mm; folding clasp.

Suggested price: $39,100

LIMELIGHT STELLA REF. G0A40110

Movement: automatic-winding 584P caliber; 42-hour power reserve; pink-gold-colored oscillating weight.
Functions: hours, minutes; moonphase at 12.
Case: 18K pink gold; Ø 36mm; sapphire crystal caseback.
Dial: white; pink-gold hour markers; moonphase underlined with 14 diamonds (approx. 0.06 carat).
Strap: brown alligator leather.
Suggested price: $20,500

LIMELIGHT STELLA REF. G0A40111

Movement: automatic-winding 584P caliber; 42-hour power reserve; black oscillating weight.
Functions: hours, minutes; moonphase at 12.
Case: 18K white gold; Ø 36mm; set with 126 brilliant-cut diamonds (approx 0.65 carat); sapphire crystal caseback.
Dial: white; white-gold hour markers; moonphase underlined with 14 diamonds (approx. 0.06 carat).
Strap: blue alligator leather.
Suggested price: $29,700

LIMELIGHT STELLA REF. G0A40123

Movement: automatic-winding 584P caliber; 42-hour power reserve; pink-gold-colored oscillating weight.
Functions: hours, minutes, seconds; moonphase at 12.
Case: 18K pink gold; Ø 36mm; set with 126 brilliant-cut diamonds (approx. 0.65 carat); sapphire crystal caseback.
Dial: white; pink-gold hour markers; moonphase underlined with 14 diamonds (approx. 0.06 carat).
Strap: taupe alligator leather.
Suggested price: $28,600

HIGH JEWELLERY LIMELIGHT STELLA REF. G0A40039

Movement: automatic-winding 580P caliber; black oscillating weight.
Functions: hours, minutes, seconds; moonphase at 12.
Case: 18K white gold; set with diamonds.
Dial: white mother-of-pearl; baguette-cut diamonds in center; moonphase underlined with diamonds.
Strap: slate gray alligator leather.
Suggested price: $37,800

LIMELIGHT GALA MILANESE — REF. G0A41212

Movement: quartz 690P caliber.
Functions: hours, minutes.
Case: 18K white gold; Ø 32mm; set with 62 brilliant-cut diamonds (approx. 1.75 carats).
Dial: silvered; silver-toned Roman numerals.
Bracelet: 18K white-gold Milanese mesh; integrated sliding clasp.
Suggested price: $36,000

LIMELIGHT GALA MILANESE — REF. G0A41213

Movement: quartz 690P caliber.
Functions: hours, minutes.
Case: 18K pink gold; Ø 32mm; set with 62 brilliant-cut diamonds (approx. 1.75 carats).
Dial: silvered; pink-gold-colored Roman numerals.
Bracelet: 18K pink-gold Milanese mesh; integrated sliding clasp.
Suggested price: $34,500

LIMELIGHT GALA — REF. G0A38160

Movement: quartz 690P caliber.
Functions: hours, minutes.
Case: 18K white gold; Ø 32mm; set with 62 brilliant-cut diamonds (approx. 1.8 carats).
Dial: silvered; black Roman numerals.
Strap: black satin; ardillon buckle set with 1 brilliant-cut diamond.
Suggested price: $33,300

LIMELIGHT GALA — REF. G0A41291

Movement: manual-winding 430P caliber.
Functions: hours, minutes.
Case: 18K pink gold; Ø 32mm; set with 62 brilliant-cut diamonds; pink-gold crown; sapphire crystal caseback.
Dial: mother-of-pearl.
Strap: black satin.
Suggested price: $32,000

PIAGET BLACK TIE EMPERADOR COUSSIN REF. G0A32017

Movement: automatic-winding 850P caliber.
Functions: hours, minutes; small seconds at 4; date at 12; day/night indicator and dual time at 8.
Case: 18K red gold.
Dial: silvered sunburst guilloché; red-gold index appliqués.
Strap: brown alligator leather.
Suggested price: $29,300

PIAGET EMPERADOR COUSSIN XL REF. G0A38019

Movement: automatic-winding 1290P caliber; thickness: 4.8mm; 40-hour power reserve; 407 components; 44 jewels; 21,600 vph; finishing on the back: circular Côtes de Genève, hand-beveled and hand-drawn bridges, sunburst satin-brushed wheels, pink-gold-toned platinum oscillating weight; finishing on the front: hand-beveled and hand-drawn sunburst satin-brushed and guilloché mainplate.
Functions: hours, minutes; minute repeater.
Case: 18K pink gold; Ø 48mm, thickness: 9.4mm; sapphire crystal; sapphire crystal caseback; water resistant to 2atm.
Dial: skeletonized.
Strap: brown alligator leather; 18K pink-gold folding clasp.
Suggested price: $271,000

PIAGET EMPERADOR COUSSIN TOURBILLON SKELETON REF. G0A40041

Movement: automatic-winding 1270S caliber; thickness: 5.05mm; 40-hour power reserve; 225 components; 35 jewels; 21,600 vph; finishing: haute horology finishing, hand-beveled and polished satin-brushed mainplate, hand-beveled and polished satin-brushed bridges, hand-drawn mainplate and bridges, beveled and satin-brushed barrel, black PVD-coated, satin-brushed, hand-beveled and polished oscillating weight.
Functions: hours, minutes; tourbillon at 1.
Case: 18K white gold; Ø 46.5mm, thickness: 8.85mm; sapphire crystal caseback.
Dial: skeletonized.
Strap: black alligator leather; 18K white-gold double folding clasp.
Suggested price: $194,000

PIAGET EMPERADOR COUSSIN XL REF. G0A38058

Movement: automatic-winding 1270P caliber; platinum oscillating weight.
Functions: hours, minutes, seconds; power reserve indicator on the caseback.
Case: 18K red gold paved with diamonds; Ø 46mm; 18K red-gold crown paved with diamonds; sapphire crystal; sapphire crystal caseback.
Dial: skeletonized; gilded indexes.
Strap: brown alligator leather.
Suggested price: $219,000

RICHARD MILLE

ALWAYS ON THE MOVE

Known for its restlessness and creativity, Richard Mille **UPDATES ITS ROSTER WITH CAREFULLY CONCEIVED DESIGN, REVOLUTIONARY NEW MATERIALS AND BRILLIANT HOMAGES** to a fellow fearless pioneer.

RM 11-03 AUTOMATIC FLYBACK CHRONOGRAPH

Restyling is a crucial element in the life cycle of any product. A watch must be vital, integrated into the natural stylistic development of a brand. A fixture of the Richard Mille collection since 2007, the RM 011 is taking its final bows. Retiring at the height of its glory, it will make way for the new RM 11-03 Automatic Flyback Chronograph.

The RM 11-03 Flyback Chronograph is in every sense a sports watch, proudly displaying the brand's new aesthetic and heavily inspired by automotive history. The guiding principle for Richard Mille was to imbue the new automatic RMAC3 calibre with a three-dimensional quality and to bring its complexity to the fore visually. The glossy, beveled rims marked with intermediate times surrounding the colored counters of the flyback chronograph and seconds window confer depth. This sense of volume is further accentuated by an upper bridge in satin-brushed grade-5 titanium that contrasts with the movement (which is also crafted of titanium, but with a PVD coating). The combination creates a visual itinerary that sweeps around the annual calendar with its oversize date, as well as the 12-hour counter and countdown function of the flyback chronograph.

The maze continues on the back of the caliber with a satin-brushed PVD-treated lower bridge that highlights the double barrel mechanism and modern lines of the brand's new variable-geometry rotor in grade-5 titanium, inspired by the aerodynamic appendages seen in Formula 1 racing. This technical solution, a Richard Mille exclusive, makes it possible to adjust automatic winding of the watch to the wearer's activity level by varying the inertia of the rotor thanks to two microblasted and chamfered wings in 18K white gold. Offering six possible positions, the grade-5, satin-brushed, PVD-treated titanium rotor is mounted on ceramic ball bearings.

Performance is another focus of the watch, thanks to the new RMAC3 automatic caliber. The entire flyback chronograph movement is designed for optimal rigidity, and the grade-5 titanium employed for the baseplate and bridges ensures high-performance functioning of its gear trains. Two barrels, mounted side by side, ensure stable coupling while providing a power reserve of around 55 hours. The 4Hz free-sprung balance is highly resistant to shocks and can be tuned more precisely than a traditional balance wheel.

The brand's designers have also reworked the three-part tonneau case, modernizing its lines and lending it a sportier, more dynamic character while keeping the essence of the watch

The RM 11-03 Flyback Chronograph is in every sense a sports watch, proudly displaying the brand's new aesthetic and heavily inspired by automotive history.

Skilled workmanship and extremely protracted machining times are required to achieve the level of ergonomics and finishing—unique in the world of haute horology—that this case exhibits. Chamfering and buffing the surfaces, which is completed entirely by hand, is a delicate and time-consuming task. This silhouette, which first appeared on the RM 27-01 Rafael Nadal, has become a distinguishing characteristic of all of Richard Mille's sports watches, differentiating them from lifestyle models while reinforcing their structural integrity.

Design details reminiscent of automobile racing abound in the RM 11-03. The grade-5 titanium crown borrows the design of competition wheel rims and tire treads. Also machined in titanium, grooved pushers recall the surface of pedals, and boast covers made of another ubiquitous material in Formula 1: NTPT carbon. As always with Richard Mille, the entire mechanism can be admired through the antireflective coated sapphire crystal that reveals the caliber. The case, available in red gold or titanium, is held together by 20 grade-5 titanium spline screws.

◄ ▲ **RM 11-03**

Formula 1-inspired touches help to modernize and streamline Richard Mille's new version of a legendary flyback chronograph.

GEM SET CARBON TPT™, GOLD CARBON TPT™ & QUARTZ TPT™ FOR RM 037 and RM 07-01

In 2016, Richard Mille introduced the North Thin Ply Technology (company NTPT®) on two of its women's models: the RM 07-01 and the RM 037. To mark this occasion, the brand launched exclusive versions combining quartz or carbon with gold leaf. This new interpretation is still based on the principle of inserting layers of quartz TPT™ or carbon TPT™ at a 45° angle, in this case alternating with dozens of gold leaf layers, none of which are more than 10 microns thick. As gold is a noble material in chemical terms, it was very difficult for the company NTPT® and Richard Mille engineers to ensure it "fused" correctly with carbon and quartz.

This procedure accentuates the specific characteristics of these materials, which in turn enhance the contours of the cases they adorn thanks to the unique play of light they create and their extremely attractive graduation of golden tones. The overall look is enhanced by a satin-brushed 5N red-gold caseband with polished pillars, and a dial set with hundreds of diamonds and a center in either mother-of-pearl or black onyx.

Carbon TPT™ has revealed a feminine side with the RM 07-01 and the RM 037, boasting a gem-set carbon TPT™ of unsurpassed elegance.

▲ **RM 07-01 GOLD & QUARTZ TPT™**

Layering infinitesimal sheets of gold, quartz and carbon was only one challenge presented by the use of NTPT® in this extraordinary model.

▶ **RM 037 GEM SET CARBON TPT™**

Using special machinery to create the settings in an unprecedented material, Richard Mille achieved a perfectly flush surface for 250 diamonds.

At the slightest wrist movement, all eyes are riveted by a striking contrast between the sparkle of clear diamonds and the matte carbon contour that graces both of these automatic timepieces.

Setting gemstones in carbon TPT™ is a new adventure for the brand. Unlike gold, which can be worked directly with tools to create the prongs that will hold the diamonds, the hardness and resistance of carbon TPT™ mean special computer-controlled milling machines, equipped with diamond tools, are required to drill the holes involved in a pavé setting. Hand-polished prongs in red or white gold are produced separately and then inserted around the many 0.25mm bearings destined to firmly contain diamonds—as many as 250 in the case of an RM 037 Set model. The perfectly flush surface of each creation bears witness to an absolute mastery of this art.

A COLLECTION DEDICATED TO JEAN TODT TO CELEBRATE 50 YEARS IN THE FIELD

Fifty years of automotive passion. Fifty years down an exceptional career path. At Chantilly Art & Elegance 2016 the brand celebrated alongside the man who wrote the greatest pages of motor sports history with an amazing Jubilee. In honor of his friend, Richard Mille has now dedicated three models to him, each bearing Jean Todt's name and favorite colors: the RM 11-03, RM 050 and RM 056 Jean Todt 50th Anniversary.

Jean Todt and Richard Mille have forged a strong friendship based on their shared passions: watchmaking, extreme fondness for technology and all things automotive. "I love the watches designed by Richard. I love their lightness, their technicity and their exclusivity," shares Todt.

The two men share a mutual recognition as equally obsessive, detail-oriented and demanding in their respective fields, as is clearly illustrated by the special Jean Todt series.

The RM 11-03 Jean Todt 50th Anniversary is protected by a new blue and white quartz TPT™ case. Extremely resistant and light, this composite is obtained by stacking 600 layers of silica only 45 microns thick, which are then impregnated with an exclusive Richard Mille blue resin. The assembly is then heated to 120°C before being machined in the watch brand's factory.

Blue quartz TPT™ is also used for the case of the RM 050 Jean Todt 50th Anniversary. This caliber houses a split-seconds chronograph regulated by a tourbillon. The extreme skeletonization of the bridges and baseplate, combined with the use of titanium and carbon nanofiber, made it possible to obtain a particularly light movement, weighing only 9.5g but offering startling performance. This exceptional mechanism also animates the final piece of the Jean Todt collection: the RM 056, which is housed in a sapphire case. Its construction and curvature require both human ingenuity and very long machining times, essential to achieving this level of ergonomics and finish, unique even in fine watchmaking. This model required no fewer than 1,000 hours of machining per case, including 430 hours devoted to grinding and 350 hours of polishing.

The 11-03, RM 050 and RM 056 in the Jean Todt collection are produced in limited editions of 150, five and three pieces, respectively.

▲ **RM 056 JEAN TODT 50TH ANNIVERSARY**

With just three models in existence, the exclusivity of the RM 056 Jean Todt is due in part to the extensive time—1,000 hours—devoted to machining its case to perfection.

◀ **RM 11-03 JEAN TODT 50TH ANNIVERSARY**
(facing page left)

Blue and white quartz TPT™ lends this commemorative limited edition watch its striking hue.

◀ **RM 050 JEAN TODT 50TH ANNIVERSARY**
(facing page right)

Using high-tech materials and sophisticated techniques such as skeletonization, Richard Mille created a high-performance movement weighing just 9.5g.

ROGER DUBUIS

HORLOGER GENEVOIS

GROUNDBREAKING LUXURY

Presenting five timepieces that share the manufacture's devotion to imagination and individuality, Roger Dubuis **EXPANDS OUR CONCEPTION OF HOROLOGY USING UNIQUE GEOMETRY, UNLIKELY UNIONS OF MATERIALS AND EXCEPTIONAL MECHANICAL MOVEMENTS**.

The Excalibur Spider Skeleton Flying Tourbillon epitomizes the manufacture's audacious individuality and drive to disrupt the status quo. Rugged masculinity, micro-mechanical intricacy and precious gems find harmonious coexistence within a design full of depth and texture. Housed in a 45mm black-DLC titanium case, and visible through the open-worked dial design, the timepiece's RD505SQ caliber complements its central time display with a flying tourbillon, at 7 o'clock, that appears to orbit weightlessly beneath its iconic carriage. The hand-wound movement, comprised of 179 components, adorns the timepiece with a structural spiderweb element, its firm lines and star-shaped motif flowing through the asymmetrical dial. Roger Dubuis's innovative horological spirit ventures beyond the heartbeat of the watch. The manufacture demonstrates spectacular mastery of unconventional materials by setting blue sapphires, red rubies or black spinels directly into the bezel's rubber molding. The patented feat—which requires a complex technique based on plastic deformation—gives the timepiece a striking layer of contrast and sets off the luxurious sheen of its 60 baguette-cut stones. Worn on a black rubber strap and certified with the exclusive Poinçon de Genève, the Excalibur Spider Skeleton Flying Tourbillon is limited to eight pieces per model.

◂ **EXCALIBUR SPIDER SKELETON FLYING TOURBILLON**

Adorned with a groundbreaking setting of blue sapphires directly into a rubber bezel, this sophisticated timepiece represents a modern age of luxurious masculinity.

The varied heights of functional elements, as well as the combination of shapes and textures, lend the Excalibur Automatic Skeleton Carbon a rich effect of multi-dimensionality.

A showcase for meticulous mechanical craftsmanship coated in a high-tech armor, the Excalibur Automatic Skeleton Carbon takes contemporary haute horology to the next level. Roger Dubuis takes a page from the aerospace industry, housing its 167-component movement in a case composed of carbon-fiber sheet-molding compound (SMC). The ultra-strong, lightweight material, traditionally utilized to increase the fuel efficiency of aircrafts, boldly asserts the timepiece's sporty personality. At 11 o'clock on the skeletonized dial, the owner is treated to a stunning view of the RD820SQ caliber's sophisticated micro-rotor, which sacrifices none of its power despite its reduced dimensions. Joining the oscillating weight, the movement's exquisitely hand-finished components are united visually by the manufacture's iconic star, centered at 5 o'clock. The varied heights of elements, as well as the combination of shapes and textures, lend the watch a rich effect of multi-dimensionality. The Excalibur Automatic Skeleton Carbon indicates the hours and seconds with optimal legibility thanks to two red-tipped hands.

▸ **EXCALIBUR AUTOMATIC SKELETON CARBON**

This 42mm timepiece reveals its movement's high-efficiency micro-rotor through a skeletonized dial and is housed in an innovative carbon-fiber sheet-molding compound case.

▲ **VELVET SECRET HEART**

A luxurious row of diamonds shimmers in the transcendent depth of this feminine wristwatch's blue dial.

Roger Dubuis bears its celebrated design codes into the realm of feminine haute horology with the Velvet Secret Heart. The self-winding timepiece vivaciously contrasts the manufacture's bold white Roman numerals with a bright blue backdrop that catches the eye with its mesmerizing depth of color. On the flange, 64 brilliant-cut diamonds further illuminate the design, playing off the elevation and reflective quality of the two white-gold appliqué numerals at 12 and 6 o'clock. Concealed beneath the dial, the 33-jewel RD821 caliber drives a display of the hours and minutes, matching its mechanical precision with a stunning finish in Côtes de Genève. The Velvet Secret Heart's 36mm white-gold case demonstrates the brand's imaginative vision of watch-making with its unique take on geometry. At 12 and 6 o'clock, in line with the dial's two highlighted numerals, two apertures allow the structure to seemingly lock into the strap, elongating the design and ingeniously accentuating its refined femininity. An ultramarine alligator strap richly echoes the dial's vivid tones.

With the Black Velvet Paraiba, Roger Dubuis sets a tone of rebellious femininity by way of a world-first testament to the manufacture's technical expertise. In a feat never before achieved in haute horology, the self-winding timepiece boasts 66 Paraiba tourmalines set directly into the carbon bezel. The unprecedented combination of materials brilliantly juxtaposes two luxurious forms—sparkling gemstones and high-tech material—into a single harmonious design. The dial poses an equally captivating narrative of balance through surprising contrasts, as 10 white Roman numerals and two white-gold appliqué numerals, at 12 and 6 o'clock, complement the colorful depth and natural motifs of a carbon backdrop. The interplay of tones, materials and textures gives the Black Velvet Paraiba a personality unlike any other: rugged and modern, yet unassailably feminine. Housed in a 36mm carbon case, the 88-piece limited edition derives its power from the RD821 caliber oscillating at a frequency of 28,800 vph.

Intricate marquetry and precious materials come together to give the Blossom Velvet Blue its irresistible character of artful luxury. Framing two graceful hands in the center of an ornate mother-of-pearl dial, 48 diamonds grace the contour of a tonneau-shaped inner barrel within the timepiece's round 36mm white-gold case. As each diamond reflects the rays of incoming light, a magnificently crafted bouquet, composed of sculpted Grand Feu enamel flowers (each set with a central gem of its own), creates a sinuous tableau filled with depth and lively tones. The Blossom Velvet Blue's case ensures a maximum degree of luxurious intensity with an additional 86 diamonds that follow the captivating shape of the bezel and lugs. Driving the timepiece's indicators with an oscillating frequency of 28,800 vph and a power reserve of 48 hours, the 172-component RD821 caliber boasts a delicate finish in Côtes de Genève. Enlivened by enthralling luminous effects and delicately graded shades of color, the self-winding ladies' timepiece brilliantly captures the spirit of its blossoming muses.

▲ **BLACK VELVET PARAIBA**

A tour-de-force in feminine haute horology, the Black Velvet Paraiba showcases a world-premiere setting of precious stones into a carbon bezel.

▶ **BLOSSOM VELVET BLUE**

This ladies' timepiece combines mother-of-pearl, Grand Feu enamel sculpture and 154 sparkling diamonds for a sumptuous floral bouquet.

EXCALIBUR 36 REF. RDDBEX0275

Movement: automatic-winding RD821 caliber; 11 ½ lines, thickness: 3.43 mm; 172 components; 33 jewels; Hallmark of Geneva certified.
Functions: hours, minutes; small seconds at 6.
Case: pink gold; Ø 36mm; bezel set with 48 brilliant-cut diamonds (0.99 carat); water resistant to 3atm.
Dial: silver rhodium-plated satin sunburst; black Roger Dubuis Roman numerals.
Strap: slate gray genuine alligator leather.
Suggested price: $31,900

EXCALIBUR 36 REF. RDDBEX0378

Movement: automatic-winding RD821 caliber; 11 ½ lines, thickness: 3.43mm; 172 components; 33 jewels; Hallmark of Geneva certified.
Functions: hours, minutes; small seconds at 6.
Case: stainless steel; Ø 36mm; bezel set with 48 brilliant-cut diamonds (0.99 carat); water resistant to 3atm.
Dial: blue; white Roger Dubuis Roman numerals.
Strap: ultramarine blue genuine alligator leather.
Suggested price: $20,100

EXCALIBUR 42 REF. RDDBEX0535

Movement: automatic-winding RD830 caliber; thickness: 4.16mm; 183 components; 27 jewels.
Functions: hours, minutes; small seconds and date at 6.
Case: stainless steel; Ø 42mm; water resistant to 3atm.
Dial: blue satin sunburst; white Roger Dubuis Roman numerals.
Strap: storm blue genuine alligator leather.
Suggested price: $12,400

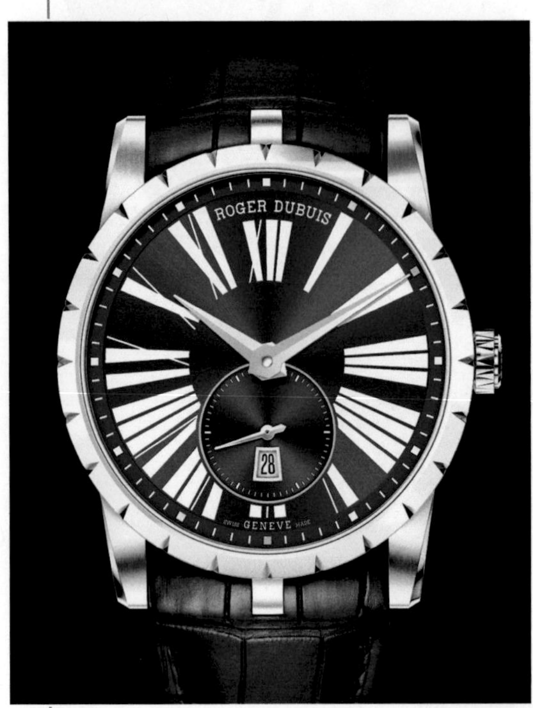

EXCALIBUR 42 REF. RDDBEX0538

Movement: automatic-winding RD830 caliber; thickness: 4.16mm; 183 components; 27 jewels.
Functions: hours, minutes; small seconds and date at 6.
Case: pink gold; Ø 42mm; water resistant to 3atm.
Dial: silver satin sunburst; black Roger Dubuis Roman numerals.
Strap: charcoal black genuine alligator leather.
Suggested price: $24,300

EXCALIBUR 42 — REF. RDDBEX0507

Movement: automatic-winding RD820SQ caliber; 16 lines, thickness: 6.38mm; 167 components; 35 jewels; Hallmark of Geneva certified.
Functions: hours, minutes; tourbillon at 8.
Case: white gold; Ø 42mm; water resistant to 3atm.
Dial: skeletonized charcoal gray flange.
Strap: charcoal black genuine alligator leather.
Suggested price: $74,900

EXCALIBUR 42 — REF. RDDBEX0422

Movement: automatic-winding RD820SQ caliber; Hallmark of Geneva certified.
Functions: hours, minutes.
Case: 18K pink gold; Ø 42mm; Excalibur signature fluted bezel; water resistant to 3atm.
Dial: skeletonized; charcoal gray flange; white minute circle and Roger Dubuis transfers.
Strap: brown alligator leather; pink-gold folding clasp.
Suggested price: $70,600

EXCALIBUR 42 — REF. RDDBEX0473

Movement: automatic-winding RD820SQ caliber; Hallmark of Geneva certified.
Functions: hours, minutes.
Case: black DLC-coated titanium; Ø 42mm; Excalibur signature fluted bezel; water resistant to 3atm.
Dial: skeletonized; Roger Dubuis and minute indexes transferred on the flange.
Strap: black alligator leather; black DLC-coated titanium folding clasp.
Suggested Price: $57,800

EXCALIBUR 42 — REF. RDDBEX0508

Movement: automatic-winding RD820SQ caliber; 16 lines, thickness: 6.38mm; 167 components; 35 jewels; Hallmark of Geneva certified.
Functions: hours, minutes.
Case: carbon; Ø 42mm; water resistant to 3atm.
Dial: skeletonized charcoal gray flange.
Strap: charcoal black genuine alligator leather.
Suggested price: $63,600

EXCALIBUR SPIDER — REF. RDDBEX0572

Movement: manual-winding RD509SQ caliber; 16 lines, thickness: 4.28mm; 60-hour power reserve; 179 components; 19 jewels; 21,600 vph; decoration: plate, bridges and tourbillon upper cage in multi-layered carbon; Hallmark of Geneva certified.
Functions: hours, minutes; small seconds on tourbillon at 7.
Case: carbon; Ø 45mm, thickness: 14.02mm; multi-layered carbon bezel decorated with vulcanized red rubber; water resistant to 5atm.
Dial: skeletonized upper flange in multi-layered carbon; skeletonized hands with SuperLumiNova.

Strap: black rubber with red technical fabric inlay and red stitching.
Suggested price: $190,000
Note: limited edition of 28 pieces.

EXCALIBUR SPIDER — REF. RDDBEX0545

Movement: manual-winding RD505SQ caliber; Hallmark of Geneva certified.
Functions: hours, minutes; small seconds on tourbillon at 7.
Case: titanium; Ø 45mm; water resistant to 5atm.
Dial: skeletonized; racing red ring under skeletonized flange; Roger Dubuis and minute indexes transferred on the ring.
Strap: rubber; titanium folding clasp.
Suggested price: $150,500
Note: limited edition of 88 pieces.

EXCALIBUR 42 — REF. RDDBEX0392

Movement: manual-winding RD505SQ caliber; 16 lines, thickness: 4.28mm; 179 components; 19 jewels; Hallmark of Geneva certified.
Functions: hours, minutes; tourbillon at 7.
Case: pink gold; Ø 42mm; water resistant to 3atm.
Dial: skeletonized black flange.
Strap: chestnut brown genuine alligator leather.
Suggested Price: $159,500

EXCALIBUR 45 — REF. RDDBEX0395

Movement: manual-winding RD01SQ caliber; Hallmark of Geneva certified.
Functions: hours, minutes; double tourbillon at 5 and 7.
Case: 18K pink gold; Ø 45mm; Excalibur signature fluted bezel; water resistant to 5atm.
Dial: skeletonized; charcoal flange; white minute circle and Roger Dubuis transfers; pink-gold indexes.
Strap: brown alligator leather; pink-gold folding clasp.
Suggested price: $307,000

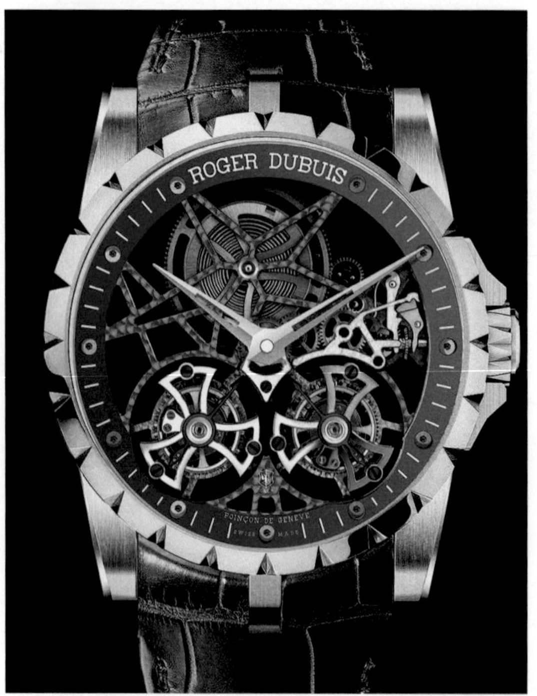

VELVET — REF. RDDBVE0041

Movement: automatic-winding RD821 caliber; 12 ½ lines, thickness: 3.43mm; 172 components; 33 jewels; Hallmark of Geneva certified.
Functions: hours, minutes.
Case: pink gold; Ø 36mm; flange set with 64 brilliant-cut diamonds (approx. 0.24 carat); water resistant to 3atm.
Dial: white; black Roman numerals; pink-gold appliqués at 6 and 12.
Bracelet: pink gold.
Suggested price: $35,300

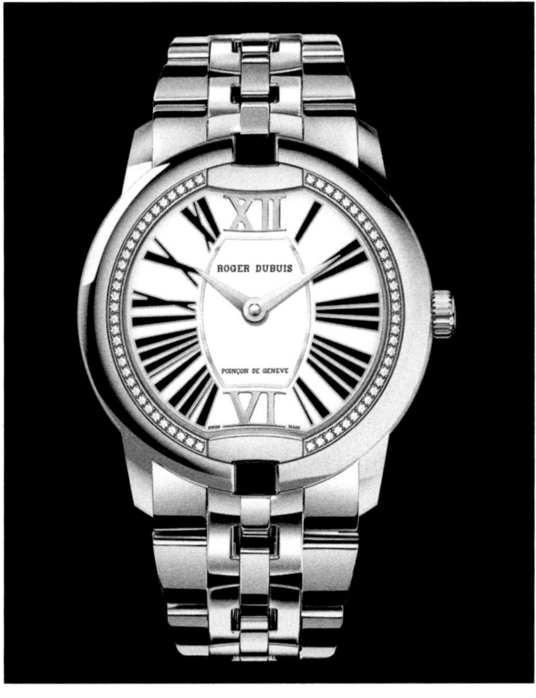

VELVET — REF. RDDBVE0048

Movement: automatic-winding RD821 caliber; 12 ½ lines, thickness: 3.43mm; 172 components; 33 jewels; Hallmark of Geneva certified.
Functions: hours, minutes.
Case: white gold; Ø 36mm; flange set with 64 brilliant-cut diamonds (approx. 0.24 carat); water resistant to 3atm.
Dial: blue; white Roman numerals; white-gold appliqués at 6 and 12.
Strap: ultramarine blue genuine alligator leather.
Suggested price: $20,900

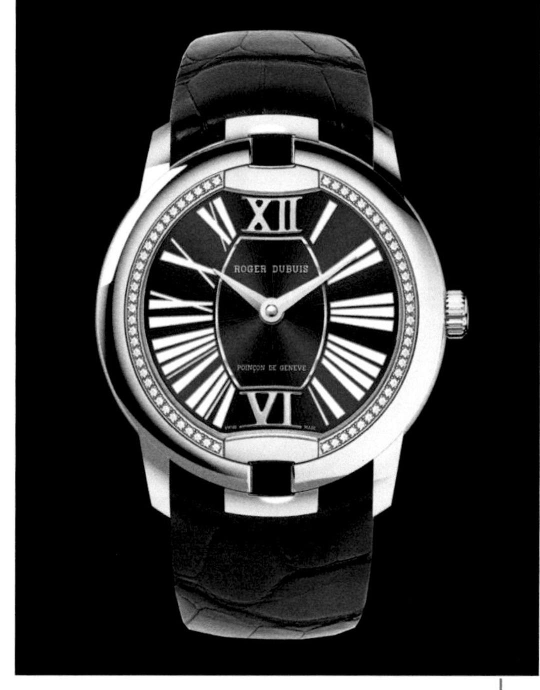

BLACK VELVET — REF. RDDBVE0050

Movement: automatic-winding RD821 caliber; 11 ½ lines, thickness: 3.43mm; 48-hour power reserve; 172 components; 33 jewels; 28,800 vph; decoration: rhodium-plated, Côtes de Genève; Hallmark of Geneva certified.
Functions: hours, minutes.
Case: carbon; Ø 36mm, thickness: 8.77mm; bezel and décor set with 66 black spinels (approx. 1.3 carats); water resistant to 3atm.
Dial: white mother-of-pearl; black Roman numeral transfers; white-gold appliqués at 6 and 12; black Roger Dubuis and Poinçon de Genève transfers.
Strap: black alligator leather; black DLC titanium adjustable folding clasp.
Suggested price: $33,500
Note: limited edition of 88 pieces.

BLOSSOM VELVET — REF. RDDBVE0054

Movement: automatic-winding RD821 caliber; 12 ½ lines, thickness: 3.43mm; 172 components; 33 jewels; Hallmark of Geneva certified.
Functions: hours, minutes.
Case: white gold; Ø 36mm; bezel and lugs set with brilliant-cut diamonds; brilliant-cut diamonds around the barrel; water resistant to 3atm.
Dial: mother-of-pearl; sculpted grand feu enamel flowers; diamonds set at center of flowers.
Strap: blue satin-finish fabric; white-gold adjustable folding buckle set with brilliant-cut diamonds.
Note: limited edition of 88 pieces; set with 154 brilliant-cut diamonds (approx. 1.9 carats).
Suggested price: $80,900

THE EVOLUTION OF PERFECTION

Synonymous with horological excellence, Rolex presents four timepieces that **ENDOW THE BRAND'S SIGNATURE AESTHETIC WITH CALIBERS OF THE HIGHEST PERFORMANCE**.

Inextricably linked to its motor sports pedigree, the Cosmograph Daytona builds on the collection's celebrated tradition of racing-inspired timepieces.

Every turn displays another instance of timekeeping perfection as the wristwatch achieves an immaculate balance of performance and aesthetic refinement. Housed in a 40mm case of 904L stainless steel (a highly resistant super-alloy), the timepiece provides a sheen further accentuated by the innovative material of its bezel. Composed of high-tech monobloc Cerachrom in black ceramic, this element endows the design with a smooth lustrous appeal while boasting a number of extraordinary properties, from its corrosion and scratch resistance to the tenacity of its rich color. A demanding process developed by Rolex allows the molded, platinum PVD-coated graduations and numerals of its tachometric scale to stand out with vibrant clarity. On the dial, contrast and legibility remain of primordial importance. No matter the speed at which the wearer is racing, the Cosmograph Daytona's bold use of contrast ensures an unambiguous display of each timekeeping indication. Joining a central three-hand display of the hours, minutes and chronograph seconds, three subdials, framed in bold black tracks against the dial's white background, indicate the small seconds as well as 30-minute and 12-hour counters of the timepiece's self-winding 4130 caliber. Finished with screw-down chronograph pushers that ensure water resistance to 100m, the new Cosmograph Daytona takes on a magnificent legacy, dating back to 1963, that has set the standard for racing timepieces.

◂ **COSMOGRAPH DAYTONA**

This racing-inspired timepiece complements its high-legibility design with an innovative bezel in high-tech Cerachrom.

A leader in aviation timepieces during the field's golden age, Rolex has long epitomized the values of meaningful sporting timekeeping.

Rolex takes to the skies with a wristwatch with a design that evokes the flawless aesthetics of the brand's aeronautic-inspired creations of the 1930s and '50s. A preeminent leader in aviation timepieces during the field's golden age of the 1930s, Rolex has long epitomized the values of meaningful sporting timekeeping. The new Air-King is no exception. Housed in a robust 40mm case in corrosion-resistant 904L stainless steel, the self-winding wristwatch puts excellent legibility at the forefront of its design—a requirement in the world of high-speed aeronautics. A deep black dial offers the perfect contrast to the Air-King's time indicators. With hands and hour markers in 18-karat white gold and enhanced with Chromalight, as well as a bright green seconds hand, the Air-King provides an unmistakable reading of the time at a single glance. A prominently numbered minutes/seconds scale confirms the timepiece's role as an optimal navigational companion. At the heart of the Air-King, the 3131 caliber ensures reliable performance, even in the harshest of conditions. Equipped with a blue Parachrom hairspring, the movement boasts extraordinary insensitivity to magnetic fields and stability in the face of temperature variations. Finished with a Rolex overcoil and a paramagnetic nickel-phosphorus escape wheel, the 3131 caliber, precise to -2/+2 seconds per day, justifies the Air-King's identity as a timekeeping instrument of the highest order.

▶ **AIR-KING**

A nod to Rolex's ties with aviation's golden age, this three-hand timepiece pairs a state-of-the-art caliber with a dial designed for unparalleled clarity.

With the Oyster Perpetual Pearlmaster 39, Rolex demonstrates a stunning wealth of gem-setting savoir-faire. Equipped with its own gemology laboratory, the Swiss horologer treats every stone with meticulous attention to detail, from selection to precise alignment, as well as finishes. On the dial, 713 sparkling pavé-set diamonds create a radiant sense of texture further accentuated by the contrast of 11 hour markers and three hands in 18-karat pink gold. The luxurious dual-tone interplay extends throughout the watch; the Oyster Perpetual Pearlmaster 39's case, composed of a solid block of 18-karat Everose gold, brings warmth and luster to the design and splendidly complements the 18-karat white-gold bezel's 36 scintillating brilliant-cut diamonds. The harmonious balance envelops the bracelet as well, where 144 brilliant-cut stones, arranged as two elegant rows, bring dazzling light to links in 18-karat Everose gold. For Rolex, luxury is not a mere matter of aesthetics. Driving the timepiece with excellent precision and supreme reliability, the new-generation 3235 caliber complements the hand-guided indications of the hours, minutes and central seconds with a magnified date aperture at 3 o'clock for ideal legibility amidst a sea of diamonds. Fitted with the patented Chronergy escapement, a paramagnetic blue Parachrom hairspring, a traversing balance bridge, a Rolex overcoil, and a large variable-inertia balance wheel, the self-winding 28,800 vph movement triumphantly matches its mechanical prowess to the breathtaking beauty of the timepiece's exterior.

The pinnacle of timeless horological elegance, the Oyster Perpetual Datejust 41 combines the flawless classicism of Rolex's DNA with a caliber of superlative performance. The 41mm timepiece achieves a vibrant aesthetic balance thanks to the brand's signature Rolesor concept, a marriage of materials dear to Rolex since 1933. Highly resistant stainless steel combines with 18-karat yellow gold for a seamless combination of strength and luxury as the case, bezel and bracelet boast alternating tones that invigorate the design without compromising its understated refinement. On a sunray-finished, champagne-colored dial, three 18-karat yellow-gold hands indicate the hours, minutes and seconds. The date, positioned at 3 o'clock in the place of a Chromalight-enriched hour marker, achieves ideal clarity thanks to a Cyclops lens integrated into the watch's sapphire crystal. Housed beneath the golden vivacity of the design, the new-generation 3235 caliber ensures outstanding timekeeping performance thanks to a construction, protected by 14 patents, that optimizes everything from shock- and magnetism resistance to precision, high-energy efficiency and dependability. Endowed with a generous power reserve of 70 hours, the 31-jewel caliber fittingly carries the Superlative Chronometer certification.

◂ OYSTER PERPETUAL PEARLMASTER 39

This self-winding timepiece invigorates its Everose-gold construction with decadent gem settings on the dial, bezel and bracelet.

▸ OYSTER PERPETUAL DATEJUST 41

Driven by the new-generation 3235 caliber, this self-winding timepiece pairs Rolex's unmistakable codes of design with a 14-patent pinnacle of micro-mechanical know-how.

CELLINI TIME — REF. 50505

Movement: automatic-winding Manufacture Rolex caliber; 48-hour power reserve; 31 jewels; 28,800 vph; blue Parachrom hairspring with Rolex overcoil; COSC-certified chronometer.
Functions: hours, minutes, seconds.
Case: 18K Everose gold; Ø 39mm; fluted double bezel; flared screw-down winding crown with Rolex emblem; domed sapphire crystal; domed screw-down caseback; water resistant to 5atm.
Dial: white lacquer; 18K pink-gold hour markers; 18K pink-gold hands.
Strap: brown alligator leather; 18K Everose gold buckle.
Price: available upon request.

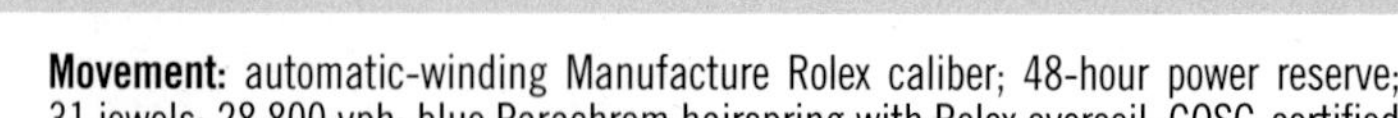

CELLINI DATE — REF. 50519

Movement: automatic-winding Manufacture Rolex caliber; 48-hour power reserve; 31 jewels; 28,800 vph; blue Parachrom hairspring with Rolex overcoil; COSC-certified chronometer.
Functions: hours, minutes, seconds; date at 3.
Case: 18K white gold; Ø 39mm; fluted double bezel; flared screw-down winding crown with Rolex emblem; domed sapphire crystal; domed screw-down caseback; water resistant to 5atm.
Dial: blue guilloché; 18K white-gold hour markers; 18K white-gold hands.
Strap: blue alligator leather; 18K white-gold buckle.
Price: available upon request.

CELLINI DUAL TIME — REF. 50525

Movement: automatic-winding Manufacture Rolex caliber; 48-hour power reserve; 31 jewels; 28,800 vph; blue Parachrom hairspring with Rolex overcoil; COSC-certified chronometer.
Functions: hours, minutes, seconds; second time zone with day/night indicator at 6.
Case: 18K Everose gold; Ø 39mm; fluted double bezel; flared screw-down winding crown with Rolex emblem; domed sapphire crystal; domed screw-down caseback; water resistant to 5atm.
Dial: brown guilloché; 18K pink-gold hour markers; 18K pink-gold hands.

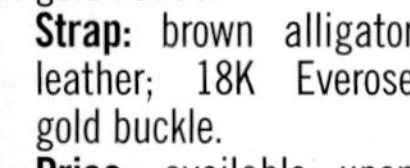

Strap: brown alligator leather; 18K Everose gold buckle.
Price: available upon request.

CELLINI TIME — REF. 50609 RBR

Movement: automatic-winding Manufacture Rolex caliber; approx. 48-hour power reserve; 31 jewels; 28,800 vph; blue Parachrom hairspring with Breguet overcoil; COSC-certified chronometer.
Functions: hours, minutes, seconds.
Case: polished 18K white gold; Ø 39mm; fluted double bezel set with 96 diamonds; flared screw-down winding crown with Rolex emblem; domed sapphire crystal; domed screw-down caseback; water resistant to 5atm.
Dial: black lacquer; 18K white-gold hour markers set with diamonds; 18K white-gold hands.
Strap: semi-matte black alligator leather; 18K white-gold buckle.

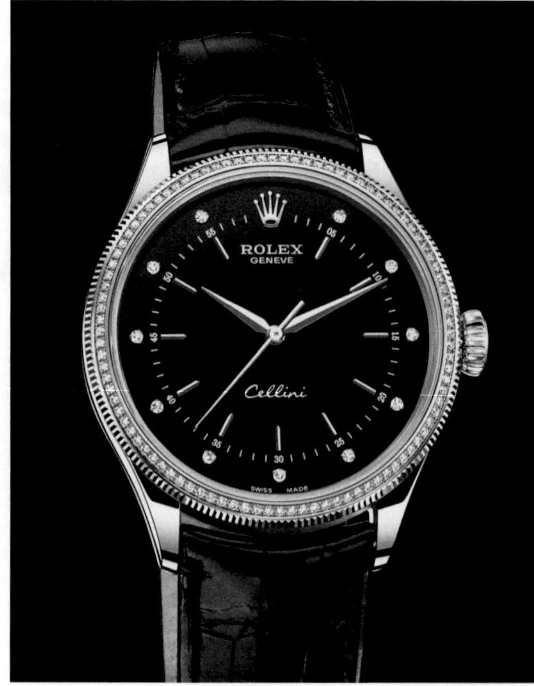

OYSTER PERPETUAL AIR-KING — REF. 116900-71200

Movement: automatic-winding Manufacture Rolex 3131 caliber; 48-hour power reserve; 31 jewels; 28,800 vph; blue Parachrom hairspring with Rolex overcoil; large balance wheel with variable inertia; COSC-certified chronometer.
Functions: hours, minutes, seconds.
Case: 904L steel; Ø 40mm; screw-down winding crown, Twinlock double waterproofness system; scratch-resistant sapphire crystal; screw-down caseback with Rolex fluting; water resistant to 10atm.
Dial: black; 3, 6 and 9 in 18K white gold; white transferred minute numerals; 18K white-gold hands with Chromalight; green seconds hand.
Bracelet: 904L steel; folding Oysterclasp.
Price: available upon request.

OYSTER PERPETUAL COSMOGRAPH DAYTONA — REF. 116500LN-78590

Movement: automatic-winding Manufacture Rolex 4130 caliber; 72-hour power reserve; 44 jewels; 28,800 vph; blue Parachrom hairspring with Rolex overcoil; large balance wheel with variable inertia; COSC-certified chronometer.
Functions: hours, minutes; small seconds at 6; chronograph: central seconds hand, 30-minute counter at 3, 12-hour counter at 9.
Case: 904L steel; Ø 40mm; monobloc Cerachrom in black ceramic bezel; screw-down winding crown, Triplock triple waterproofness system; scratch-resistant sapphire crystal; screw-down caseback with Rolex fluting; water resistant to 10atm.
Dial: white lacquer; black snailed counters; 18K white-gold appliqué hour markers with Chromalight; 18K white-gold hands with Chromalight.
Bracelet: 904L steel; Oysterlock folding safety clasp.
Price: available upon request.

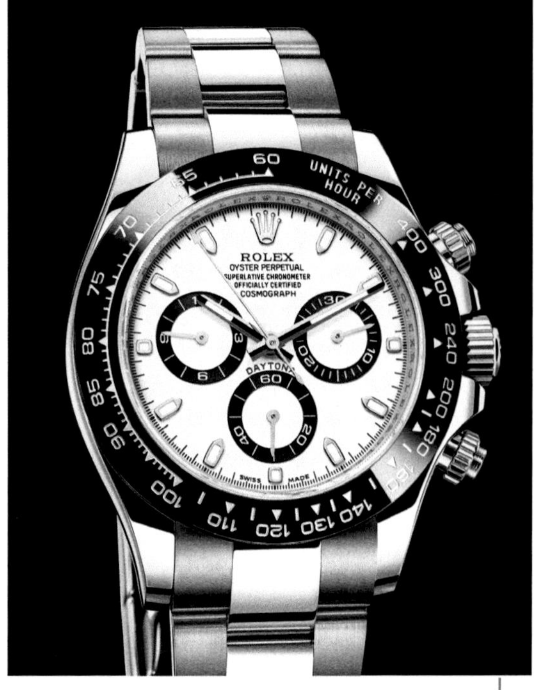

OYSTER PERPETUAL COSMOGRAPH DAYTONA — REF. 116500LN-78590

Movement: automatic-winding Manufacture Rolex 4130 caliber; 72-hour power reserve; 44 jewels; 28,800 vph; blue Parachrom hairspring with Rolex overcoil; large balance wheel with variable inertia; COSC-certified chronometer.
Functions: hours, minutes; small seconds at 6; chronograph: central seconds hand, 30-minute counter at 3, 12-hour counter at 9.
Case: 904L steel; Ø 40mm; monobloc Cerachrom in black ceramic bezel; screw-down winding crown, Triplock triple waterproofness system; scratch-resistant sapphire crystal; screw-down caseback with Rolex fluting; water resistant to 10atm.
Dial: black lacquer; gray snailed counters; 18K white-gold appliqué hour markers with Chromalight; 18K white-gold hands with Chromalight.
Bracelet: 904L steel; Oysterlock folding safety clasp.
Price: available upon request.

OYSTER PERPETUAL DATEJUST 41 — REF. 126333-62613

Movement: automatic-winding Manufacture Rolex 3235 caliber; 70-hour power reserve; 31 jewels; 28,800 vph; blue Parachrom hairspring with Rolex overcoil; large balance wheel with variable inertia; COSC-certified chronometer.
Functions: hours, minutes, seconds; date at 3.
Case: 904L steel and 18K yellow gold; Ø 41mm; fluted bezel; screw-down winding crown, Twinlock double waterproofness system; scratch-resistant sapphire crystal; screw-down caseback with Rolex fluting; water resistant to 10atm.
Dial: champagne; 18K yellow-gold appliqué hour markers with Chromalight; 18K yellow-gold hands with Chromalight.
Bracelet: 904L steel and 18K yellow gold; Oysterclasp folding clasp.
Price: available upon request.

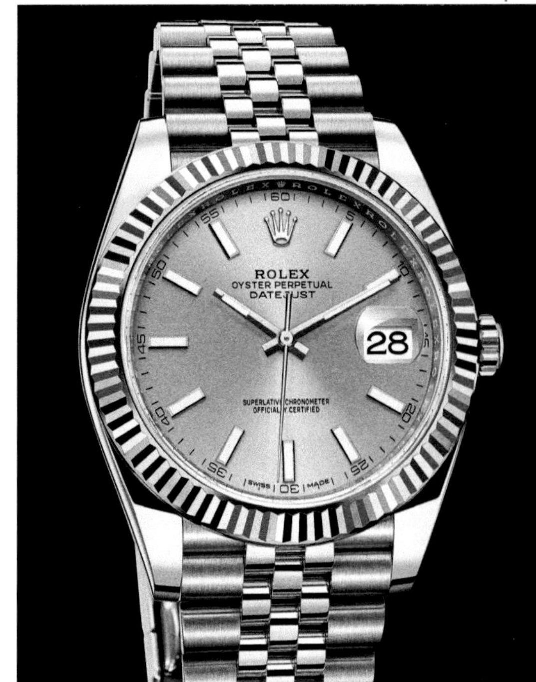

OYSTER PERPETUAL DATEJUST 41 — REF. 126301-72611

Movement: automatic-winding Manufacture Rolex 3235 caliber; 70-hour power reserve; 31 jewels; 28,800 vph; blue Parachrom hairspring with Rolex overcoil; large balance wheel with variable inertia; COSC-certified chronometer.
Functions: hours, minutes, seconds; date at 3.
Case: 904L steel and 18K Everose gold; Ø 41mm; screw-down winding crown, Twinlock double waterproofness system; scratch-resistant sapphire crystal; screw-down caseback with Rolex fluting; water resistant to 10atm.
Dial: sundust; 18K pink-gold hour markers set with diamonds; 18K pink-gold hands.

Bracelet: 904L steel and 18K Everose gold; Oysterclasp folding clasp.
Price: available upon request.

OYSTER PERPETUAL EXPLORER — REF. 214270-77200

Movement: automatic-winding Manufacture Rolex 3132 caliber; 48-hour power reserve; 31 jewels; 28,800 vph; blue Parachrom hairspring with Rolex overcoil; large balance wheel with variable inertia; COSC-certified chronometer.
Functions: hours, minutes, seconds.
Case: 904L steel; Ø 39mm; screw-down winding crown, Twinlock double waterproofness system; scratch-resistant sapphire crystal; screw-down caseback with Rolex fluting; water resistant to 10atm.
Dial: black; 3, 6 and 9 in 18K white gold; 18K white-gold appliqués; 18K white-gold hands with Chromalight.

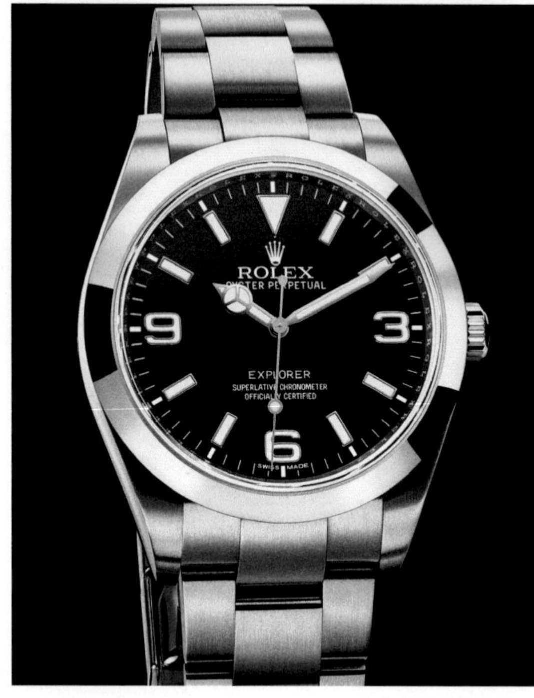

Bracelet: 904L steel; Oysterlock folding clasp.
Price: available upon request.

OYSTER PERPETUAL YACHT-MASTER 40 — REF. 116621-78801

Movement: automatic-winding Manufacture Rolex 3135 caliber; 48-hour power reserve; 31 jewels; 28,800 vph; blue Parachrom hairspring with Rolex overcoil; large balance wheel with variable inertia; COSC-certified chronometer.
Functions: hours, minutes, seconds; date at 3.
Case: 904L steel and 18K Everose gold; Ø 40mm; 18K Everose gold bidirectional rotating bezel; screw-down winding crown, Triplock triple waterproofness system; scratch-resistant sapphire crystal; screw-down caseback with Rolex fluting; water resistant to 10atm.
Dial: chocolate; 18K pink-gold hour markers with Chromallight; 18K pink-gold hands with Chromalight.
Bracelet: 904L steel and 18K Everose gold; Oysterlock folding clasp.
Price: available upon request.

OYSTER PERPETUAL PEARLMASTER 39 — REF. 86286-42745

Movement: automatic-winding Manufacture Rolex 3235 caliber; 70-hour power reserve; 31 jewels; 28,800 vph; blue Parachrom hairspring with Rolex overcoil; large balance wheel with variable inertia; COSC-certified chronometer.
Functions: hours, minutes, seconds; date at 3.
Case: 18K Everose gold; Ø 39mm; 18K white-gold bezel set with 36 brilliant-cut diamonds; screw-down winding crown, Twinlock double waterproofness system; scratch-resistant sapphire crystal; screw-down caseback with Rolex fluting; water resistant to 10atm.
Dial: aubergine; 18K pink-gold hour markers set with 8 diamonds; 6 and 9 in 18K pink gold set with 16 diamonds; 18K pink-gold hands.

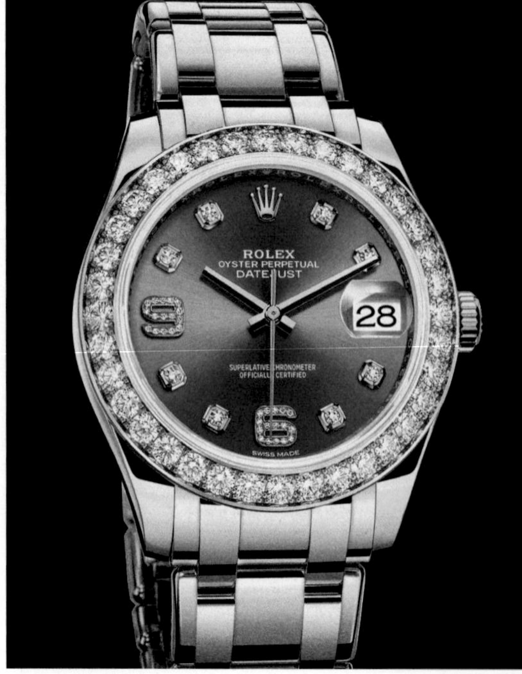

Bracelet: 18K Everose gold; Crownclasp folding clasp.
Price: available upon request.

OYSTER PERPETUAL PEARLMASTER 39 REF. 86286-44745

Movement: automatic-winding Manufacture Rolex 3235 caliber; 70-hour power reserve; 31 jewels; 28,800 vph; blue Parachrom hairspring with Rolex overcoil; large balance wheel with variable inertia; COSC-certified chronometer.
Functions: hours, minutes, seconds; date at 3.
Case: 18K Everose gold; Ø 39mm; 18K white-gold bezel set with 36 brilliant-cut diamonds; screw-down winding crown, Twinlock double waterproofness system; scratch-resistant sapphire crystal; screw-down caseback with Rolex fluting; water resistant to 10atm.
Dial: 18K pink gold; paved with 713 diamonds; 18K pink-gold Roman numerals; 18K pink-gold hands.
Bracelet: center and outer links in 18K Everose gold; intermediate links in 18K white gold set with 144 brilliant-cut diamonds; Crownclasp folding clasp.
Price: available upon request.

OYSTER PERPETUAL LADY-DATEJUST 28 REF. 279381RBR-63341

Movement: automatic-winding Manufacture Rolex 2236 caliber; 55-hour power reserve; 31 jewels; 28,800 vph; silicon Syloxi hairspring with patented geometry; balance wheel with variable inertia; COSC-certified chronometer.
Functions: hours, minutes, seconds; date at 3.
Case: 904L steel and 18K Everose gold; Ø 28mm; bezel set with 46 brilliant-cut diamonds; screw-down winding crown, Twinlock double waterproofness system; scratch-resistant sapphire crystal; screw-down caseback with Rolex fluting; water resistant to 10atm.
Dial: white mother-of-pearl; 18K pink-gold hour markers set with 10 diamonds; 18K pink-gold hands.
Bracelet: 904L steel and 18K Everose gold; Crownclasp folding clasp.
Price: available upon request.

OYSTER PERPETUAL LADY-DATEJUST 28 REF. 279173-72343

Movement: automatic-winding Manufacture Rolex 2236 caliber; 55-hour power reserve; 31 jewels; 28,800 vph; silicon Syloxi hairspring with patented geometry; balance wheel with variable inertia; COSC-certified chronometer.
Functions: hours, minutes, seconds; date at 3.
Case: 904L steel and 18K yellow gold; Ø 28mm; fluted bezel; screw-down winding crown, Twinlock double waterproofness system; scratch-resistant sapphire crystal; screw-down caseback with Rolex fluting; water resistant to 10atm.
Dial: champagne; 18K yellow-gold Roman numerals; 18K yellow-gold hands.
Bracelet: 904L steel and 18K yellow gold; Oysterclasp folding clasp.
Price: available upon request.

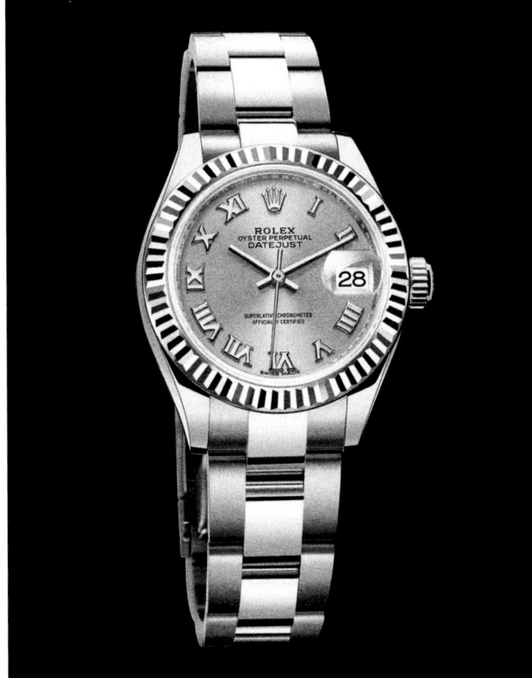

OYSTER PERPETUAL LADY-DATEJUST 28 REF. 279135 RBR-83345

Movement: automatic-winding Manufacture Rolex 2236 caliber; approx. 55-hour power reserve; 31 jewels; 28,800 vph; Syloxi hairspring in silicon with patented geometry; balance wheel with variable inertia; COSC-certified chronometer.
Functions: hours, minutes, seconds; date at 3; stop seconds for precise time setting.
Case: polished 18K Everose gold; Ø 28mm; bezel set with 44 brilliant-cut diamonds; screw-down winding crown, Twinlock double waterproofness system; scratch-resistant sapphire crystal; screw-down caseback with Rolex fluting; water resistant to 10atm.
Dial: chocolate sunray finish; hour markers: 9 diamonds in 18K pink-gold "star" settings, 18K pink-gold IX set with 8 diamonds; 18K pink-gold hands.
Bracelet: 18K Everose gold; three-piece solid links; polished center links and satin-finished outer links with polished edges; concealed folding Crownclasp.
Also available: 950 platinum case, silver dial, 950 platinum bracelet (ref. 279166-83346); 18K yellow-gold case, silver dial, 18K yellow-gold bracelet (ref. 279178-63348).

OYSTER PERPETUAL 39 — REF. 114300-70400

Movement: automatic-winding Manufacture Rolex 3132 caliber; approx. 48-hour power reserve; 31 jewels; 28,800 vph; paramagnetic blue Parachrom hairspring with Breguet overcoil; large balance wheel with variable inertia; COSC-certified chronometer.
Functions: hours, minutes, seconds; stop seconds for precise time setting.
Case: satin-finished 904L steel; Ø 39mm; domed bezel; screw-down winding crown, Twinlock double waterproofness system; scratch-resistant sapphire crystal; screw-down caseback with Rolex fluting; water resistant to 10atm.
Dial: dark rhodium sunray finish; hour markers: 18K white-gold baton appliqués, 18K white-gold appliqués with phosphorescent material at 3, 6 and 9; blue hour transfers; 18K white-gold hands with phosphorescent material.
Bracelet: satin-finished 904L steel with polished edges; folding Oysterclasp.

OYSTER PERPETUAL 34 — REF. 114200-70190

Movement: automatic-winding Manufacture Rolex 3130 caliber; approx. 48-hour power reserve; 31 jewels; 28,800 vph; paramagnetic blue Parachrom hairspring with Breguet overcoil; large balance wheel with variable inertia; COSC-certified chronometer.
Functions: hours, minutes, seconds; stop seconds for precise time setting.
Case: satin-finished 904L steel; Ø 34mm; domed bezel; screw-down winding crown, Twinlock double waterproofness system; scratch-resistant sapphire crystal; screw-down caseback with Rolex fluting; water resistant to 10atm.
Dial: champagne sunray finish; 18K white-gold appliqué hour markers with phosphorescent material; 18K white-gold hands with phosphorescent material.
Bracelet: satin-finished 904L steel with polished edges; folding Oysterclasp.

OYSTER PERPETUAL 31 — REF. 177200-70160

Movement: automatic-winding Manufacture Rolex 2231 caliber; approx. 48-hour power reserve; 31 jewels; 28,800 vph; hairspring with Breguet overcoil; balance wheel with variable inertia; COSC-certified chronometer.
Functions: hours, minutes, seconds; stop seconds for precise time setting.
Case: satin-finished 904L steel; Ø 31mm; domed bezel; screw-down winding crown, Twinlock double waterproofness system; scratch-resistant sapphire crystal; screw-down caseback with Rolex fluting; water resistant to 10atm.
Dial: red grape sunray finish; III, IV and IX in 18K white gold; pink Roman numeral hour ring; 18K white-gold hands.
Bracelet: satin-finished 904L steel with polished edges; folding Oysterclasp.

OYSTER PERPETUAL 26 — REF. 176200-70130

Movement: automatic-winding Manufacture Rolex 2231 caliber; approx. 48-hour power reserve; 31 jewels; 28,800 vph; hairspring with Breguet overcoil; balance wheel with variable inertia; COSC-certified chronometer.
Functions: hours, minutes, seconds; stop seconds for precise time setting.
Case: satin-finished 904L steel; Ø 26mm; domed bezel; screw-down winding crown, Twinlock double waterproofness system; scratch-resistant sapphire crystal; screw-down caseback with Rolex fluting; water resistant to 10atm.
Dial: olive green sunray finish; 18K white-gold appliqué hour markers with phosphorescent material; 18K white-gold hands with phosphorescent material.
Bracelet: satin-finished 904L steel with polished edges; folding Oysterclasp.

OYSTER PERPETUAL DATEJUST PEARLMASTER 39 REF. 86348 SABLV-42748

Movement: automatic-winding Manufacture Rolex 3235 caliber; approx. 70-hour power reserve; 31 jewels; 28,800 vph; paramagnetic blue Parachrom hairspring with Breguet overcoil; large balance wheel with variable inertia; COSC-certified chronometer.
Functions: hours, minutes, seconds; date at 3; stop seconds for precise time setting.
Case: polished-finish 18K yellow gold; Ø 39mm; bezel set with a blue to green gradient of 48 baguette-cut sapphires; screw-down winding crown, Twinlock double waterproofness system; scratch-resistant sapphire crystal; screw-down caseback with Rolex fluting; water resistant to 10atm.
Dial: olive green sunray finish; hour markers: 8 diamonds in 18K yellow-gold settings, 6 and 9 in 18K yellow gold each set with 16 diamonds; 18K yellow-gold hands.
Bracelet: polished-finish 18K yellow gold; concealed folding Crownclasp.
Also available: bezel set with an orange to yellow gradient of 48 baguette-cut sapphires, cognac sunray finish dial (ref. 86348 SAJOR-42748); 18K white-gold case, bezel set with a blue to fuchsia gradient of 48 baguette-cut sapphires, red grape sunray finish dial, 18K white-gold bracelet (ref. 86349 SAFUBL-42749).

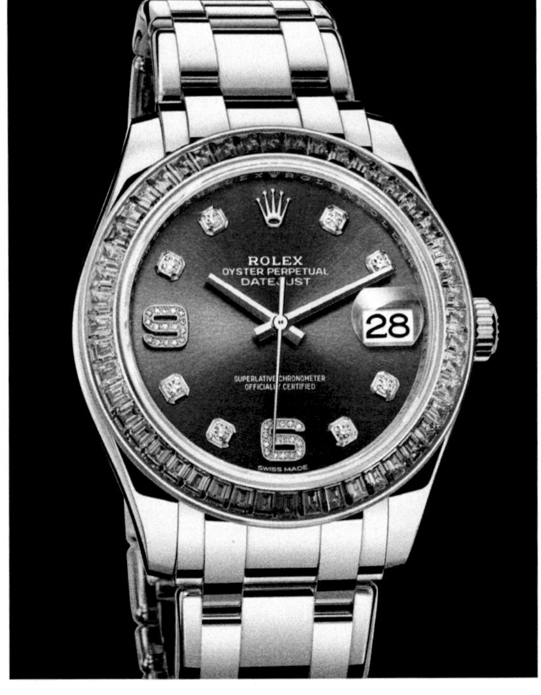

OYSTER PERPETUAL DATEJUST PEARLMASTER 34 REF. 81348 SARO-72848

Movement: automatic-winding Manufacture Rolex 2236 caliber; 55-hour power reserve; 31 jewels; 28,800 vph; Syloxi hairspring in silicon with patented geometry; balance wheel with variable inertia; high-precision regulating via two gold Microstella nuts; traversing balance bridge; high-performance Paraflex shock absorbers; COSC-certified chronometer.
Functions: hours, minutes, seconds; date at 3; stop seconds for precise time setting.
Case: 18K yellow gold, polished finish; Ø 34mm; bezel set with 12 baguette-cut pink sapphires and 24 baguette-cut light pink sapphires; screw-down winding crown, Twinlock double waterproofness system; screw-down caseback with Rolex fluting; scratch-resistant sapphire crystal; water resistant to 10atm.
Dial: 18K yellow-gold pavé with 455 diamonds; 18K yellow-gold Roman numeral hour marker appliqués; 18K yellow-gold hands.
Bracelet: 18K yellow gold, polished finish; concealed folding Crownclasp.

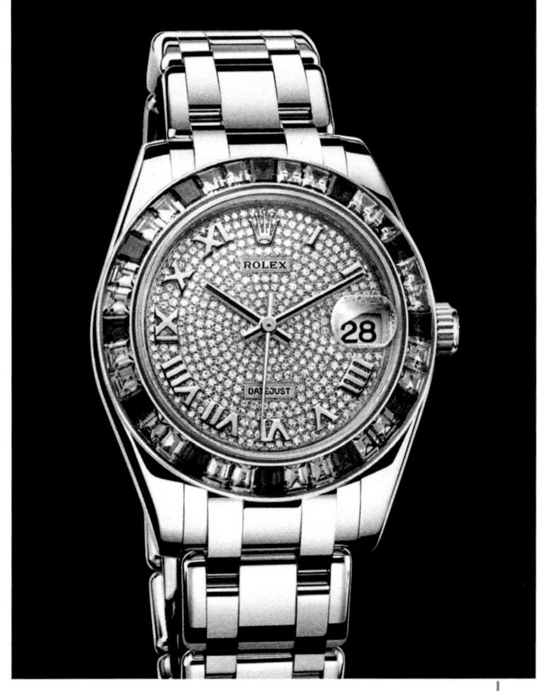

OYSTER PERPETUAL GMT-MASTER II REF. 116719 BLRO-78209

Movement: automatic-winding Manufacture Rolex 3186 caliber; 48-hour power reserve; 31 jewels; 28,800 vph; paramagnetic blue Parachrom hairspring with Breguet overcoil; large balance wheel with variable inertia; high-precision regulating via four gold Microstella nuts; traversing balance bridge; COSC-certified chronometer.
Functions: hours, minutes, seconds; date at 3; GMT: 24-hour display via additional hand, second time zone via independent rapid setting of hour hand; stop seconds for precise time setting.
Case: 18K white gold, satin and polished finish; Ø 40mm; bidirectional rotating 24-hour graduated bezel with two-color Cerachrom insert in red and blue ceramic, engraved numerals and graduations coated with platinum via magnetron sputtering (PVD); screw-down winding crown, Triplock triple waterproofness system; screw-down caseback with Rolex fluting; scratch-resistant sapphire crystal; water resistant to 10atm.
Dial: black lacquer; highly legible Chromalight hour marker appliqués in 18K white gold; 18K white-gold Chromalight hands; red 24-hour hand.
Bracelet: 18K white gold; polished center links and satin-finished outer links with polished edges; Oysterlock folding safety clasp.

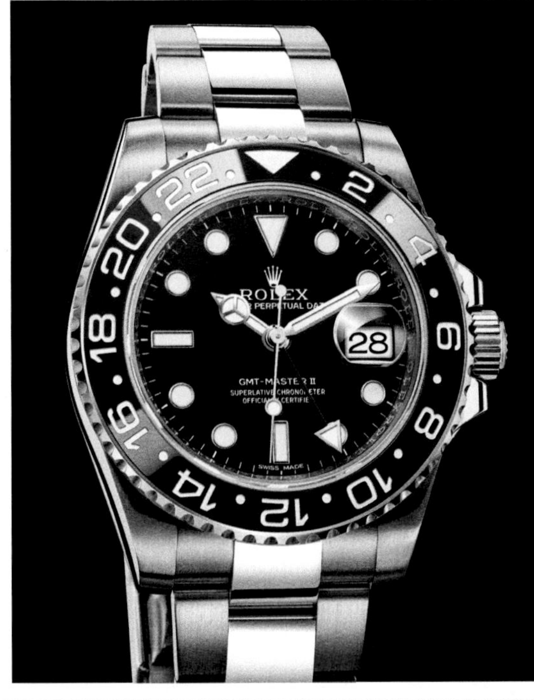

MILGAUSS REF. 116400 GV-72400

Movement: automatic-winding Manufacture Rolex 3131 caliber; 48-hour power reserve; 31 jewels; 28,800 vph; paramagnetic blue Parachrom hairspring with Breguet overcoil; large balance wheel with variable inertia; Paramagnetic nickel-phosphorus escape wheel; high-precision regulating via four gold Microstella nuts; traversing balance bridge; COSC-certified chronometer.
Functions: hours, minutes, seconds; stop seconds for precise time setting.
Case: 904L stainless steel superalloy, polished finish; Ø 40mm; smooth bezel; screw-down winding crown, Twinlock double waterproofness system; scratch-resistant green sapphire crystal; water resistant to 10atm.
Dial: Z blue; highly legible Chromalight hour marker appliqués in 18K white gold; 18K white-gold Chromalight hands; orange lightning-bolt-shaped seconds hand.
Bracelet: 904L stainless steel superalloy; polished center links; satin-finished outer links with polished edges; folding Oysterclasp.

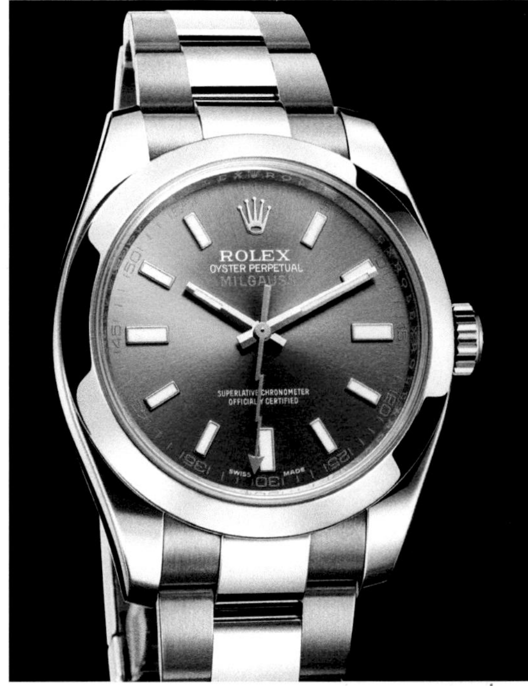

TAG Heuer

SWISS AVANT-GARDE SINCE 1860

A SPORTING PEDIGREE

TAG Heuer **CONTINUES ITS BRILLIANT SPORTING LEGACY** with four timepieces that find elegance in the purposeful nature of their compositions.

The Swiss watchmaker injects one of its most iconic timepieces with a jolt of power. A timepiece fit for the world's most challenging conditions, the Aquaracer 300M has now grown to 43mm, accentuating its robust personality. The watch's sporting elegance, however, remains intact, founded firmly in the Aquaracer 300M's uncompromising functionality. Housed in a satin-finished steel case, the timepiece boasts a restyled black ceramic bezel whose engraved silver-lacquer numerals reaffirm the design's rugged masculinity. Unidirectional in rotation and endowed with twelve sides for an optimal grip, the bezel reaches its fullest potential when in the heart of the action, ensuring the protection of the diver while submerged under water.

The dial combines extreme functionality and flawless understatement. Against a rich black backdrop, 12 hour markers and three hands achieve optimal legibility thanks to their generous luminescent coating. At 3 o'clock, a date aperture follows the theme with the help of an ingenious magnifying window. An authentic diver's watch first and foremost, the Aquaracer 300M boasts an extraordinary water resistance to 300 meters beneath the surface—a fitting achievement, given that the first-ever patent for a watertight case was filed by Edouard Heuer in 1852.

TAG Heuer complements the alluring dark tone of the Aquaracer Lady 300M's main structure with the luxurious warmth of 18-karat rose gold on the hands, indexes and bezel.

The Aquaracer Lady 300M utilizes a superb material to adorn the wearer with a timepiece as visually stunning as it is practical. Housed in a black ceramic case and worn on a black ceramic bracelet, the 35mm timepiece finds exceptional beauty in a material primarily sought after for its remarkable physical properties. From its extreme hardness, scratch resistance and light weight to its hypoallergenic qualities and ability to preserve the purity of its color, ceramic is ideal for a wristwatch meant for active use. TAG Heuer complements the alluring dark tone of the timepiece's main structure with the luxurious warmth of 18-karat rose gold on the hands, indexes and black-PVD unidirectional bezel. The precious metal's rich tones deepen the impact of the black ceramic by providing a bold yet harmonious contrast. Water resistant to 300m and finished with a date window at 3 o'clock, the Aquaracer Lady 300M embraces the power of femininity, with a watch that finds grace and refinement in its strength and sporting determination.

▸ **AQUARACER LADY 300M**

By combining the rich black hue of its ceramic case and bracelet with the luxurious warmth of a pink-gold bezel, this feminine wristwatch creates beauty through the excellence of its construction.

◂ **AQUARACER 300M**

This resolute diver's timepiece complements its rugged construction with a black ceramic bezel perfectly suited for the high stakes of deep-sea exploration.

By revealing the technical sophistication of its caliber through a riveting skeletonized architecture, the Carrera Heuer 01 achieves a brilliant sense of mechanical dynamism. Housed in a 45mm modular steel case with alternating finishes, the self-winding timepiece captivates with a vibrant exhibition of the HEUER-01 caliber's distinguished inner workings. Atop an openworked display of the column-wheel chronograph's construction, the timepiece asserts its high-tech personality with a trio of skeletonized subdials that indicate the small seconds as well as the stopwatch's 30-minute and 12-hour counters. To ensure maximum legibility, all three of the timepiece's chronograph hands stand out from the rest of the design thanks to a sharp blue hue that perfectly opposes the tones of the mechanical display as well as those of the luminously enhanced accents of the hour and minute hands. From its piston-like pushers at 2 and 4 o'clock to a tachometric scale on its black ceramic bezel, the Carrera Heuer 01 confirms its resolute sporting personality at every turn, including a perforated blue rubber strap that immediately evokes the spirit of high-speed racing.

◄ **CARRERA HEUER 01**

This self-winding timepiece reveals the intricacies of its sophisticated column-wheel-chronograph caliber through a skeletonized dial architecture.

TAG Heuer returns to its historic roots, honoring a groundbreaking 1969 creation with a reinterpreted vision. Housed in a square case like its celebrated predecessor, the first square-shaped water resistant automatic chronograph in Swiss watchmaking history, the Monaco Calibre 11 pays particular homage to its racing heritage with a daring combination of colors evocative of vintage motorsports. On a metallic blue dial graced by a number of red and white accents, the 39 x 39mm timepiece complements its display of the hours, minutes and central chronograph seconds with a date aperture and subdials for the small seconds and 30-minute counter. At the heart of the timepiece, the Calibre 11, equipped with a Dubois Dépraz chronograph module, boasts a 40-hour power reserve. Finished with a crown at 9 o'clock to honor the design codes of its 1969 ancestor, the Monaco Calibre 11 grants its wearer a brilliant view of the movement's gears through a transparent sapphire crystal on the watch's caseback.

▸ MONACO CALIBRE 11

A revival of an iconic 1969 timepiece, the Monaco Calibre 11 exemplifies the racing spirit of the brand with a design profoundly imbued with a motoring persona.

MONACO CALIBRE 11 CHRONOGRAPH — REF. CAW211P.FC6356

Movement: automatic-winding TAG Heuer Calibre 11.
Functions: hours, minutes; small seconds at 3; date at 6; chronograph: central seconds hand, 30-minute counter at 9.
Case: polished and fine-brushed steel; Ø 39mm; sapphire crystal; sapphire crystal caseback; water resistant to 10atm.
Dial: matte blue; faceted polished hour and minute hands with luminescent coating; faceted hour markers with luminescent tips; red central chronograph hand; "MONACO" – "AUTOMATIC CHRONOGRAPH" – "CALIBRE 11" lettering; printed vintage TAG Heuer logo.
Strap: black perforated calfskin; steel deployant buckle.
Price: available upon request.

CARRERA CHRONOGRAPH CALIBRE HEUER 01 — REF. CAR201Z.FT6046

Movement: automatic-winding TAG Heuer Calibre Heuer 01.
Functions: hours, minutes; small seconds at 9; date at 3; chronograph: central seconds hand, 30-minute counter at 12, 12-hour counter at 6.
Case: fine-brushed steel; Ø 43mm; fine-brushed ceramic bezel; sapphire crystal and fine-brushed steel caseback; water resistant to 10atm.
Dial: black; polished, satin-brushed and hand-applied indexes with white luminescent coating; polished and sanded hour and minute hands with luminescent coating; polished chronograph and small seconds hands with red tip; "CARRERA HEUER 01" and "AUTOMATIC CHRONOGRAPH" lettering; hand-applied TAG Heuer logo.
Strap: black perforated rubber; titanium deployant buckle.
Price: available upon request.

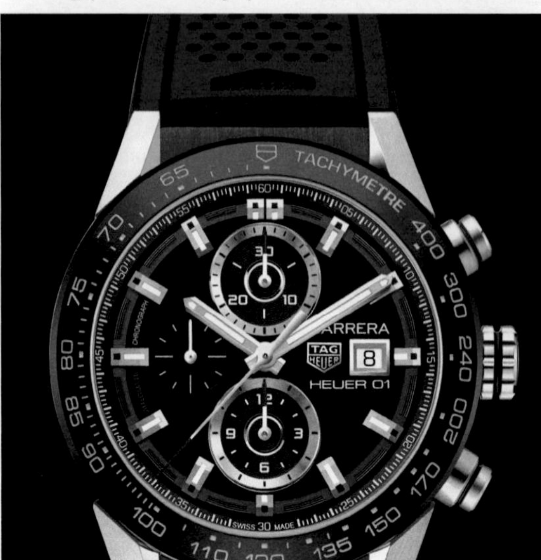

CARRERA CHRONOGRAPH CALIBRE HEUER 01 — REF. CAR2A1Z.FT6044

Movement: automatic-winding TAG Heuer Calibre Heuer 01.
Functions: hours, minutes; small seconds at 9; date between 3 and 4; chronograph: central seconds hand, 30-minute counter at 12, 12-hour counter at 6.
Case: steel; Ø 45mm; black ceramic bezel; antireflective sapphire crystal; sapphire crystal and fine-brushed steel caseback; water resistant to 10atm.
Dial: skeletonized; polished and sanded hour and minute hands with luminescent coating; red chronograph and small seconds hands; "CARRERA HEUER 01" and "CHRONOGRAPH" lettering in white; "AUTOMATIC" lettering in red; hand-applied TAG Heuer logo.
Strap: black perforated rubber; steel deployant buckle.
Price: available upon request.

CARRERA CHRONOGRAPH CALIBRE HEUER 01 — REF. CAR2A5A.FT6044

Movement: automatic-winding TAG Heuer Calibre Heuer 01.
Functions: hours, minutes; small seconds at 9; date between 3 and 4; chronograph: central seconds hand, 30-minute counter at 12, 12-hour counter at 6.
Case: titanium and 18K 5N rose gold; Ø 45mm; black ceramic bezel; antireflective sapphire crystal; sapphire crystal and titanium caseback; water resistant to 10atm.
Dial: black; 18K 5N rose-gold-plated indexes with black luminescent coating; 18K 5N rose-gold-plated hour and minute hands with black luminescent coating; 18K 5N rose-gold-plated small seconds and chronograph hands with red tips; "CARRERA HEUER 01" – "CHRONOGRAPH" – "AUTOMATIC" lettering; 18K 5N rose-gold-plated hand-applied TAG Heuer logo.
Strap: black perforated rubber; black titanium deployant buckle.
Price: available upon request.

CARRERA CHRONOGRAPH CALIBRE HEUER 01 — REF. CAR2A90.FT6071

Movement: automatic-winding TAG Heuer Calibre Heuer 01.
Functions: hours, minutes; small seconds at 9; date between 3 and 4; chronograph: central seconds hand, 30-minute counter at 12, 12-hour counter at 6.
Case: black ceramic; Ø 45mm; black titanium crown; antireflective sapphire crystal; sapphire crystal caseback; water resistant to 10atm.
Dial: skeletonized black ceramic; polished, fine-brushed and hand-applied indexes with black luminescent coating; black polished and sanded hour and minute hands with black luminescent coating; "CARRERA HEUER 01" – "CHRONOGRAPH" – "AUTOMATIC" gray lettering; hand-applied TAG Heuer logo.
Strap: black perforated rubber; black titanium deployant buckle.
Price: available upon request.

CARRERA CALIBRE 16 CHRONOGRAPH — REF. CV2A1R.BA0799

Movement: automatic-winding TAG Heuer Calibre 16.
Functions: hours, minutes; small seconds at 9; day and date at 3; chronograph: central seconds hand, 30-minute counter at 12, 12-hour counter at 6.
Case: polished steel; Ø 43mm; polished steel bezel with a ceramic band; antireflective sapphire crystal; sapphire crystal caseback; water resistant to 10atm.
Dial: black opaline; hand-applied Arabic numerals; polished, fine-brushed and faceted hour and minute hands with luminescent coating; "CALIBRE 16 – CARRERA" lettering; hand-applied TAG Heuer logo.
Bracelet: steel; steel deployant buckle.
Price: available upon request.
Also available: black alligator leather strap.

CARRERA CALIBRE 16 CHRONOGRAPH — REF. CV201AK.FT6040

Movement: automatic-winding TAG Heuer Calibre 16.
Functions: hours, minutes; small seconds at 9; date at 3; chronograph: central seconds hand, 30-minute counter at 12, 12-hour counter at 6.
Case: polished steel; Ø 41mm; sapphire crystal; caseback adorned with FANGIO decoration and "Juan Manuel Fangio" inscription; water resistant to 10atm.
Dial: black opaline; polished, faceted and hand-applied indexes; polished, fine-brushed and faceted hour and minute hands with luminescent coating; red chronograph and small seconds hands; "CALIBRE 16 – CARRERA" lettering; printed TAG Heuer logo.
Strap: black rubber; steel deployant buckle.
Price: available upon request.
Also available: steel bracelet.

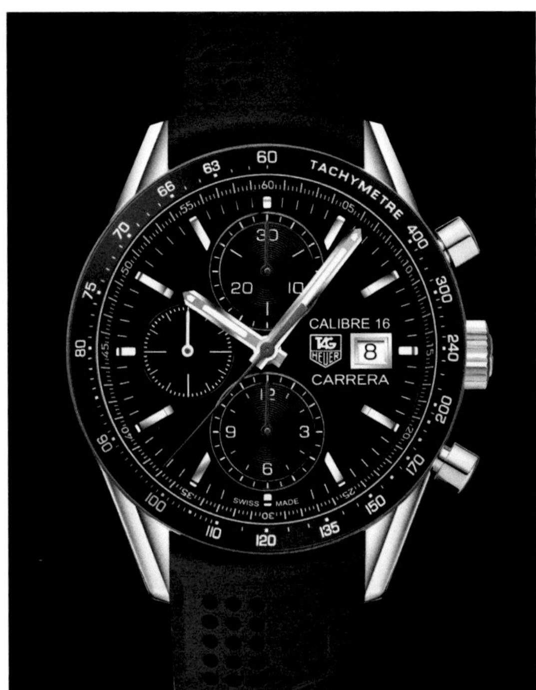

CARRERA CALIBRE 5 — REF. WAR201C.BA0723

Movement: automatic-winding TAG Heuer Calibre 5.
Functions: hours, minutes, seconds; day and date at 3.
Case: polished steel; Ø 41mm; antireflective sapphire crystal; sapphire crystal caseback; water resistant to 10atm.
Dial: black; polished, faceted, hand-applied and rose-gold-plated indexes; polished and faceted rose-gold-plated hour and minute hands with luminescent coating.
Bracelet: steel; steel deployant buckle.
Price: available upon request.

CARRERA CALIBRE 5 REF. WAR201E.FC6292

Movement: automatic-winding TAG Heuer Calibre 5.
Functions: hours, minutes, seconds; day and date at 3.
Case: polished steel; Ø 41mm; antireflective sapphire crystal; sapphire crystal caseback; water resistant to 10atm.
Dial: blue; polished, fine-brushed, faceted and hand-applied indexes; polished and faceted hour and minutes hands with luminescent coating; "CARRERA" and "CALIBRE 5 – automatique" lettering; hand-applied TAG Heuer logo.
Strap: blue alligator leather; steel deployant buckle.
Price: available upon request.
Also available: steel bracelet.

AQUARACER 300M CHRONOGRAPH REF. CAY111B.BA0927

Movement: quartz Ronda 5040 B Calibre.
Functions: hours, minutes; small seconds at 3; date at 6; chronograph: central seconds hand, 30-minute counter at 9, 1/10th-second counter at 6.
Case: polished and fine-brushed steel; Ø 43mm; unidirectional rotating polished and fine-brushed aluminum bezel; antireflective sapphire crystal; fine-brushed caseback stamped with diving decoration; water resistant to 30atm.
Dial: blue; polished and faceted hand-applied indexes with luminescent coating; polished and faceted skeletonized hour and minute hands with luminescent coating; "AQUARACER" – "300M" – "1/10th" lettering; printed TAG Heuer logo.
Bracelet: polished and fine-brushed steel; fine-brushed steel deployant buckle.
Price: available upon request.

AQUARACER 300M REF. WAY111Z.BA0910

Movement: quartz Ronda 4020 Calibre.
Functions: hours, minutes; small seconds at 3; date at 6; alarm at 9.
Case: polished and fine-brushed steel; unidirectional rotating bezel; antireflective sapphire crystal; caseback stamped with diving decoration; water resistant to 30atm.
Dial: black; faceted hand-applied indexes with luminescent coating; faceted hour and minute hands with luminescent coating; "AQUARACER – 300 m / 1000 ft" and "ALARM" lettering; printed TAG Heuer logo.
Bracelet: polished and fine-brushed steel; fine-brushed steel deployant buckle.
Price: available upon request.

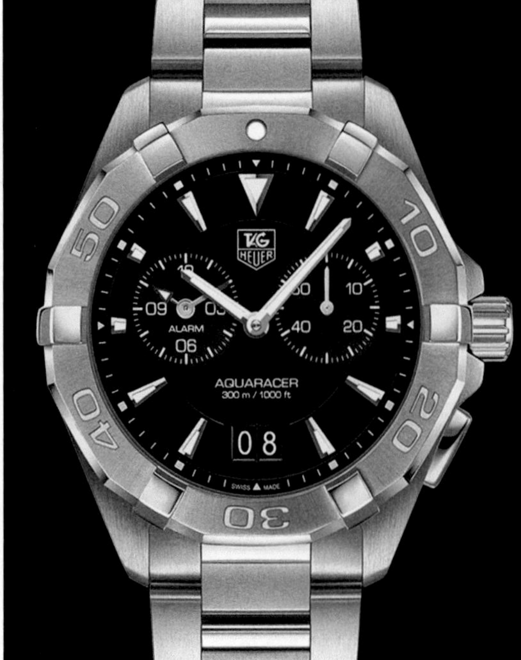

AQUARACER 300M REF. WAY111C.BA0928

Movement: quartz Ronda 6003.D Calibre.
Functions: hours, minutes, seconds; date at 3.
Case: polished and fine-brushed steel; Ø 41mm; unidirectional rotating blue aluminum bezel; antireflective sapphire crystal; fine-brushed caseback with diving decoration; water resistant to 30atm.
Dial: blue; polished and faceted hand-applied indexes with blue luminescent coating; polished and faceted hour and minute hands with blue luminescent coating; "AQUARACER" and "300 m / 1000 ft" lettering; printed TAG Heuer logo.
Bracelet: fine-brushed steel; steel deployant buckle.
Price: available upon request.

AQUARACER 300M CALIBRE 5 REF. WAY201A.BA0927

Movement: automatic-winding TAG Heuer Calibre 5.
Functions: hours, minutes, seconds; date at 3.
Case: polished and fine-brushed steel; Ø 43mm; unidirectional rotating black ceramic bezel; antireflective sapphire crystal; fine-brushed steel caseback with diving decoration; water resistant to 30atm.
Dial: black with horizontal lines; polished and faceted hand-applied indexes with luminescent coating; polished and faceted hour and minute hands with luminescent coating; "AQUARACER" and "CALIBRE 5 – AUTOMATIC – 300 m / 1000 ft" lettering; printed "TAG Heuer" logo.
Bracelet: fine-brushed steel; steel deployant buckle.
Price: available upon request.

TAG HEUER FORMULA 1 CALIBRE 16 CHRONOGRAPH REF. CAZ2010.BA0876

Movement: automatic-winding TAG Heuer Calibre 16.
Functions: hours, minutes; small seconds at 9; date at 3; chronograph: central seconds hand, 30-minute counter at 12, 12-hour counter at 6.
Case: polished and fine-brushed steel; Ø 44mm; sapphire crystal; fine-brushed caseback with checkerboard pattern; water resistant to 20atm.
Dial: black; polished hand-applied indexes with luminescent coating; polished hour and minute hands with luminescent coating; chronograph hands with red tips; "CALIBRE 16" and "FORMULA 1" lettering at 3; printed TAG Heuer logo.
Bracelet: fine-brushed steel; fine-brushed steel buckle.
Price: available upon request.

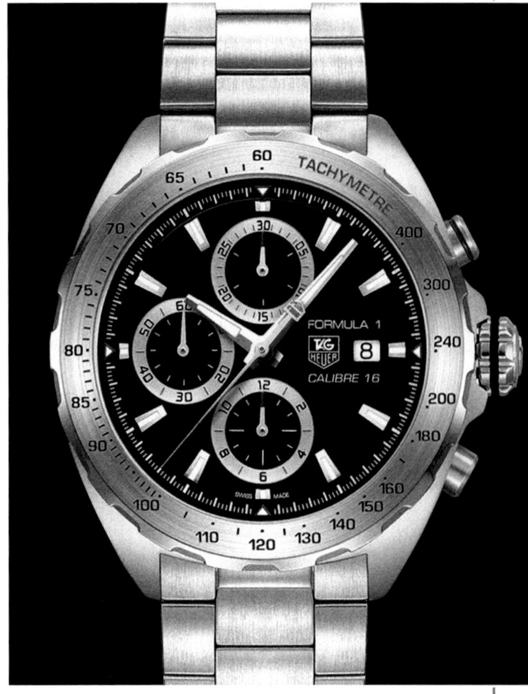

TAG HEUER FORMULA 1 CHRONOGRAPH REF. CAZ1014.BA0842

Movement: quartz Ronda 5040D Calibre.
Functions: hours, minutes; small seconds at 3; date at 4; chronograph: central seconds hand, 30-minute counter at 9, 10-hour counter at 6.
Case: polished and fine-brushed steel; Ø 43mm; polished and sanded steel and matte blue aluminum bezel; sapphire crystal; fine-brushed steel caseback with checkerboard pattern; water resistant to 20atm.
Dial: blue; polished hand-applied indexes with luminescent coating; polished and faceted hour and minute hands with luminescent coating; chronograph and small seconds hands with orange tip; "TAG HEUER – FORMULA 1" lettering; printed TAG Heuer logo.
Bracelet: steel; fine-brushed steel deployant buckle.
Price: available upon request.

TAG HEUER FORMULA 1 REF. WAZ111A.BA0875

Movement: quartz Ronda 4120B Calibre.
Functions: hours, minutes; small seconds at 3; date at 6; alarm at 9.
Case: polished and fine-brushed steel; Ø 41mm; sapphire crystal; fine-brushed steel caseback stamped with checkerboard pattern.
Dial: black opaline; polished hand-applied indexes; polished hour and minutes hands with luminescent coating; "TAG HEUER – FORMULA 1" lettering; printed TAG Heuer logo.
Bracelet: steel; steel deployant buckle.
Price: available upon request.

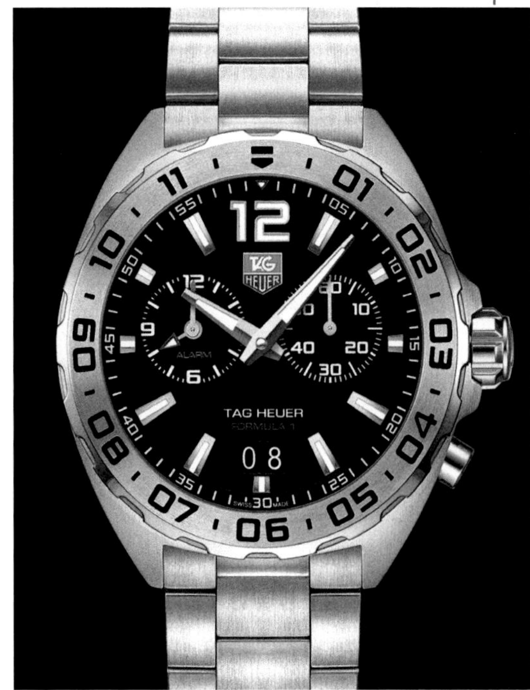

TAG HEUER FORMULA 1 — REF. WAZ2113.BA075

Movement: automatic-winding TAG Heuer Calibre 5.
Functions: hours, minutes.
Case: fine-brushed and polished steel; Ø 41mm; scratch-resistant sapphire crystal; water resistant to 20atm.
Dial: black.
Bracelet: fine-brushed steel.
Price: available upon request.

CARRERA LADY — REF. WAR1114.FC6391

Movement: quartz ETA 955.112 Calibre.
Functions: hours, minutes; date at 3.
Case: polished steel; Ø 39mm; bezel set with 72 diamonds (0.79 carat); antireflective sapphire crystal; water resistant to 10atm.
Dial: blue; faceted and hand-applied rose-gold-plated indexes; rose-gold-plated hour and minute hands with white luminescent coating; rose-gold-plated seconds hand; "CARRERA" lettering and TAG Heuer logo at 12.
Strap: blue quilted leather; polished steel deployant buckle.
Price: available upon request.

CARRERA LADY — REF. WAR1115.FC6392

Movement: quartz ETA 955.112 Calibre.
Functions: hours, minutes; date at 3.
Case: fine-brushed and polished steel; Ø 39mm; black anodized aluminum bezel set with 72 diamonds (0.79 carat); antireflective sapphire crystal; fine-brushed and polished caseback; water resistant to 10atm.
Dial: anthracite; faceted and hand-applied rose-gold-plated indexes; rose-gold-plated hour and minute hands with black luminescent coating; rose-gold-plated seconds hand; "CARRERA" lettering and TAG Heuer logo at 12.
Strap: black quilted leather; fine-brushed deployant buckle.
Price: available upon request.

CARRERA LADY — REF. WAR1314.BA0773

Movement: quartz RONDA 704 Calibre.
Functions: hours, minutes; date at 3.
Case: polished steel; Ø 32mm; antireflective sapphire crystal; water resistant to 10atm.
Dial: white mother-of-pearl; 12 diamond indexes (0.097 carat); polished and faceted hands; "CARRERA" lettering; polished TAG Heuer logo at 12.
Bracelet: polished steel; steel deployant buckle.
Price: available upon request.

CARRERA LADY REF. WAR1353.BD0774

Movement: quartz Ronda 704 Calibre.
Functions: hours, minutes; date at 3.
Case: steel and 18K 5N rose gold; Ø 32mm; bezel set with 64 diamonds (0.62 carat); antireflective sapphire crystal; water resistant to 10atm.
Dial: white mother-of-pearl; polished, faceted and hand-applied rose-gold-plated indexes; polished and faceted rose-gold-plated hands; "CARRERA" lettering; TAG Heuer logo at 12.
Bracelet: polished steel and rose gold; steel deployant buckle.
Price: available upon request.

AQUARACER LADY 300M REF. WAY131G.BA0913

Movement: quartz ETA 955.112 Calibre.
Functions: hours, minutes, seconds; date at 3.
Case: polished steel; Ø 35mm; steel unidirectional rotating bezel with black ceramic coating; antireflective sapphire crystal; steel caseback; water resistant to 30atm.
Dial: black; faceted and hand-applied indexes with luminescent coating; faceted hour and minute hands with luminescent coating; "AQUARACER" and "300 METERS – 1000 ft" lettering; TAG Heuer logo at 12.
Strap: black ceramic and steel; polished butterfly clasp.
Price: available upon request.

AQUARACER LADY 300M REF. WAY1395.BH0716

Movement: quartz ETA 955.112 Calibre.
Functions: hours, minutes, seconds; date at 3.
Case: polished steel; Ø 35mm; black ceramic unidirectional rotating bezel with 60 diamonds (0.27 carat); antireflective sapphire crystal; steel caseback with diving decoration; water resistant to 30atm.
Dial: black; faceted hand-applied indexes with luminescent coating; faceted hour and minute hands with luminescent coating; "AQUARACER" and "300 METERS – 1000 ft" lettering; TAG Heuer logo at 12.
Bracelet: black ceramic; polished butterfly clasp.
Price: available upon request.

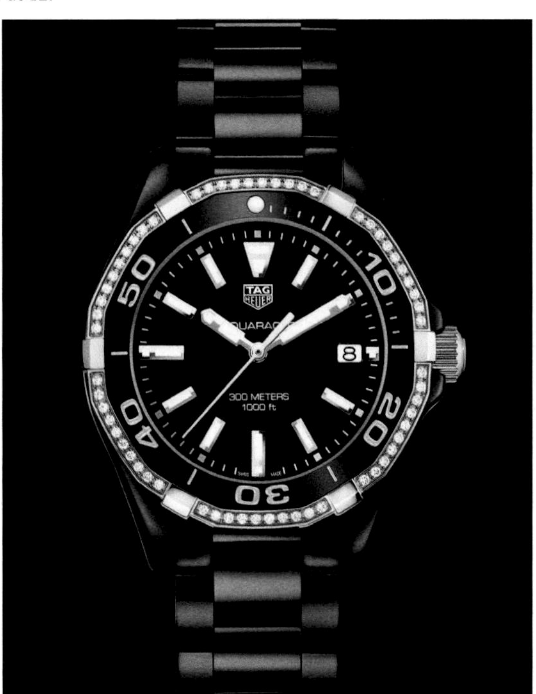

AQUARACER LADY 300M REF. WAY1396.BH0717

Movement: quartz ETA 955.112 Calibre.
Functions: hours, minutes, seconds; date at 3.
Case: polished and fine-brushed steel; Ø 35mm; white ceramic unidirectional rotating bezel with 60 diamonds (0.27 carat); antireflective sapphire crystal; steel caseback with diving decoration; water resistant to 30atm.
Dial: white; faceted hand-applied indexes with luminescent coating; faceted hour and minute hands with luminescent coating; "AQUARACER" and "300 METERS – 1000 ft" lettering; TAG Heuer logo at 12.
Bracelet: white ceramic; polished butterfly clasp.
Price: available upon request.

VACHERON CONSTANTIN

Manufacture Horlogère. Genève, depuis 1755.

AN ICON, REVISITED

Vacheron Constantin pays glowing tribute to its classic 1996 creation, the Overseas timepiece, with three wristwatches that take **A RESOLUTELY MODERN APPROACH TO A TIMELESS CONCEPT**.

With the Overseas World Time, the Swiss watchmaking legend sends its wearer on a voyage to the deepest corners of the planet. Exquisitely designed to display the time in multiple global locations simultaneously, the 43.5mm timepiece indulges its owner with the integration of an impressive 37 total time zones. While the traditional world-time concept displays the time in 24 zones, this self-winding stainless steel interpretation also incorporates lesser-displayed destinations offset from UTC by increments of 30 and 15 minutes. Two luminously enhanced 18-karat gold hands indicate the hours and minutes against a disc, which is highlighted by a two-tone design to unmistakably differentiate day and night in any of the 37 locales. In the center of the dial, a delicately finished "Lambert" projection map of the Northern hemisphere firmly asserts the timepiece's identity as a decisive accessory for the globetrotting lifestyle. Powering the watch at an oscillation frequency of 28,800 vph, the 255-component 2460 WT caliber completes its display with a central sweeping stem for the seconds.

▲ **OVERSEAS WORLD TIME**

This sophisticated traveller's timepiece goes the extra mile, displaying a total of 37 time zones on a single dial.

A six-sided bezel, a signature of the manufacture, plays off the subtle curvature of the Overseas' 41mm stainless steel case and establishes an intriguing flow of geometric lines.

A modern reinterpretation of Vacheron Constantin's iconic 1996 timepiece, itself inspired by the maison's numerous achievements in the field of sporting time instruments, the Overseas combines functional excellence and contemporary presence within a design of timeless elegance. A six-sided bezel, a signature of the manufacture, plays off the subtle curvature of the timepiece's 41mm stainless steel case and establishes an intriguing flow of geometric lines. Performance, however, remains at the forefront of the watch. Housed within the case, a soft iron ring protects the timepiece's movement from magnetic interference, ensuring excellent performance in the most challenging of conditions. A date aperture, at 3 o'clock, complements a three-hand display of the hours, minutes and sweeping seconds upon a dial finely embellished with a sunburst satin-finished base. Through its transparent caseback, the Hallmark-of-Geneva-certified timepiece reveals the inner workings of the 37-jewel 5100 caliber and its stunning 22-karat gold Overseas oscillating weight.

▲ **OVERSEAS**

A modern take on a Vacheron Constantin classic, this stainless steel wristwatch protects its movement from magnetic fields via a soft iron cage integrated in the case.

Beneath the elegant sobriety of its design, the Overseas Chronograph delivers a striking statement of performance emblematic of the watchmaking house that began its celebrated tradition of excellence more than two and a half centuries ago. The 5200 caliber at the heart of the timepiece, the result of a five-year development process, drives the dial's indications with unparalleled precision and smoothness of animation, the latter achieved by way of a vertical coupling clutch that prevents any sudden jerking motion upon activation of the chronograph's seconds hand. The Overseas Chronograph's stopwatch, boasting a column-wheel construction for ideal synchronicity, accompanies its central seconds hand with traditional subdials, at 3 and 6 o'clock, depicting the complication's 30-minute and 12-hour counters respectively. A small seconds indicator, at 9 o'clock, and date aperture, between 4 and 5 o'clock, complete a design that blends traditional codes and contemporary aesthetics on a translucent silver-toned or blue lacquered dial for a bold colorful personality. Housing the 263-component, 54-jewel caliber, the timepiece's 42.5mm stainless steel case boasts a soft iron cage for protection from magnetic interference. The wearer may seamlessly admire the movement's immaculate construction, finishes and 22-karat gold oscillating weight through a transparent sapphire crystal opening on the back of the watch. A demonstration of multi-faceted watchmaking excellence, the Overseas Chronograph is worn on a choice of three easily interchangeable straps in steel with half-Maltese-Cross-shaped links, hand-stitched Mississippiensis alligator leather with large scales, or black/blue rubber.

▲▶ OVERSEAS CHRONOGRAPH

This self-winding chronograph ensures excellent precision and smoothness of animation thanks to its caliber's column-wheel construction and vertical coupling clutch.

The Overseas Small Model enhances its diminutive 37mm case with an expert setting of precious stones that brings light and luxurious energy to the timepiece's captivating tones and minimalist dial architecture. An 18-karat pink-gold model complements the warmth of its case with a dial in translucent rosy-beige lacquer that offers a stunning blend of passion and refinement. On the case, 84 round-cut diamonds take advantage of the bezel's unique geometry to illuminate the timepiece while honoring Vacheron Constantin's rich history with a nod to the manufacture's famous Maltese Cross. A single subdial, positioned at 9 o'clock, creates a subtle off-centered effect and endows the uncluttered dial with a sense of dynamism. Driven by the 128-component 5300 caliber, two hands, in 18-karat gold and enhanced with a luminescent material, indicate the hours and minutes against 12 gold hour markers to complete the simple and graceful choreography of the face. The movement, protected from magnetic interference by a soft iron cage, may be admired through a sapphire crystal caseback, where the owner is treated to a delightful view of the winding system's 22-karat-gold Overseas oscillating weight. On the other end of the temperature spectrum, a stainless steel Overseas Small Model uses its shimmering gems to accentuate the sharp, cool tones of a contemporary design. This time more subtly framed within the metallic accents of the case, the 84 round-cut diamonds execute a harmonious play of light against the dial's blue-lacquered finish. On the face, two hands and 12 hour markers, all in 18-karat white gold, perfectly echo the color palette of the timepiece's exterior while imbuing the dial with a touch of precious luster. The Overseas Small Model oscillates at a frequency of 28,800 vph and boasts a power reserve of 44 hours.

▸ **OVERSEAS SMALL MODEL**

The Overseas Small Model adorns its understated dial architecture with a uniquely shaped setting of 84 sparkling diamonds on the bezel.

PATRIMONY — REF. 1110U/000R-B085

Movement: manual-winding 4400AS caliber; Ø 28mm, thickness: 2.8mm; 65-hour power reserve; 127 components; 21 jewels; Hallmark of Geneva certified.
Functions: hours, minutes; small seconds at 6.
Case: 18K 5N pink gold; Ø 42mm, thickness: 7.6mm; sapphire crystal caseback; water resistant to 3atm.
Dial: metal opaline.
Strap: dark brown Mississippiensis alligator leather.
Suggested price: $20,000

PATRIMONY PERPETUAL CALENDAR — REF. 43175/000R-9687

Movement: automatic-winding 1120QP caliber; Ø 29mm, thickness: 4.05mm; 40-hour power reserve; 276 components; 36 jewels; Hallmark of Geneva certified.
Functions: hours, minutes; perpetual calendar: date at 3, day of the week at 9, month at 12, leap year at 12; moonphase at 6.
Case: 18K 5N pink gold; Ø 41mm, thickness: 8.9mm; sapphire crystal caseback; water resistant to 3atm.
Dial: metal opaline.
Strap: dark brown Mississippiensis alligator leather; 18K 5N pink-gold buckle.
Suggested price: $76,000

PATRIMONY RETROGRADE DAY-DATE — REF. 86020/000G-9508

Movement: automatic-winding 2460R31R7 caliber; Ø 27mm, thickness: 5.4mm; 40-hour power reserve; 276 components; 27 jewels; Hallmark of Geneva certified.
Functions: hours, minutes; retrograde date between 9 and 3; retrograde day of the week between 5 and 7.
Case: 18K white gold; Ø 42.5mm, thickness: 5.4mm; sapphire crystal caseback; water resistant to 3atm.
Dial: metal opaline.
Strap: black Mississippiensis alligator leather.
Suggested price: $45,700

PATRIMONY ULTRA-THIN CALIBRE 1731 — REF. 30110/000R-9793

Movement: manual-winding 1731 caliber; Ø 32mm, thickness: 3.9mm; 65-hour power reserve; 265 components; 36 jewels; Hallmark of Geneva certified.
Functions: hours, minutes; small seconds at 8; minute repeater.
Case: 18K 5N pink gold; Ø 41mm, thickness: 8.1 mm; sapphire crystal caseback.
Dial: sand-blasted 18K 5N pink gold opaline.
Strap: black Mississippiensis alligator leather; 18K 5N pink-gold buckle.
Suggested price: $376,000

PATRIMONY SMALL MODEL REF. 4100U/110R-B180

Movement: automatic-winding 2450Q6 caliber; Ø 26mm, thickness: 3.6mm; 40-hour power reserve; 196 components; 27 jewels; Hallmark of Geneva certified.
Functions: hours, minutes, seconds; date at 6.
Case: 18K 5N pink gold; Ø 36mm, thickness: 8.1mm; sapphire crystal caseback; water resistant to 3atm.
Dial: metal opaline.
Bracelet: 18K 5N pink gold.
Suggested price: $39,600

PATRIMONY SMALL MODEL REF. 85515/000G-9841

Movement: automatic-winding 2450Q6/2 caliber; Ø 26mm, thickness: 3.6mm; 40-hour power reserve; 196 components; 27 jewels; Hallmark of Geneva certified.
Functions: hours, minutes, seconds; date at 6.
Case: 18K white gold; Ø 36.5mm, thickness: 9.1mm; bezel set with 117 round diamonds (0.97 carat); water resistant to 3atm.
Dial: metal opaline; gem set.
Strap: dark blue Mississippiensis alligator leather.
Suggested price: $36,500
Also available: red Mississippiensis alligator leather strap.

TRADITIONNELLE REF. 82172/000R-9382

Movement: manual-winding 4400AS caliber; Ø 28mm, thickness: 2.8mm; 65-hour power reserve; 127 components; 21 jewels; Hallmark of Geneva certified.
Functions: hours, minutes; small seconds at 6.
Case: 18K 5N pink gold; Ø 38mm, thickness: 7.7mm; sapphire crystal caseback; water resistant to 3atm.
Dial: metal opaline.
Strap: dark brown Mississippiensis alligator leather; 18K 5N pink-gold buckle.
Suggested price: $19,500

TRADITIONNELLE 14-DAY TOURBILLON REF. 89600/000P-9878

Movement: manual-winding 2260 caliber; Ø 29mm, thickness: 6.8mm; 336-hour power reserve; 231 components; 31 jewels; Hallmark of Geneva certified.
Functions: hours, minutes; small seconds on tourbillon at 6; power reserve indicator at 12.
Case: platinum 950; Ø 42mm, thickness: 12.2mm; bezel and lugs set with 80 baguette diamonds (4 carats); sapphire crystal caseback; water resistant to 3atm.
Dial: metal opaline.
Strap: black Mississippiensis alligator leather; platinum 950 deployant buckle.
Suggested price: $325,000

TRADITIONNELLE WORLD TIME — REF. 86060/000G-8982

Movement: automatic-winding 2460WT caliber; Ø 36mm, thickness: 7.55mm; 40-hour power reserve; 255 components; 27 jewels; Hallmark of Geneva certified.
Functions: hours, minutes, seconds; world time with day/night indication.
Case: 18K white gold; Ø 42.5mm, thickness: 11.6mm; sapphire crystal caseback; water resistant to 3atm.
Dial: 18K white gold.
Strap: black Mississippiensis alligator leather; 18K white-gold deployant buckle.
Suggested price: $48,000

TRADITIONNELLE MOONPHASE AND POWER RESERVE SMALL MODEL — REF. 83570/000R-9915

Movement: manual-winding 1410 caliber; Ø 26mm, thickness: 4.2mm; 40-hour power reserve; 175 components; 20 jewels; Hallmark of Geneva certified.
Functions: hours, minutes; small seconds at 6; moonphase between 8 and 9; power reserve indicator at 11.
Case: 18K 5N pink gold; Ø 36mm, thickness: 8.9mm; bezel and lugs set with 81 round diamonds (1.1 carats); sapphire crystal caseback; water resistant to 3atm.
Dial: mother-of-pearl.
Strap: gray Mississippiensis alligator leather; 18K 5N pink-gold ardillon buckle.
Suggested price: $37,900

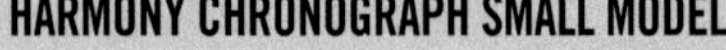

HARMONY DUAL TIME — REF. 7810S/000G-B050

Movement: automatic-winding 2460DT/260 caliber; Ø 28mm, thickness: 5.4mm; 40-hour power reserve; 233 components; 27 jewels; Hallmark of Geneva certified.
Functions: hours, minutes, seconds; second time zone at 4; day/night indicator at 8.
Case: 18K white gold; 40x49.28mm, thickness: 11.4mm; sapphire crystal caseback; water resistant to 3atm.
Dial: metal opaline.
Strap: dark brown Mississippiensis alligator leather; 18K white-gold deployant buckle.
Note: limited edition of 625 pieces.
Suggested price: $40,000

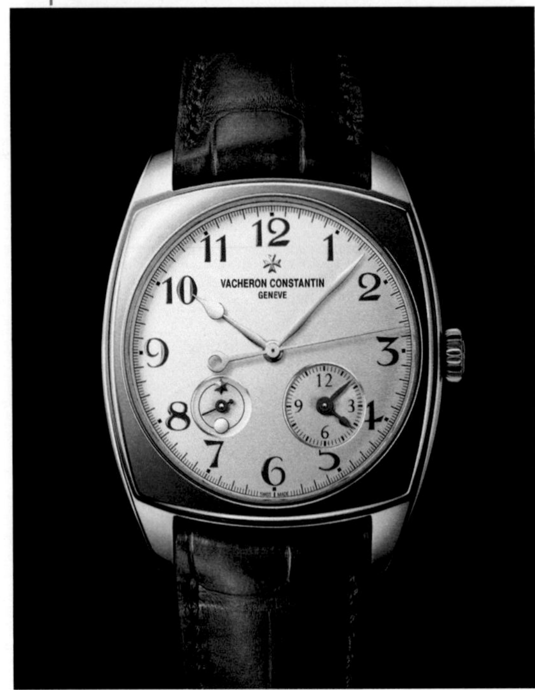

HARMONY CHRONOGRAPH SMALL MODEL — REF. 5005S/000R-B053

Movement: manual-winding 1142/260 caliber; Ø 27mm, thickness: 5.57mm; 48-hour power reserve; 164 components; 21 jewels; Hallmark of Geneva certified.
Functions: hours, minutes; small seconds at 9; chronograph: central seconds hand, 30-minute counter at 3.
Case: 18K 5N pink gold; 37x46.6mm, thickness: 11.7mm; bezel set with 84 round diamonds (1.2 carats); sapphire crystal caseback; water resistant to 3atm.
Dial: metal opaline.
Strap: warm gray Mississippiensis alligator leather; 18K 5N pink-gold deployant buckle.
Note: limited edition of 260 pieces.
Suggested price: $65,000

MALTE REF. 82230/000G-9185

Movement: manual-winding 4400AS caliber; Ø 28mm, thickness: 2.8mm; 65-hour power reserve; 127 components; 21 jewels; Hallmark of Geneva certified.
Functions: hours, minutes; small seconds at 6.
Case: 18K white gold; 36.7x47.61mm, thickness: 9.2mm; sapphire crystal caseback; water resistant to 3atm.
Dial: gray sand-blasted metal.
Strap: gray Mississippiensis alligator leather; 18K white-gold ardillon buckle.
Suggested price: $24,700

MALTE SMALL MODEL REF. 81515/000G-9891

Movement: manual-winding 1400AS caliber; Ø 20mm, thickness: 2.6mm; 40-hour power reserve; 98 components; 20 jewels; Hallmark of Geneva certified.
Functions: hours, minutes; small seconds at 6.
Case: 18K white gold; 28.4x38.67mm, thickness: 7.7mm; bezel set with 50 round diamonds (0.93 carat); sapphire crystal caseback; water resistant to 3atm.
Dial: silvered sand-blasted metal.
Strap: dark blue Mississippiensis alligator leather; 18K white-gold ardillon buckle.
Suggested price: $31,500

MALTE MOONPHASE REF. 7000M/000R-B109

Movement: manual-winding 1410AS caliber; Ø 26mm, thickness: 4.2mm; 40-hour power reserve; 179 components; 20 jewels; Hallmark of Geneva certified.
Functions: hours, minutes; small seconds at 6; moonphase at 9; power reserve indicator between 10 and 11.
Case: 18K 5N pink gold; thickness: 10.4mm.
Dial: sand-blasted metal; Roman numerals at 12 and 6.
Strap: dark brown Mississippiensis alligator leather.
Suggested price: $35,000

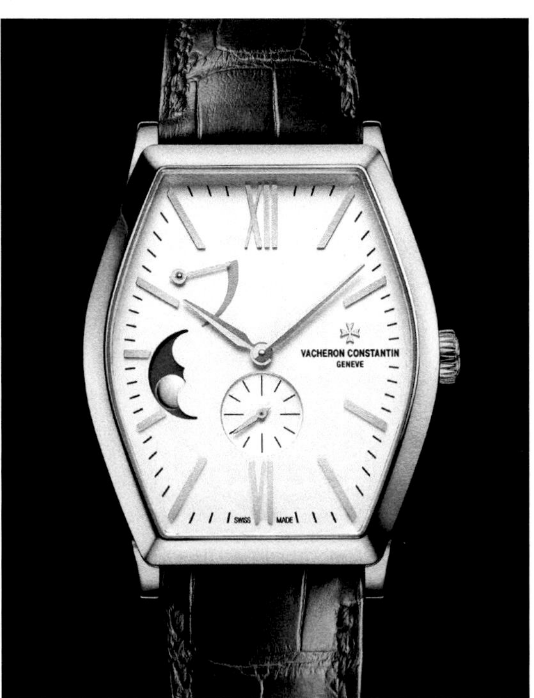

MALTE TOURBILLON OPENWORKED REF. 30135/000P-9842

Movement: manual-winding 2790SQ caliber; Ø 28mm, thickness: 6.1mm; 45-hour power reserve; 246 components; 27 jewels; Hallmark of Geneva certified.
Functions: hours, minutes; small seconds on tourbillon at 6; date via hand at 2; power reserve indicator at 10.
Case: platinum 950; 38x48.24mm, thickness: 12.7mm; sapphire crystal caseback; water resistant to 3atm.
Dial: skeletonized.
Strap: black Mississippiensis alligator leather; platinum 950 deployant buckle.
Suggested price: $230,000

QUAI DE L'ILE RETROGRADE ANNUAL CALENDAR REF. 86040/000R-I0P29

Movement: automatic-winding 2460QRA caliber; Ø 26mm, thickness: 5.4mm; 40-hour power reserve; 326 components; 27 jewels; Hallmark of Geneva certified.
Functions: hours, minutes; small seconds at 9; annual calendar: date via hand at 3, month via hand between 6 and 7; moonphase at 9.
Case: 18K 5N pink gold; Ø 53.78mm, thickness: 13.5mm; water resistant to 3atm.
Dial: vertical satin-finished metal opaline.
Strap: dark brown Mississippiensis alligator leather; 18K 5N pink-gold buckle.
Suggested price: $65,000

Also available: dark brown rubber strap.

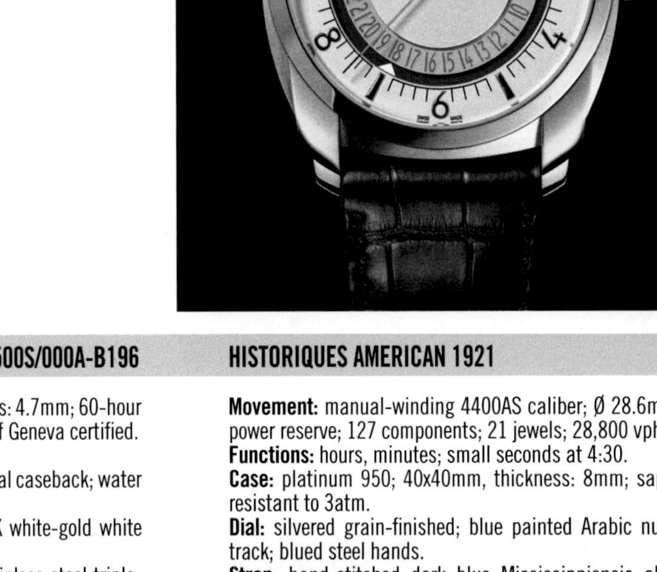

QUAI DE L'ILE ACIER REF. 4500S/000A-B195

Movement: automatic-winding 5100/1 caliber; Ø 30.6mm, thickness: 4.7mm; 60-hour power reserve; 172 components; 37 jewels; 28,800 vph; Hallmark of Geneva certified.
Functions: hours, minutes, seconds; date via central ring.
Case: stainless steel; Ø 41mm, thickness: 11.75mm; sapphire crystal caseback; water resistant to 3atm.
Dial: silver-toned; white luminescent Arabic numerals and indexes; 18K white-gold white luminescent hour and minute hands.
Strap: hand-stitched brown Mississippiensis alligator leather; stainless steel triple-blade folding clasp; delivered with a second black rubber strap.
Suggested price: $14,900

QUAI DE L'ILE ACIER REF. 4500S/000A-B196

Movement: automatic-winding 5100/1 caliber; Ø 30.6mm, thickness: 4.7mm; 60-hour power reserve; 172 components; 37 jewels; 28,800 vph; Hallmark of Geneva certified.
Functions: hours, minutes, seconds; date via central ring.
Case: stainless steel; Ø 41mm, thickness: 11.75mm; sapphire crystal caseback; water resistant to 3atm.
Dial: black; white luminescent Arabic numerals and indexes; 18K white-gold white luminescent hour and minute hands.
Strap: hand-stitched brown Mississippiensis alligator leather; stainless steel triple-blade folding clasp; delivered with a second black rubber strap.
Suggested price: $14,900

HISTORIQUES AMERICAN 1921 REF. 82035/000P-B168

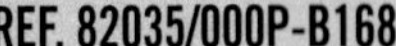

Movement: manual-winding 4400AS caliber; Ø 28.6mm, thickness: 2.8mm; 65-hour power reserve; 127 components; 21 jewels; 28,800 vph; Hallmark of Geneva certified.
Functions: hours, minutes; small seconds at 4:30.
Case: platinum 950; 40x40mm, thickness: 8mm; sapphire crystal caseback; water resistant to 3atm.
Dial: silvered grain-finished; blue painted Arabic numerals; black painted minute track; blued steel hands.
Strap: hand-stitched dark blue Mississippiensis alligator leather; platinum 950 buckle.
Suggested price: $44,000

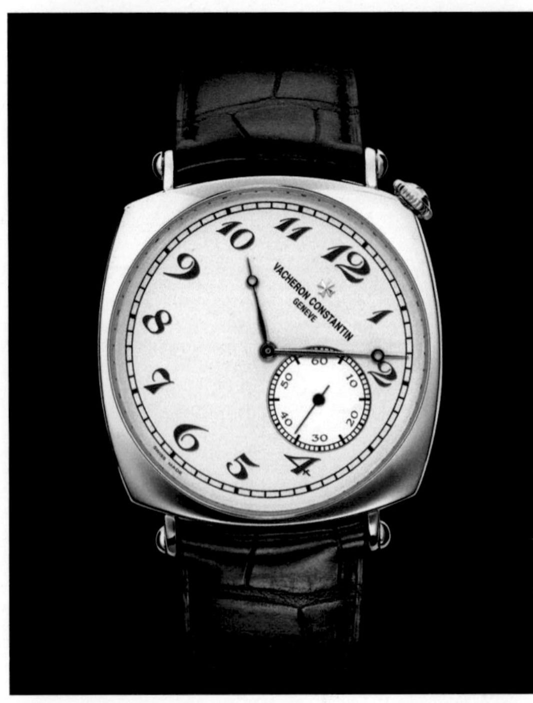

HISTORIQUES CORNES DE VACHE 1955 REF. 5000H/000P-B058

Movement: manual-winding 1142 caliber; Ø 27mm, thickness: 5.57mm; 48-hour power reserve; 164 components; 21 jewels; 21,600 vph; Hallmark of Geneva certified.
Functions: hours, minutes; small seconds at 9; chronograph: central seconds hand, 30-minute counter at 3.
Case: platinum 950; Ø 38.5mm, thickness: 10.9mm; sapphire crystal caseback; water resistant to 3atm.
Dial: silvered opaline; platinum 950 applied hour markers; blued steel chronograph hands.
Strap: hand-stitched blue Mississippiensis alligator leather; platinum 950 ardillon buckle.
Suggested price: $53,600

HISTORIQUES ULTRA-FINE 1955 REF. 33155/000P-B169

Movement: manual-winding 1003 caliber; Ø 21.1mm, thickness: 1.64mm; 31-hour power reserve; 117 components; 18 jewels; 18,000 vph; Hallmark of Geneva certified.
Functions: hours, minutes.
Case: platinum 950; Ø 36mm, thickness: 4.13mm; sapphire crystal caseback; water resistant to 3atm.
Dial: silvered opaline; blue painted hour markers; 18K gold baton hands.
Strap: dark blue Mississippiensis alligator leather; platinum 950 buckle.
Suggested price: $38,500

HISTORIQUES ARONDE 1954 REF. 81018/000R-9657

Movement: manual-winding 1400AS caliber; Ø 20mm, thickness: 2.6mm; 40-hour power reserve; 98 components; 20 jewels; Hallmark of Geneva certified.
Functions: hours, minutes; small seconds at 6.
Case: 18K 5N pink gold; 32.01x44.5mm, thickness: 9.9mm; solid caseback; water resistant to 3atm.
Dial: 18K white gold hand-guilloché.
Strap: dark brown Mississippiensis alligator leather; 18K 5N pink-gold ardillon buckle.
Suggested price: $29,500

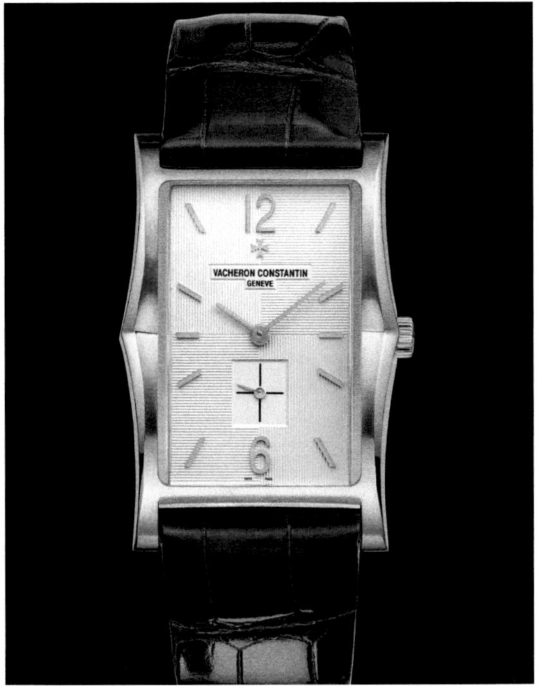

METIERS D'ART MECANIQUES AJOUREES REF. 82020/000G-9926

Movement: manual-winding 4400SQ caliber; Ø 28mm, thickness: 2.8mm; 65-hour power reserve; 127 components; 21 jewels; Hallmark of Geneva certified.
Functions: hours, minutes.
Case: 18K white gold; Ø 40mm, thickness: 7.5mm; sapphire crystal caseback; water resistant to 3atm.
Dial: 18K white gold skeletonized.
Strap: dark gray Mississippiensis alligator leather; 18K white-gold ardillon buckle.
Suggested price: $69,000

CHRONOGRAPHS FOR THE AGES

Like the man whose courage and conviction saved the brand during mechanical horology's darkest hour, Zenith understands that **THE PAST MUST BE RECOGNIZED, EVEN AS ONE ADVANCES UPON THE FRONTIERS OF MODERNITY**.

Inspired by the Café Racer principle of maximum performance with no superfluous components, the Heritage Pilot Ton-Up perfectly combines an understated aesthetic and high-performance "engine."

A celebrated champion of military and aviation-grade chronographs, the Swiss watchmaker pays tribute to one of its most iconic models. In presenting the Heritage Cronometro TIPO CP-2, Zenith reinvigorates a timepiece that equipped the wrists of Italian pilots from the 1960s onwards. Boasting the same 43mm diameter as its predecessor, the stainless steel timepiece ensures its wearer the optimal legibility that made the original TIPO CP-2 such a natural choice for the strict standards of 20th-century military personnel. While the DP146 caliber that powered the original model endowed the wristwatch with an exceptional degree of precision, the Heritage Cronometro TIPO CP-2 now takes on the 21st century with a mechanical movement as iconic as the brand that brought it to life. The Zenith El Primero caliber, oscillating at the extraordinary rate of 36,000 vph, powers the dial's indicators with indispensable reliability. The 254-component self-winding movement, equipped with a column-wheel chronograph, animates the hours, minutes and small seconds as well as a high-precision chronograph comprised of a central seconds hand and complementary 30-minute counter at 3 o'clock. An authentic flight instrument, the limited edition timepiece achieves ideal visibility thanks to the stark contrast of its numerous SuperLumiNova-enhanced indicators against its rich black dial and bezel. Finished with a transparent caseback through which the wearer can admire the movement's Côtes-de-Genève finishing, the Heritage Cronometro TIPO CP-2 is worn on a black calfskin strap and boasts a power reserve of 50 hours.

Zenith takes its vintage watchmaking spirit on the road, honoring the British "Café Racer" biker movement of the 1950s and '60s. Inspired by the Café Racer principle of maximum performance with no superfluous components, the Heritage Pilot Ton-Up perfectly combines an understated aesthetic and high-performance "engine." The 45mm timepiece's case, in aged stainless steel, finds a fitting complement in a slate-gray dial whose grained pattern gives the watch an irresistible sense of texture and depth. By enhancing the Arabic numerals and primary hands with coatings in beige SuperLumiNova, Zenith ensures flawless legibility at whatever speed the wearer chooses to careen around street corners, while providing a unique color palette that sets the timepiece apart. The self-winding wristwatch does its most impressive work beneath the frame, powering the timepiece with excellent precision and reliability. The column-wheel-chronograph El Primero 4069 caliber drives its indications of the hours, minutes, small seconds, central chronograph seconds and 30-minute counter with a precision to the tenth of a second thanks to its oscillation frequency of 36,000 vph. Finishing the rugged vintage design of the watch, a green oily-nubuck leather strap provides the Heritage Pilot Ton-Up with a chic, lived-in aesthetic while ensuring a comfortable grip against the wrist of its high-speed wearer.

◄ **HERITAGE CRONOMETRO TIPO CP-2**

This revival of an icon of military timekeeping boasts a self-winding caliber oscillating at an impressive frequency of 36,000 vph.

▲ **HERITAGE PILOT TON-UP**

This self-winding timepiece's vintage, understated aesthetic perfectly captures the free-spirited attitude of the "Café Racer" biker movement.

The El Primero 410 Tribute to Charles Vermot is more than mere homage; it is a statement of gratitude to one of Zenith's unforgettable heroes. When the quartz crisis in the 1970s led Zenith's new management to abandon the automatic chronograph and place its complete energy toward the production of electronic watches, senior engineer Charles Vermot pled for them to reconsider. Told he was merely being sentimental to a bygone era, Vermot stuck firmly to his conviction, defying orders and hiding equipment parts and instructions inside the manufacture's attic, convinced that mechanical horology would rise once again. Without him, the historic El Primero caliber would never have seen the light of day again. Zenith itself might not have survived had it not been able to fill sudden orders, in the 1980s, for the iconic caliber—an impossible feat without the appropriate equipment, cams and blueprints. Zenith was reborn. The El Primero 410 Tribute to Charles Vermot honors the courage and strength of its savior with a sophisticated personality perfectly in line with the brand's unmistakable design codes. Housed in a 42mm stainless steel case, the automatic-winding El Primero 410 caliber drives a full time display, complemented by a calendar with day, date and month, a moonphase indication at 6 o'clock and a two-counter chronograph with a central seconds hand beating at 36,000 vph—the frequency of the caliber that Charles Vermot saved from extinction.

◂ **EL PRIMERO 410 TRIBUTE TO CHARLES VERMOT**

This hyper-sophisticated timepiece with full calendar and column-wheel chronograph pays tribute to the man whose belief in the El Primero caliber saved the movement from certain extinction and propelled it toward its unparalleled success.

▸ **EL PRIMERO – RANGE ROVER**

Designed in partnership with Land Rover / Range Rover, this self-winding timepiece houses its 36,000 vph caliber within a spectacular case in ceramised aluminum.

Inspired by its collaboration with Land Rover / Range Rover, Zenith presents a timepiece that plays with materials and tones to achieve a unique aesthetic as sleek and powerful as the vehicles of Zenith's partner. On a brushed-gray dial, the El Primero – Range Rover achieves a harmonious monochromatic choreography thanks to its seamless integration of three counters using subtly shaded accents that ensure optimal legibility without rupturing the dark serenity of the design. Housed in a 42mm case in ceramised aluminum, the 326-component El Primero 400B caliber drives the hours, minutes, small seconds, date, and a column-wheel chronograph complete with central seconds, 30-minute and 12-hour totalizers. The rhodium-plated hands and hour markers provide essential daytime contrast thanks to their white accents and nighttime visibility by way of their generous luminous enhancements. Worn on a black rubber strap coated with ivory-toned or blue perforated calfskin, the El Primero – Range Rover boasts a transparent caseback that reveals the movement's special oscillating weight, which is adorned with Zenith and Range Rover logos.

EL PRIMERO CHRONOMASTER — REF. 03.2520.4061/69.C714

Movement: automatic-winding El Primero 4061 caliber; Ø 30mm, thickness: 6.6mm; 50-hour power reserve; 282 components; 31 jewels; 36,000 vph; oscillating weight with "Côtes de Genève" motif; COSC-certified movement.
Functions: hours, minutes; small seconds at 9; chronograph: central seconds hand, 12-hour counter at 6; 30-minute counter at 3; tachometer scale.
Case: stainless steel; Ø 45mm, thickness: 14.05mm; antireflective domed sapphire crystal; sapphire crystal caseback; water resistant to 10atm.
Dial: silver-toned sunray-patterned; two different-colored counters; rhodium-plated faceted hour markers coated with SuperLumiNova; rhodium-plated faceted hands coated with SuperLumiNova.
Strap: black alligator leather; protective rubber lining; stainless steel triple-folding clasp.
Suggested price: $8,600

EL PRIMERO CHRONOMASTER OPEN — REF. 03.2040.4061/51.C700

Movement: automatic-winding El Primero 4061 caliber; Ø 30mm, thickness: 6.6mm; 50-hour power reserve; 282 components; 31 jewels; 36,000 vph; oscillating weight with "Côtes de Genève" motif; COSC-certified movement.
Functions: hours, minutes; small seconds at 9; chronograph: central seconds hand, 12-hour counter at 6, 30-minute counter at 3; tachometer scale.
Case: stainless steel; Ø 42mm, thickness: 14.05mm; antireflective domed sapphire crystal; sapphire crystal caseback; water resistant to 10atm.
Dial: blue-toned sunray-patterned; rhodium-plated faceted hour markers coated with SuperLumiNova; rhodium-plated faceted hands coated with SuperLumiNova.
Strap: black rubber; stainless steel triple-folding clasp.
Suggested price: $8,600

EL PRIMERO 410 — REF. 03.2091.410/01.C494

Movement: automatic-winding El Primero 410 caliber; Ø 30mm, thickness: 7.7mm; 50-minute power reserve; 390 components; 31 jewels; 36,000 vph; oscillating weight with "Côtes de Genève" motif.
Functions: hours, minutes; small seconds at 9; chronograph: central seconds hand, 12-hour counter at 6, 30-minute counter at 3; tachometer scale; moonphase at 6; calendar: day at 10, date between 4 and 5, month at 2; tachometer scale.
Case: stainless steel; Ø 42mm, thickness: 12.75mm; antireflective domed sapphire crystal; sapphire crystal caseback; water resistant to 5atm.
Dial: silver-toned sunray-patterned; rhodium-plated faceted hour markers coated with SuperLumiNova; rhodium-plated facted hands coated with SuperLumiNova.
Strap: brown alligator leather; stainless steel triple-folding clasp.
Suggested price: $9,700

EL PRIMERO ORIGINAL — REF. 03.2520.400/69.C713

Movement: automatic-winding El Primero 400B caliber; Ø 30mm, thickness: 6.6mm; 50-hour power reserve; 326 components; 31 jewels; 36,000 vph; oscillating weight with "Côtes de Genève" motif.
Functions: hours, minutes; small seconds at 9; date at 4:30; chronograph: central seconds hand, 12-hour counter at 6, 30-minute counter at 3; tachometer scale.
Case: stainless steel; Ø 45mm, thickness: 14.05mm; antireflective domed sapphire crystal; sapphire crystal caseback; water resistant to 10atm.
Dial: silver-toned sunray-patterned; three different-colored counters; rhodium-plated faceted hour markers coated with SuperLumiNova; rhodium-plated faceted hands coated with SuperLumiNova.
Strap: brown alligator leather; protective rubber lining; stainless steel triple-folding clasp.
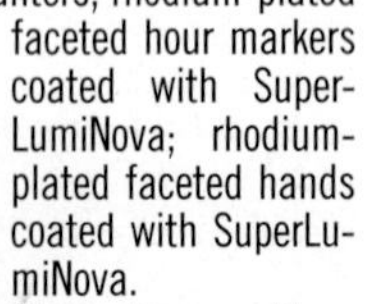
Suggested price: $6,700

ELITE 6150 REF. 18.2270.6150/01.C498

Movement: automatic-winding Elite 6150 caliber; Ø 30mm, thickness: 3.92mm; 100-hour power reserve; 195 components; 35 jewels; oscillating weight with "Côtes de Genève" motif.
Functions: hours, minutes, seconds.
Case: rose gold; Ø 42mm, thickness: 9.45mm; antireflective domed sapphire crystal; sapphire crystal caseback; water resistant to 5atm.
Dial: silver-toned sunray-patterned; engraved and gold-plated hour markers; leaf-shaped gold-plated hands.
Strap: brown alligator leather; protective rubber lining; rose-gold pin buckle.
Suggested price: $14,100

ELITE CHRONOGRAPH CLASSIC REF. 03.2270.4069/01.C493

Movement: automatic-winding El Primero 4069 caliber; Ø 30mm, thickness: 6.6mm; 50-hour power reserve; 254 components; 31 jewels; 36,000 vph; oscillating weight with "Côtes de Genève" motif.
Functions: hours, minutes; small seconds at 9; chronograph: central seconds hand, 30-minute counter at 3.
Case: rose gold; Ø 42mm, thickness: 11.8mm; antireflective domed sapphire crystal; sapphire crystal caseback; water resistant to 5atm.
Dial: silver-toned sunray-patterned; engraved and rhodium-plated hour markers; leaf-shaped rhodium-plated hands.
Strap: brown alligator leather; protective rubber lining; stainless steel triple-folding clasp.
Suggested price: $6,900

ELITE LADY MOONPHASE REF. 03.2320.692/80.C714

Movement: automatic-winding Elite 692 caliber; Ø 25.6mm, thickness: 3.97mm; 50-hour power reserve; 195 components; 27 jewels; 28,800 vph; oscillating weight with "Côtes de Genève" motif.
Functions: hours, minutes; small seconds at 9; moonphase at 6.
Case: stainless steel; Ø 36mm, thickness: 9.1mm; antireflective domed sapphire crystal; sapphire crystal caseback; water resistant to 5atm.
Dial: white mother-of-pearl; engraved and gold-plated hour markers; leaf-shaped gold-plated hands.
Strap: brown alligator leather; protective rubber lining; stainless steel pin buckle.
Suggested price: $7,400

EL PRIMERO 36,000 VPH REF. 03.2046.400/25.C771

Movement: automatic-winding El Primero 400B caliber; Ø 30mm, thickness: 6.6mm; 50-hour power reserve; 326 components; 31 jewels; 36,000 vph; oscillating weight with "Côtes de Genève" motif.
Functions: hours, minutes; small seconds at 9; date at 6; chronograph: central seconds hand, 12-hour counter at 6, 30-minute counter at 3; tachometer scale.
Case: stainless steel; Ø 42mm, thickness: 12.75mm; antireflective domed sapphire crystal; sapphire crystal caseback; water resistant to 3atm.
Dial: silver-toned sunray-patterned; three different-colored counters; rhodium-plated faceted hour markers coated with SuperLumiNova; rhodium-plated faceted hands coated with SuperLumiNova.
Strap: brown calfskin leather; stainless steel triple-folding clasp.
Suggested price: $6,900

EL PRIMERO CHRONOMASTER OPEN — REF. 03.2040.4061/51.C700

Movement: automatic-winding El Primero 4061 caliber; Ø 30mm, thickness: 6.6mm; 50-hour power reserve; 282 components; 31 jewels; 36,000 vph; oscillating weight with "Côtes de Genève" motif.
Functions: hours, minutes; small seconds at 9; chronograph: central seconds hand, 12-hour counter at 6, 30-minute counter at 3; tachometer scale.
Case: stainless steel; Ø 42mm, thickness: 14.05mm; antireflective domed sapphire crystal; sapphire crystal caseback; water resistant to 10atm.
Dial: silver-toned sunray-patterned; rhodium-plated faceted hour markers coated with SuperLumiNova; rhodium-plated faceted hands coated with SuperLumiNova.
Strap: brown alligator leather; protective rubber lining; stainless steel triple-folding clasp.
Suggested price: $8,600

PILOT TYPE 20 ANNUAL CALENDAR — REF. 03.2430.4054/21.C721

Movement: automatic-winding El Primero 4054 caliber; Ø 30mm, thickness: 8.3mm; 50-hour power reserve; 341 components; 29 jewels; 36,000 vph; oscillating weight with "Côtes de Genève" motif.
Functions: hours, minutes; small seconds at 9; annual calendar: day/month at 3, date at 6; chronograph: central seconds hand, 60-minute counter at 6.
Case: stainless steel; Ø 48mm, thickness: 15.8mm; screw-down crown; antireflective domed sapphire crystal; caseback engraved with the Zenith flying instruments logo; water resistant to 10atm.

Dial: matte black; Arabic numerals in SuperLumiNova; black ruthenium-plated and satin-finished hands.
Strap: brown alligator leather; protective rubber lining; stainless steel pin buckle.
Suggested price: $9,900

PILOT TYPE 20 GMT — REF. 03.2430.693/21.C723

Movement: automatic-winding Elite 693 caliber; Ø 25.6mm, thickness: 3.94mm; 50-hour power reserve; 186 components; 26 jewels; 28,800 vph; oscillating weight with "Côtes de Genève" motif.
Functions: hours, minutes; small seconds at 9; 24-hour dual-time indicator.
Case: stainless steel; Ø 48mm, thickness: 15.8mm; antireflective domed sapphire crystal; caseback engraved with the Zenith flying instruments logo; water resistant to 10atm.
Dial: matte black; Arabic numerals in SuperLumiNova; black ruthenium-plated and satin-finished hands.
Strap: brown calfskin leather; protective rubber lining; stainless steel pin buckle.
Suggested price: $7,100

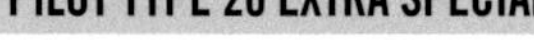

PILOT TYPE 20 EXTRA SPECIAL — REF. 29.2430.679/21.C753

Movement: automatic-winding Elite 679 caliber; Ø 25.6mm, thickness: 3.85mm; 50-hour power reserve; 126 components; 27 jewels; 28,800 vph; oscillating weight with "Côtes de Genève" motif.
Functions: hours, minutes, seconds.
Case: bronze; Ø 45mm, thickness: 14.25mm; antireflective domed sapphire crystal; titanium caseback engraved with the Zenith flying instruments logo; water resistant to 10atm.
Dial: black; Arabic numerals in SuperLumiNova; gold-plated faceted hands coated with SuperLumiNova.
Strap: oily nubuck leather; protective rubber lining; titanium pin buckle.
Suggested price: $6,700

ELITE CHRONOGRAPH CLASSIC REF. 03.2270.4069/01.C493

Movement: automatic-winding El Primero 4069 caliber; Ø 30mm, thickness: 6.6mm; 50-hour power reserve; 254 components; 31 jewels; oscillating weight with "Côtes de Genève" motif.
Functions: hours, minutes; small seconds at 9; chronograph: central seconds hand, 30-minute counter at 3.
Case: stainless steel; Ø 42mm, thickness: 11.8mm; antireflective domed sapphire crystal; sapphire crystal caseback; water resistant to 5atm.
Dial: silver-toned sunray-patterned; engraved and rhodium-plated hour markers; leaf-shaped rhodium-plated hands.
Strap: black alligator leather; protective rubber lining; stainless steel triple-folding clasp.
Suggested price: $6,900

HERITAGE CRONOMETRO TIPO CP-2 REF. 03.2240.4069/21.C774

Movement: automatic-winding El Primero 4069 caliber; Ø 30mm, thickness: 6.6mm; 50-hour power reserve; 254 components; 35 jewels; 36,000 vph; oscillating weight with "Côtes de Genève" motif.
Functions: hours, minutes; small seconds at 9; chronograph: central seconds hand, 30-minute counter at 3.
Case: stainless steel; Ø 43mm, thickness: 12.85mm; antireflective domed sapphire crystal; antireflective domed sapphire crystal caseback; water resistant to 10atm.
Dial: black; Arabic numeral hour markers in SuperLumiNova; rhodium-plated faceted hands coated with SuperLumiNova.
Strap: black calfskin leather; protective rubber lining; stainless steel triple-folding clasp.
Note: limited edition of 1,000 pieces.
Suggested price: $7,700

HERITAGE PILOT TON-UP REF. 11.2430.4069/21.C773

Movement: automatic-winding El Primero 4069 caliber; Ø 30mm, thickness: 6.6mm; 50-hour power reserve; 254 components; 35 jewels; 36,000 vph; oscillating weight with "Côtes de Genève" motif.
Functions: hours, minutes; small seconds at 9; chronograph: central seconds hand, 30-minute counter at 3.
Case: aged stainless steel; Ø 45mm, thickness: 14.25mm; antireflective domed sapphire crystal; titanium caseback with "Pilot Ton-Up" engravings; water resistant to 10atm.
Dial: slate gray toned with grained pattern; Arabic numerals with beige SuperLumiNova; black ruthenium-plated faceted hands coated with beige SuperLumiNova.
Strap: green oily nubuck leather; protective rubber lining; titanium pin buckle.
Suggested price: $7,100

ACADEMY TOURBILLON GEORGES FAVRE-JACOT REF. 49.2520.4805/98.R576

Movement: manual-winding El Primero 4805 caliber; Ø 37mm, thickness: 5.9mm; 50-hour power reserve; 807 components; 32 jewels; 36,000 vph.
Functions: hours, minutes; tourbillon at 6; power reserve indicator at 4:30.
Case: black ceramic; Ø 45mm, thickness: 14.65mm; antireflective domed sapphire crystal; sapphire crystal caseback; water resistant to 5atm.
Dial: black elements screwed to the movement; ruthenium-plated faceted hour markers coated with SuperLumiNova; ruthenium-plated faceted hands coated with SuperLumiNova.
Strap: black rubber; black PVD-coated titanium triple-folding clasp.
Suggested price: $76,700

EL PRIMERO CHRONOMASTER REF. 16.2150.4062/91.C760

Movement: automatic-winding El Primero 4062 caliber; Ø 30mm, thickness: 6.6mm; 50-hour power reserve; 253 components; 31 jewels; 36,000 vph; oscillating weight with "Côtes de Genève" motif; COSC-certified movement.
Functions: hours, minutes; small seconds at 9; chronograph: central seconds hand, 30-minute counter at 3.
Case: stainless steel; Ø 38mm, thickness: 12.45mm; bezel set with 122 brilliant-cut diamonds (~0.65 carat); antireflective domed sapphire crystal; sapphire crystal caseback; water resistant to 5atm.

Dial: slate gray velvet-finish; rhodium-plated and faceted hour markers; rhodium-plated and faceted hands.
Strap: slate gray alligator leather with protective rubber lining; stainless steel triple-folding clasp.
Suggested price: $8,600

EL PRIMERO TOURBILLON REF. 03.2280.4035/21.C714

Movement: automatic-winding El Primero 4035 D caliber; Ø 37mm, thickness: 7.66mm; 50-hour power reserve; 381 components; 35 jewels; 36,000 vph; gold oscillating weight with "Côtes de Genève" motif.
Functions: hours, minutes; tourbillon at 11; chronograph: central seconds hand, 12-hour counter at 6, 30-minute counter at 3.
Case: stainless steel; Ø 46mm, thickness: 15.6mm; antireflective domed sapphire crystal; sapphire crystal caseback; water resistant to 10atm.
Dial: black lacquered; rhodium-plated and faceted hour markers coated with SuperLumiNova; rhodium-plated and faceted gold hands coated with SuperLumiNova.
Strap: black alligator leather.
Suggested price: $52,900

EL PRIMERO CHRONOMASTER POWER RESERVE REF. 18.2080.4021/01.C494

Movement: automatic-winding El Primero 4021 caliber; Ø 30mm, thickness: 7.85mm; 50-hour power reserve; 248 components; 39 jewels; 36,000 vph; oscillating weight with "Côtes de Genève" motif; COSC-certified movement.
Functions: hours, minutes; small seconds at 9; power reserve indicator at 6; chronograph: central seconds hand, 30-minute counter at 3; tachometer scale.
Case: rose gold; Ø 42mm, thickness: 14.05mm; antireflective domed sapphire crystal; sapphire crystal caseback; water resistant to 10atm.
Dial: silver-toned sunray-patterned; gold-plated and faceted hour markers coated with SuperLumiNova; gold-plated and faceted hands coated with SuperLumiNova; blued faceted chronograph hands coated with SuperLumiNova.
Strap: brown alligator leather
Suggested price: $19,000

EL PRIMERO CHRONOMASTER GRANDE DATE REF. 18.2160.4047/01.C713

Movement: automatic-winding El Primero 4047 caliber; Ø 30.5mm, thickness: 9.05mm; 50-hour power reserve; 332 components; 32 jewels; 36,000 vph; oscillating weight with "Côtes de Genève" motif; COSC-certified movement.
Functions: hours, minutes; small seconds at 9; date at 2; moon and sunphase indicator at 6; chronograph: central seconds hand, 30-minute counter at 3; tachometer scale.
Case: rose gold; Ø 45mm, thickness: 15.6mm; antireflective domed sapphire crystal; sapphire crystal caseback; water resistant to 5atm.

Dial: silver-toned sunray-patterned; gold-plated and faceted hour markers coated with SuperLumiNova; gold-plated and faceted hands coated with SuperLumiNova; blued faceted chronograph hands coated with SuperLumiNova.
Strap: brown alligator leather.
Suggested price: $25,100

EL PRIMERO SPORT REF. 03.2270.4069/01.C493

Movement: automatic-winding El Primero 400 B caliber; Ø 30mm, thickness: 6.6mm; 50-hour power reserve; 326 components; 31 jewels; 36,000 vph; oscillating weight with "Côtes de Genève" motif.
Functions: hours, minutes; small seconds at 9; date at 6; chronograph: central seconds hand, 12-hour counter at 6, 30-minute counter at 3; tachometer scale.
Case: stainless steel; Ø 45mm, thickness: 14.05mm; antireflective domed sapphire crystal; sapphire crystal caseback; water resistant to 20atm.
Dial: slate gray velvet-finish; rhodium-plated and faceted hour markers coated with SuperLumiNova; rhodium-plated and faceted hands coated with SuperLumiNova.
Strap: black alligator leather.
Suggested price: $7,700

EL PRIMERO CHRONOGRAPH REF. 03.2110.400/22.C493

Movement: automatic-winding El Primero 400 B caliber; Ø 30mm, thickness: 6.6mm; 50-hour power reserve; 326 components; 31 jewels; 36,000 vph; oscillating weight with "Côtes de Genève" motif.
Functions: hours, minutes; small seconds at 9; date at 6; chronograph: central seconds hand, 12-hour counter at 6, 30-minute counter at 3.
Case: stainless steel; Ø 42mm, thickness: 12mm; antireflective domed sapphire crystal; sapphire crystal caseback; water resistant to 5atm.
Dial: black sunray-patterned; rhodium-plated and faceted hour markers; rhodium-plated and faceted hands.
Strap: black alligator leather with protective rubber lining; stainless steel triple-folding clasp.
Suggested price: $6,700

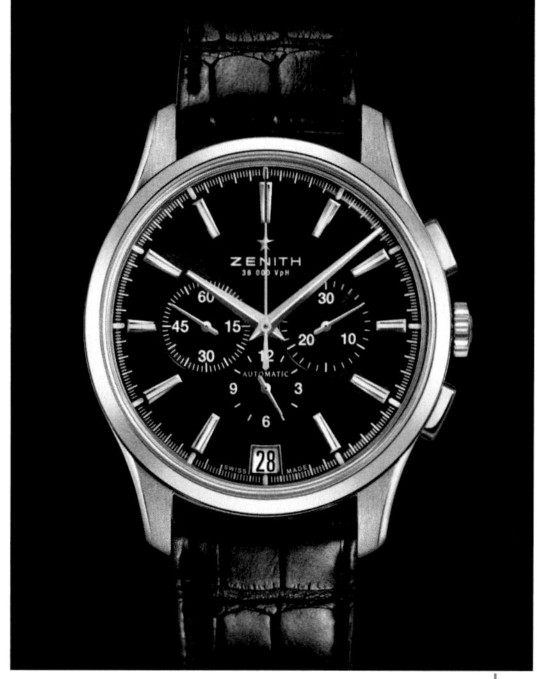

EL PRIMERO SYNOPSIS REF. 18.2170.4613/01.C713

Movement: automatic-winding El Primero 4613 caliber; Ø 30mm, thickness: 5.58mm; 50-hour power reserve; 160 components; 19 jewels; 36,000 vph; oscillating weight with "Côtes de Genève" motif.
Functions: hours, minutes; small seconds at 9.
Case: rose gold; Ø 40mm, thickness: 11.7mm; antireflective domed sapphire crystal; sapphire crystal caseback; water resistant to 10atm.
Dial: silver-toned sunray-patterned; gold-plated and faceted hour markers coated with SuperLumiNova; gold-plated and faceted hands coated with SuperLumiNova.
Strap: brown alligator leather with protective rubber lining; rose-gold pin buckle.
Suggested price: $13,600

ELITE ULTRA THIN REF. 03.2010.681/01.C493

Movement: automatic-winding Elite 681 caliber; Ø 25.6mm, thickness: 3.47mm; 50-hour power reserve; 128 components; 27 jewels; 28,800 vph; oscillating weight with "Côtes de Genève" motif.
Functions: hours, minutes; small seconds at 9.
Case: stainless steel; Ø 40mm, thickness: 8.3mm; antireflective domed sapphire crystal; sapphire crystal caseback; water resistant to 5atm.
Dial:silver-toned sunray-patterned; rhodium-plated and faceted hour markers; rhodium-plated and faceted hands.
Strap: black alligator leather with protective rubber lining; stainless steel pin buckle.
Suggested price: $6,900

Brand Directory

ALPINA
3 Chemin de la Galaise
1228 Plan-les-Ouates
Switzerland
Tel: 41 22 860 87 40
USA: 954 312 3600

ARNOLD & SON
38 Boulevard des Eplatures
2300 La Chaux-de-Fonds
Switzerland
Tel: 41 32 967 97 97
USA: 213 622 1133
Arije: 33 1 47 20 72 40

ATELIERS deMONACO
32 Chemin du Champ des Filles
1228 Plan-les-Ouates
Switzerland
Tel: 41 22 860 04 63

AUDEMARS PIGUET
Route de France 18
1348 Le Brassus
Switzerland
Tel: 41 21 642 39 00
USA: 212 758 8400
Arije: 33 1 47 20 80 80

BLANCPAIN
6 Chemin de l'Etang
1094 Paudex
Switzerland
Tel: 41 21 796 36 36
USA: 877 520 1735
France: 33 1 53 81 22 40
Arije: 33 1 47 20 72 40

BOUCHERON
20, rue de la Paix
75002, Paris
France
Tel: 33 1 42 44 42 44
Arije: 33 1 47 20 72 40

BREGUET
1344 L'Abbaye
Switzerland
Tel: 41 21 841 90 90
USA: 866 458 7488
France: 33 1 53 81 22 33
Arije: 33 1 47 20 72 40

BVLGARI
34 Rue de Monruz
2000 Neuchâtel
Switzerland
Tel: 41 32 722 78 78
USA: 212 315 9700
France: 33 1 56 89 32 26
Arije: 33 1 47 20 72 40

CARL F. BUCHERER
1805 South Metro Parkway
Dayton, OH 45459
USA: 800 395 4306
Switzerland: 41 41 369 74 80

CARTIER SA
8 Boulevard James-Fazy
1201 Geneva
Switzerland
Tel: 41 22 721 24 00
USA: 212 446 3400
France: 33 1 58 18 15 96
Arije: 33 1 47 20 72 40

CHOPARD
8 Rue de Veyrot
1217 Meyrin Geneva 2
Switzerland
Tel: 41 22 719 3131
USA: 212 821 0300
Arije: 33 1 47 20 72 40

CHRISTOPHE CLARET
2 Route du Soleil d'Or
2400 Le Locle
Switzerland
Tel: 41 32 933 80 80
USA: 305 812 3344

CORUM
Rue du Petit Chapeau 1
2301 La Chaux de Fonds
Switzerland
Tel: 41 32 967 0877
USA: 954 279 1220
Arije: 33 1 47 20 72 40

de GRISOGONO
39 Chemin du Champs des Filles
Bâtiment E
1228 Plan-les-Ouates
Switzerland
Tel: 41 22 817 81 00
France: 33 1 42 99 69 54
USA: 212 439 4220
Arije: 33 1 47 20 72 40

FREDERIQUE CONSTANT SA
32 Chemin du Champ des Filles
1228 Plan-les-Ouates
Switzerland
Tel: 41 22 860 04 40
USA: 954 312 3600
Arije: 33 1 47 20 72 40

GIRARD-PERREGAUX
1 Place Girardet
2301 La Chaux-de-Fonds
Switzerland
Tel: 41 32 911 33 33
France: 33 1 42 44 09 45
USA: 201 355 4523
Arije: 33 1 47 20 72 40

GLASHÜTTE ORIGINAL
1 Altenberger Strasse
01768 Glashütte/Sachsen
Germany
Tel: 49 3 50 53 460
France: 33 1 53 81 22 68
USA: 201 271 1400
Arije: 33 1 47 20 72 40

GREUBEL FORSEY
Eplatures-Grise 16
PO Box 670
2301 La Chaux-de-Fonds
Switzerland
Tel: 41 32 925 45 45
USA: 310 205 5555

GUY ELLIA
7 rue Lincoln
75008 Paris
France
Tel: 33 1 53 30 25 25
USA: 212 888 0505
Arije: 33 1 47 20 72 40

HARRY WINSTON SA
8 Chemin du Tourbillon
1228 Plan-les-Ouates
Switzerland
Tel: 41 22 716 29 00
USA: 212 245 2000
Arije: 33 1 47 20 72 40

HUBLOT
33 Chemin de la Vuarpillière
1260 Nyon 2
Switzerland
Tel: 41 22 990 90 00
USA: 800 536 0636
Arije: 33 1 47 20 72 40

JACOB & CO.
1 Chemin de Plein-Vent
1228 Arare
Switzerland
Tel: 41 22 310 69 62
USA: 212 719 5887
Arije: 33 1 47 20 72 40

JAEGER-LECOULTRE
Rue de la Golisse 8
1347 Le Sentier
Switzerland
Tel: 41 21 845 02 02
USA: 212 308 2525

JAQUET DROZ SA
2 Allée du Tourbillon
2300 La Chaux-de-Fonds
Switzerland
Tel: 41 32 924 28 88
France: 33 1 53 81 22 00
USA: 201 271 1400
Arije: 33 1 47 20 72 40

LONGINES
Saint-Imier 2610
Switzerland
Tel: 41 32 942 54 25
USA: 201 271 1400

LOUIS VUITTON
101 av. des Champs-Élysées
75008 Paris, France
Tel: +33 1 53 57 52 00
USA: 866 VUITTON

MANUFACTURE ROYALE
Zone Industrielle Le Day
1337 Vallorbe
Switzerland
Tel: 41 21 843 01 01

OMEGA
Rue Jakob Staempfli 96
2500 Bienne 4
Switzerland
Tel: 41 32 343 9211
France: 33 1 53 81 22 00

PATEK PHILIPPE
141 Chemin du Pont du Centenaire
1228 Plan-les-Ouates
Switzerland
Tel: 41 22 884 20 20
USA: 212 218 1240

PERRELET
7 Rue Bubenberg
2502 Biel/Bienne
Switzerland
Tel: 41 32 346 26 26
USA: 305 812 3344

PIAGET
37 Chemin du Champ-des-Filles
1228 Plan-les-Ouates
Switzerland
Tel: 41 22 884 48 44
USA: 212 891 2440
Arije: 33 1 47 20 72 40

RICHARD MILLE
11 rue du Jura
2345 Les Breuleux Jura
Switzerland
Tel: 41 32 959 43 53
France: 33 2 99 49 19 00
USA: 310 205 5555

ROGER DUBUIS
1217 Meyrin 2 Geneva
Switzerland
Tel: 41 22 808 48 88
France: 33 1 58 18 14 67
USA: 888 738 2847
Arije: 33 1 47 20 72 40

ROLEX
3-5-7 Rue François Dussaud
1211 Geneva 26
Switzerland
Tel: 41 22 302 22 00
USA: 212 758 7700
Arije: 33 1 47 20 72 40

TAG HEUER
6A Louis-Joseph Chevrolet
2300 La Chaux-de-Fonds
Switzerland
Tel: 41 32 919 80 00
USA: 973 467 1890
Arije: 33 1 47 20 72 40

VACHERON CONSTANTIN
10 Chemin du Tourbillon
1228 Plan-les-Ouates
Switzerland
Tel: 41 22 930 20 05
USA: 212 713 0707
Arije: 33 1 47 20 72 40

ZENITH
2400 Le Locle
Switzerland
Tel: 41 32 930 62 62
USA: 973 467 1890